READING THE IRISH LANDSCAPE

Reading the Irish Landscape

Frank Mitchell
&
Michael Ryan

TownHouse
Dublin

First published in Ireland in 1986, reprinted 1987.
Revised edition 1990, reprinted 1993.

This edition (revised) published in 1997 by
Town House and Country House
Trinity House
Charleston Road
Ranelagh
Dublin 6

British Library Cataloguing in Publication Data.
A catalogue record for this book is available
from the British Library.

ISBN: 0-946172-54-4

Front cover illustration:
Lough Shindile, near Maam Cross, Connemara, courtesy of Fergus Bourke
Cover design by Wendy Williams
Designed by identikit design consultants
Typeset by Typeform Repro Ltd, Dublin
Printed in Ireland by Betaprint

CONTENTS

ACKNOWLEDGMENTS

We have had numerous discussions with helpful colleagues and those most often turned to were: Terry Barry, Mary Cahill, Michael Conry, Russell Coope, Pete Coxon, George Eogan, John Feehan, Peter Harbison, Beatrice Kelly, Fergus Kelly, Marshall McCabe, Con Manning, Paddy Matthews, Fraser Mitchell, Billy O'Brien, Michael O'Connell, John Quinn, Matthew and Geraldine Stout, David Sweetman, Pat Tuite, Bill Watts, Brian Williams, Robin Wingfield and Peter Woodman. Tom Condit was particularly helpful and he, Gabriel Cooney and Barry Raftery gave us the use of unpublished photographs as well as the benefit of their views on many issues. Dermot Burke, Director of the National Monuments and Historic Properties Service, kindly gave permission to reproduce many photographs and we acknowledge our debt to him and his colleagues, Con Brogan and John Scarry. The Director of the Ordnance Survey also gave permission for the use of aerial photographs and his colleagues, John Danaher and Dick Lanigan were unstinting of their time, as was William Aliaga-Kelly of University College Dublin.

PREFACE

Ireland is a small island in an archipelago off the north-western shore of the European mainland. Its position has in the past encouraged people to regard it as in some sense apart from all the great processes that have formed – or happened on – the European landmass. True, the fact that Ireland is *now* surrounded by sea influences the climate and the attitudes of its inhabitants and confers both advantages and disadvantages economically and politically. But Ireland's isolation is an illusion – the rocks, the soils and the cultures of its peoples were all shaped by processes that operated much more widely. However important to us who live here, Ireland and its history represent but a tiny part of a much greater whole. There is no nationalism in geological structures, climatic changes are no respecters of man-made frontiers. Our interdependency on this planet has been brought home to many of us by our increasing knowledge of the processes of environmental change at work today; volcanic eruptions far away can be seen to affect climate; one country's industry pollutes the air or the rivers of its neighbours; social or economic change in distant places or discoveries in obscure laboratories can have rapid and far-reaching effects on all of us. Ireland cannot be studied in isolation. We have been struck by how much contemporary attitudes have been moulded by our knowledge of, or assumptions about, what happened in the past. Since the first edition of this book, our knowledge of that past has been expanding rapidly. For reasons of space we have been selective; much had to be excluded and so we were keenly aware that what we have been writing is merely an interim sketch of our one small piece of a vast four-dimensional jigsaw puzzle.

Writing about the history of the Irish landscape is a somewhat perilous venture. The many disciplines that have contributed to our understanding – geology, botany, climatology, pedology, history, archaeology and many more – can set traps for the unwary generalist. Some attempt, however risky, to bring these various themes together between two covers seems to us to be still a useful exercise in an increasingly specialist world. So we have taken as our motto the old adage that the best is the enemy of the good, and have ploughed our own furrow. We have been fortunate in our friends and colleagues who have endured our interrogations about the arcana of their research and who have often voluntarily ridden to our rescue in an effort to prevent us from straying into error. Whether they have been successful or not, time and the reader will tell. If we have ventured unwisely down certain paths, the responsibility is entirely our own. To see even a little further, we have stood on the shoulders of giants: we owe an enormous debt to the generations of scholars on whose published work we have relied, to those who taught us and to those with whom we have worked. A tribute to all of them is implicit in everything which we have written, but we remember here especially Kinahan, Charlesworth,

Praeger, Jessen, Godwin, Wilde, Coffey, Armstrong, Mahr and Ó Ríordáin, who have long departed the scene, to be joined more recently by Synge, Webb, Jackson, O'Kelly, De Valera and Raftery.

We have stuck to the chronological scheme of the earlier editions of this book. Dating of events from the beginning up to the arrival of the first farmers and the first significant evidence for man-made change in the environment is expressed generally in terms of years ago or BP (before the present). From the Neolithic Period onwards we have preferred BC/AD dating because that seems to us to be more familiar to the general reader of human history. In the overlap, Mesolithic, period (from about 9000 years BP to about 6200 BP – about 7000-4200 BC), both systems of dating are used to effect the transition more conveniently for the reader. Radiocarbon dating, the method on which the chronology for the post-glacial period is based, has become much better understood in recent years and when suitably calibrated against true solar years greater precision has been achieved. We have chosen in the main not to quote individual dates: instead we have given a broad chronological framework for events in prehistoric times based on a range of radiocarbon dates and other chronological evidence where it was available. In doing so we felt that it was necessary to present the best guess that we could make about what happened and that a finicky discussion of detail was out of place in a book of this kind. We have also retained the practice of previous editions of explaining technical issues and terms as they arise. Where necessary we have felt it advisable to repeat or amplify these explanations at other places in the text.

In addition to what has been passed into Irish law lately, a number of new measures to protect the natural and built environment are planned. This gradual development of better environmental preservation has been brought about by European Union pressures including the requirements of development grant-aid and by the belated recognition by tourism interests that a clean environment is a priceless asset. In this area official policy has lagged behind public opinion. But time is running out for some irreplaceable parts of our inheritance from the past, there is not a moment to lose.

1. THE GROWTH OF THE ROCK FOUNDATION

BEFORE 600 MILLION YEARS AGO

The rock structures out of which the Irish landscape has been carved have not only an extent in space, but also a history in time. Of the latter, as the famous Scottish geologist James Hutton said so long ago, we have 'no vestige of a beginning, no prospect of an end.'

As far as the beginning is concerned, geologists now reckon that the oldest rock so far dated has an age of more than 4000 million years, and that the earth must have had a rocky crust stretching back still farther in time. In Ireland our oldest rock, 1700 million years in age, is found on the small island of Inishtrahull, 8km north-west of the Inishowen coast in Donegal (*Illus. 1*). All these early rocks have been very much deformed and metamorphosed by later upheavals and it is difficult to sort out their sequence.

When geologists attempt to decipher the sequence of rock deposition and metamorphism, and hence the history of the earth, they rely on a variety of

*Illus. 1
Inishtrahull,
Co. Donegal. The
rocks are 1700
million years old and
their disturbed nature
is clearly seen from
the air; a fault cuts
diagonally across the
bottom of the picture.*

methods of dating, some physical, some chemical, some biological. When molten material solidifies into rock, or is torn into ash particles by a volcanic explosion, both rock and ash contain small quantities of radioactive elements which proceed to break down into simpler materials at a constant rate; for example, uranium breaks down into lead. If we determine the amount of uranium originally present, the rate of breakdown and the amount of lead formed, we can calculate for how long the process has been going on, and hence the age of the rock. This is the *radiometric* method.

The solidification process also provides another method, the *paleomagnetic* method. The earth has a powerful magnetic field, with north and south poles; the field is not constant, but varies with time. Molten rock usually has a content of minerals, such as oxides of iron, which are influenced by the magnetic field and align themselves with it. When the rock solidifies, they are locked in position and so record the direction of the field at the moment of solidification. Later earth movements may alter the geographical position of the rock; we can detect these by reading the magnetic record of the rock and so follow its wanderings across the surface of the globe.

From time to time, for unexplained reasons, the magnetic field of the earth reverses itself. Such reversals are recorded, not only in solidifying rocks, but in many other deposits, and as the reversal is simultaneous throughout the world, it is most valuable in correlating geological deposits in different parts of the globe.

Well-organised life was certainly established on the earth 1000 million years ago, with primitive forms going back perhaps 1400 million years. Gradually individual animals and plants evolved and their hard parts changed and developed. As successive rocks were deposited, some of these hard parts were preserved in them as fossils. If the fossils in the different layers of rock can be placed in an evolutionary sequence, their relative ages will become apparent. This gives us a *biological* method of dating, which is of the greatest importance.

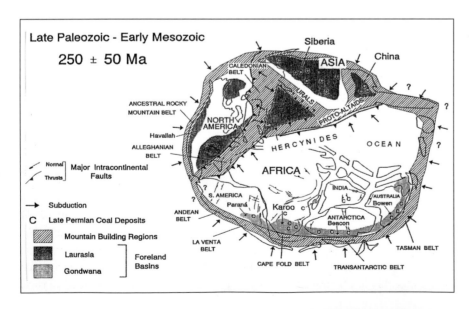

Illus. 2
Final re-assembly of Pangea before the dispersal of its plates around the globe.

As the primeval earth formed, it seems to have passed through a liquid stage. Solid crust then began to crystallise and appears to have formed one great single continent, *Pangea*. Pangea showed a tendency to split and re-form, being only finally separated into the modern continents about 250 million years ago (*Illus. 2*). But at the beginning, perhaps 4000 million years ago, the crust was thin and was subjected to violent and repeated disturbances. Fluids at very high temperatures and pressures were capable of carrying large quantities of dissolved metals, including platinum, gold, silver, selenium and tellurium. If temperature and pressure fell, minerals containing these elements were precipitated in veins and strings through the surrounding rocks; platinum and gold appeared in the metallic form.

It has recently been shown that a narrow interrupted reef of rock, containing gold in sufficient quantity to make its extraction profitable, runs from south-west Scotland across the north of Ireland to reach the Atlantic coast not far from Croagh Patrick. Proposals to mine for gold in Scotland, Tyrone and Mayo have been brought forward, but have met with intense local opposition mainly on three grounds: general disturbance of scenic areas, creation of unsightly dumps of broken rock, and pollution from chemicals used to leach the gold from the crushed rock. Economic abstraction is possible if four tons of crushed rock yields one ounce of gold.

An application for planning permission in Tyrone stated that the area occupied by the mining operation would extend to 60 hectares and that each full working day would produce 2000 tons of waste rock. The rate at which crushed rock would rise into huge dumps can easily be imagined. Nothing can grow on these dumps; the mining dumps in the Avoca valley in Wicklow are as ugly and as bare as they were when the mines were abandoned over one hundred years ago. With the possibility of pollution from spills of the powerful chemicals needed to leach the gold from the crushed rock, it was proposed to discharge the spent water used into a tributary of the River Foyle. Obviously if such mining proceeds, there will be very serious consequences for the environment. 'To mine or not to mine'– important decisions will have to be made.

After 600 million years ago, disturbances to the earth's crust were less profound and with the aid of fossils and other methods of dating, it is possible to follow crustal events fairly closely. The temperatures in the earth's interior remained high.

The sea covered the area we call Wales – although the Romans had earlier called it Cambria. In that sea there were many forms of animal life and these left fossils in the local rocks which are known as *Cambrian*. The vast majority of still older rocks have either no fossils or only a very limited range of them and have largely defeated attempts so far to sort them out in detail. As a result, they are usually treated together as *Pre-Cambrian,* although two major units – Archaean and Proterozoic – are becoming increasingly clearly defined.

Geologists and geographers have long commented on the way some of the modern continents could be made to fit together. South America, for example, would fit quite neatly against the west coast of Africa. Moreover we find rock types on the east coast of South America that would be quite at home in Africa and similarities can also be traced in fossils of earlier periods. The Pre-Cambrian rocks of Inishtrahull have no relationship with the nearby rocks of Donegal or Derry; they match up quite neatly however with rocks in the Hebrides and Greenland. Scientists played with the idea of 'continental drift', although they could not imagine what forces moved the continents.

More recent studies have suggested the mechanism – though not as yet the forces – and so we talk about *plate tectonics*. We picture the globe as covered by a series of rigid plates, which fit together like pieces in a jigsaw puzzle, though the pieces are of very different sizes. On average they are about 100km thick and are supported on less rigid material, which thus allows them to move relative to one another (*Illus. 3*). Each plate has a crust of which there are two forms. Under the oceans we have oceanic crust; a thin uniform rind about 8km thick of fine-grained rock composed of minerals rich in iron and magnesium, which make it dark and heavy. When this type of rock appears at the surface on land (as it does at the

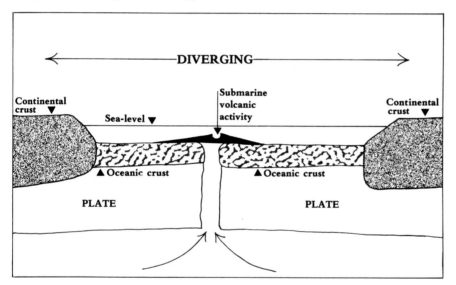

Illus. 3a
As the plates diverge and the oceanic plate splits, molten material rises in the crack. Contact with the cold sea water causes it to solidify, building onto the walls of the crack, thus expanding the plate. Normally the volcanoes along the escape line are below sea level, but occasionally, as in Hawaii, they rise above it. As a result of divergence the sea floor spreads and the ocean widens or spreads.

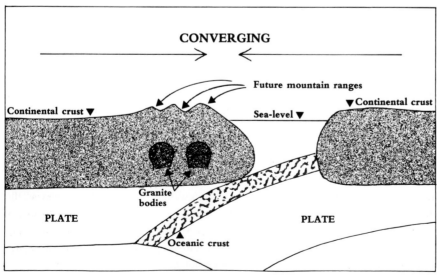

Illus. 3b
As the plates converge one plate is forced down below the other, whose margin buckles. These bucklings later appear as mountains. Within the continental plate masses of molten rock are forced up. On cooling they will form coarsely crystalline rock, such as granite. As a result of convergence, the ocean narrows and finally disappears.

Giant's Causeway in Antrim (*Col. 8*)) then we know it as *basalt*. Under the continents we have continental crust, a layer variable in both thickness (on average about 35km) and composition. This crust shows a wide variety of rock types which are generally light in colour and relatively light in weight. This is because they are composed of minerals rich in aluminium and silicon. Silicon combines with oxygen to form the mineral quartz which in very thin slices (as a silicon chip) forms the heart of a computer. Quartz is an important ingredient of the pale rock, granite, which occurs in the Wicklow Mountains and in the past was used extensively in Dublin as a building stone.

Continental crust is lighter than oceanic crust and where it occurs the plate surface is at a higher level. This crust is therefore largely found above sea level, whereas the oceanic crust lies mainly below sea level. The contact between the two, however, is not at the shoreline, as the continental crust usually extends outwards under water for some distance as a shallow continental shelf.

When the plates move, three kinds of relative motion are possible. In the simplest motion the two plates slip past one another. However, if grating occurs, the consequent vibrations may cause severe earthquakes. The San Andreas Fault in California marks the contact between two plates and movement along this contact caused the disastrous San Francisco earthquake of 1906. Movement on this fault still continues as demonstrated by a severe earthquake in 1992 which brought about the extensive collapse of motorway flyovers.

In recent geological time, the North American plate and the European plate have been moving away from one another in the second relative motion. As they diverge (*Illus. 3a*), molten rock rises up between them and solidifies on the ocean floor, thus extending the plates. By reading the magnetic print-out on the newly-formed rock we can date the spreading of the sea floor. The modern Atlantic Ocean is the product of such spreading.

In the third motion, the plates converge on one another and shrinking of the surface must follow (*Illus. 3b*). Buckling up may take place, or one plate may be forced down below the other and melt away when, under enormous pressures, it reaches the higher temperatures nearer the earth's interior. Original rock characteristics are drastically metamorphosed and bodies of molten rock may be forced up to higher levels where they cool into coarsely crystalline rocks, such as granite. If we look down from the air at the rocks of Inishtrahull (*Illus. 1*), our first glance reveals the degree to which its Pre-Cambrian rocks have been crumpled by converging pressures. Later, one block of the island has moved relative to the other and a crack or 'fault' (shown clearly in the photograph) has developed.

Elsewhere in Donegal we find other Pre-Cambrian rocks that started off as unsorted glacial deposits containing striated boulders but have since lithified into hard rock. If the superficial layers of the earth's surface freeze and thaw repeatedly, characteristic structures are created and we can see these structures near the glacial deposits. These will be looked at in detail when we come to the more recent ice age and see that although millions of years separate them the same freezing processes were involved.

The temperature of the earth and the composition of its atmosphere at that time were not the same as today's and it is difficult to imagine the presence of polar ice sheets. Given its position on the earth's surface at the time, this Donegal ice must have come from the South Pole and not the North Pole.

Although the plates move only very slowly, perhaps a few millimetres a year, geological time has been long enough to carry them enormous distances. Ireland was first at the level of South Africa in the southern hemisphere about 500 million years

ago (*Illus. 5*). Always moving northwards, it took 200 million years to reach the Equator. Under the equatorial climate, rainforests flourished and great quantities of decaying vegetable material provided the raw matter for coals. 150 million years ago, Ireland lay at the level of the Canary Islands and warm shallow seas were about to invade its surface. From there it moved slowly on to reach its present temperate position.

Illus. 4
Benbulbin, Co. Sligo. Uplifted horizontal beds of carboniferous limestone are dramatically dissected by faulting followed by prolonged weathering.

600 TO 400 MILLION YEARS AGO

When viewing our chronological route through successive events, we can picture ourselves as looking through a time telescope. Unfortunately, when we try to look at events that took place hundreds of millions of years ago, we find that our telescope is not good enough to give us a clear picture and we can only get a hazy impression of events. As we move forward in time, our telescope improves. We will no longer have to deal in millions of years, but will be able to resolve events lasting just thousands of years. Ultimately, our scale will be hundreds and even tens of years.

Geologists are gradually building up a picture of the sequence of events that unrolled themselves as the years went by. These events are set out in Table 1 and a map shows where different rock formations occur in Ireland (*Col. 5*).

When Pre-Cambrian time ended, about 600 million years ago, a wide ocean (the proto-Atlantic or Iapetus Ocean) lay between the

Illus. 5
Ireland's drift on the earth's surface.

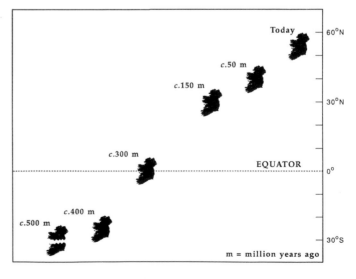

North American plate and the European plate. At that time the fragment of the earth that we call Ireland was in the southern hemisphere at about the latitude of South Africa and was divided into two parts lying on opposite sides of the Iapetus Ocean.

Off the shores of the plates there were basins with abundant marine life; a distinct North American fauna to the west and a European fauna on the eastern shore. There was already a considerable variety of plant and animal life in the oceans. However, only one fossil of this age, and an intriguing one at that, has been found in Ireland. Slates at Bray Head in Co. Wicklow, dating from about 550 million years ago, carry numerous small fan-like impressions probably of some small alga. They are named *Oldhamia antiqua* (*Illus. 6a*) in honour of Thomas Oldham who discovered them over 150 years ago.

Illus. 6a
Oldhamia antiqua.
At the time of their discovery at Bray Head in Co. Wicklow by an Irish geologist, Thomas Oldham, these frond-like fossil impressions with an age of about 550 million years were the oldest fossils yet discovered.

Illus. 6b
Doolin fossils. These brachiopods and other marine creatures lived in a warm sea at Doolin in Co. Clare about 350 million years ago.

Illus. 6c
Vertebrate forms were now developing rapidly and these amphibian fossils from the Kilkenny lagoon clearly have backbones and limbs.

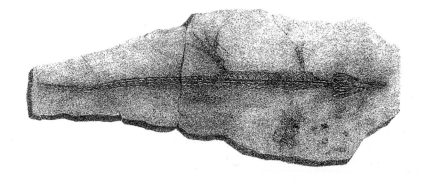

On the north Co. Dublin coast, between Portrane and Skerries, the rocks are
a little younger, about 450 million years old, and contain a range of marine fossils
(*Illus. 6b*). There are trilobites, jointed animals with hard outer coats like the
modern beetle, brachiopods with paired calcareous shells rather like the modern
cockle, and graptolites or thin rods which look like lines drawn on the rocks with a
soft pencil. Graptolites have no close parallels in the modern seas, but little cups on
the rods suggest an affinity with the coral group. Bony plates from armour-plated

Table 1

	CLIMATE	ENVIRONMENT	
Today	Temperate Oscillating phases going from very cold to warm Frosts appear	Arable land, grassland and woodland. Forests of modern aspect appear in temperate phases Tundra appears in cold phases Palms disappear; hemlock appears Swamp forests with palms	
25			
65		Erosion active as sea retreats; karst development renewed	
100	Warm	Chalk seas cover Ireland Sediments (some with high organic content) accumulate in various basins	
180 200	Arid with temporary lakes	Eroding limestone starts to develop karstic features Ireland largely above sea level; sandstones form	
300	Tropical marine Seasonal rainfall	Plant debris (later changed into coal) accumulates in swamps Warm seas (with corals), in which limestone forms, flood over the land The landscape becomes green, as land plants extend As the land erodes, great rivers transport large quantities of sand, which harden into sandstone Ireland largely above sea level	
400 430			
450		Sediments continue to accumulate in marine basins	
500		Wide development of marine basins with many forms of life	
600 1200		**PRE-CAMBRIAN TIME** (Rocks of this age give only rare signs of contemporary plants and animals)	
1800	Cold	Ice in Donegal	
2400			
Millions of years ago			

fish are exceedingly scarce and are only very rarely found, but they do show that vertebrate life was beginning to take shape. There are also scraps of the earliest land plants – primitive forms perhaps related to the modern horse-tails.

The opposite shores of the Iapetus Ocean finally collided about 440 million years ago. Just before the final closure there was opportunity for the two different shore faunas to mingle, and in the rocks just north of Clogher Head in Co. Louth and for some distance inland from there, a mixture of two facies of life, American and European, can be found.

EARTH MOVEMENTS	
Rift carries Greenland away from Europe; modern Atlantic Ocean nearly complete	25
Volcanic activity in north-east Ireland and south-west Scotland creates the framework of the Mourne Mountains and the Antrim plateau	65
As the North American and the European plates begin to separate, a rift – which will widen into the modern Atlantic Ocean – opens from the South	100
	180
	200
Extension creates marine basins around the Irish land mass	
Hercynide rock deformation (due to plate movement in central Europe) creates framework of the east-west mountain ridges of the south of Ireland	300
Further deformation occurs when the two halves of Ireland finally collide and are fused into one	400
	430
Intrusions of granite provide the framework for the mountains of Wicklow and other hills in Ireland The framework for the mountains of Connemara and Donegal is created As the two shores get closer to one another, rocks on the western shore are intensely deformed all the way from Newfoundland, through the north-west of Ireland and Scotland on into western Scandinavia (Caledonide rock deformation)	450
The two shores of the proto-Atlantic begin to move towards one another	500
	600
Repeated cycles	1200
of	1800
intense rock formation	2400
	Millions of years ago

As the shores grew closer (*Illus. 7*), rock deformation was much more severe for some reason on the American side than on the European side and great folded structures, running north-east/south-west, were formed across what is now Newfoundland, north-west Ireland, Scotland, Scandinavia and Greenland. Subsequent denudation left the core of these structures standing up as mountain ranges. Caledonia was an old name for Scotland and because of their common origin geologists call these mountain ranges the *Caledonides,* whether they occur in Newfoundland, Ireland, Scotland or Scandinavia.

Continental plate materials got involved in the disturbances and, becoming molten, were injected in large masses into older rocks, where they cooled slowly. Such cooling allowed coarse crystals to develop, and in this way the coarsely crystalline rock granite was formed. Subsequent dissection by denudation has left large upstanding bosses of granite, such as those in the Wicklow Mountains (*Col. 3*) and at several localities in Donegal.

400 TO 225 MILLION YEARS AGO

The area now occupied by Ireland found itself in a totally new environment. It was above sea level and exposed to atmospheric erosion. The main trend of the drainage was from north to south. The rivers flowed sluggishly at some times, and at other times were swollen into torrential floods. These flooding rivers transported great masses of silt, sand and gravel, which is now cemented into *sandstone,* long known as Old Red Sandstone. Such fluctuations in river activity suggest marked

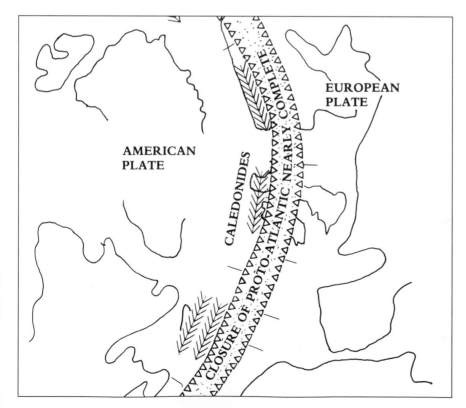

Illus. 7
About 450 million years ago, plate convergence was bringing America and Europe closer together and the early Atlantic (proto-Atlantic) ocean was being pinched out. Intense rock crumpling on the American side ultimately resulted in a long mountain chain running from Newfoundland through north-west Ireland and north-west Scotland and on into Scandinavia.

seasonal changes, and this type of climate tends to favour rapid erosion. The seashore probably lay a short distance south of the present south coast.

The generally arid landscape was dotted with occasional freshwater ponds with fringes of trees around them and active life in the water. These trees have survived in fossil form at Kiltorcan in Co. Kilkenny and it is clear that they were very primitive compared with modern trees. They had a coniferous appearance, but they did not produce seeds or cones; instead they reproduced themselves from spores, like the modern fern. In the water there were fish armed with bony plates and also arthropods, crustacea and a large freshwater mussel very similar to the swan mussel living in many Irish lakes. These ponds were probably active about 375 million years ago.

On Valencia Island in Co. Kerry, outcrops of pressure-cleaved slate are common. The slate is thought to be 350 million years old. Recently when examining some of these outcrops, Dr I Stössel of Zurich made a most exciting and important discovery. He saw, impressed in the slate, a track of footprints of a four-footed creature; the track could be traced for a distance of about 10m (*Illus. 8*). It was made by a small four-footed amphibian, perhaps about 1m long, moving across a tidal flat of fine-grained sediment. The importance of the discovery can be judged from the fact that only five other records of amphibian tracks of this age are known, and these occur in Australia and Brazil.

Once more there must have been tectonic disturbance, and either Ireland and much of Britain subsided below sea level, or sea level rose and engulfed them. In any event north-west Europe, then lying on the Equator, was invaded by a great sea whose waters were warm and rich in the element calcium. Animals and plants were able to combine the calcium with carbon and oxygen also present in the seawater and formed supporting skeletons of calcium carbonate (*calcite*). Great coral reefs were built up. When the shellfish and the plants died, their skeletons largely disintegrated into calcareous debris which accumulated on the sea floor, although some shells did survive more or less intact in the debris to become fossils. Great thicknesses of debris built up and the lower layers became consolidated into *limestone*. Despite later disturbance and erosion, today this limestone occupies about two-thirds of Ireland's rock mantle. At this time the sea was one of clear water, but then sand and clay began to be carried in. These consolidated into sand-stone and shale, which lay on top of the limestone. Eventually, the water became so shallow that tropical forests invaded its margins and vegetable debris

Illus. 8
About 375 million years ago, a four-legged amphibian wandered across soft muds in Valencia Island, Co. Kerry. Though the muds have been metemorphosed into hard slates, the footprints survive.

accumulated in backwaters and swamps. With the passage of time, this debris became transformed into coal. While trees in the rainforests still reproduced themselves by spores, life in the water was advancing rapidly.

Around Castlecomer in Co. Kilkenny, some deposits of coal were exploited in the last century and one particular seam which had accumulated in a meandering channel, the Jarrow Channel, was particularly rich in fossils. Among these were amphibians with limbs adapted for walking (as at Valencia Island) and these animals must have spent part of their life ashore (*Illus. 8*). The air was invaded as well as the land, for there are fossil remains of spiders and dragonflies.

Geologists regard this sequence of clearwater sea, then muddy sea, then swamp forest as a single sedimentary cycle and because of the presence of coal, it is called the *Carboniferous* period. In Ireland, however, a better name would be Carbonexodus period, because subsequent denudation stripped away virtually all the coal that formerly covered much of the Irish area. Limited deposits, too uneconomic to work today, survive at Castlecomer and Arigna in Co. Roscommon, with two further tiny patches at Bridgetown in Co. Wexford. A larger deposit exists below the Kish Bank in Dublin Bay.

Dramatic tectonic movements brought the Carboniferous cycle to an end about 300 million years ago when there was relative movement of the European and the African plates. In central Germany, the Harz Mountains were thrust up and as this area was known in classical time as Hercynia; the geological features then created are called *Hercynide*. The disturbance was beginning to lose force as it approached Ireland and its main effect was confined to the south of the country, where a great lateral thrust from the south caused dramatic rock deformation (*Illus. 9*). The Old Red Sandstone and the overlying Carboniferous deposits were folded and faulted (that is, broken across and shifted) into pleats which ran east/west. Farther north, the thrust progressively died away. Its weakened effects were influenced by the older Caledonide structures and so tended to follow a north-east/south-west trend.

These movements probably began before the deposition of Carboniferous deposits had ended. At depth, the water in the accumulating deposits was very hot and capable of bringing metals – notably copper, lead and zinc – into solution. The Hercynian earth movements brought the Old Red Sandstone and the Carboniferous rocks into contact, fracturing them as it did so. The fracture cracks

Illus. 9
Section along a line running approximately from Tuam, Co. Galway to Cork showing tectonic features created by a lateral thrust of Hercynide age.

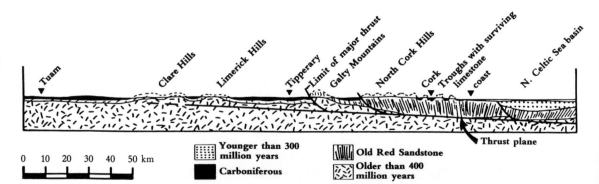

Younger than 300 million years

Carboniferous

Old Red Sandstone

Older than 400 million years

Thrust plane

0   10   20   30   40   50 km

provided channels along which the metal-rich hot waters could move upwards. As temperature and pressure fell, great quantities of ore deposits, usually sulphides, were formed at points along the contact between the Old Red Sandstone and the Carboniferous rock.

Through a very much later development, the outcrops of these ore deposits were almost buried beneath glacial deposits and up until only thirty years ago their existence was unknown. At that time, a new technique of exploration, called *geochemistry*, was introduced to Ireland. Using this technique, a drainage basin is chosen and the metal content of the water of all its contributing streams is analysed moving methodically upstream. If the metal values rise significantly in any area, then a drilling programme is carried out. Using this technique, at least ten ore deposits capable of economic working have been located since 1963 and Ireland, whose mineral deposits were formerly considered as almost negligible, is now recognised as having some of the richest metallogenic provinces in Europe. The deposits are chiefly in the south of Ireland, with the deposits at Navan in Co. Meath estimated to be at least 80 million tonnes.

Most of the mining developments opened up in the past ten years have endeavoured to keep environmental considerations in mind when laying out and developing their operations. There is one major problem, however, and that is the disposal of *tailings*. This is the finely-crushed rock debris that becomes valueless after the minerals in it have been removed by chemical action. The general practice is to construct huge tailings ponds into which running water deposits the debris, much of which still has a small content of metals. When production ceases, the tailings ponds may dry out, leaving a thin skin of dangerous material lying exposed to the atmosphere.

Most recent mining developments have been sited near to rivers into which the effluent could be discharged after suitable treatment. But interest has recently shifted to an area near Durrow in Co. Laois, where a karstic landscape (see p. 14) on limestone has been concealed by glacial deposits and there is no surface drainage pattern. Mining operations in this area will not only require large quantities of water for some procedures, but local pumping will also be necessary to keep the vicinity of the mines dry. It is almost impossible to forecast what the net effect might be on the local water table. Some local farm wells will be seriously affected.

Wetlands can also be affected by mining. Between Durrow and Rathdowney, 12km to the west, there is a large area of wetland, The Curragh, where surface streams trickle across marshes. If the water table drops as a consequence of the mines interfering with the water balance of the area, there will be serious consequences for the local wildlife.

At Galmoy, near Rathdowney, where planning permission has been granted, it is estimated that the mine will have a life of ten years. An additional problem has been revealed here. The tailings are extremely heavy and the thick layer of debris lying on the floor of the tailings pond will be of considerable weight. Local objectors claim that the underlying limestone, perforated as it is by karstic cavities, will collapse beneath the weight. Only time will tell. The developers have to provide a sum of £4.5 million towards the subsequent rehabilitation of the area. But time as well as money is a factor, and it will be many, many years before a stable natural environment is re-established.

About 250 million years ago, Ireland was in the northern hemisphere at about the latitude of Egypt today and had a desert climate. After the tectonic disturbances, atmospheric denudation proceeded to whittle away the uplifted rocks and erosion was very vigorous. The coal deposits quickly disappeared, as did much of the sandstone and shale, until limestone was exposed over much of central Ireland. In the south, where the rocks had been crushed into east/west folds, the limestone was thinner, and much of it was removed by erosion. However, some limestone did survive in the troughs of the folds, separated by ridges of sandstone.

Moving from north to south, we can see the east/west ridge of the Galty and Ballyhoura Mountains, then the low-lying limestone areas around Mitchelstown, then the Knockmealdown Mountains, then the Blackwater valley, then another sandstone ridge and finally the valley of the Lee. Further west we have similar structures in the mountains of west Cork and Kerry, where the highest peak, Carrauntoohil, rises to a height of 1000m. Today this mountain is only a pygmy compared with its former size; it probably once rose to a height of at least 3000m. The earlier sediments which were thrust upwards by the Hercynide earth pressures contained eroded fragments of coal. The applied forces bleached the black of the coal to shades of yellow; the depth of surviving colour is related to the temperatures involved and therefore it can be estimated that the present mountain range was once at least 2km higher.

As soon as extensive areas of Carboniferous limestone were exposed, they were attacked by a different process of denudation, which resulted in a karstic landscape, one type of which we see today in the Burren (*Col. 9, 17*). Along the Dalmatian Coast, karstic landscapes are well developed and have long been studied in detail; it is from there that the words *karst* and *doline* (see below) came into international geomorphological terminology.

The essence of karstic conditions is that surface water disappears down vertical passages, instead of moving laterally as a surface stream. The original sediment was laid down in layers or *strata* and during earth movements these were broken across by cracks or *joints*. Carbon dioxide in the atmosphere dissolves in the water droplets in clouds. When these droplets fall to earth as rain, the rain is slightly acidic and so is capable of dissolving the calcite of which the limestone is chiefly composed. Elaborate consequences follow (*Illus. 10*).

The rainwater enters the fissures and enlarges them by dissolving away the rock walls. One fissure becomes a master fissure and a *sink-hole* is created; some sink-holes develop into large closed depressions, *dolines,* which come to dominate the landscape. When the descending water reaches the water table (a level below which all the spaces in the rock are filled with standing water) it begins to move laterally, enlarging its channel by dissolving the rock as it flows. If the water table drops, the moving water follows it down and the former channel is abandoned as a cave. As

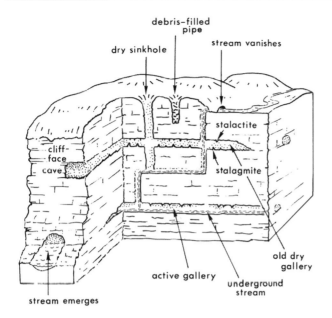

debris–filled pipe

dry sinkhole

stream vanishes

stalactite

cliff-face

cave

stalagmite

old dry gallery

active gallery

underground stream

stream emerges

Illus. 10
Features created by
underground karst
erosion.

with river flow, the level at which the water table lies is related to contemporary sea level. In Ireland, many sink-holes and solution-channels descend below modern sea level and at the time of their creation, sea level must have been far below its present position. The Blue Grotto in Capri and the drowned caves of Bermuda are modern examples of drowned solution-channels.

In normal landscape development, small streams in small valleys join to become large rivers in large valleys, bringing the products of erosion they are carrying to the sea. In karstic landscape development, surface water quickly disappears down sink-holes and innumerable smaller sink-channels. In recent years in the Gort area of Galway, there have been floods on a very large scale, some of which have been slow to drain away. More and more farmers are using enormous quantities of plastic sheeting, either as bags for fertilisers or as sheets to protect silage. After use, the plastic debris often blows away and comes to rest in hedges or streams. Some must inevitably be carried by water into sink-channels, where sooner or later they will lodge in an inaccessible position. If a substantial number of sink-channels become blocked, there will be very serious consequences to the local surface drainage.

Solution of rock is not confined to the sink-holes. As the rainwater moves across the rock surface towards the sink-holes, it dissolves some rock and gradually frets the surface into a series of pinnacles and minarets. Well-developed examples of these features can be seen in tropical Africa (*Col. 12*). In China and North Vietnam this process reached an exaggerated degree, giving a 'mountains of the moon' landscape with rising towers of limestone, a scene well-loved by Chinese artists. Unfortunately when ice later swept over Ireland, such spectacular irregularities were almost completely abraded away, and a smoothed surface was created. The time that has elapsed since the ice disappeared has been too short for these features to develop again, but provided ice stays away long enough, they will reappear. Some vestiges of pinnacles still remain near Fenit in Co. Kerry (*Illus. 11*). Knocknarea, which rises to 330m just west of Sligo town, is a massive isolated block. Dissected blocks still surround the east end of Lough Gill in the same county. The basins of some of our largest lakes, notably Lough Ree on the Shannon, have probably been deepened by solution.

This relentless erosion was enhanced by the fact that since the Irish land mass was raised by the Hercynide mountain-building phase, it seems to have remained as a positive block relative to the surrounding areas. About 250 million years ago in the Irish Sea basin, there was spasmodic foundering perhaps due to tension, and

Illus. 11
Limestone pinnacle
near Fenit, Co. Kerry.

many small basins, some of considerable depth, acted as traps for the insoluble products of erosion. Most of these are completely submerged today, but two basins have their south-west ends exposed. Belfast Lough lies on the south-west side of a basin, the Lough Neagh/Arran Basin which continues north-east below the Firth of Clyde; Lough Foyle is at the end of a smaller basin, the Rathlin Trough, which only reaches as far as Islay. At Larne the deposits are over 3000m thick.

At first, seawater had intermittent access to the basins and there was some accumulation of limestone. Land-derived sediments then became dominant and thick red deposits – first of sand and later of clay – accumulated. Temporary lagoons developed as the sea level oscillated and layers of rock salt and gypsum were laid down. Rock salt has long been quarried at Carrickfergus, on the north shore of Belfast Lough. Scrabo Hill, south of Newtownards, which has been extensively quarried for its red sandstone, still rises to a height of 160m.

225 TO 65 MILLION YEARS AGO

At this time, 225 million years ago, reptiles were beginning to expand, both in the size of their bodies and in the habitats they occupied, ultimately being found on land, in the water and high in the sky. The distribution of the dinosaurs was almost worldwide; some forms must have frequented Ireland, but of them we can find no trace. One record exists from near Scrabo Hill, where a small reptile, crossing the muddy edge of a pond, left a trail of footprints, each about 7cm long.

Near the west shore of Dublin Bay, just off Dun Laoghaire, there is a large bank of sand, the Kish Bank, which has caused many shipwrecks and is today marked by a lighthouse. Paradoxically it overlies a deep fault-bounded basin, the Kish Bank Basin, which holds a remarkable number of rock types (*Illus. 12*). There are marine clays and limestones, whose fossil content indicates an age of about 180 million years; these may be up to 2500m thick. There are also older sedimentary rocks similar to those at Larne, possibly 3000m thick. Most surprisingly of all, there is a block of rock of Carboniferous age, containing coals of a high quality not matched by any of the coals that still survive above water in Ireland. Technically it would be possible to mine this coal, most probably by driving a tunnel out from the coast, but at today's fuel prices it would be quite uneconomic. The recent laying of a gas pipeline across the Irish Sea indicates that in the short term at least our fuel will come from the gas fields of Europe rather than domestic sources.

Offshore along the south coast of Ireland from Carnsore Point to Clear Island and beyond, in what is called the Celtic Sea, there is a huge elongated basin largely divided into two halves by a central ridge, which runs east/west. In this basin, the red sandstones seen farther north are overlain by a very thick series of younger rocks, marine on the whole but with some brackish and even freshwater deposits, accompanied by massive deposition of rock salt. Deposition in the basins seems to have extended from about 200 to 65 million years ago.

At all times the sea has been rich in organic debris, perhaps derived from seaweeds and with the passage of time this debris transformed itself into oil and gas. Being light, these substances tended to migrate upwards. If by chance some compact rock had been folded upwards into an arch-like structure, the movement of the fuels was checked and they accumulated below the arch.

Illus. 12
Map showing basins
around Ireland.

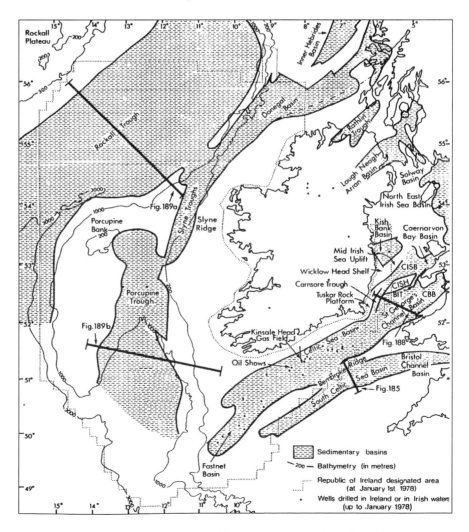

Such features are sought out by oil companies; if they drill a hole through the compact arch, the oil and gas will rise upwards in an Artesian well. Most of the basins round Ireland have now been explored, but only the North Celtic Sea Basin, offshore from Kinsale, has produced commercial quantities of gas.

By about 150 million years ago, continued erosion over much of western Europe seems to have produced a land surface of very low relief, with rivers incapable of carrying substantial amounts of sediment into the sea. At that time seawater flooded across Europe from Ireland to the Caucasus, and in it a remarkably pure form of calcareous sediment was formed. Tiny floating organisms with calcareous shells drifted in the sea and when they died and sank to the sea floor, a fine oozy sediment, free from sand and clay, accumulated there. This was later consolidated and uplifted as a fine-grained white limestone or *chalk*. Siliceous debris in the ooze later coagulated as *flint*.

In the Celtic Sea basins, chalk accumulated to a thickness of at least 1000m. It seems that the rise in sea level was sufficient to flood mainland Ireland also and chalk must once have covered almost the whole of Ireland, in places to a thickness of more than 100m. This was almost completely stripped away by later erosion and to accept that it was once there almost requires an act of geological faith. We have no problem, however, in north-east Ireland. Although some chalk was removed by erosion – much of it of a karstic nature, as chalk is a readily-soluble limestone – later great outpourings of basaltic lava buried the remaining chalk and so protected it from further erosion. Off the south and west coasts of Ireland chalk also occurs over wide areas of the sea floor. However, between north-east and south-west Ireland only one vestige of chalk remains. The main road from Tralee to Killarney in Co. Kerry runs through a narrow valley at Ballydeanlea, not far south of Farranfore. Here farmers found a small deposit of white limestone, which they quarried for burning in a limekiln where it was roasted to lime (an oxide of calcium) and used as a fertiliser. The deposit was noted by the Geological Survey over one hundred years ago, but as the accepted dogma was that chalk did not occur in the south of Ireland, it was not recognised as such. It was re-found in 1966 by Dr Peter Walsh of the City University in London, who not only identified it as typical chalk, but also noted that it was lying in a karstic sink-hole, which must have formed more than 100 million years ago. At Ballydeanlea, the shale that was deposited on top of the limestone in Carboniferous times has not yet been eroded away; none the less many millions of years ago water percolated down cracks in the shale into the limestone, where it created solution-cavities. These ultimately grew to such a size that in places the roof of shale was left unsupported and collapsed down into the cavity, opening a sink-hole at the point of collapse.

Such sink-holes were standing open when the chalk-seas flooded the area and chalk was deposited in them, just as on the surrounding sea floor. When the area once more came above sea level and erosion was renewed, all the local chalk was removed, except for the fragment preserved in the pipe of the sink-hole. The tiny quarry at Ballydeanlea is one of Ireland's most remarkable, as well as most informative, sites and should be preserved as a Natural Heritage Area (NHA).

As well as Ballydeanlea, we have two other conundrums to contemplate. Near Cloyne in Co. Cork, and not far above modern sea level, there is a karstic hollow in the Carboniferous limestone. In the hollow is a sandy lacustrine clay with plant fossils of about 180 million years old. Therefore, at some time the waters in the Celtic Sea must have risen and laid thin deposits on the limestone lowland; these deposits may once have been quite extensive. Near Kingscourt in Co. Cavan, a well-developed fault runs north/south. West of the fault are rocks that are about 400 million years old; east of the fault, a great block of rock has dropped down carrying half a small basin with it. The contents of the surviving half are about 500m thick, and are similar to those in the Belfast Basin, with sandstone, clay and gypsum formed about 250 million years ago. Gypsum is the raw material for plaster of Paris, and is also used in the cement-making and building industries. It is currently being extensively mined (*Col. 6*).

If we turn north round Mizen Head, on the south-west corner of Ireland, then we have, though on a scale much greater than in the Celtic Sea, another double basin or trough offshore from and more or less parallel to the Irish west coast. A ridge separates the narrow Porcupine Trough nearer land from the much broader Rockall Trough further out. Beyond the trough the Rockall Plateau rises and from this plateau one tiny spike of rock rises to a height of 20m to become an island called Rockall. Small as it is, Rockall is a source of controversy in international jurisdiction. Is it an offshore island of Ireland, or Great Britain, or the Faröes? The question is not an academic one, as it brings into question oil exploration rights in the neighbouring basins. There has been very little drilling in the area, but the rock sequences generally resemble those in the other basins and the possibility of significant quantities of fuels remains. There is one important difference in that the subsidence of the Porcupine Basin must have begun much earlier than in other basins as the base of the depositional sequence is of rocks of Carboniferous age, laid down about 300 million years ago. The sequence continues on up into the chalk and even higher, as we shall see later on.

But even before the chalk was deposited, other dramatic events were taking place about 180 million years ago which were to bring about profound changes in the geographical location of Ireland. We have seen that about 400 million years ago the North American and the European plates were welded together along a seam that included Ireland. These plates then split and diverged and by sea-floor spreading created a new Atlantic Ocean, which would ultimately separate the continents by thousands of kilometres of water. In 1858, Valencia Island was first joined to Newfoundland by cable. At that time it was recorded that 2000 miles (3200 kilometres) of wire had been necessary; 180 million years ago the points now joined by the two cable ends were quite close together.

65 to 25 Million Years Ago

Spreading of the plates continued and an area involving north-east Ireland, south-west Scotland, Iceland and Greenland were split by fissuring (*Illus. 13*). The fissures were most numerous in the vicinity of the North Channel and here, about 65 million years ago, there was tremendous volcanic activity. At weak points in the

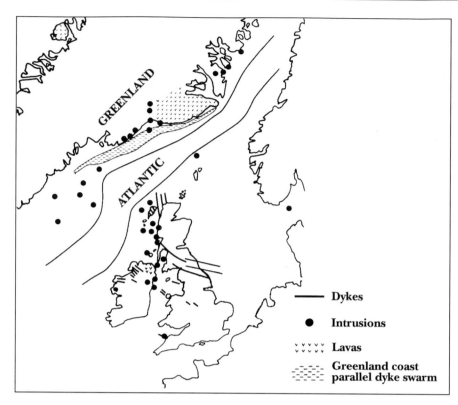

Illus. 13
Map of north
Atlantic area about
55 million years ago
showing an early
stage of the modern
Atlantic ocean and
outpourings and
intrusions of molten
rock.

—— **Dykes**

● **Intrusions**

⌄⌄⌄⌄ **Lavas**

⁻⁻⁻⁻ **Greenland coast**
parallel dyke swarm

crust, material was pushed upwards hurling molten material to great heights. As it fell back to earth it built up a cone of debris, as Vesuvius does intermittently today. Where linear cracks occurred in the crust, great quantities of molten material welled up from below and flowed out over the surrounding countryside, burying it beneath great sheets of *basalt (Col. 1)*. Fingal's Cave in Staffa can be taken as an epitome of this volcanic phase in Scotland, while the Giant's Causeway provides a good example in the North of Ireland (*Col. 8*).

If the molten material solidified in the fissure before it reached the surface of the ground it formed a *dyke*; dykes with a north-west/south-east trend are known throughout the northern half of Ireland. Lava flows may formerly have covered much more of Ireland than they do today.

As well as regional lava flows, intrusions of molten rock occurred both on a large and on a small scale. Large-scale intrusions created the Mourne Mountains and Carlingford Mountain, while on a small scale Doon Hill in Connemara was formed; eruptions like those of Hawaii and of Vesuvius must have been common at this time. Igneous activity, though on a very small scale, also took place in Wales and south-west England. Beginning about 65 million years ago, it continued for 15 million years.

Basalt rock was formed at the beginning of the volcanic phase and we are fortunate that this basalt has preserved a record of both the climate and the vegetation allowing us to imagine a warm Irish landscape covered with dense tropical forest. After a first outpouring of lava, there was a lull during which the surface of the lava weathered into soil and became covered by vegetation. A second series of lava flows buried and preserved the soil and the plant fossils. Molten rock is rich in silicon, oxygen, aluminium and other metals and when the rock solidifies the metals combine with the silicon and oxygen to form complex *silicate* molecules. When weathered under cool temperate climates such as we have in Ireland today, the silicates tend to take up water while retaining the silicon and the aluminium and turn into tiny plate-like particles of hydrated aluminium silicate or *silicate clay*; the other metals are removed in solution. However, under warm moist conditions, very different changes take place. It is the silicon that is now carried away in solution, while the aluminium and the iron are left behind to take up water and become hydrous oxide clays, again in tiny particles; the other metals are removed in solution. If developed in sufficient quantity, the hydrous aluminium oxide clay forms the ore of aluminium, *bauxite,* and its iron equivalent forms *limonite*; in the past both of these ores were mined in the weathered inter-basaltic layer in north-east Ireland.

It is one of the ironies of the Irish economic situation that although the country has small quantities of a wide range of economically desirable substances ranging from gold to coal, only lead and zinc (and possibly gold) occur in quantities that make modern economic working possible. At Aughinish Island in the Shannon estuary, Ireland has one of the largest alumina factories in the world; the bauxite it processes comes not from Ireland but from Guinea in west Africa and from Brazil.

The evidence of warm conditions given by the inter-basaltic soils is confirmed by the plant remains that they contain, chiefly in the form of *lignites* which were formed by the alteration of lake muds or peats in which tree stumps and logs were embedded. Among the conifers, pine (*Pinus*), cypress (*Cupressus*) and monkey-puzzle (*Araucaria*) were present and there was a wealth of deciduous leaf debris, including leaves of alder (*Alnus*). Ferns were also present, but herbs were only poorly represented. At this time, Ireland was on the same latitude as the forested Great Smoky Mountains in the central United States.

Minor earth movements had accompanied the outpouring of basalt and these continued in north-east Ireland after the volcanic activity had ceased. About 35 million years ago, renewed downward warping of the Lough Neagh Basin, extending a distance of 70km from Ballymoney to Portadown, enabled a large lake surrounded by swamp forest to form. Trees, confined today to North America, such as redwood (*Sequoia*), swamp cypress (*Taxodium*) and black gum (*Nyssa*) were present, together with more familiar forms such as alder, holly (*Ilex*), lime (*Tilia*) and oak (*Quercus*). There were also palms (*Palmae*).

Rivers carried clay, sand and plant debris out into the lake where they accumulated as a sequence of clays and lignites to a thickness of 350m and Lough Neagh can be regarded as the much shrunken descendant of the basin. The marine basins west of Mull, off the Dublin coast, in Tremadoc Bay, in the St. George's Channel, in the Bristol Channel and in the Celtic Sea continued to build up sediments.

The vegetable debris that accumulated in the Antrim depression was slowly transformed into thick beds of lignite or brown coal. While this is a bulky fuel of lower calorific value than true coal, it is very valuable if costs of extraction are low. The lignite is close to the surface – only covered by a thin skin of glacial deposits – and it is a wonder that it was not discovered long ago. The near-surface lignite could easily be extracted by open-cast mining, but due to its low calorific value, it cannot profitably bear the cost of long-distance transport. The only possibility of development, therefore, would be an open-cast mine feeding power stations in the

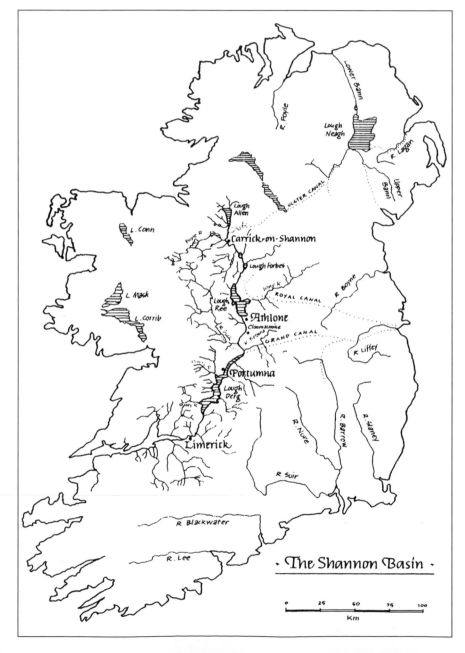

Illus. 14
The Shannon and its winding tributaries which drain lakes and bogs suggest that there has been tectonic subsidence which created a kidney-shaped basin in central Ireland. It is only with difficulty that the drainage water escapes to the sea.

immediate vicinity. Needless to say, this would wreak havoc in an agricultural landscape and would-be developers are pondering as to their next move. Meanwhile the privatisation of electricity production in the North, the restoration of the inter-connector between the North and the South and the building of a gas pipeline across the Irish Sea have altered the playing field and today there is a rather uncertain truce among the players.

It is possible that a trough, similar to that that developed in Antrim, was produced in the area now occupied by the Shannon drainage basin (*Illus. 14*) and perhaps also in the Erne Basin. The drainage of the Shannon is one of Ireland's long-standing electoral carrots. Nearly every winter there is extensive flooding along the margins of the river and the call goes up for its drainage. But the Shannon can only be drained – whatever magnificent engineering works may be carried out – if there is a sufficient gradient between the water level in the basin and the water level in the sea for the flood waters to be discharged rapidly.

It may well be that the basin was lowered to its present level by tectonic sagging. At today's level, there is probably not sufficient fall for unassisted gravity discharge. Colossal pumps might be installed, but pumping would be hopelessly uneconomic. The annual pumping season would be very short and the land to be drained is not of high quality. The best solution would be to compensate the farmers for flood losses and preserve the river margins as water meadows. These would shelter many birds including the much-threatened corncrake.

Meteorologists today discuss 'Storms of the Century' when extreme conditions occur perhaps for only a short while. If the flood heights likely to be attained in the Shannon under such conditions could be set out on a map, then no further domestic or agricultural building should be permitted below that level. Such a measure might be Draconian, but it would prevent the pictures that appear so regularly on our television screens in winter of the flooding of relatively new homes.

About 35 million years ago, the prevailing tropical weathering had powerful effects on nearly all types of rock and not only on those composed of silicates; quartzite alone might have had some chance of survival (*Illus. 15*). The calcite of limestone and chalk can be directly dissolved by percolating water. As solution proceeds, the small amounts of clay that are also present in the rock are left behind as a superficial mantle. In the case of chalk, the embedded flints disappear more slowly than the calcite and a capping of 'clay with flints' develops. In southern England where large areas of chalk survive to the present day, such 'clay with flints' caps the chalk over wide areas.

In some parts of Antrim, the old chalk surface underneath the basalt carries a capping of flint debris; this shows that the weathering away of the chalk had started even before the lavas were poured out. Karstic features can also be seen. South of Cork city there is a large area of high ground; here an unusually high number of pieces of flint are scattered through the modern soil. These may be the last remnants of a former deposit of 'clay with flints'.

Once the chalk was removed, Carboniferous limestone appeared over a large part of central Ireland, and karstic attack on it resumed. However, as the calcite of

the limestone was carried away in solution, the small amount of clay it contained was left behind and gradually accumulated as a superficial mantle. In the limestone there were siliceous nodules of black chert, just as there were brown nodules of flint in chalk. The siliceous chert did not succumb to chemical weathering and the residual clay often contained a substantial number of nodules of chert. On occasion, mineral exploration drillings have encountered layers of chert nodules; as chert is harder than steel there was very heavy wear on the drilling bits. Such nodules may well have been lying in a layer of 'clay with chert'.

As the protective mantle developed, the rate at which the calcite could be removed was slowed down and perhaps halted altogether. Any metallic ores that existed in the limestone were also attacked by weathering and complex hydrated compounds were formed. This seems to have been the case at the valuable lead and zinc deposit at Tynagh, Co. Galway, where the upper altered part of the ores lay in karstic hollows. The finding of a log of cypress wood in the ore supports the suggested age of about 35 million years.

Illus. 15
Errigal, Co. Donegal.
A residual cone of
quartzite at 750m is
mantled by frost-
shattered scree. At its
base, at 60m, beyond
the cottages, ridges of
moraine are banked
against the lower
slopes.

Over considerable areas of Ireland and of western Britain, the limestone is perforated by vertical karstic pipes which contain weathered material. In one such pipe at Ballymacadam near Cahir, the fill material contains pollen that indicates woodland of the same general type as that of the Lough Neagh clays and is presumably also of similar age. Exploratory drillings for minerals in the karstic country around Abbeyleix also penetrated clays and lignites at depth. The fill material must have developed in a depression in a land surface at a once higher level. How much higher? Is the fill material the last remnant of the sediment that formerly occupied a now vanished basin? These are questions which are of the greatest significance for the origin of the modern Irish landscape.

In Co. Clare today, the limestone which has been scoured by later ice sheets lies naked at the surface without any protective mantle of clay and is being dissolved away at a rapid rate. One estimate suggests that the limestone surface is being lowered at a rate of 0.053mm per annum. If this rate is projected backwards, it means that the surface was lowered by 53m in one million years and that a layer of limestone more than 1000m thick vanished during the last 25 million years. That the rate of weathering can be rapid cannot be denied. At Carrigacappeen near Kenmare, a large insoluble boulder of sandstone sits precariously on top of a pedestal of solid limestone 1.5m high (*Illus.16*). The boulder was deposited from ice on the limestone surface about 18,000 years ago; 1.5m of rock has disappeared since then. In parts of the Burren, field walls, which cannot be more than 5000 years old, were once built on a level rock surface. Now the walls stand on a shallow plinth of solid rock which is protected from solution, while the surface of the adjacent rock has been lowered by several centimetres.

Such rapid erosion as seen in the Burren would long since have destroyed not only the Ballymacadam pipe fill but also the ore deposit at Tynagh. We are driven to

Illus. 16
Carrigacappeen near Kenmare, Co. Kerry. As ice melted away 18,000 years ago, this erratic boulder of sandstone came to rest on a relatively even limestone surface. Since then, solution by rainfall has removed 1.5m of limestone except where it was protected by the erratic which now stands perilously perched.

the conclusion, therefore, that the karstic limestone surface of the Irish midlands, ranging between 60 and 120m in height, must be a very old one and that it has only been able to survive due to the former possession of a protective mantle of clay and woodland. The modern rapid rate of solution set in only after that protective mantle was torn away by later frost and ice.

25 MILLION TO 2 MILLION YEARS AGO

About twenty-five million years ago, Ireland was nearing its present position of latitude and was only very slowly moving away from North America. An irregular fall in temperature was beginning; periods of lowering were followed by periods of recovery, but always with a downward trend. These changes in temperature appear not to have been due to Ireland changing its position on the earth's surface, but were climatic in origin and worldwide in extent. About 13 million years ago, icecaps were beginning to form in north polar regions. The quantity of ice present was under constant change, but there was never complete melting.

By this time, except for upstanding pinnacles of limestone in karstic areas, there were probably very few exposed areas of solid rock to be seen in Ireland. In granitic areas, such as the Wicklow Uplands and the Mourne Mountains, the rock as it contracted on cooling had developed shrinkage-cracks or joints at right angles to one another. Cubical blocks were thus created and weathering was most severe on the corners. Gradually, the surface of the rock became mantled with surviving spherical lumps of relatively unaltered rock, generally called *core-stones*. Gabbros and some types of sandstone were similarly affected.

In most places, the soil mantle was very thick and relatively uniform; original differences, due to the character of the underlying rocks, were largely eliminated by the vigour of the chemical weathering processes. The surface layer was probably brown or grey due to the presence of small quantities of decayed vegetable debris or humus and the absence of iron. The colour of the underlying weathered hydrous oxide clays was probably red or yellow due to the presence of fully oxidised iron. Gradually, this weathered clay merged into the unaltered rock below, probably at a depth of several tens of metres. In places where the soil was of considerable depth and its surface was so leached of nutrient that plants could not grow, the soil was dissected by stream flow after rain. Such landscapes can be seen in the western United States where they are known as 'badlands'; they may well have existed in Ireland at this time.

On low-lying ground, where soil drainage was poorer, there was a greater accumulation of humus and a black clayey soil was formed. Where soil conditions permitted, the whole country was densely wooded by trees, many of which would have been unfamiliar to our modern eyes. If we wish to see these trees growing today, we must look to the mountains of eastern North America and China.

This period, therefore, was one of falling temperatures and diminishing vigour on the part of the soil-forming agencies. But the altered conditions could not give anything back to the already heavily-depleted soils and they probably altered little. Rainfall may have increased and there may have been some erosion of the soil mantle, with increased deposition of clays, sands and gravels on lower grounds. There are extensive deposits of plant remains of this age in northern Europe and they indicate a warm temperate woodland, again similar to that seen in eastern North America today.

Magnolias, sweet gums (*Liquidambar*), black gums, swamp cypress and palms occurred and the hemlock (*Tsuga*) made its first appearance. Some of the conifers appear to have been identical with modern species. There were also raised bogs, perhaps not very different from those we know today. One Irish deposit, again in a solution pipe, has an age of perhaps 15 million years and may be from this period. At Hollymount, north of Carlow town, where the ground has a height of about 70m, a well which was expected to hit Carboniferous limestone at about 10m, went instead to a depth of over 60m in a pipe (almost down to modern sea level) before it was abandoned without hitting solid rock. The fill sediment contained finely-divided powdery quartz with lignite and pollen at some levels. As well as leaves of heather (*Erica*), pollens of the heather family (including *Rhododendron*) were very common and there were some spores of *Sphagnum* moss. Coniferous trees were represented by pollen of pine, redwood, hemlock and umbrella pine (*Sciadopitys*) and among the broad-leaved trees were alder, birch (*Betula*), hazel (*Corylus*), holly, hornbeam (*Carpinus*) and willow (*Salix*). Palms still survived. The plant evidence suggests a forest, rich in varieties of trees, growing when temperatures were higher and seasonally more uniform than at present. Sphagnum and heathers grew in wet hollows as these plants require acid conditions. Here again is evidence that the underlying calcareous limestone rock was mantled by a layer of clayey soil out of which all lime had been leached by deep weathering.

Hollymount lies beside the River Barrow which at this point flows into an open limestone valley at a height of 70m. But 50km farther south, where the river is almost at sea level, a ridge of very much older granite rises through the limestone to lie across its path. The river is not deflected; at Graiguenamanagh it enters a gorge with incised meanders whose rock walls rise to a height of 75m on either side. To add to the puzzle, although the gorge is 40km from the point where Waterford Harbour opens out into the sea at Hook Head, spring tides flow up through the gorge as far as Graiguenamanagh.

How do we explain the paradox set by the Graiguenamanagh gorge? Some geomorphologists would claim that at this time in this part of south-east Ireland, there was a high planation surface (a surface thought to have been smoothed by erosion, either sub-aerial or marine) at about 225m and that the river pattern we see today was initiated on this surface. As the surface was washed away through denudation and older rocks began to be revealed below, the strength of river flow was sufficient to cut down into the older rocks and so maintain the flow. If the Hollymount plants were growing on this surface, then the pipe must have been over 250m deep and it seems impossible to think that plant debris could work its way down more than 200m without being completely destroyed en route.

This rather passive view is rejected and it is considered that the older rocks were raised tectonically above an already low-lying landscape and that the river trenched through the rising blocks. In south-east Ireland, not only the Barrow but also the Nore and the Slaney are spectacularly indifferent to the geological structures across which they pick their way; all have cut narrow gorges through the granite ridge which seems to bar their course. As the granite block was slowly raised, the rivers trenched across it as fast as it rose. Thus by maintaining their original course, they found themselves leaving open country, passing through a steep-sided gorge and emerging to open country once more. The present steepness of the gorges may be partly due to the discharge, during the melting of the later ice sheets of the midlands, of great quantities of melt-water through them to a sea level lower than that of today. Such major landforms, however, cannot have been initiated by melt-water overflow.

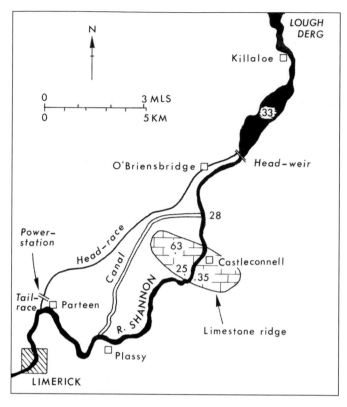

On a smaller scale, the same paradox arises at two points on the course of the Shannon between Clonmacnoise and Limerick. Over certain places, the limestone was more resistant to solution than at others and a residual knoll, known to geomorphologists as a *hum*, gradually rose up. If the river's course crossed such an area, as at Meelick north of Portumna, the river was not deflected. However, the Grand Canal, which followed the river as far possible, had to negotiate some locks.

Castleconnell, seven miles north-east of Limerick (*Illus. 17*) lies on another hum. While the river ploughed on through the hum in a gorge, the canal followed lower ground to the west. Much the same route as the canal was taken by the head-race to the Ardnacrusha power station. The race drew water from the river south of Killaloe and the flow of water through the gorge near Castleconnell was very greatly reduced and its rapids have become much less spectacular.

Illus. 17
As at Meelick further north, the Shannon at Castleconnell in Co. Limerick cuts across an upstanding ridge of limestone, although lower ground lies to the west.

This is the view of French geomorphologists who consider that by this time, many millions of years ago, the relief of the modern landscape was already blocked out, its river valleys were in existence and sea level was similar to that of today. In southern Brittany, the corresponding sediments were deposited within already existing river valleys when they were flooded by the sea, either by a rising in sea level or by sinking of the land. The landscape of south-east Ireland has much in common with that of south Brittany and rivers such as the Barrow in Ireland and the Vilaine in France exhibit the same paradox – their valleys are incised into the landscape while their lower reaches are drowned by the sea with the result that the tide runs up these rivers for many kilometres inland.

Several years ago, Professor Herries Davies, when discussing the age of the Wicklow Mountains, suggested that there might have been late tectonic movement in this part of Ireland. The mountains are eroded out of pre-existing granite. To have achieved its coarsely crystalline texture, the molten granite, which was intruded 400 million years ago, must have cooled slowly below a thick insulating roof of older rock. Despite such burial, granitic debris appears in the nearby Old Red Sandstone, showing that already by that early date erosion had exposed at least part of the granite at the surface. If erosion had continued without interruption, one would think that all of the protecting cover would have been removed. The highest point on the range today, the summit of Lugnaquilla at about 1000m, is not of granite, however, but is part of the roof which has not yet been completely removed. It seems possible, therefore, that for much of its long geological history this part of the Wicklow granite lay at a lower level protected by younger sediments above. At a later date, it was uplifted as a block and erosion is now attacking it once more.

Images taken from satellites can indicate landscape features in a remarkable way. The summit of Lugnaquilla lies in the centre of the Landsat-2 image (*Illus. 18a*). In the east, we see the older rocks into which the granite was intruded some 400 million years ago. In the north centre, we see the deeply-dissected dome of granite which has been exposed by denudation. On its north-west side, it rises steeply above the older rocks, separated from them by a break in slope with a remarkably straight course. To the south-west, a straight-edged salient of low ground outlined by a break in slope thrusts into the highlands. In the lowland, Carboniferous limestone deposited 300 million years ago rests on a weathered granite surface.

It is probable that the break in slope resulted from recent tectonic uplift on the east and downthrow on the west. In consequence, the top of the granite stands at 925m on the uplift side, while the glacial deposits and the limestone on the downthrow side lie on a surface, more than 800m lower, to which the granite had been cut down by weathering.

We probably see tectonic movement again in western Ireland where, to the west of Lough Mask, patches of rock 325 million years old lie on the top of Maumtrasna at elevations between 600 and 700m. To the east of the lough, the same rocks are buried beneath younger rocks whose karstic surface lies at an elevation of less than 70m.

Lough Hyne, south-west of Skibbereen in Co. Cork, is a very remarkable place (*Illus. 19*). It is a small lake, square in outline with sides about 1km long and more than 40m deep in places; it is very close to the sea. At the end of the Ice Age, its waters were fresh, but a later rise in sea level enabled salt water to flow in along a narrow channel, the Rapids, where at low water the depth may be less than a metre. The channel has enabled a rich marine flora and fauna to enter the lake and so make it a Mecca for marine biologists.

The setting of Lough Hyne suggests relatively recent subsidence as the lake lies in terrain with some indication of a planation surface at about 80m. North-west of the lough, there is a hill that rises to almost 200m while the present floor of the basin has a depth of 45m. The basin must hold a considerable quantity of recent unconsolidated debris and the rock floor probably lies at a substantially lower level. It has been suggested that the rock basin is a corrie excavated by ice when the sea level was lower than it is at present; but no corrie-like features are apparent. Nor does it seem possible that it was gouged out by a flow of glacier ice. It cannot have been created by wave erosion nor by river erosion as no rivers flow into or through it. The surrounding rock is of Old Red Sandstone so it cannot be a solution hollow. Differential movement of the order of at least 300m, which created a hill on one side and a hollow below sea level on the other, becomes a possibility. But this hypothesis is rejected by many hard-rock geologists who say that they cannot see any traces of fault movement in the surrounding rocks. The mystery remains unsolved.

We meet with a different mystery when we look at the great rivers of Co. Cork – the Blackwater, the Lee and the Bandon – which are set in a planation surface with their trellis-patterns of long eastward-flowing stretches truncated by short southward-flowing discharge channels. One hundred years ago, J B Jukes, a distinguished director of the Geological Survey, thought that the north/south element was the older having been initiated on a south-sloping surface of chalk and cutting down into older rocks as the chalk vanished through denudation. As we have seen, the older rocks were deposited as two types of sediment, sandstone below and limestone above. Earth pressure then pleated these into east/west folds. Where limestone capped a ridge, it quickly disappeared to reveal a ridge of sandstone, but its removal from a trough was slower. Jukes thought that the limestone was still in the troughs when chalk was deposited on top and that after the chalk had gone, the later east/west tributaries pushed gradually westwards as the limestone was removed.

Illus. 18a Landsat-2 image (13.11.76) of part of south-east Ireland showing block elevation of part of granite massif.

However, as we stated earlier, a low-level karstic depression was found in the limestone near Cloyne which contained a deposit older than the chalk. Therefore, much of the limestone was removed from the east/west troughs before the chalk was deposited and of course the chalk would also have filled the troughs. It is possible – as Jukes thought – that the south-flowing elements of the pattern did start on a chalk surface and succeeded in cutting through the sandstone ridges as they emerged through the chalk, thus continuing their north/south course to the sea.

Although we know little of rates of erosion and of later earth movements, we cannot see in the Irish river systems any substantial legacy from a chalk surface formed 70 million years ago and so the relief of the modern landscape must be younger. But how much younger? At Poulnahallia near Headford in Co. Galway, there is a karstic area of Carboniferous limestone at about 70m above sea level. One large depression contains a layer of lignite about 5m thick which is covered first by blown sand and then by glacial deposits. Pollen of palms has vanished and pollen of hemlock has appeared, but many of the older tree forms, such as redwood, swamp cypress, and umbrella pine, are still represented. Quantities of ericaceous pollen again suggest acid soil conditions. An age of 3 million years might be suggested. Thin patches of lignite, giving similar pollen counts, occur in the immediate vicinity. Here again we have a paradox; we are told that limestone is very vulnerable to erosion, yet no significant amounts have been removed here in the past 3 million years or even in the past 35 million years as the picture at Ballymacadam suggests.

Illus. 18b
Diagram indicating
features in the
Landsat-2 image.

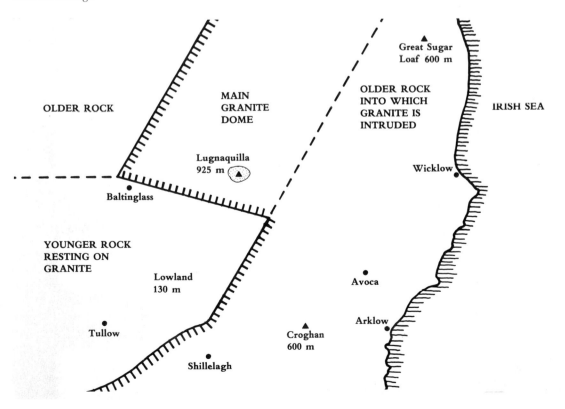

Illus. 19
Lough Hyne in
Co. Cork is connected
to the sea by the
channel on the right
(the picture shows
high tide). We look
north and as soil
cover is thin, the
east/west rock
structure imposed by
folding 300 million
years ago can be seen.
The heavily shadowed
scarp may be due to
later earth movements
which raised a block
of rock and lowered
the floor of the lough.
In the blind arm on
the left there is
'submerged' peat. In
the rocky foreground
there are small fields
made at a time of
greater population.

Across the channel at St. Erth in Cornwall, we get a pollen-diagram similar to that at Poulnahallia and perhaps of the same age. Here on sandy terrain, a coniferous woodland with pine, fir (*Abies*) and hemlock and a ground vegetation dominated by heathers, surrounded a small lagoon in which a marine clay was deposited. As well as the plant fossils, the clay also had shellfish and other marine organisms. *Foraminifera* suggest an age of about 4 million years. The clay was at a height of 40m, but again the usual ambiguity presented itself as to whether the sea was 40m above its present level when the deposit was being formed, or whether we are dealing with a basin which was formerly at a lower level and has since been raised to its present height. Late tectonic uplift was recently demonstrated in the Portsmouth area in southern Britain.

The problem of minor tectonic movements is a complex one. If we go to the vicinity of Lismore and Cappoquin and turn north, the valley wall of the Blackwater gives way to a remarkably flat surface slightly below 250m which can be up to 5km wide. A cliff then appears and the Knockmealdown Mountains rise quickly up (*Illus. 20*). How was the surface, which has been described as a peneplane, formed? Erosion by waves at a time when sea level was markedly higher was the first suggestion. Telling objections can be raised to this view and normal atmospheric weathering has also been suggested. The surface must be 'young' or else it would have been destroyed by erosion.

We have seen that where chemical weathering is involved there can be an abrupt horizon between deeply-weathered and fresh rock. The horizon was often relatively level, or at least followed the surface topography, just as the modern water table does. When frost action developed in the subsequent glacial episodes, the

Illus. 20
Etch-plain near
Cappoquin,
Co. Waterford.

mantle of weathered clay was quickly swept away and a relatively flat rock surface was exposed. Weathering processes were strongest where slopes increased and with time the base of the slopes steepened into cliffs and the surface expanded. Flats that developed in this way are known as etch-plains. They are very well-developed in the western United States.

The flat surfaces of the Lismore area are etch-plains. Well-developed etch-plains are also seen in west Kerry. The road from Kells to Caherciveen has two impressive flat-floored horseshoes at about 100m surrounded by high rims on their southern side; these are drained by the Ferta and Carhan Rivers. On the other side of the road and across a major fault, Knocknadobar soars to almost 700m. If we look south from Portmagee towards the broadcasting masts standing on top of a horseshoe-shaped ridge, we see a gentle rise of about 2° which extends inland for a distance of 3km before the ground steeply rises to the ridge-crest at 300m. Although the low, almost flat, area has been partly buried by peat, it is drained by a fan of small streams running on rock; these converge to reach the sea at Portmagee. This area must be an etch-plain.

Etch-plains are also numerous in the Dingle Peninsula. At its west end, only a narrow arrête of high ground survives to link Mount Eagle to the Brandon massif. The etch-plains of Dingle and Ventry lie to the south-east and the extensive cluster of etch-plains around Smerwick Harbour are to the north-west (*Col. 2*). If we stand on the top of Mount Eagle and look westwards, it is clear that this type of relief continues on below the modern sea. Beyond the ridge-crest of the Blasket, we see a small archipelago of unsubmerged hilltops.

All of these etch-plains have been partly invaded by the sea to create harbours. Does this indicate that in this area the relative levels of the sea and the coast are out of balance? The etch-plains have been flooded and wave attack has created high cliffs, which are subject to constant rock-falls. Just south-west of Portmagee, a hog-backed ridge of rock running west-north-west has been deeply cut into, creating a range of magnificent cliffs (*Col. 7*). Puffin Island nearby is crumbling away under wave attack, yet there is no wave-cut platform lying at a shallow depth below the face of the cliffs. Skellig Michael tells the same story. There is no wave-cut platform; the cliffs continue to below 40m on the south face, and to much greater depths on the north face, and the marine life that grows on them is a source of constant wonder to visiting scuba-divers.

Narrow pinnacles such as Skellig Michael and the Tearacht (one of the islands off the Blaskets) protrude high above the sea. The waters of the surrounding seas were not surveyed to the standard expected today, but there are suggestions that submerged pinnacles are common in these waters. If modern sea levels were to drop by 100m in this area, a dramatic archipelago would appear.

About 25 million years ago, ice began to build up in Antarctica. In Europe, grasslands and open vegetation replaced the forests and when the woodland broke up, many plants disappeared. At a date probably about 2 million years ago, severe conditions of cold established themselves in north-west Europe.

2. The Ice Age 1,700,000 to 13,000 years ago

Dating Methods

As we get nearer and nearer to the present day, the detail we can see with our time telescope increases rapidly and we can begin to measure events in thousands instead of millions of years. This is because we are able to use more precise methods of dating (magnetic, radiometric and chemical) to assist us in placing deposits in chronological order.

As we have already seen, the earth's magnetic field reverses its direction at rather lengthy, irregular intervals and the time of such reversals can be measured by radiometric dating at favourable localities. One such locality is the famous Olduvai Gorge in Uganda. In the past, there was a lake here and the lake basin filled up with stratified layers of volcanic ash. Important fossil material was buried in the ash, not only bones of animals but also implements used by Palaeolithic (Early Stone Age) man. A later river cut a gorge down through the ash and the walls of the gorge reveal a splendid sequence of deposits. By measuring the magnetism of the deposits, a reversal in a layer of ash can be dated to about 1.7 million years ago. This reversal can also be traced in many other parts of the earth. The early human material can also be dated to the same time. So, because the reversal here is most valuable for dating purposes, its date is chosen for the formal opening of the Ice Age. It may seem curious to choose a site in tropical Africa to herald an Ice Age, but with more recent precision it is hoped to make this timing valid throughout the whole globe.

Geologists have divided the older fossiliferous rocks of the earth into three great divisions characterised by the appearance of more and more advanced types of life. The appearance of man was regarded as marking a further advance and a new division, the Quaternary or fourth, was opened. The growing and ebbing of great masses of ice was a great feature of this division and so it is loosely described as the Ice Age.

A new technique used in dating Ice Age deposits is essentially chemical and is based on oxygen isotope ratios. Oxygen is available in seawater, and tiny organisms which float in the sea, *Foraminifera*, extract oxygen from the water to build up calcareous shells. There are two main forms (or isotopes) of oxygen atom present, one lighter and one heavier; organisms take up the two forms as they occur in the water. If the proportions of the two forms change with time, then shells from one generation will differ from later shells in the proportion of the two forms of oxygen

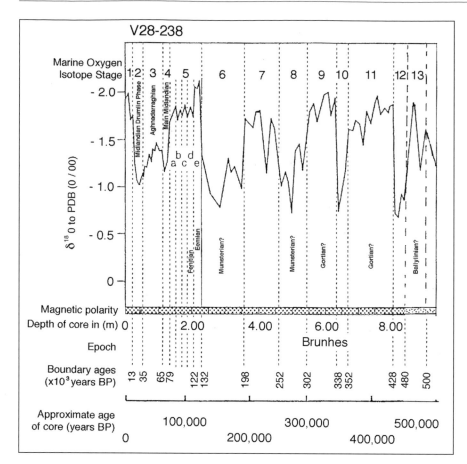

Illus. 21
The later Marine
Oxygen Isotope Stage
with Irish phases
inserted at the
appropriate points.

they contain. The difference is very small, but can be measured using sensitive instruments. When ice sheets form, oxygen from the seawater is locked in them and the ice preferentially takes up the lighter form. Consequently, the proportion of the heavier form in the remaining water increases and this change is recorded in the foraminiferal shells.

When the organisms die, their shells sink to the ocean floor where they accumulate in layers; each layer recording the oxygen proportions of its time. Again, using very sophisticated equipment, a cored vertical column of sediment can be recovered from the sea floor and analysed. The varying proportions of oxygen can be traced and hence the varying amount of ice on the earth's surface can be calculated. The assumption can then be made that large amounts of ice indicate cold conditions and small amounts of ice indicate warm conditions.

Since the concept first arose about 25 years ago, fantastic developments have taken place and we can now 'read' the thermal history of the surface of the ocean throughout the last million years. These new studies of sea floor deposits show that there have been a considerable number of climatic oscillations in the not too distant geological past. In the British Isles, Quaternary deposits suggest that ice deposited melt-out material on quite a number of occasions. There are a smaller number of records of warm-stage vegetation, but it is proving a very difficult task to assign these to their appropriate place in the oceanic record. Twenty-three cold/warm Marine Oxygen Isotope Stages (here abbreviated to MS) have been recognised in the oceanic record; these have been numbered, counting downwards from the top. In each stage, a short cold phase is followed by a longer warm phase and the change from cold to warmth and vice versa takes place extremely rapidly. The earlier stages have an overall duration of about 100,000 years, but in the youngest upper layers of the sea floor the record is preserved in great detail and – rather confusingly – five stages have been defined in the deposits of the last 132,000 years. This means that the last five stages, which are relatively short, are given the same status in the numbering system as the very much longer, earlier stages. In at least two of these later stages – the first beginning about 79,000 years ago and the second beginning about 35,000 years ago – conditions were cold enough to allow masses of ice to build up in the British Isles.

The complete record available from the oceans stretches back for more than 1.5 million years, but the earlier part is only of academic interest to us in Ireland. The curve for the last 500,000 years is shown in *Illus. 21*; some Irish localities are entered on the curve, and are recorded in Table 2. However, these placings can only be regarded as highly tentative. The reasoning behind these placings will be discussed later when the deposits are being described (see also p. 57).

Table 2

POSSIBLE RELATIONSHIP BETWEEN MARINE OXYGEN ISOTOPE STAGES AND CLIMATIC EVENTS IN IRELAND DURING THE PAST 500,000 YEARS

MS	Years Ago	
1	13,000-10,000	Late-gacial
2	35.000-13,000	Midlandian (Drumlin) Cold
3	65,000-35,000	Aghnadarraghian Mild
4	79,000-65,000	Midlandian (Main) Cold
5d	122,000-100,000	Fenitian Mild
5e	132,000-122,000	Eemian Warm
6	198,000-132,000	} Munsterian Cold
	or	
8	302,000-252,000	
9	338,000-302,000	} Gortian Warm
	or	
11	428,000-352,000	
13	500,000-480,000	Ballylinian Warm

As there is no reason to think that the relatively genial climate of today is any more firmly established than that of previous transient 'warm stages', the view will be taken here that the so-called 'postglacial' in which we live is merely another 'warm stage', now named in Ireland the Littletonian Warm Stage, which will in all probability be succeeded in due course by yet another 'cold stage'.

We can check on the latest stages – for the past 40,000 years – of the oceanic

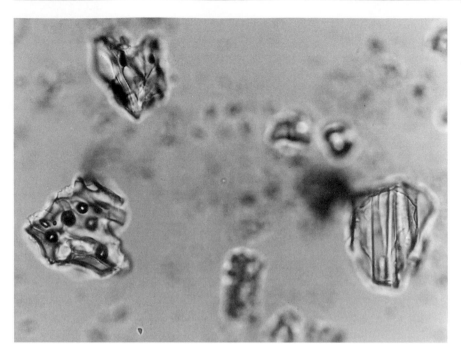

Illus. 22
Volcanic ash
fragments in peat,
Croagharn East,
Co. Mayo.

record by another method, that of radiocarbon dating. The atmosphere contains a very rare and radioactive form of carbon with an atomic weight of 14, called ^{14}C in chemical shorthand. Most living organisms contain some amount of radioactive carbon. After their death, the content of radioactive carbon gradually decays. By measuring the quantity that remains, scientists can tell the number of years before the present that have elapsed since the organism died (e.g. 23,000 BP). Radiocarbon dating or ^{14}C dating is of immense importance to geologists and archaeologists. However, it has only a limited range because when 40,000 years have elapsed, the amount of ^{14}C surviving is too small to be measured accurately. There are problems associated with this method and a discussion of these begins on p. 68.

Today two other methods – tephrochronology and dendrochronology (see p. 69) – are beginning to develop. Tephrochronology involves studying molten lava and ash from eruptions. The chemical composition of molten lavas in the earth's crust is constantly changing. If an eruption occurs, both the lava and the ejected ash (glass fragments) will have the same mineralogical make-up and can be traced back to their source. Depending on wind patterns, some ash will travel for long distances before falling to the ground. If that ground is a growing bog, then the ash will form a thin layer in the accumulating deposit. This ash can be traced back to its parent volcano. Most Irish ash, which has been recorded from Antrim to Kerry, comes from volcanoes in Iceland, where many eruptions are well dated (*Illus. 22*). At least six layers of ash have been calendrically dated.

FROST AND ICE IN COLD STAGES

In Ireland, the deposits laid down by ice have been studied for more than one hundred years, but the study of the effect of cold unaccompanied by masses of ice is

Illus. 23
Quaternary geology
of Ireland.

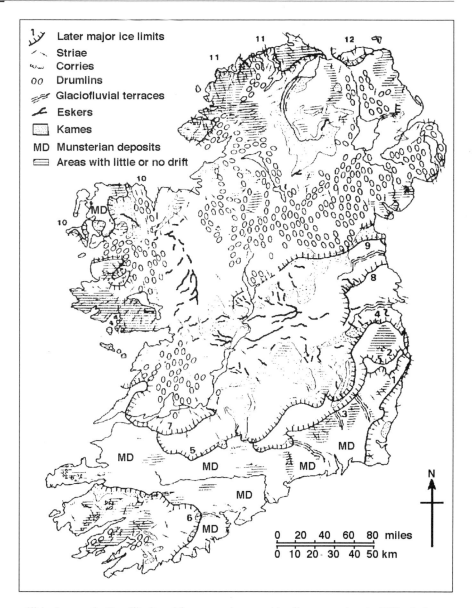

still in its youth. Familiarity with our moist oceanic climate makes it difficult for us to picture Ireland in the dry grip of perennial frost with a landscape typical of cold polar deserts. Round the margins of modern ice sheets, climatic conditions are severe and frost processes are active; such a region and the processes can both be described as *periglacial*. However, these processes are largely brought about by the energy produced by water as it expands and contracts in volume on freezing and thawing and this freeze-thaw activity is not confined to regions in the vicinity of ice sheets. Periglacial processes flourish best where summer thaws do not entirely melt away the frosts of previous winters and where, at some times of the year, there is repeated oscillation of temperature across the freezing-point of water.

If winter freeze consistently exceeds summer thaw, then an ever-thickening

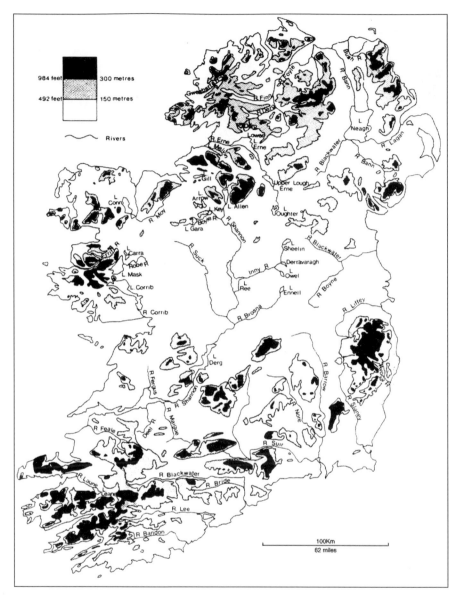

*Illus. 24
Major geographical
features of Ireland.*

*Illus. 25
Modern ice-wedge in
frozen silt near
Fairbanks, Alaska
(rule is 50cm).*

*Illus. 26
(Opposite left)
Fossil ice-wedge-cast
in Late Midlandian
outwash gravels,
Gorticross, Co. Derry
(matchbox gives
scale).*

layer of permanently frozen subsoil or *permafrost* will develop. Heat flow from the
earth's interior will inhibit freezing below a limiting depth, but in Siberia today the
permafrost extends beyond 500m in depth. It is not known to what depth the
permafrost formed in Ireland – perhaps to about 20m – but structures characteristic of it were formed in more than one cold stage. Marked contraction of the
surface layer of the ground during the cold of winter caused tapering shrinkage-
cracks to develop. Repeated layers of hoar-frost on the walls of the crack gradually
filled it with a wedge-shaped tongue of ice (*Illus. 25*) If, when the ice later melted,
earth took its place, an *ice-wedge-cast* was formed and such structures are widely
known in Ireland (*Illus. 26*). Sometimes the shrinkage-cracks were arranged in a
polygonal pattern and *ice-wedge-polygons*, whose patterns can still be traced today,

*Illus. 27
(Opposite right)
Fossil ice-wedge-
polygons probably of
Midlandian age,
Broomhill Point,
Co. Wexford.*

were formed (*Illus. 27*). They can even be seen in the very old lithified glacial deposits in Donegal (see p. 5).

If, in summer, the surface thaws while a still-frozen layer remains below, then water cannot drain away downwards. As a result, the surface layers become supersaturated with water and highly mobile forming the so-called *active layer*. Where the surface has a slope of even as much as 1°, the active layer will move downslope in a generally unsorted condition and when it eventually comes to rest it will form a deposit of *head*. Deposits of head are common in Ireland; on Skellig Michael in Kerry, gullies hold streams of immobilised head. If slopes are steep, as seen on the south of Lower Lough Erne, blocks of rock may become detached and glide laterally down the slope (*Illus. 28*).

Where the slope is less than 1°, gravity may not be able to draw the material away and the supersaturated material will remain in a stagnant condition. Water that is near its freezing-point varies in density due to slight changes in temperature. These variations produce movements analogous to convection-currents in the supersaturated layer and under the influence of these movements, the materials of the active layer become

sorted into coarser and finer units. In plan, a net-like pattern may appear with finer material in the interstices of the net and coarser material along the strands. In section, irregular columns of stones arranged with their long axes vertical underlie the strands while below the interstices irregular material has the appearance of a basin-fill. Polygonally *patterned ground* – not to be confused with ice-wedge-polygons – is formed and such patterned ground can be seen from Wexford to Kerry. Less regular currents churn the active layer in a tumultuous manner and strings of stones are drawn out into irregular bands or involutions, a process known as *cryoturbation*. Where the ground does slope very slightly, the sorted stones may be drawn out into *stone-*

stripes running downhill. Both involutions and stone-stripes are common in Ireland.

Illus. 28
Mass downslope rock movement by periglacial sliding.

As summer gives way to autumn, the surface of the active layer re-freezes, trapping a layer of as yet unfrozen water between the frozen ground below and the thickening rind of re-freezing material above. Sooner or later this trapped pocket of water will itself freeze and as it does so it must create space in which it can expand on changing from liquid to solid. Under certain special circumstances, not yet clearly understood, the expanding water forces its way upwards, elevates the frozen surface layer with its contained soil and turns itself into a dome-like mass of ice; an ice-cored mound is thus created. Such mounds are well known in arctic Canada today and are called by the Eskimo name of *pingo* (*Illus. 29*). When such a structure starts to thaw, the outer layer with its contained soil melts first and starts to slump down surrounding the still unmelted central ice with a ring of earth and soil (*Illus. 30*). When melting is complete, the former pingo is represented by a residual central hollow surrounded by a raised rim. Fossil structures of this type are very common in south-east Ireland (*Illus. 31*).

In Ireland, therefore, we have ample evidence that in certain stages of the Ice Age the general aspect of the landscape must have been essentially identical to that seen in arctic Canada and arctic Siberia today. By contrast, Greenland today is buried by ice up to 2300m thick and there is also evidence to show that Ireland too once carried an extensive ice-cover with large areas at all levels completely buried by a great thickness of ice. If such large masses of ice were to have formed, the amount of snow that fell in the winter must have exceeded the amount that was melted away in the summer.

The first stage of accumulation took place on higher ground. Irish upland topography has many hills and hollows. Hollows that faced north-east received the least sun and there the snow was slowest to melt. Where snow failed to melt in

*Illus. 29
Modern pingo near
Yakutsk, Siberia.*

*Illus. 30
Collapsing pingo in
permafrost with ice-
wedge-polygons near
Tuktoyaktuk, North
Western Territories.*

*Illus. 31
Fossil pingos,
Camaross,
Co.Wexford.*

summer, a permanent snow-patch was formed. Above the patch, the wedging action of the freeze-thaw process was breaking up the ground and loosened debris slid down across the frozen surface of the snow-patch to accumulate at its base as a ramp-like deposit of broken rock or talus. Errigal and Muckish mountains in Donegal show splendid examples of *pro-talus ramparts* (*Illus. 15*). The thick snow in the patch gradually consolidated into a small lens of ice which itself began to slide downhill. As it did so, a gap appeared between it and the rock slope against which it was resting. Again freeze-thaw action detached pieces of rock from the slope and these fell against the ice and became incorporated in it. The ice now had rock 'teeth' and as it moved, these tore away the underlying rock and gradually a hollow or *corrie* (*Illus. 32*) was excavated in the rock of the hillside. Some lenses never expanded beyond this stage, but elsewhere domes of ice built up on the high ground and from these, tongues of ice or glaciers stretched away downslope. As the glacier moved along, it took advantage of the existing relief, especially river valleys. Armed with its contained pieces of rock, it deepened the V-shaped valley into a U-shaped trench. The magnificent results of recent valley glaciation of this type can be seen in the Wicklow Mountains (*Col. 10*) and in the Brandon mountain group in Kerry.

Illus. 32
Corrie above
Gulkana glacier,
Alaska.

Around Brandon, there was not a sufficient area of high ground for a local icecap to develop. Farther to the south and centring on the Kenmare estuary, there was sufficient high ground and the last of such icecaps formed here relatively recently. The high ground was not continuous but was dissected into ridges and valleys and these exercised a strong control on the directions of possible ice movement. In places, a tongue of ice forced its way across a ridge, gouging out a deep valley as it did so, as for example at the Gap of Dunloe. The ice-scoured country around the Upper Lake at Killarney gives further evidence of the erosive power of the ice while the drumlins at Bantry and the end-moraines around

Killarney and Caragh Lake show the materials that the ice transported and deposited. At an earlier stage, a similar tongue of ice cut across the Knockmealdown Mountains and created a short gorge, The Gap, through which the road from Caher to Lismore runs at a height above 600m.

At other times, more general ice developed, sometimes on a massive scale (*Col. 13*). As its weight increased, it depressed the surface of the land on which it rested. A very large icecap built up over the mountains of Scotland and from its south-west sector great masses of ice moved into northern Ireland and far down the Irish Sea. Ailsa Craig, which lies in the Firth of Clyde, is a conical peak of an unusual and easily-identified type of granite. Pieces of this rock were carried by glacial transport as far as Cork Harbour.

As the ice advanced, it picked up the superficial weathered material that lay in its path and thus came in contact with the underlying rock. It was now armed with incorporated sand and pebbles and could abrade the rock producing a surface that, in general, was rounded but on closer examination shows scratches or *striae* (*Illus 33*); these were produced when stones embedded in the base of the ice were dragged across the rock. The ice carried along not only the pebbles and clay it picked up as it advanced, but also new material plucked from the underlying rock; such material ranged in size from blocks of rock several cubic metres in volume to the finest of rock-flour.

Illus. 33
Striae at Mount
Gabriel, Co. Cork.

At times as the ice moved along, it deposited some of its basal load without possibility of sorting and so rocks, pebbles, sand and clay were disgorged in an indiscriminate mixture to form what used to be called boulder clay, but is now generally termed *till* or *diamict*. The latter term carries no implication of origin; it merely implies that the deposit is unsorted. Such deposits can be of considerable thickness. Some stones which have been carried for some distance from their original outcrop are deposited as *erratics* (*Illus. 34*).

If the ice continues to advance, a discontinuity may develop near the base of

the load it is carrying. When the ice
disappears, the material below the discontinuity is moulded into small ovoid masses
aligned with the direction of ice flow and a
swarm or field of small hills known as *drumlins*
is created (*Illus. 35*). This feature was first
recognised in Ireland and the name
'drumlin' is a blundered form of the Irish
word for a small hill. Drumlins usually occur
in clusters or fields and a broad swathe of
them extends across north central Ireland
from Down to Mayo. No satisfactory explanation has been given for their origin. Many
sections expose only till, but often, as in Clew
Bay, where wave action has cut deep sections,

the basal material is stratified gravel deposited by water; onto this a skin of till has
been plastered. Some sections exhibit small units of material which can only have
been deposited by running water. It is difficult to picture water channels existing in
material that must have been heavily compacted by the weight of the overlying
material. As we see the drumlins today, we have to ask: Are they primary
depositional features, or did moving ice cut them out of earlier material?

*Illus. 34
Erratic near
Kenmare, Co. Kerry.*

Between Roundstone and Slyne Head in Connemara, there are great areas
of ice-scoured rock. Scattered across this bare surface are occasional isolated
'typical' drumlins. Oughtdarnid (300m) is a hill 7km south-west of Donegal town.
The area is heavily ice-scoured, but at a point where a ridge rises from flatter
ground the notch has had a drumlin (on which there is a farm) inserted in it by
the passing ice. It is difficult to picture what conditions must have been like at
the base of the moving ice, if on the one hand it was capable of eroding rock and on
the other hand of excreting drumlins constructed of disturbed sediment entrapped
in the ice.

Ice disappeared or *ablated* from the ice mass in two ways, either by direct
evaporation into the air from the entire surface or by melting into water which
drained away from the margins. As the melt-water flowed away, it carried with it

*Illus. 35
Drumlins, The
Temple, Co. Down.*

*Illus. 36
Midlandian end-
moraine with kettle-
holes near Blackwater
in Co. Wexford
showing very
irregular topography
in a 'young'
landscape.*

some of the ice-enclosed debris released by the melting. If through a decrease in snowfall the rate at which the ice was ablating came to equal the rate at which the ice was advancing, the front of the ice appeared to stand still and the debris that had been dispersed throughout the ice was released along the line of the apparently stationary front. In this way, great quantities of sand and gravel were built up into an *end-moraine* (*Illus. 36*) while the escaping melt-water carried the clay fraction away in suspension. Where the melt-water stream flowed into a lake, *deltas* were built up. If the rate at which the ice was ablating overtook the rate at which it was advancing, then the ice mass became almost stationary or 'dead' and ablated away in situ, often producing a very confused topography of sand and gravel. Detached lumps of ice became embedded in gravel and when they later melted out, small lake basins or *kettle-holes* were formed.

Melt-water on the ice surface sank down through fissures in the ice to its base where major discharge tunnels were gradually established. The water in the tunnels often flowed vigorously under hydrostatic pressure and was capable of cutting the floor of the tunnel down into the ground below the ice and creating a *tunnel-valley*. As a result, on the final disappearance of the ice, a segment of incised valley usually bearing no relation to the modern surface drainage was exposed. Similarly, changes in discharge routes might lead to a section of tunnel being abandoned by the main

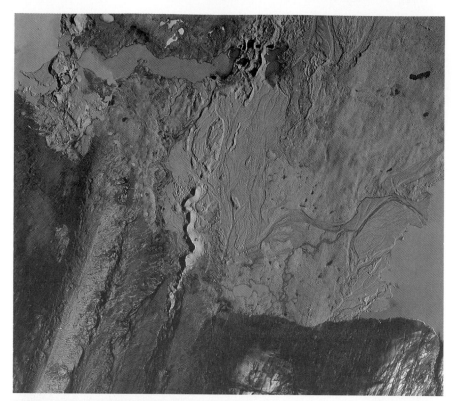

*Illus. 37
Eskers being exposed
as ice sheet melts
away,
Breidamerkurjokull,
Iceland.*

*Illus. 38
Bifurcating fossil
eskers near
Ballinlough,
Co. Roscommon.
Discharge water
flowed from bottom to
top of picture. Note
road on crest of esker
in lower right-hand
corner.*

stream flow and it would then silt up with sand and gravel. When the ice ultimately disappeared, the tunnel fill would emerge as a ridge (*Illus. 37, 38*) running across country often for several kilometres and bearing no relation to the local topography. In boggy country, such ridges provided natural causeways or eskers (Ir *eiscir*) and this Irish word has also passed into international geological usage.

Where the ice-fronts abutted against hilly ground, complicated situations developed and often great quantities of sand and gravel were deposited. Interpretations of the ways in which that deposition took place have steadily changed. The simplest of these was that ice dammed the valley mouths to create lakes in the valleys and where melt-waters discharged sand and gravel into the lake, great deltas were formed. Such deltas form important sources for concrete

Illus. 39
North of Galbally,
Co. Limerick, a rock
ridge of Hercynide
origin formed the
watershed between the
Shannon and the
Blackwater rivers. Ice
from the midlands
ponded melt-water
against the north face
of the ridge; the
ponded water over-
topped a low point on
the ridge and as it
gushed southwards it
cut a deep channel in
the ridge. The
watershed was thus
breached and some
water which formerly
went to the Shannon
now turns south to
the Blackwater.

aggregate. There are enormous deposits of such sand and gravel near Blessington in Co. Wicklow where an entire landscape is being quarried away. Where standing water spilt from one valley across a ridge into the next valley, a deep *overflow channel* was formed (*Illus. 39*). There are splendid examples of such deltas and channels in many parts of Ireland.

Interpretation has now been carried one stage further, and it is suggested that the detail of the complicated structures seen in the sands and gravels, often on a small scale, could only have been created in a vast lake completely roofed by ice. The debate seems set to continue.

The features that have just been described apply to land-based ice, but for a long time it had been noted that marine cliffs cut in glacial deposits such as those along the west shore of the Irish Sea from Belfast Lough to Cork Harbour and those around Donegal Bay exhibit features not known in inland Ireland. Some of these features suggest that water as well as ice was involved in their deposition.

Such old controversy has recently been given new life. When the geology of Ireland was first being surveyed in the second half of the last century, the surveyors could cope with the solid rocks, but were greatly puzzled as to the origin of the unconsolidated deposits that capped them, especially by the long ridges of poorly-stratified sand and gravel that ran uphill and downhill across the country. It was finally decided that they were marine deposited at a time when much of lowland Ireland was below sea level and their deposition was ascribed to the Esker Sea. But in 1867, it was demonstrated incontrovertibly at the Conor Pass in Dingle that the polishing and grooving seen on the local rocks could only have been produced by the action of moving ice and the Esker Sea vanished from sight.

The west shore of the Irish Sea presents an almost continuous section through glacial deposits and here some atypical features were noted. Some sections exhibited a very fine-grained mud or rock-flour whose very small particles could only have settled in almost current-free water. But scattered at random through the mud were isolated stones, sometimes of considerable size; if the mud was laminated, the laminae below the stones were disturbed. When the clay was being deposited, there must have been floating icebergs above and these released contained stones as they melted; the stones fell as *drop-stones* down into the mud below.

Today at the Ross Ice Shelf in Antarctica, the margin of the ice is afloat and it has been claimed recently that an ice sheet which stretched from central Ireland to central Wales about 22,000 years ago was similarly afloat where it crossed the Irish Sea. Fifty years ago, this would have been thought impossible because it was assumed that at times when there were great ice masses on the earth's surface, worldwide sea levels were low and ice margins could not float.

This older view has recently received new support. The British Geological Survey put down a boring into the bed of the Irish Sea, 80km south-west of Milford Haven in Wales. Below a water depth of 120m, a core of shelly debris 6m long was brought to the surface. The evidence from the fossils showed that they were late glacial in age and that sea level at the time of their deposition was probably 100m below that of today. If this was the case, then the earlier ice in the Irish Sea could not have been floating.

Illus. 40
The ice in two valleys
coalesces and flows
on into the sea. As it
becomes afloat it
breaks up into
icebergs and floes.

The floating theory pictures that about 17,000 years ago the end of an ice mass which had advanced down the Irish Sea was afloat except where it was stranded across the Isle of Man *(Illus. 41a)*. The end of the floating ice is shown in perspective in *Illus. 41b* and a section through the ice along the line AB is shown in *Illus. 42*. Before the ice became waterborne it had been shaping drumlins, but once afloat the debris it carried fell to the sea floor as dispersed morainic gravel and sand. Where water-bearing tunnels existed below the ice, the coarser material that was being carried along was dumped in a heap at the mouth of the tunnel. The tunnel was blocked by debris from time to time and when the temporary dam gave way, the

Illus. 41
a Ice mass at north
end of Irish Sea;
b perspective
drawing of floating
ice-edge.

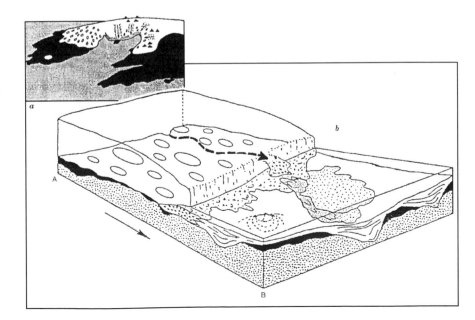

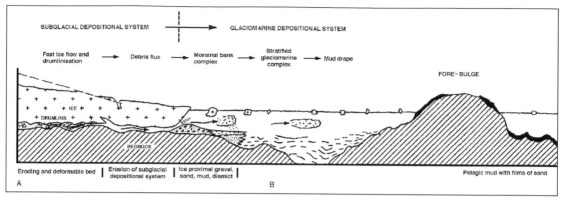

Illus. 42 Section though floating ice-edge and fore-bulge.

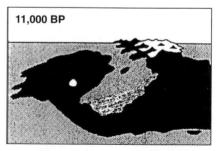

surging exit-waters carried gravel for quite some distance into the sea. The finer debris in the surge took more time to settle and was ultimately deposited as a sheet of mud. Icebergs laden with debris broke away from the ice-edge and slowly melted as they floated around. Occasional larger stones fell into the mud below as drop-stones.

When these deposits were later raised above sea level and exposed in wave-cut coastal sections, the picture presented was usually more complicated than that in inland sections. Where pent-up material had been released in a turbulent plume from the mouth of a sub-glacial tunnel, the debris fell to the sea floor in a relatively unsorted condition; such a deposit had a close resemblance to gravel deposited directly from ice. The fine rock-flour with its entrapped drop-stones had no parallel in inland sections.

The concept that as an icecap increased in weight it depressed the crust below it has been in circulation for many years. The displaced material rose as an annular *fore-bulge* surrounding the ice. Such equalising movements are called isostatic, while movements of sea level as ice masses expand and contract are known as eustatic. A schematic section through such a fore-bulge is shown in *Illus. 42*. The bulge moves away from the ice and rises if the ice mass expands; when the mass contracts, the bulge moves nearer to the ice and falls in level.

A recent detailed study by Robin Wingfield of the British Geological Survey suggests how the phenomenon may have developed in the Irish sea which is, in essence, a straight-sided canal. At 17,000 BP (before present), the last icecap was in retreat; its drumlins had been formed and more and more

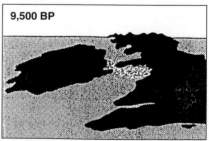

Illus. 43 Diagram to show migration of fore-bulge up Irish Sea.

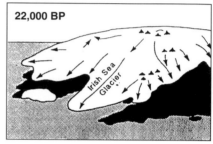

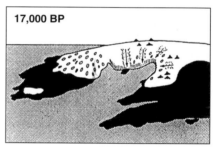

melt-water with its contained debris was being delivered into the north end of the Irish Sea (*Illus. 43*). At 11,000 BP, the fore-bulge moved into the south end of the Irish Sea and linked Carnsore Point to Devon. On the north side of the bulge, land level and sea level were both low as the boring off Milford Haven shows. Temperatures were still low and environmental patterns were static. Ice-melt continued and the bridge crept gradually northwards with soil development beginning on the glacial deposits of marine origin that capped the bulge. Soon it was serving as a bridge for the plants and animals that were streaming north from their distant refuges. But at about 9500 BP the bridge was severed, and immigration of new forms of life into Ireland ended, leaving the country without many forms that continued to have access to Britain where a land-bridge spanned the English Channel till a later date.

VEGETATIONAL DEVELOPMENT IN WARM STAGES

So far we have dealt with the deposits and structures that were produced as glacial conditions first waxed and then waned in Ireland. We can now try to form a generalised picture of what happened in the warm stages which could have been of minor or major duration.

When the temperature rises at the end of a cold stage, the ground surface either emerges from below massive ice or is released from the grip of frost and soil development can start. The plants begin to return from areas to which they were dispersed by the cold and soon the hardier types clothe the ground with vegetation. If, at this time, the climatic trend is reversed and the climate again gets colder, the plants will again retreat. Such minor episodes of amelioration – very many of which can be traced in the Ice Age record – have been given the rather unsatisfactory name of *interstadial* implying a minor phase of warmth characterised by vegetation which had not developed into closed woodland. This is in contrast to a major episode which is called *interglacial* or a warm stage. Closed woodland is the climax vegetation of north-west Europe today. If we picture that the cold of the Ice Age is over and that we are living in the postglacial, then if a past stage of warmth was to merit the title of interglacial, corresponding in rank with the postglacial, it must have been of sufficient warmth and length for closed woodland to develop in it.

For classification purposes, therefore, this first phase of vegetational development will be regarded as belonging to the preceding cold stage which may or may not be ending and will be called the Absence phase (IWA) meaning that closed woodland is absent from Ireland. If amelioration continues and the trees return and gradually spread until they cover the whole countryside, then we are entering a true warm stage; if renewed deterioration sets in after only a short space of time, we have been merely concerned with yet another interstadial.

The events of a full warm stage are shown in diagrammatic form (*Illus. 44*). The stage is divided into phases, and each phase is given a label, e.g. IWX, in which I stands for Ireland, W stands for woodland and X indicates the particular phase. The return of trees and their spread are not simple functions of climate and of time. Even granted maximal conditions for expansion, trees will spread at different rates according to their methods of propagation. There is, therefore, a period of

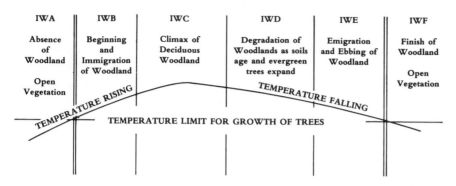

IWA	IWB	IWC	IWD	IWE	IWF
Absence of Woodland	Beginning and Immigration of Woodland	Climax of Deciduous Woodland	Degradation of Woodlands as soils age and evergreen trees expand	Emigration and Ebbing of Woodland	Finish of Woodland
Open Vegetation					Open Vegetation

TEMPERATURE RISING

TEMPERATURE FALLING

TEMPERATURE LIMIT FOR GROWTH OF TREES

Illus. 44
Successive phases of
woodland
development in a
warm stage. See text
for explanation of
IWA etc.

immigration during which the woodlands cannot reach a position of stability and this is called the Beginning phase (IWB) implying that woodland development is beginning as tree immigration proceeds. This phase opened when the first pioneer trees – in Ireland the juniper (*Juniperus*) – led off an expansion of woodland that continued without interruption until high forests were established.

Geographical barriers such as mountain ranges and stretches of water also affected immigration. As great ice masses grew in cold stages, they abstracted water from the oceans and as sea level fell, Ireland was joined to Britain and Britain to Europe. Amelioration of climate reversed this trend, but at the beginning of the warm stage, sea level would still have been low and immigration from Europe into Britain and Ireland would have been easy. However, rising sea level gradually re-flooded the old channels, drowning the land-bridges and eventually overland migration into Ireland was no longer possible.

The materials on which the soils of the warm stage developed were constituted during the preceding cold stage, first by the carrying away of earlier exhausted soil by ice or solifluction, second by fresh rock being broken into fragments by the grinding action of ice and third by subsoil being brought to the surface through the churning action of frost processes. Thus when the warm stage opened, the soil parent materials were again rich in nutrient elements and luxuriant plant growth quickly led to the development of deciduous woodland. In north-west Europe, deciduous trees are thought of, perhaps illogically, as giving a richer aesthetic spectacle than coniferous trees and so woodland composed of oak (*Quercus*), lime (*Tilia*) and elm (*Ulmus*) is regarded as climax woodland. Accepting this opinion, we can picture the climax of this phase as a time of tall deciduous woodlands on deep forest soils and label it IWC, the Climax phase.

As time progressed, leaching gradually reduced the fertility of the soils and there was a tendency to acidity and to a replacement of the deciduous trees by conifers and heath; this process may have been accelerated by falling temperature. Again accepting the perhaps mistaken opinion that coniferous woods are of lower aesthetic value than deciduous woods, we can picture the climax of this phase as a time of soil degradation leading to consequent degradation of the woodlands and label it IWD, the Degradation phase.

Eventually, the cyclical fluctuations of the Ice Age began to draw the warm stage to a close and temperatures fell. All but the hardiest trees – in Ireland birch

(*Betula*) and pine (*Pinus*) – were eliminated from the woodlands. Again, we can picture the climax of this phase as a time of ebbing of woodland and subsequent disappearance of all but the hardiest trees and name it IWE, the Ebbing phase.

A further increase in severity of climate caused even the boreal woods to break up and, as continuous woodland is our criterion for a warm stage, here the warm stage ended. The woodlands were finished, but some hardy herbs and grasses would have struggled on in clumps which were continually shrinking in size, until even they too were eliminated as full polar desert conditions became established. We name this phase IWF, the Finished phase, and picture the climax of this phase as a time when the trees have fled to distant refuges and all vegetation is on the retreat as the rigorous climate of the next cold stage develops.

As we have seen, there were a considerable number of warm stages during the Ice Age. If in each warm stage the vegetational cycle and the plants that composed it had repeated themselves identically, the study of plant fossils from the organic deposits of a stage could not establish that the deposits belonged to one particular warm stage rather than any other. However, several factors work against such simple repetition.

First, the climatic conditions of each warm stage were not identical. The amount of solar energy received on different parts of the earth's surface does have an important effect on climate and this amount is not constant, but is subject to several variables. The tides in the Irish Sea change every day in response to changes in the combined gravitational effects of the sun and the moon. The variables controlling the amount of solar energy received can combine with, or oppose, one another in very complicated patterns which extend over thousands of years and each pattern has a specific climatic influence. It is becoming increasingly clear that this sequential changing of the patterns has an influence on a wide range of terrestrial developments.

Second, the possible migration routes of the warm stages were not identical; animals and plants which may have expanded freely in one warm stage may have found their movements restricted in another. Therefore, different possibilities for vegetational developments existed in the different warm stages and detailed studies may reveal key characteristics by which the particular deposits of each warm stage may be identified.

During the warm stages, peats and muds slowly accumulated, trapping within their deposits as they grew in thickness successive generations of pollen grains liberated from flowering plants. Studies of the contained pollen grains are particularly useful in revealing vegetational differences, even on a small scale. A vertical series of samples is taken at suitable intervals from the top to the bottom of the deposit. As many types of pollen as possible are identified and several hundred grains are counted in all. The values for the different pollens are then expressed as a percentage either of their relative proportions or of the total amount (concentration) present. The values for each sample are then shown as a pollen-diagram where the sample values are arranged one below another in the same way as the samples were located in the deposit. The different values for the different

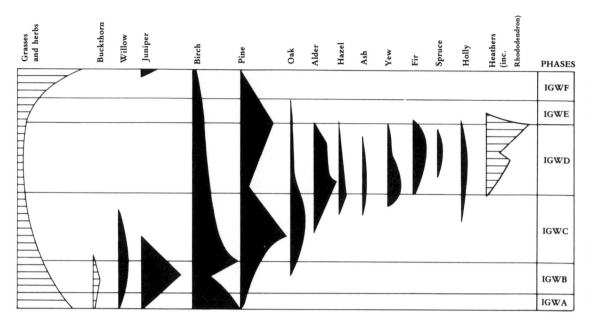

pollens are expressed by bars of appropriate length. The bars may stand independently or they may be linked to give a curve.

Within the whole column of samples, a sequence – of shorter or longer length – may give broadly similar pollen counts, indicating a relatively stable plant community throughout the period of time represented by the accumulation of the sediment from which the sequence came. The counts will be dominated by certain pollens, presumably derived from plants that were prominent in the neighbourhood at the time and so we can establish a type of pollen phase, for example a hazel-pine phase, from which we can infer that pine and hazel were then common in the local woodlands. A second sequence of samples immediately above the first may show increased amounts of oak and elm giving a further pollen phase from which we can infer that relatively open woodland with pine and hazel was replaced by denser woodland with tall deciduous trees (*Illus. 45*).

For many years, systematic pollen counts only recorded the relative proportions of the different pollens in the samples and interpretation of such figures was often treacherous. If the amount of one pollen fell drastically in quantity, say pollen of elm due to an outbreak of disease, then the figures for the other pollens rose automatically to fill the gap. However, it did not follow from this that the importance of these plants showing higher pollen counts had increased in the local countryside. Today, efforts are being made to determine the total number of pollen grains contained in a unit volume of a deposit and to assess the time it took for the unit volume to be deposited. In this way an impression can be formed of the absolute amount of pollen contributed by different plants to the accumulating deposit in a given length of time. Under tundra conditions, total pollen production by herbs and grasses is low while under closed woodland conditions, pollen production by trees is high. By making absolute counts, it is

Illus. 45
Schematic pollen-diagram to illustrate the phases of woodland development in the Gortian Warm Stage.

possible to follow the expansion and contraction of the woodland cover as climate changed, as well as to see how the different trees building up that cover waxed and waned in importance. However, we can only hope to make good absolute counts if we can find a deposit, such as a lake-mud, which is uniform in composition and which accumulated at a uniform rate; the rate of deposition can be checked by radiocarbon datings. Very occasionally, the mud itself is laminated and the laminae can be counted. If the deposition of a lamina is an annual event, then we can estimate the length of time the deposit took to accumulate and compare this with our pollen changes. Our absolute counts enable us to check on our percentage counts, although the percentage diagram is more useful when we try to compare woodland from region to region.

Sophisticated statistical treatment makes it possible to assess absolute values for one particular tree, say birch, against another, say hazel. Thus if the hazel count rises, is it because that tree has expanded its territory or is it because birch has been smitten by disease and is no longer producing the same quantity of pollen? Trends in forest development can thus be pinned down.

In addition to pollen grains, other small fossils such as diatom skeletons and fungus spores can be identified and counted with profit. Larger fossils – wood, epidermis, seeds, insect parts, mollusc shells (often loosely called macrofossils) may also be preserved and their detailed study can provide a great deal of valuable information. Vertebrate bones are also of help, but because of the mobility of the typical mammal their interpretation is often difficult. During examination of the sample, shards of volcanic ash may also be noted (*Illus. 22*) and as we have seen already these can provide dating information of the highest value.

It is clear, therefore, that even a small amount of material can yield a surprising amount of information to specialised treatment, while a deposit whose thickness is measured in metres may hold a complete record of a warm stage from the first replacement of the preceding tundra, through the full development of the woodlands, to their final collapse and replacement by the succeeding tundra of the next cold stage. With younger material, a detailed series of ^{14}C dates through the deposit is also of great help. However, even after an organic deposit obviously from a warm stage has been subjected to a most meticulous examination, some ambiguity may still remain as to the particular warm stage to which it should be assigned.

The deposits of the cold stages also present difficulties. In all of the cold stages, the action of ice and frost produced broadly similar deposits and their appropriate assignation is difficult. The younger deposits are not neatly stacked on top of the older ones because a younger ice sheet could cut away older deposits and replace them with its own deposits. An ice sheet can simultaneously deposit till in one area, melt-water sands and gravels in a second area and glacio-marine materials in a third. If the ice sheet is moving, the three types of deposit may merge laterally into one another. Life is sparse in cold stages and fossils are correspondingly rare. A moving ice sheet may engulf a fossiliferous deposit, redeposit the fossils elsewhere and so give rise to confusion.

Therefore, it is exceedingly difficult to sort out Ice Age deposits into their correct chronological sequence and this difficulty exists even within a single country, let alone on a continental or worldwide scale. For this reason, the suggested sequence of events in Ireland which follows cannot be regarded as more than tentative.

Today in regard to Ireland's glacial deposits we find ourselves in the embarrassing position that in the hope of determining their age and so being able to place them in the worldwide scheme of climatic variations – in spite of the fact that we can study their physical characteristics, that is the size and identity of the contained stones; examine the proportions of sand and silt in the finer material; and can look for signs of late ice-thrusting or other disturbances, in greater and greater detail – we have almost completely failed to arrive at any satisfactory results. The same embarrassment arises when we look at Ireland's warm stage deposits. Although we can identify more and more types of pollen; identify more and more macrofossils (seeds (*Illus. 46*), leaves, woods, bones,

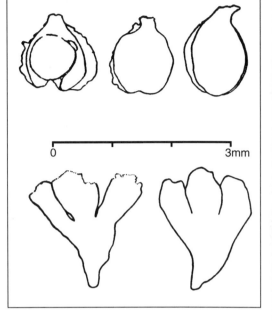

teeth, etc.); make more and more sophisticated statistical analysis of our various counts, we have again failed to fit them into a general scheme.

Illus. 46
Fossil fruits <u>above</u> and catkin-scales <u>below</u> of the dwarf birch (Betula nana) which no longer grows in Ireland.

TENTATIVE CHRONOLOGICAL AND STRATIGRAPHICAL SEQUENCE

Here, we embark on the hazardous task of describing Ireland's known warm and cold Quaternary deposits in a tentative stratigraphic order. Our scheme is based on the *Marine Oxygen Isotope Stages* (here labelled MS), which are gaining more and more recognition. The last part of the curve, dating back to 500,000 years ago, is shown in *Illus. 21*. Different phases of heat and cold during that period in Ireland have been recognised and given names and those names are inserted at tentative positions in the curve.

The Ballylinian Warm Stage (MS 13?) 500,000 to 480,000 Years Ago?

At Ballyline, south of Castlecomer in Co. Kilkenny, a drilling in a karstic sink-hole went through 25m of lacustrine clay. The pollen content suggests open country with a considerable variety of trees scattered through it. Most of the trees seen in Ireland today were there, with the addition of fir (*Pinus*), spruce (*Picea*) and hornbeam (*Carpinus*) and one straggler from much earlier days, the wing-nut (*Pterocarya*) which still survives in Turkey. This was clearly a warm stage and is perhaps the oldest of our Quaternary deposits. An age of 500,000 years in MS13 can be suggested.

The Gortian Warm Stage (MS 9 or 11?) 425,000 to 300,000 Years Ago?

Our next deposit is near Gort in Co. Galway, where there is one unit that seems reasonably complete. More than 100 years ago, a distinguished Irish geologist, G H Kinahan, discovered 'a peaty accumulation' below a thick cover of 'glacial drift' in a river valley near Gort. Pine, spruce and hazel (*Corylus*) were recorded and Kinahan considered that 'the presence of such trees in Ireland during intraglacial times' was proved by his discovery. In 1949, the deposit was re-investigated by Knud Jessen and Svend Andersen, both experts in Danish interglacial deposits and Tony Farrington, a Dublin glacial geologist. They confirmed that it did indeed belong to a warm stage which they named *Gortian*. Since then, similar deposits have turned up in about twelve other localities in Ireland and it is now possible to build up a picture of the vegetational events of the stage. These partial records have been put together into a schematic pollen-diagram (*Illus. 45*) to suggest the course of woodland development in Ireland through the whole stage. As the woodlands of the warm stage in which we are living at present have been wrecked by man's activities, it is interesting to look at an undisturbed record.

The re-investigation at Gort was done by means of a special boring and towards the bottom of the borehole there was a change in deposit from fine sandy clay below to muddy clay above. In the sandy clay, pollen of herbs and of birch (probably the dwarf form *Betula nana*) were common, indicating the immigration of pioneer vegetation on to still unstable soils as the preceding cold stage was ending. This is the Absence phase and on the right-hand margin of the diagram this level is marked IGWA (G being inserted to stand for Gortian) showing the approach to the Gortian Warm Stage with woodland still absent. Therefore, it is clear that cold conditions preceded the Gortian Warm Stage in Ireland, though we have not yet recognised deposits that belong to them.

Illus. 45 then shows an upsurge in pollen of juniper (*Juniperus*), presumably in response to a rise in temperature to a level sufficient to allow this tree to spread widely and to flower freely. This rise marks the beginning of woodland expansion and the Beginning phase (IGWB) opened the Gortian Warm Stage. Birch, juniper, pine and willow (*Salix*) were the most important trees in this early phase.

The Climax phase (IGWC) started when oak appeared in strength and birch declined and the climax woodland was made up of oak and pine with smaller amounts of alder. As the climax phase ended, hazel, ash (*Fraxinus*), yew (*Taxus*) and holly (*Ilex*) appeared. The climax woods of this Gortian stage were thus very different from those of the warm stage in which we are living at present – the Littletonian – where elm and hazel have much greater importance. Fir then made its appearance and as it increased in quantity, yew (*Taxus*) also increased. Spruce then arrived, followed by the spread of box (*Buxus*), a small tree not now native in Ireland and which we chiefly know in clipped garden hedges.

As the larger trees disappeared, pollen of the heather family, among which that of rhododendron is important, also appeared in quantity. Here we see the trend towards soil acidity, encouraging coniferous woodland and heath, marking the opening of the Degradation phase (IGWD). Fir and spruce did not establish themselves in the Littletonian woodlands in Ireland, although today they are widely planted. *Rhododendron ponticum* is also here today, but only as a result of introduction in the late eighteenth century. It is clear that once introduced, it found conditions ideal on Ireland's acid soils and it has since run like wildfire through woods and over upland bogs. At Glenveigh in Co. Donegal, Killarney in

Co. Kerry and Castle Archdall in Co. Fermanagh, strenuous efforts are being made towards its eradication. This is a classic example of a tree that had a wider distribution in an earlier warm stage and was then driven by cold far back into Europe – it now centres to the south and west of the Black Sea, with a few outlying localities in Spain and Portugal; it has been prevented by barriers, probably geographical in this case, from returning to areas where it formerly grew, but can now flourish again after introduction by man.

Among the heaths were Mackay's heath (*Erica mackaiana*), Dorset heath (*Erica ciliaris*) and St. Dabeoc's heath (*Daboecia cantabrica*). Today the first two are confined to the Roundstone area of Co. Galway while Daboecia occurs more widely in the same region. All have their main distribution from south-west France to Portugal, but are found especially in the Cantabrian Mountains of Spain where they occur in heathy woodland. There were also filmy ferns which only flourish in areas with acid soils and high rainfall. Of these, the Killarney fern (*Trichomanes*) is the extreme example as it is happiest in the spray zone of waterfalls. It used to be common in south-west Ireland, but was made almost extinct by wholesale collecting in Victorian times to supply the ferneries which were then so popular. We can safely postulate an oceanic high-rainfall climate, similar to that of south-west Ireland today, affecting all or most of Ireland.

At Derrynadivva, near Castlebar in Co. Mayo, Pete Coxon and Gina Hammond of Trinity College Dublin have carried the Gortian record almost to its end. The pollen counts suggest that trees fell away and the heathers gave way to the crowberry (*Empetrum nigrum*). This plant seems to flourish in cold wet oceanic climates, as when the ice had finally disappeared from Ireland and the post-glacial vegetation was endeavouring to establish itself; *Empetrum* heaths were again well developed in western Ireland. At Derrynadivva, we see the disappearance of closed vegetation in the Ebbing phase (IGWE) and the establishment of tundra, heralding the next cold stage.

It is clear, therefore, that the Gortian climax woodlands were very different from those of the current Littletonian Warm Stage, not so much in the difference in the trees found as in the different proportions in which they were present. The later phases of the Gortian forests with fir, yew and alder (*Alnus*) and smaller amounts of spruce are, of course, unrepresented in modern Ireland; the European woods that most resemble them today are on the southern slopes of the Caucasus. Several of the trees of those later Gortian forests – fir, spruce, hornbeam, box and rhododendron – have been introduced by man into Ireland; it is unlikely that they could have reached the country unless assisted in this way.

In all, about one hundred taxa of higher plants have been identified for this Gortian Warm Stage, and of these about twenty are not native in Ireland today. Three plants that are no longer here are essentially North American in their modern distribution and show that as the Ice Age progressed there was a progressive elimination from Europe of plants that had earlier grown freely on both sides of the Atlantic Ocean. Two water plants, *Eriocaulon septangulare* and *Naias flexilis*, common in North America today and recorded in the Gortian deposits, still grow in the west of Ireland.

An exciting discovery of rich deposits has recently been made in preliminary works for a road tunnel below Cork Harbour, where a marine facies has been found. Here over 15m of organic deposits lie below 17m of gravels. Organic silty clays contain *Foraminifera*, *Ostracoda* and diatoms in addition to vegetable matter. Calcareous shells contain amino acids and the relative proportions of the various acids change with time. The datings obtained suggest an age between 430,000 and 300,000 years ago, which would place the deposit in either MS 9 or MS 11. The 'true' Gortian Warm Stage may lie in MS 7 or MS 9 and the question arises: Are the Cork and Gort deposits of the same age? The topography of Cork Harbour is controlled by the east to west rock ridges of the Hercynian structures which lie below it. There is no deep channel at the point where the harbour joins the sea at Roche's Point. There may be interglacial deposits of very considerable extent in the harbour.

Illus. 47
General directions of
ice sheet movement
during the
Munsterian Cold
Stage.

Freshwater deposits in Britain where they are known from the type-site in East Anglia as *Hoxnian* and marine deposits in Germany where they are known as *Holsteinian* are probably of comparable age.

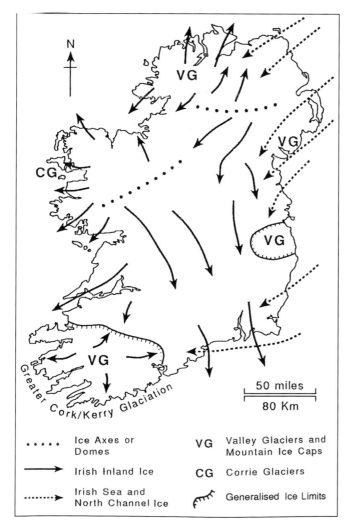

What are we to say about the earlier materials lying below the Gortian deposits which vary greatly from site to site? At Kill in Co. Waterford, they rested on deeply-rotted rock whose base was not reached; did the weathering take place in an earlier warm stage? At Ballykeerogemore in Co. Wexford, the deposit had been deformed by later overriding ice, but earlier glacial material could not be traced. At Derrynadivva in Co. Mayo, later overriding ice had torn up the Gortian deposits and carried them along as 'rafts'. In Cork Harbour, the deposits are marine, but what lies below them is as yet unknown.

The same problem arises when we try to move forward in time. Much of south-west Ireland is covered by glacial deposits, mostly heavily cryoturbated in their upper layers; they have been named *Munsterian* (*Illus. 47*). These deposits have obviously been subjected to severe periglacial conditions. The northern limit, where they can be seen at the surface, follows a fairly well-developed line of younger moraine –

Map legend:

Symbol	Description
.....	Ice Axes or Domes
→	Irish Inland Ice
·····▶	Irish Sea and North Channel Ice
VG	Valley Glaciers and Mountain Ice Caps
CG	Corrie Glaciers
〰	Generalised Ice Limits

50 miles
80 Km

called the South Irish end-moraine of Charlesworth – which runs approximately from the Saltee Islands in Co. Wexford, round the north of the Wicklow Mountains and then heads out to the Shannon Estuary. North of this line, there is no record of severe cryoturbation of the deposits after they were laid down. Evidence is accumulating that the younger moraine dates to about 80,000 years ago, placing this phase of cold in MS 4 which is thought to have lasted from 80,000 to 65,000 years ago. However, the ocean record shows that there were two major phases of cold, MS 6 and MS 8, between the probable end of the Gortian Warm Stage and 80,000 years ago. How are we to fill this gap? One school of thought places the deposition of the cryoturbated materials of the south of Ireland as late as MS 4, thus making all Irish glacial deposits relatively young.

The Munsterian Cold Stage (MS 6 or 8?) 300,000 to 130,000 Years Ago?
In the Munsterian Cold Stage, although both frost and ice were active, we can as yet say little about their relative importance at different parts of the stage. Large ice masses formed and most of Ireland was probably covered by ice for at least some part of the stage. Ice carried erratic material to a height of at least 520m on the Knockmealdown Mountains and cut a deep gash through them known as The Gap; the floor of The Gap is at 350m. It is possible that limited areas of higher ground in the south and west may have remained ice-free, rising as *nunataks* above the surrounding ice.

It is hazardous to try to trace ice movements by means of the present distribution of erratics, that is blocks of rock carried by the ice from their original outcrop and deposited elsewhere. If these erratics were first carried in early glacial times, later ice may have picked them up and re-deposited them elsewhere. But yet we cannot ignore them. On the modern beach, both at Ballybunnion in north Kerry, and at Ballinskelligs some 70km to the south, there is a large boulder of Galway granite (over 7.5m in diameter) whose nearest outcrop is 80km north of Ballybunnion. In the beaches at Rough Point (7km north of Castlegregory in Kerry), cobbles of Pre-Cambrian gneiss from north Mayo (200km to the north) can be found. We can of course say that they were dropped from icebergs of unknown age, but they do hint at an early north/south movement of ice. This is supported by the presence on Valencia Island, at an altitude of 100m, of striae aligned north/south cut into a reef of quartz.

Later, we have a slightly clearer picture. An enormous elongated dome of ice, oriented north-east/south-west, lay across central Mayo and from it ice flowed freely to the south and west (*Illus. 47*). Erratic cobbles of Galway granite on the high ground east of Abbeyleix in Co. Laois, 130km from their nearest outcrop, may have first been transported in this phase.

A second elongated ice dome, oriented east/west, lay across central Tyrone; this ice moved freely north and west over Donegal, but in the south-west, it met Mayo ice moving in the opposite direction. Mutual deflection took place and the joint ice streams moved north-west into Donegal Bay and south-east across the midlands.

The Tyrone ice also met opposition in the north-east, where it was met by ice of Scottish origin. Scotland has higher mountains than Ireland and its icecaps were correspondingly greater. South west-flowing Scottish ice was powerful enough to surmount the cliffed edge of the Antrim coast and push inland for a certain distance, before it was halted by the Tyrone ice, which turned aside to flow north and south. It is not difficult to document the Scottish ice, because in order to reach Ireland it had to cross a stretch of sea floor. Here it picked up fine-grained calcareous marine clays and the fossil shells that they contained and when it melted away, it deposited a till which was fine in texture and speckled with shell debris. South-flowing Scottish ice found a ready-made exit down the North Channel and the Irish Sea basin. We can picture an enormous *mer-de-glace* flowing along between Britain and Ireland pushing laterally inland where coasts were low and being deflected where blocks of higher ground occurred, as in the Mourne and Wicklow Mountains on the west and in the Lake District and Snowdonia on the east. The massifs carried independent icecaps of their own and these added a contribution to the passing Scottish ice. Once it had passed Carnsore Point in Co. Wexford and St. David's Head in Wales, the Scottish ice fanned out. In Britain, it flowed along the Cornish coast to reach its outer limit in the Isles of Scilly. In Ireland, it turned west along the coast to reach its limit in Ballycotton Bay just east of Cork Harbour. As the Scottish ice advanced from the Irish Sea into the Celtic Sea, south of Waterford and Cork, it probably became a floating ice shelf as many of the coastal sections in Cork show deposits of typical glacio-marine facies.

We can be quite positive that this ice did get as far as Cork because as we have seen it carried with it, as an erratic, a very specialised Scottish rock type. Ailsa Craig rises as a rock-cone in the Firth of Clyde; the rock which composes it is an unusual type of granite, fine in grain and containing rare minerals which give it a characteristic blue-green hue making it easily recognisable. Ailsa Craig shed great quantities of this rock into the passing ice and some of it was transported as far as the Cork coast, where it was recognised by a famous Irish geologist, W B Wright, more than eighty years ago.

Irish ice centres were still active after the Scottish ice had ceased to advance; on the Waterford coast, shelly till of Scottish origin is covered by a till containing only Irish rocks. At Garryvoe in Ballycotton Bay where the Scottish till is at its limit, it is covered by a till containing rocks from farther west in Cork and Kerry.

The mountains of Cork and Kerry carried their own icecap, perhaps centred over the Derrynasaggart Mountains. To the west and south, the ice flowed freely towards the sea. On the east, it reached its limit at Garryvoe. On the north it abutted against ice of northern inland origin.

If we try to form a general picture of Ireland during the Munsterian Cold Stage, our main impression is of great masses of ice waxing and waning from time to time in different parts of the country, with only small patches of higher ground here and there remaining ice-free. But before it was buried by ice, low-lying ground, even along the shore of the Atlantic Ocean, was experiencing a cold polar desert climate, while on higher ground conditions were even more severe; under these circumstances, only the hardiest of plants and animals could have survived. Where then were the temperate trees and shrubs that had clothed Ireland during the

Gortian Warm Stage? Recent studies suggest that in general during periods of maximum harshness in cold stages, a broad band of tundra stretched south of the ice from the English Channel to Kiev and still farther eastwards. South of the tundra, steppes stretched south almost to the shores of the Mediterranean. Extensive forest growth was possible over much of south-west Spain and Portugal and on the north shore of the Black Sea. More open coniferous forest with some broad-leaved trees grew in the foothills of the Carpathians and the ranges of mountains in the Peleponnese. It is not without significance, therefore, that Jessen placed the refugees from the Gortian Warm Stage in the Black Sea area.

The Eemian Warm Stage (MS 5e?) 130,000 to 120,000 Years Ago?

During the Eemian Warm Stage, forests returned to Europe and show a developmental succession not unlike that of the Gortian Warm Stage. Hornbeam was common in the central phases, while spruce became more common later; fir was absent. There was some marine flooding in the south of England and in the Netherlands and from a type site in Holland the stage is known as *Eemian*.

In England, there is no uninterrupted record of the full stage and it is possible that some deposits may belong to another, as yet not fully identified Warm Stage. Ireland has no typical deposits, only four slight and puzzling pictures, probably younger.

The Fenitian Warm Stage (MS 5d?) 122,000-100,000 Years Ago?

Near Fenit in Tralee Bay, in the south-west of Ireland, a tantalising cliff section shows periglacial deposits resting on peaty muds; below are beach deposits higher than those of the modern beach (raised beach) and then a wave-cut shore platform. A Dutch group, led by Henrik Heijnis, using radiometric dating methods based on the progressive breakdown of uranium into thorium, has placed an age of between 115,000 and 120,000 years on the mud. This would place it in MS 5d, immediately after the end of the Eemian Warm Stage (MS 5e) or the beginning of the last Cold Stage (see p.37). In any case, it establishes that the Munsterian Cold Stage should lie between 300,000 and 130,000 years ago. At Fenit, where the deposits in the low cliff appear to lie conformably on one another without signs of marked disturbance, we must take it that the raised beach and the wave-cut shore platform on which it rests are older and were perhaps formed in Eemian times.

Such associated features – a wave-cut platform and an overlying raised beach, generally about 4-6m above modern mean sea level – are exposed intermittently on the south-west coast of Ireland, running from Waterford to Mayo (*Illus. 48*). They appear on the Saltee Islands at the limit of the last major advance of Scottish ice down the Irish Sea. They disappear at Clonakilty in Cork, just east of where deposits of the last independent icecap in the Kerry Mountains – thought to be contemporaneous with the last advance down the Irish Sea – reach the coast. The beaches reappear in Tralee Bay, where the Fenit deposit lies. The deposits of the independent icecap end at Fenit. There are good exposures in the Dingle Peninsula and an important exposure at Ballybunnion. Ice thought to be of the same age as the Irish Sea ice passed out to sea in mid-Clare. It is probable that this

Illus. 48
Wave-cut platform
near Kinsale,
Co. Cork.

ice failed to reach Belmullet and its limit in Achill Island is controversial; but there is one deposit of raised beach on the Atlantic coast of Achill where glacial deposits appear to overlie the beach. Apart from a small area around Malin Beg in north-west Donegal, the rest of the Irish coast from Ballycastle round to Kilmore quay in Wexford was overrun by late ice and the beach as a feature is not seen.

At Ballybunnion, where we get our second glimpse, the shore platform is cut, not in rock but in till and has typical beach resting on it; the beach is buried by later solifluction-deposits. William Warren of the Irish Geological Survey attaches special significance to this section, accepting the beach as Eemian in age and the underlying till as a Munsterian deposit. On Beginish, a small island in Valencia Harbour in Co. Kerry, within the area of the last icecap, the beach has been disturbed by ice-thrusting and an injection of silt (*Illus. 49*). The age of the deforming ice is not known.

Illus. 49
Photograph and
diagram to show
disturbed raised beach
at Beginish Island,
Co. Kerry.

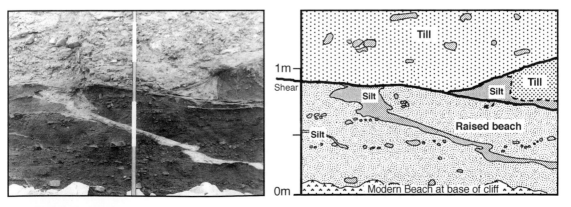

This beach and its underlying platform have been and still are the subject of considerable controversy. Some regard them as the result of wave action in a temperate Eemian sea, higher in level than that of today. Unfortunately, no fossils have ever been found in these beaches in Ireland, though analogous beaches in Wales have marine molluscs of Eemian age. Others see them as transient features of glacial age and of little stratigraphical importance. The rock platform is regarded as quickly cut, possibly by cold ice-bearing waves and the beach as a fleeting feature thrown up by a sea whose level was constantly changing. The relatively constant level of the beach does suggest a period of general stillstand, but until it yields some fossils its dating must remain uncertain.

The third glimpse came not long ago, when Marshall McCabe of the University of Ulster was examining younger glacial deposits exposed on the Wexford coast near Blackwater, north of Wexford town. He picked out from the cobbles one which was not of rock, but of dried mud. The counting of its embedded pollen showed a typical Eemian picture. The ice that carried it had moved from north to south, so at one time typical Eemian deposits must have lain to the north of Wexford. The fourth glimpse came at Shortalstown in the same county, where a deeply-cut farm drainage-trench showed a mass of estuarine sand with till above and below it. The pollen-diagram shows a Climax phase of deciduous woodland with abundant pollen of oak (*Quercus*); the pollen-diagram agrees very closely with the Climax phase of Eemian pollen-diagrams from England. Though at a low level, pollen of elm (*Ulmus*) was consistently present at Shortalstown, whereas it was very rare in Gortian deposits and never reached the values shown at Shortalstown. The Wexford sand could be Eemian in age, but may well come from a deposit of another, as yet unidentified, warm stage.

The Main Phase of the Midlandian Cold Stage (MS 4?) 80,000 to 65,000 Years Ago?
Tony Farrington introduced an element of order to the Irish glacial record about 70 years ago. At that time, great attention was focused on the fresh-looking glacial deposits of central Ireland and the name *Midlandian* was given to them. However, later studies have shown that this name conceals a succession of events in which the main development of ice came early; hence the qualification of the name to *Midlandian Main Phase*.

In the Midlandian Main Phase (*Illus. 50, 51*), as in the Munsterian – but on a much smaller scale – there was an elongated western ice dome, although its axis was a little farther to the south-east, running from Galway City to Castlerea in Co. Roscommon. There was another elongated dome to the north, lying along much the same line as its predecessor, from Belfast to Donegal town. Scottish ice advanced again and although it did not surmount the Antrim coast, it forced the east-flowing Irish ice to turn to the north and the south. The Scottish ice sent a lobe down the Irish Sea and this may have become waterborne as it passed along the coasts of Wicklow and Wexford, where its deposits became clay-rich. It barely managed to round the corner at Carnsore Point, failing to advance farther westwards than the Saltee Islands. In Britain, it did not cross the Bristol Channel.

The Irish inland ice advanced down through the midlands to reach its limit

*Illus. 50
Generalised
Midlandian ice sheet
flows in Ireland and
the Irish Sea Basin.*

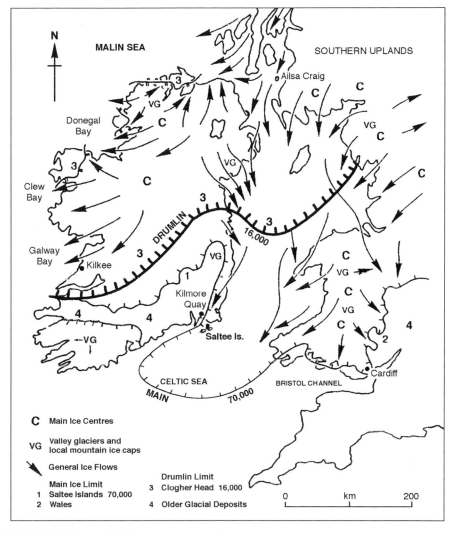

*Illus. 51
Transatlantic ice
limit, perhaps 70,000
years ago.*

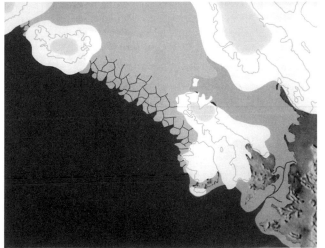

along an arcuate line from Kilrush in the Shannon Estuary down to Tipperary town and then curved back round the Wicklow uplands to reach the east coast at Wicklow Head. Well-developed morainic features mark most of its course. These were first noted by Carvill Lewis, a distinguished American glacial geologist, as long ago as 1894. They were given further precision as the 'South Irish end-moraine' by J K Charlesworth, Professor of Geology in Queen's University Belfast, in 1928. From its outer limits, the ice shrank back irregularly, sometimes maintaining a stillstand and sometimes re-advancing. When it retreated, it left till, morainic mounds of sand and gravel, sheets of outwash sands and eskers in its wake.

There were also small independent icecaps in the Wicklow Mountains and in the mountains of Cork and Kerry. Unlike its Munsterian predecessor, the southern icecap did not get as far east as Cork Harbour, but built up its end-moraine at Kilumney, west of the city. Today the sand and gravel of the moraine are being rapidly carried away for building work in Cork city.

From about 40,000 years ago onwards we can now begin to use radiocarbon dating as an important yardstick. As mentioned earlier, this is a means of dating organic materials by virtue of their containing some atoms of the radioactive form of the carbon atom (see p.38). The atmosphere contains a vast number of atoms of carbon and among these is a very rare form with an atomic weight of 14 as opposed to the usual 12; in chemical terms it is called ^{14}C. This form is unstable, and with the passage of time it breaks down by radioactive emission at a relatively steady rate into nitrogen. As they grow, certain organisms build carbon from the atmosphere into the tissues of their bodies and so acquire a content of radioactive carbon. After their death the content of radioactive carbon gradually dies away and if scientists measure the quantity that remains in comparison with that of today, they can tell the number of years that have elapsed since the plant died. Hence we get radiocarbon or ^{14}C dating, which is of immense importance to geologists and archaeologists. But it has only a limited range, because by the time 40,000 years have elapsed, the amount of ^{14}C surviving is too small to be measured accurately. All calcareous shellfish, as well as *Foraminifera,* draw carbon from the water to build up their shells, and after death the date of the formation of the shell can be established by ^{14}C dating. Animals also build carbon into their tissues, especially those with a vegetable diet, and so animal remains, such as bones, can also be ^{14}C dated.

While we cannot extend the range of this method backwards in time, we can improve the technology. In the past, relatively large samples were needed if they were to yield a satisfactory date. Now, only small specimens are required; it is possible to date samples no bigger than a mustard seed.

A radiocarbon date is usually accompanied by a range (±) figure which indicates that the date given is not an absolute one, because technical difficulties make exact dating impossible, but that the real date probably lies within the range of figures given. The ± figures have in the past been given to one standard error; this means that there is a sixty-eight per cent chance that the true date falls within the given range. The absolute width of the range will depend on the nature and age of the original sample and the technical abilities of the laboratory dating the material. Thus 1000 ± 180 BP indicates that the true date most probably lies between 1180 and 820 BP, but there is around a three in ten chance that it may not. However, widening the ± figures to two standard errors improves the probability that the date lies within the given range to around ninety-five per cent.

The technique was first developed by W F Libby in Chicago. For the first forty years radiocarbon dates were regarded as infallible, but now problems have appeared. Many workers are interested in the complicated climatic changes of the late glacial period, but numerous datings suggest that between 11,000 and 10,000 years ago, the radiocarbon clock must have run erratically. As a result, a blur lies over this part of the late glacial, when accurate dates would be of the greatest help. Problems also arise in the post-glacial. Another major blur occurs in the millennium after the birth of Christ. In addition, it has also been realised that all conventional ^{14}C dates are not readily expressed in calendar years because ^{14}C years not only have a different length to calendar years, but also vary in length from one ^{14}C year to the next.

One new dating method currently emerging is that of *dendrochronology*. Over the temperate zone of the world, trees grow seasonally and this seasonal growth is recorded by an interruption in the growth of the wood, which produces an annual ring; the age of the tree can be determined by counting the rings. The breadth of each ring is related to the nature of the growing season and rings of different width succeed one another. If a series of tree trunks of different ages are compared, the same sequences of rings may be found at differing distances from the centre of the tree and so overlaps can be found. With ingenuity, such overlaps can be extended and so the technique of dendrochronology emerges, enabling the dating of a tree-ring that is perhaps thousands of years old. Some trees, such as the bristle-cone pine of the White Mountains in western America, are very long-lived. Others, such as oaks in Ireland, are shorter lived but more common; in Queen's University Belfast, Gordon Pearson, Mike Baillie and Jon Pilcher have produced a long oak chronology.

About twenty years ago, workers including the Queen's group used dendro-chronological techniques to look at annual tree-ring growths in long-living trees on a wider scale. Linking from younger trees to older trees, they gradually built up an extended dendrochronological record in calendrical age (BC/AD dates).

This dendrochronological record was then compared with the ^{14}C record and some important developments followed. It became apparent that on entering the time range of human activity in north-west Europe, the tree-ring evidence can be called on to make a calibration of the ^{14}C age with calendrical age. (Samples of wood whose calendrical age is known exactly from tree-ring analysis can be re-analysed using the ^{14}C technique and the results provide a calibration curve, which is the basis for correcting the ^{14}C record.) In other words, all ^{14}C dates can now be converted to estimated calendrical dates. Again, however, there is a margin of error, and so a range of dates is given either with ± one or two standard errors. Examples of a calibrated date might be 633-665 cal. AD (using one standard error), or 617-681 cal. AD (using two standard errors).

It had been assumed that the rate of radiocarbon decay would be constant and therefore radiocarbon years would be of constant length, like calendar years and tree-ring years. But if we take the tree-ring record as truth, then the rate of radiocarbon decay must vary. We used to picture radiocarbon decay running down a hill with a constant slope, but now we begin to see that the slope is more like an interrupted cascade, with ledges of slow decay succeeded by falls of more rapid change. Workers are trying to calibrate the change in rate against calendrical years, but even if this is done, zones of uncertainty, sometimes quite substantial, still remain. We can only regard many of our dates as approximations rather than certainties.

In general, both ^{14}C dates and BC/AD dates must be taken as being close to the truth, rather than absolute truth itself. Farmers arrived in Ireland about 4000 BC and from then on there was continuous habitation of Ireland, which passed the BC/AD dating-point. In this book events later than 4000 BC are given a BC/AD figure. Before 4000 BC, datings are more hazy and such datings are given a BP figure. However, their distinction is not vigorously maintained.

The Aghnadarraghian Complex (MS3?) 65,000 to 35,000 Years Ago?

We referred previously to the lignite deposits around Lough Neagh (see p.22). At Aghnadarragh, near the village of Glenavy, on the east shore of the lake, the thin glacial deposits that cover the lignite have been stripped off over an area of some acres, so that the lignite can be studied more closely.

The Quaternary deposits exposed are of great interest and studies suggest that among them are some that belong to a late phase of considerable warmth. In an earlier book, the deposits were regarded as those of a full warm stage and given a provisional name, *Glenavian,* from the nearby village, Glenavy. Organic material gave a date of greater than 47,000 years, which suggests an age somewhere in MS 3, from 65,000 to 35,000 years ago. During this stage, the general level of the curve suggests relatively cool conditions, punctuated by five minor peaks which perhaps indicate more genial conditions of varied duration. The highest peak comes early in the sequence, at about 55,000 years ago and the Aghnadarragh deposits are now placed here, in a relatively warm interstadial. The concept of a full warm stage (Glenavian) is abandoned.

At Aghnadarragh a till, which here is regarded as of Midlandian (Main) age, rests on the lignite. Above this is a gravel that has yielded a number of elephant molar teeth, pieces of tusk (some large, many small) and some broken large bones, probably also elephant. There was one bison tooth.

The elephant remains appear to belong to the woolly mammoth (*Elephas primigenius*). We have seen that the Ice Age was not sufficiently long for many significant evolutionary developments to have taken place, but the elephants are a group which were undergoing rapid change at that time. The woolly mammoth, as its name implies, had a hairy coat; this is in contrast to the two surviving members of the elephant group, the African and the Indian forms, which both have naked skins. Though extinct, the woolly mammoth is well known, both because frozen carcasses have survived in Siberia and because Palaeolithic artists made engravings of them on ivory (*Col. 14*).

The bison was also portrayed by these early artists, both by paintings on cave walls and by clay models. In England, it is known to have been contemporaneous with the woolly mammoth. The fossil bison was probably very similar to the modern European bison, which still survives under protection in Poland and the Caucasus. The European evidence suggests that the woolly mammoth did not appear until the middle of a late interglacial warm stage, and this gives a lower limit to the age of the deposit. Therefore, at Aghnadarragh we do not have any record of the beginning of the warming, we only get a glimpse of its later phases.

Above the gravel there is a series of sands and at some horizons in this series there are seams of washed-in vegetable debris; in some places rolled pieces of wood, chiefly spruce and pine; in other places thin layers of spruce cones. There are also fruits of hazel and yew. Beetle remains are common. Higher still, the sands become finer and contain lenses of mud which was deposited in small open-water ponds under cold conditions. Cold is clearly indicated by the presence of leaves of the least willow (*Salix herbacea*), abundant in northern latitudes but surviving only on mountain tops in Ireland, and the dwarf birch (*Betula nana*), also a northern plant, now extinct in Ireland. At the top of the section, there is till which can be assigned to MS 2, the late Drumlin phase of the Midlandian Cold Stage.

What conclusions can we draw from the limited range of fossils found at Aghnadarragh? Unfortunately, most of them are not in their primary position, but have been transported – though probably not very far – by running water. Yew is a tree indicative of a mild oceanic climate, intolerant of frost and limited in its distribution by winter cold. It is absent from eastern Europe and does not go north of the Gulf of Bothnia. Hazel can tolerate slightly colder conditions and so it goes a little farther to the east and creeps north on the coasts of the Baltic and the Atlantic (*Illus. 52*). The beetle evidence is more definite; of the fifty forms found, many do not go north of the Gulf of Bothnia and there is a complete absence of high northern species. The beetles suggest that the temperature lay between: +15°C to

Illus. 52
The superimposed lines show the areas within which yew (Taxus) and hazel (Corylus) flourish in modern Europe. They are trees of the central European forests and avoid northern latitudes.

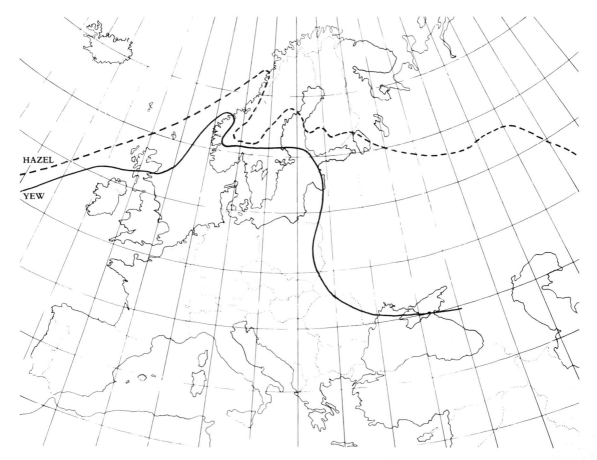

HAZEL

YEW

+16°C (July mean) and +11°C to +14° (January mean). Armagh lies within a few kilometres of Aghnadarragh; today's temperatures there are: +15.5°C (July mean) and +14°C (January mean).

At Aghnadarragh, the climate was much as today and yew and hazel today find their home in temperate closed woodland. If temperate woodland is the prerogative of a warm stage – as has been said already – then here we are dealing with a period marked by relatively warm conditions and not with a harsh interstadial. We can place the deposits in a warm interstadial where woodland with hazel and yew was beginning to develop, only to be cut back by a return of cold.

Elsewhere in Ireland, a horse bone from Shandon Cave, near Dungarvan in Co. Waterford, was dated as more than 40,000 years old, which may parallel the Aghnadarragh date. Over 100 years ago, Mr Edward Brenan of Dungarvan saw 'giants' bones' being paraded through the streets of the town. He quickly observed that the bones could not be those of a human giant, but were elephant bones. Asking where they came from, he was directed to Shandon Cave on the outskirts of the town where limestone quarrying was in progress. He found the cave richly strewn with bones and the following mammals were identified: woolly mammoth (*Elephas primigenius*) (*Col. 14*), bear (*Ursus sp.*) of perhaps more than one kind, wild horse (*Equus ferus*) and hare (*Lepus sp.*). A radiocarbon test of a horse bone indicated an age of greater than 40,000 years; more recent tests (see below) show that the bones in the cave are not all of the same age, but were assembled there over a long period of time.

Much of Co. Fermanagh is covered by drumlins which are of late Midlandian age. At Hollymount, near Lisnaskea, a river has cut a small cliff in the flank of a drumlin. Beneath the till of the drumlin, there is a silt with washed-in vegetable debris with an age of more than 40,000 years old derived from a tundra landscape. The silt passes down into arctic clay and this rests directly on unweathered till. The Hollymount plants may well have grown at the end of the Aghnadarragh Complex, as warmth gave way to cold.

The Drumlin Phase of the Midlandian Cold Stage (MS 2?) 35,000 to 13,000 Years Ago?

In Ireland, a cool interstadial seems to have opened MS 2, with massive ice developing rather later. Recent cave investigations, centred on the securing of ^{14}C dates by Peter Woodman and Nigel Monahan have given valuable results. West of Shandon and not very far away in the Blackwater valley, there is another cave in limestone at Castlepook, close to Doneraile. The fauna was richer than at Shandon, but the bones did not lie as originally deposited, as they had been redistributed by later running water. Bones of the mammoth were very common, ranging in size from adult to unborn foetus; one bone was dated to 33,500 years ago. The cave also produced the only bones so far found in Ireland of the spotted hyena (*Crocuta crocuta*); one bone was dated to 34,400 years ago. There were also bones of the giant Irish deer (*Megaloceros giganteus*) dated to 32,000 years ago and the Norway lemming (*Lemmus lemmus*) dated to 28,000 years ago. Shandon Cave yielded mammoth, dated to 32,000 years ago and red deer (*Cervus elephas*) dated to 26,000 years ago. Foley Cave, a small cave above the Awbeg River near Castletownroche, had bones of reindeer (*Rangifer tarandus*) dated to 28,000 years ago, brown bear dated to 26,000 years ago and mammoth undated.

The dates from these bones – whose complete list is woolly mammoth, brown bear, spotted hyena, Arctic fox, Irish giant deer, reindeer, red deer, mountain hare, Norwegian lemming and Greenland lemming – cluster remarkably round the time span from 34,000 to 26,000 years ago.

It is difficult to imagine Ireland with these animals wandering through it. What did the landscape look like under interstadial conditions? At Shandon, Castlepook and Foley we are south of the limits of all Midlandian ice. The caves are in the limestone of the Blackwater valley, where there will have been both shelter and fertile soil materials, and we probably had open grasslands with scattered copses of birch and willow. Here, the mammoth, giant deer and reindeer browsed and grazed and the bear and the hyena prowled around scavenging. The tree growth cannot have been dense, because the giant deer could not cope with closed woodland. On the other hand, bare tundra probably did not provide sufficient food for the mammoth and although the Ice Age range of the hyena went farther north than that of today, it is doubtful if it pushed up into the tundra zone.

The conditions described above are those of the typical interstadial. If the time period had been long enough and the climate sufficiently favourable for high forest to have formed, then Ireland would have been experiencing interglacial or full warm stage conditions. At Derryvree in Co. Fermanagh, not far away from the Hollymount site, a road-straightening operation cut right through a drumlin. Underneath the till of the drumlin, there was a thin layer of mud and moss-peat that contained tundra forms of plants and beetles with a radiocarbon age of 30,500 years. The climate had deteriorated as the interstadial was coming to an end. The organic material rested on unweathered till, probably of Midlandian age.

The time bracket of 34,000 to 26,000 years, which covers the period when many large mammal bones were being carried into Irish caves situated in the south of the country, corresponds remarkably with a time-period of 33,000 to 29,000 years, which has been blocked out in the south of Scotland. There, at Sourlie in Ayrshire a cut was made in a drumlin in the course of opencast mining, not transversely as at Hollymount, but longitudinally. Workmen noticed bones in a peaty deposit and these proved to be from woolly rhinoceros (*Coelodonta antiquitatis*) and reindeer. The peaty beds formed a rich deposit of smaller fossils, flowering plants, mosses and beetles. The whole assemblage suggests cold continental conditions, such as might be met with in parts of Siberia today. Most of the mammals recorded in Ireland would have been found in similar conditions. So, we can picture MS 2 opening in both Ireland and Scotland with a phase of dry cold which lasted for some 8,000 years.

Large masses of ice then developed in the Drumlin phase, particularly an oval mass which extended from Lough Foyle to Galway Bay. Its limit on the south-east ran from Dunany Point, on the east coast near Dundalk, across Lough Ree and onward to fill the inner part of the Shannon Estuary. It also pushed out into Galway Bay. Farther north it got thinner and failed to cover the mountains of Mayo and

Donegal, but streamed out to sea wherever coastal valleys such as Donegal Bay gave an easy passage; Lough Swilly and Lough Foyle also gave exit routes. When the ice crossed Sligo Bay, it picked up shells and deposited these in till at Belderg on the Mayo coast. The shells have a radiocarbon date of 17,000 years, thus placing the ice advance late in MS 2.

Ice from Scotland made a short incursion into the north-east tip of Antrim. It failed to cover the Isle of Man and ended on the English coast north of Morecambe Bay. Ice from Scotland was dominant in the Irish Sea and southeast-moving Irish ice merged with it. There were small independent icecaps in the Wicklow Mountains and in the mountains of Cork and Kerry and active corrie and valley glaciers in the Dingle Peninsula and in Achill Island.

For some unexplained reason, the ice of this last advance – at some stage of its development – moulded the underlying deposits it gave rise to into drumlins (*Illus. 35*); so much so that Francis Synge of the Irish Geological Survey was tempted to name it the Drumlin advance (here called the Drumlin phase).

Numbering thousands, the drumlins were often aligned in serried ranks, giving rise to the so-called 'basket-of-eggs' topography. The alignment is particularly marked where the ice was following topographically defined exit routes. Today, they stretch in a broad band across north central Ireland, from Down to Mayo. Drumlins were also formed by the independent south-west icecap, being well-developed near the town of Bantry. Many were formed below modern sea level and are today being attacked by the waves, as in Strangford Lough and Clew Bay. In areas of lower topography, drumlins blocked the surface drainage routes and were often surrounded by standing water. Thousands of years later, when separated by water and covered by dense woodland, they provided a severe obstacle to man's lines of communication. When the Midlandian ice finally disappeared, many of the areas it had covered presented an essentially 'young' landscape, that is they showed either features associated with recent ice scouring and moulding, or features associated with ice deposition, for example unweathered till, steeply-sloping drumlins, and sharp-sided eskers.

What of the areas that were not glaciated during the Midlandian, but had been covered by Munsterian ice? In many parts of Ireland, rock was left exposed at the surface of the ground when that ice disappeared. Throughout the following warm period, the rock was subject to chemical attack, a type of attack to which granite is particularly vulnerable. Earth movements brought about cracking in solid rock, and very often more than one set of cracks or joints intersected, so that the upper layers of the granite were like a mass of closely packed, if somewhat irregular, cubes, rather than solid rock. Water percolated along the cracks and from them its chemical attack moved out into the stone, being especially severe at the corners of the cubes.

The upper part of the rock thus became a weathered mush of loose debris, which contained within itself, like currants in a cake, the rounded blocks or *core-stones* of intact rock which had survived in the centre of the cubes. The contact between the weathered rind and the solid rock below was often irregular, again due to the influence of the joint-pattern.

Illus. 53
During the last warm stage the granite of the Three Rock Mountain, Co. Dublin, was partly rotted by chemical weathering to some depth. The mountain was a nunatak in the Midlandian Cold Stage and freeze-thaw

When the later cold Drumlin phase set in, and freeze-thaw processes again became active, the superficial weathered debris crept away downslope. The core-stones were left behind, littering the surface, while prominences on the irregular surface of the solid rock stood up as *tors*. If a granitic area escaped being overrun by ice – as was the case with Bloody Foreland in Donegal and Three Rock Mountain south of Dublin (*Illus. 53*) – then the core-stones and the tors survived. Where the granite was overrun by ice – as was the case with Killiney Hill near Dublin (*Illus. 54*) – the core-stones were carried off, and the upstanding tors were then drastically abraded and turned into elongated rounded bosses, the elongation being parallel with the direction of ice movement. Such bosses of abraded rock, from which the direction of ice movement can be deduced, are known to the geologist as *roches moutonnées*, because nineteenth-century observers thought their outline resembled that of a *moutonnée*, a type of sheepskin wig then in fashion.

activity moved the rotted material down the slope leaving masses of solid rock standing up as tors and rounded core-stones scattered about.

Other types of rock, though also full of cracks, were not so sensitive to chemical attack. The water in the cracks expanded on freezing and so prised off blocks and fragments which crept away downslope to accumulate as a scree of loose stones or *head* at lower levels. Croagh Patrick in Mayo and Errigal in Donegal (*Illus. 15*) are surrounded by masses of scree. The lower limit of the scree sometimes rises into a terminal ridge, which is known as a *pro-talus rampart*.

When the Munsterian ice melted away, it also had left behind irregular deposits in a young landscape. The vulnerability of these deposits to Midlandian freeze-thaw activity depended largely on the relative amounts of clay, silt, sand and gravel that they contained. Sands and gravels are not easily moved, and some eskers and kames of Munsterian age still stand with quite steep slopes. But where clay and silt dominated, freeze-thaw processes mobilised the materials and with the necessary degree of slope, great solifluction-flows were set in motion, only coming

to a halt in lake-basins, valley floors and similar places where the necessary gradient was no longer available. On these stretches of flatter ground, polygonal patterns and involutions developed.

Therefore in the areas, largely in Munster, where in the absence of ice freeze-thaw conditions dominated during the Midlandian cold, there is on the whole an 'older' smoother landscape, where sections usually show erected stones, involutions and head. Farther north, where there was Midlandian ice, the topography is younger and more irregular and sections rarely show the churning action of frost. Older generations of glacial geologists used this concept of areas of 'Newer Drift', with steep slopes and open lake-basins, as opposed to 'Older Drift' with more gentle slopes and only occasional open-water lakes. Lately, the concept has rather fallen into disrepute, but it should not be too lightly discarded. The contrast in the two landscapes is sometimes quite striking. Main Midlandian ice advanced down the Shannon estuary as far as Scattery Island in midstream and Ballylongford on the south shore. Within the Midlandian limit around Ballylongford, there is hummocky topography and well-drained soils; outside the limit and with an abrupt change there are smooth slopes of poorly-drained soils, heavily infested with rushes (*Juncus* spp).

Occasionally, the dumped masses of morainic material blocked previous lines of river flow and caused rivers to find new routes. A short distance to the south of Drumsna in Co. Leitrim, the Shannon enters Lough Boderg and at the point where it leaves the lake there is an impediment (*Illus. 55*). A narrow whale-back ridge of rock, 30km long and rising to 250m in height, lies diagonally across the course of the river. Here, there was a Hercynide upfold in the rocks and erosion has removed the overlying Carboniferous limestone to expose basal sandstones and shales; at some points even these rocks have been removed and Old Red Sandstone and still older rocks are revealed.

Today, the river leaves the lake by a cut across a low point on the ridge at Derrycarne Narrows. When barge navigation started on the river, this rock bar had to be extensively deepened by blasting. Before the last advance of ice in the area, the river failed to cross the ridge and instead flowed down the west side of it to enter Lough Ree (if it then existed) on its north-west side, somewhere south of Lanesborough. Later a lobe from the ice cut across and lowered the low point in

Illus. 54
Killiney Hill,
Co. Dublin, also of
granite, was overrun
by Midlandian ice
which carried away
the rotted material
and abraded the solid
rock, turning
upstanding blocks
into streamlined
roches moutonnées.
The ice was moving
from left to right; it
cut away the
upstream side of the
rock in the
foreground leaving it
smoothed and
rounded, but plucked
blocks off the
downstream side
giving it sharp
outlines. The rock
behind shows the
same shape.

*Illus. 55
Between Carrick-on-
Shannon and
Lanesborough a ridge
of older rocks rises
across the course of
the Shannon. Until
late in the Ice Age the
river flowed down the
western side of the
ridge. The retreating
ice blocked that
channel and a new
one was cut across
the ridge at the
Darrycarne Narrows.*

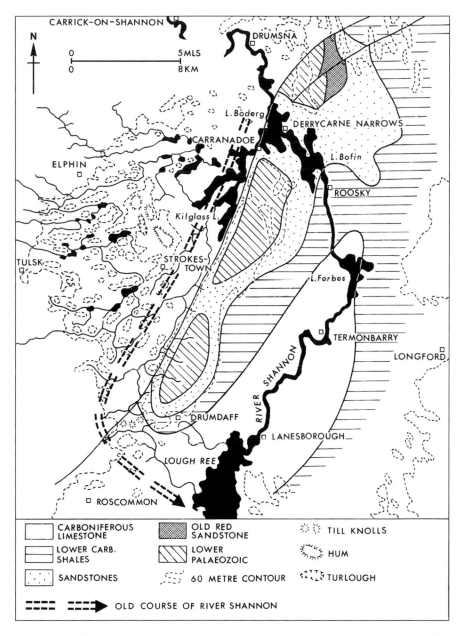

the ridge at Derrycarne. On its retreat, on the western side of the south end of the ridge, not far from Dundaff, it left a line of morainic knolls of till which rise to 65m and block the former course of the Shannon.

As a result, today all the drainage on the west side of the ridge runs back northwards from the moraine; it passes through and widens into Kilglass and other lakes, before it passes through a channel at Carranadoe to join the waters of today's Shannon in Lough Boderg.

Another version of the same process can be seen where the Shannon leaves Lough Derg (*Illus. 56*). To the south, the river is confronted by four parallel

Hercynide ridges of older rocks, aligned north-east/south-west. Differential erosion has caused the ridges, which are of hard rock, to rise through the limestone, strips of which survive in the low ground between the ridges. It would seem that the simplest course for the river would have been to follow one of these low-lying limestone corridors and to emerge on the far side of the ridges somewhere between Ennis and Limerick. Here it is regarded that in pre-glacial times the river did take such a course, following the low-lying corridor that now carries both the main road and the railway line south-west from Nenagh. The southern part of the corridor is now drained by the Kilmastulla River, which joins today's Shannon just north of O'Briensbridge. But the modern river cuts directly through one of the ridges, with the ground rising to over 150m on either side. The south shore of Lough Derg runs along the north face of the ridge in an almost straight line from Scariff in the west to Youghal Bay in the east. This line marks the boundary between low-lying limestone to the north and a steeply-rising ridge of harder rocks to the south. But this regular line is now cut into by a deep indentation, a gorge running down to Killaloe where the river exits today. It is probable that the ridge lay crosswise to the ice advancing from the north and the ice was forced to divide to the east and the west, further steepening the scarp by erosion as it did so. The ridge was interrupted by a short valley sloping to the north and a lobe of ice pressed up the valley, deeply scouring it to a depth that in places lies below modern sea level. Continuing south, the ice breached the watershed at the head of the valley and entered the head of another valley which ran south to Killaloe. Ice erosion lowered the ridge to a level across which the modern Shannon flows at a height of 30m. The ice that had followed the low-lying Kilmastulla corridor, the pre-glacial course of the Shannon, left great quantities of sand and gravel as it retreated, including a bar at 60m, across the corridor at Five Alley, about 4km south-west of Nenagh. South of the morainic bar, surface water today drains south as the Kilmastulla River; north of the bar, the water flows north to enter Lough Derg in Youghal Bay at its south-east corner.

Similar instances of the influence of former ice sheets on today's river pattern, whether by a moraine blocking a former course or a river taking advantage of a glacially cut channel can be seen in many parts of Ireland.

Illus. 56
Pre-glacial erosion of the underlying rock structures here created three small uplands; the Shannon then flowed around the southern one. Ice erosion modified the shape of the uplands and the river now cuts through the southern upland instead of flowing around it.

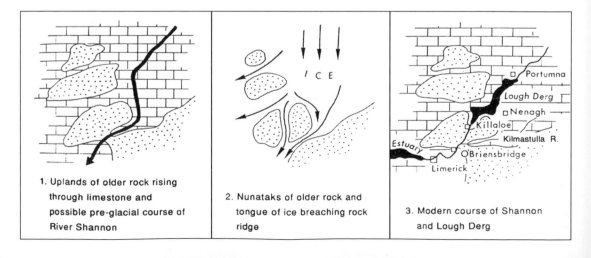

1. Uplands of older rock rising through limestone and possible pre-glacial course of River Shannon

2. Nunataks of older rock and tongue of ice breaching rock ridge

3. Modern course of Shannon and Lough Derg

After 15,000 years ago, the annual supply of snow to the ice sheets gradually fell away and the ice first became stagnant and then started a long melt-out until it had totally disappeared about 2000 years later. There was only a very limited amount of plant life, probably consisting of very sparse, scattered herbs in a landscape in which bare soil still predominated.

THE ABSENCE OF LARGE MAMMALS AND OF PALAEOLITHIC MAN

In marked contrast to Ireland, where we have only very limited mammalian faunas, many parts of the world have rich faunas which often assist in deciphering Ice Age events. In England, good assemblages are known from several warm stages, while the Irish record is almost blank. Most of the mammalian finds come from river gravels, or from cave deposits. Much of the south of England was never covered by ice and river gravels containing mammalian bones continued to build up over a long period. In Ireland, the ice cover was extensive. Nearly every major valley outside the ice limit served as a melt-water discharge channel into a sea level much lower than today's, so that any earlier gravels the valleys may have contained were scoured away. Ireland has no interglacial gravels such as those in Trafalgar Square in London, which have produced abundant remains of lion, hyena, rhinoceros, elephant and hippopotamus.

The Carboniferous limestone of Ireland contains many caves, but most of the limestone is at a relatively low altitude. All the limestone areas were probably overrun by ice during the Munsterian Stage and by far the greater part was again overrun during the Midlandian Stage. When the ice stagnated and melt-water was draining downwards, many cave systems served as escape routes for melt-water and any deposits they contained were either grossly disturbed or completely carried away. Nevertheless when all this has been said, there are in the Lee and lower Blackwater valleys in Cork many cave systems which could have provided shelter for Quaternary mammals and where the bones might have escaped disturbance. But despite sporadic excavation over the past hundred years, no temperate faunas, such as those that occur in the caves of Devon, have been found.

Much of the cave excavation of the late nineteenth century in Ireland was directed towards the discovery of 'Early Man' and all the excavators were disappointed. In the first half of this century, there was a revival of interest in the search and various claims were made. Limestone flakes from Co. Sligo were claimed by some to be the handiwork of Palaeolithic man, but were dismissed as entirely natural by others. Kilgreany Cave in Co. Waterford produced human remains in apparent association with bones of the giant deer, but a later re-examination of the cave showed that the deposits in some places had been considerably disturbed. Radiocarbon dating of some of the human bones that were claimed to be early indicated that they were Neolithic, rather than Mesolithic or Palaeolithic in age.

Two recent chance finds have drawn attention to the problem once more. A large coarsely-struck flint flake was picked up on the stripped surface of the glacial gravel of Irish Sea origin and of Midlandian age that occurs in a big quarry near Drogheda in Co. Louth. The flake (*Illus. 57*) showed signs of having been rolled and abraded by running water. It cannot be claimed to have been

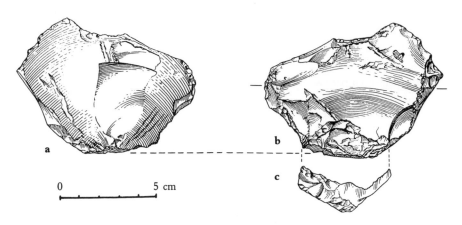

Illus. 57
Palaeolithic flint
flake from near
Drogheda,
Co. Louth:
a bulbar surface;
b dorsal surface;
c striking-platform.

in situ when found, but it would strain credibility to claim that it had been dropped on the recently-stripped gravel surface by some human visitor. Also the rolling is most easily explained if the flake belonged to the gravel and had been rolled along with it.

Gail Sieveking in the British Museum examined the flake. He is satisfied that although the flake is no more than a piece of knapper's waste, it was struck by a technique that was in vogue in southern England in Palaeolithic times. Palaeolithic implements are common in the south of England, but thin out rapidly northwards; a few have been found in central England. The Drogheda flake shows that the Palaeolithic hunters pushed still farther north-westwards out into what is now the basin of the Irish Sea. When later ice advanced southwards from Scotland, the flake – along with stones and other debris – was first picked up by the ice and subsequently washed out of the melting ice by currents which deposited it in gravel on the Irish coast.

While the occurrence of this worked flake in Co. Louth cannot be claimed to establish the presence of Palaeolithic man in Ireland, it does show that in Britain he wandered sufficiently far to the west to reach the basin of the Irish Sea.

The second occurrence is still more mysterious. A perfectly typical Palaeolithic hand-axe was found in the *chevaux-de-frise* that surrounds Dún Aengus on Inishmore in the Aran Islands. A Palaeolithic hunter, however, could not have lost a very valuable tool in a crevice which did not yet exist. Here we must see the hand of a practical joker as in the hoax of Piltdown Man.

3. THE END OF THE ICE AGE

We have referred to the increasing accuracy with which we can survey the past as the time period gets shorter and the opportunity for post-depositional damage is reduced. As we come to the very recent past, methods of investigation have become both more numerous and more accurate. This is because we are prepared to pay substantially for any information that may help us to forecast what is climatically likely to happen to our already over-crowded world.

We have seen that the earth passes through major cycles of heat and cold of approximately 100,000 years duration and that this pulse can be affected by minor cycles which, though shorter in length, can be of considerable severity. The major cold of the last Ice Age ended about 13,000 years ago, but the ensuing warmth was interrupted by a cold snap which started about 10,000 years ago and had a considerable effect on animal and plant life. In recent decades the earth's temperature has shown a tendency to rise and as the reckless consumption of fossil fuels continues to increase, worry grows about the consequences of 'Global Warming'.

If world sea level were to rise by any substantial amount, many great cities would be threatened. Tropical islands might be submerged. The general rise in temperature would also affect current agricultural practices. It is therefore of the highest importance to endeavour to predict future climatic developments and one road to this knowledge is most detailed studies of recent climatic changes.

THE NORTH ATLANTIC AREA

A substantial volume of up-to-date information covering the North Atlantic Area has recently been recently released in tabulated form by Blanchon and Sheen, and a simplified version is presented in *Illus. 58*.

Column A on the left shows timescales – one calendrical, the other ^{14}C – reading from the present back to about 20,000 years ago. We have two scales, because as we have already seen the radioactive clock appears not to run at a constant rate, but has periods of acceleration and periods of retardation. An effort has been made to match the two clock records, but here the ^{14}C clock readings will be preferred.

Column B shows changes in the North Atlantic sea surface temperature as recorded by pelagic *Foraminifera* in the manner already described. As the Ice Age ended, the low temperature rose sharply about 13,000 BP. However, there was a fall just before this sharp rise and this made the surface water cold enough for it to transport icebergs far out into the ocean. As they melted, tiny pebbles and finer debris of land origin fell to the ocean floor.

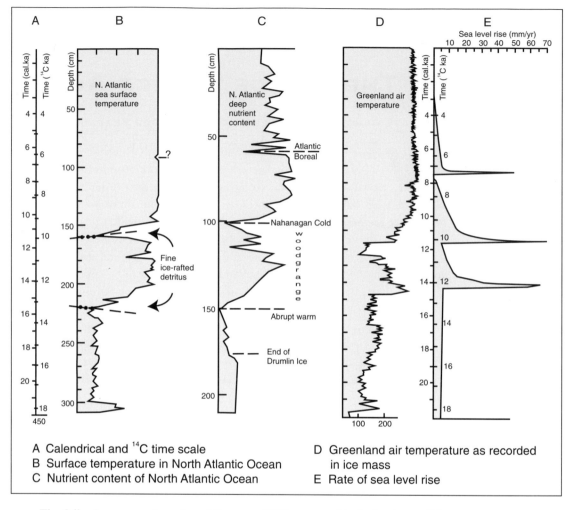

A Calendrical and ^{14}C time scale
B Surface temperature in North Atlantic Ocean
C Nutrient content of North Atlantic Ocean
D Greenland air temperature as recorded
   in ice mass
E Rate of sea level rise

The following warm phase lasted for some 3000 years and in Ireland we call it the *Woodgrange Interstadial* based on a record made in Co. Down some years ago. Ocean surface temperatures then fell very abruptly, icebergs re-appeared and more inorganic debris reached the sea floor.

After this, there was a short interlude of severe cold, which perhaps lasted no more than 500 years. In Ireland, small glaciers appeared in the Wicklow Mountains and the glacial deposits were studied at Lough Nahanagan; in Ireland this time period is named the *Nahanagan Stadial*.

We then enter what is called in Ireland the *Littletonian* or the *Postglacial Warm Stage*, when sea surface temperatures climbed to levels approximating to those of today.

Column C tells essentially the same story. It records the residual content of nutrient in the ocean sediments and hence the food productivity of the ocean, this level of productivity being related to the water temperature. Again, we see the sudden warming at about 13,000 years ago, but here note that after about 11,000 BP an irregular drop in temperature sets in, reaching its nadir about 10,000 years ago.

*Illus. 58
Records of
temperature change
over the past 20,000
years. See text for
explanation of
columns A, B etc.*

In Ireland, in the later stages of the Woodgrange Interstadial, irregular inwashes of inorganic material formed thin layers in lake-muds and it has been suggested that these were due to frost breaking the surface of the vegetation mat. When cold was most severe in the Nahanagan Stadial, more severe freezing enabled solifluction to carry large quantities of sand and clay downslope.

After 10,000 years ago, productivity bounded up as the genial conditions of the Littletonian Warm Stage developed and temperatures higher than those of today may have occurred. About 6000 years ago, there were, in short succession, two marked fallings-away in production, followed by a lower rate than before. Earlier workers in Scandinavia pictured that climate in the first stage of the postglacial as being relatively dry and continental, hence the term *Boreal*. The later postglacial climate was regarded as more oceanic, hence the term *Atlantic*. The change may have come at the time of the falling-away of production. In historical times, there have been at least two further oscillations. The amelioration in the thirteenth century AD gave the Normans the opportunity to grow bumper corn crops in northern Europe, while a late seventeenth-century deterioration brought about a 'Little Ice Age', when glaciers expanded in Norway and rivers in central Europe froze over.

Column D is established from studies of the composition of the gas entrapped in bubbles in the ice of the Greenland icecap. The cap, which has been in existence for at least 250,000 years, is built up by the accumulation of annual layers of snow which contained entrapped air. The general trends of its thermal record are essentially the same as those from the ocean.

Column E deals with sea level rise (see also *Illus. 60*). When great masses of the earth's volume of water were locked up in ice sheets, the sea level had to fall. As the ice sheets dissipated, the sea level rose, with the rate of rise depending on the rate of melting. If there were short bursts of higher temperature, then the rate of rise would increase briefly. The other columns show that there were sharp rises in temperature about 13,000 and 10,000 years ago and both are shown clearly in this record of sea-level rise. Land-based records of the post-glacial show that there was a rise in sea level about 7000 years ago and this is also seen in the record of sea-level rise.

Illus. 59
Near Malin Head, Co. Donegal, Ballyhillin village lies along the curved crest of a Late Midlandian beach raised by isostatic uplift to about 20m above modern sea level. From the crest, the beach gravels slope seawards with unfenced strip-fields on them. When about 5000 years ago sea level rose eustatically about 4m above its present level, its waves cut cliffs in the earlier beach gravels; more gravel was laid down as the waves retreated.

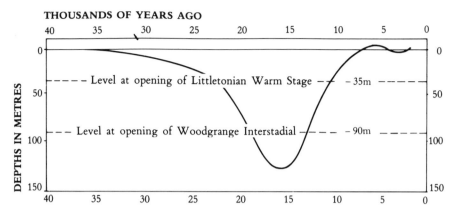

THOUSANDS OF YEARS AGO

Illus. 60
Outline curve to
indicate possible
course of sea level
around Ireland
during the last
40,000 years.

THE STORY IN IRELAND

Detailed studies of the late glacial period began in Ireland about sixty years ago, when Knud Jessen and Tony Farrington conducted excavations at Ballybetagh Bog in Co. Dublin, long known as a site where remains of the Irish giant deer (*Megaloceros giganteus*) were common. Since then, more and more investigation has been carried out, not only in Ireland but also throughout north-west Europe and a considerable volume of information has been built up. Some years ago, a generalised summary of the possible sequence of events was drawn up by V Andrieu, Michael O'Connell of Galway and others (Illus. 61).

Illus. 61
Late-glacial Ireland.
See text for
explanation of
columns A, B etc.

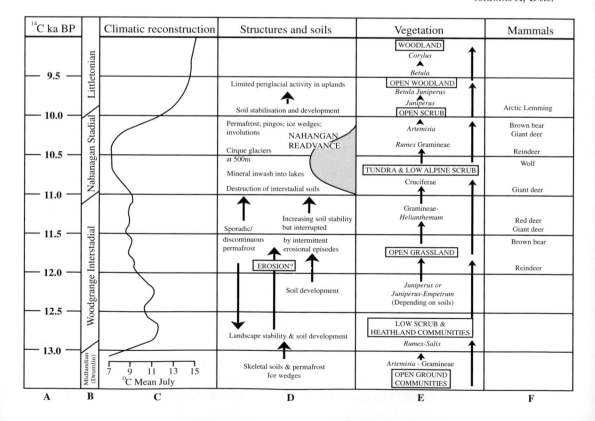

Column A gives the time-scale for the last 13,000 radiocarbon years. Column B gives the names of the Irish type sites. Column C shows temperature trends, largely based on information from fossil animals and plants rather than instrumental measurements. Column D shows geomorphological and soil developments. Column E outlines vegetational developments. Column F lists mammalian records.

The Woodgrange Interstadial 13,000 to 10,600 Years Ago

As we have seen, about 13,000 years ago a marked amelioration of climate set in. The vegetational changes that followed were first well documented in a pollen-diagram (*Illus. 62*) from Woodgrange, Co. Down and so we speak of the *Woodgrange Interstadial*; it was no more than an interstadial as it was followed by a short return to very cold conditions.

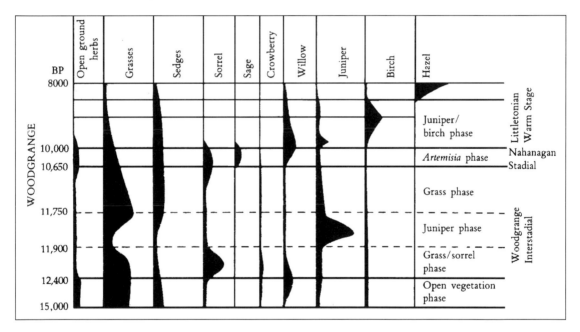

*Illus. 62
Pollen-diagram
from Woodgrange,
Co. Down.*

Since the Woodgrange studies were made, contemporary deposits in other parts of Ireland have been studied with new techniques and in greater detail, but there seems to be no reason to abandon the name of Woodgrange for the period. The vegetational developments of the interstadial were not merely an expansion of the very few plants that may have survived the cold of the Ice Age in Ireland; there was a massive immigration of new plants and animals across land-bridges from Britain and Europe.

It is clear that early movement into the Isle of Man presented no difficulty, because by 12,000 years ago at least eighty plant taxa had already reached the island and many more were pushing in; a large number of beetles and the giant deer were also present. Ireland's richest Woodgrange flora comes from a site near the Leinster coast at Mapastown, Co. Louth and the plants and the beetles must have moved on easily into Ireland. The fore-bulge bridges of glacial material must have developed a varied pattern of soil types across which a wide range of plants and animals could quickly reach Ireland.

About 13,000 years ago, climate improved rapidly and plants and animals could move freely. At first, there was room for all and local conditions in soil type, elevation and exposure had strong influence, leading to many distinct plant associations. We give precedence to the Woodgrange site and give its name to the warm interstadial into which we are entering, because it is the site that was first described in detail and it does display, at least in outline, all the characteristic features of the interstadial.

Woodgrange lies close to the east coast in Co. Down and the basin which holds the deposits lies near sea level between drumlins. As the climate improved, biological productivity was stepped up, the plant cover became complete and about 12,400 years ago clay ceased to be washed into the basin and organic mud formed instead.

The Grass-Sorrel Phase 13,000 to 12,5000 Years Ago

The mud was rich in pollen of grasses, sorrel and least willow (*Salix herbacea*). The sorrels are docks (*Rumex*) and are characteristic of heaths, grasslands and open country; as weeds they are abundant in modern Ireland. Such vegetation, as seen in northern Scandinavia today, was rich enough to support herds of reindeer and at this age we have our earliest record of reindeer in Ireland. Least willow is now rare in Ireland, being largely confined to mountain-tops. In northern Scandinavia today, winter snow that falls in hollows is slow to melt in spring and snow patches remain when the rest of the snow is gone. These snow patches provide a good habitat for sorrel and least willow. Their abundance at this time in Ireland suggests that even though climate was improving, there were still late snow patches in spring (*Col. 18*). In Achill, sheets of soliflucting sand moving down from a snow patch carried large numbers of willow leaves. In the west of Ireland, willow seems to have been less common and meadow rue (*Thalictrum*) was abundant. This is the grass-sorrel phase.

At this early phase of recovery, however, there is a conflict of evidence between the plants and the beetles; the latter tending to suggest greater warmth than the plants. But there is a gremlin lurking somewhere in the beetle dates. After 12,000 years ago, the beetle dates go hand-in-hand with plant or bone dates. However, before that time, beetle parts indicating considerable warmth are found side-by-side with plant parts that indicate cold conditions. The extreme example is a beetle *Bembidion grisvardi*. Today, this beetle is only found in the south of France. However, at many sites in Britain and one near Waterville in Kerry, it was found among fossils which generally indicate cold conditions.

Juniper Phase 12,500 to 11,750 Years Ago

Five hundred years later, the climate became sufficiently favourable for junipers and birches to spread throughout Ireland and we have the juniper phase. In the north-east, as at Woodgrange, juniper was abundant, but birch was rare. At a few locations in the south, at Killarney and near Cashel, birches flourished. In more exposed conditions near the west coast, as at Roundstone, heaths of crowberry (*Empetrum nigrum*) were widespread.

Some of the plants recorded for this period have a remarkably southern, central or western European distribution today, a fact Knud Jessen remarked on some forty years ago. Detailed studies by Russell Coope of an insect fauna of this period from near Shortalstown in Co. Wexford, show that it closely resembles insect assemblages from England and Wales that date from about the same time. These faunas suggest a climate at least as warm as, or at times even warmer than, that found in the same areas today. Finds of birch fruits show that tree birches were in Ireland at this time and if the temperature had continued to improve, birch probably would have expanded into extensive woods.

So far, this vegetation sequence suggests the opening of a full warm stage, with the temperature high enough for the immigration of major trees, but at about 12,000 years ago, short periods of colder climate began to intrude. Recent oceanic studies suggest that these deteriorations were associated with the initiation of a movement of cold polar water down the Atlantic coast of Europe. Production of juniper and other pollens fell drastically and some sand and silt were washed into the lake basins. Bill Watts was the first to recognise the significance of this change; he considers that there were short periods of climatic deterioration when the plant cover broke up, allowing bare soil to be washed into the lake-basins.

Grass Phase 11,750 to10,600 Years Ago

These breaks did not last long and grasses largely re-established the plant cover, though some bare patches may still have remained. Beetles also show that the early high temperatures were not re-established. Ireland probably had a tundra-like grassland with trees and shrubs confined to protected places. This grass phase lasted perhaps some 750 years from 11,750 to 10,600 years ago.

In Ireland, it was during this grassland phase of the Woodgrange Interstadial that the magnificent Irish giant deer (*Megaloceros giganteus*) reached the zenith of its success only to be struck down, like Lucifer in full flight, by the abrupt climatic deterioration that followed. That deterioration restored freeze-thaw conditions which broke up the plant cover and allowed sand and clay (often containing remains of arctic plants) to be washed down into lake-basins. As a result, the Woodgrange muds and peats in which the remains of the giant deer are typically found are usually sealed by a layer of sandy clay, an observation first made 250 years ago.

A letter of 1725 from Downpatrick in Co. Down, states, 'Under this appears a stratum of blue clay, half a foot thick, fully mixed with shells; then appears the right marl, commonly two, three or four feet deep, and in some places much deeper, which looks like buried lime, or the lime that tanners throw out of their lime-pits, only that it is fully mixed with shells – such as the Scots call 'fresh-water wilks'. Among this marl, and often at the bottom of it, we find very great horns, which we, for want of another name, call 'elk-horns'. We have also found shanks and other bones of these beasts in the same place.' The shells referred to are those of freshwater molluscs and investigations in the same area many years later by Arthur

Stelfox revealed fossil molluscan faunas of great interest, including arctic types no longer living in Ireland.

The same stratigraphy was also well known to Williams, an energetic nineteenth-century taxidermist and dealer in natural history specimens. The illustration which he contributed to Millais's book *British Deer and their Horns* is shown in *Illus. 63*. The method of probing is the same as that formerly used by country folk to locate buried timbers in bogs at times when wood was short in Ireland. The stratigraphy was again confirmed in 1934 by Knud Jessen when he worked at Ballybetagh Bog in Co. Dublin, a site long famous because of the large quantities of remains of giant deer and of reindeer that it had produced for Williams and other collectors. Since 1934, about forty further finds of remains of giant deer have been investigated in the field and in each case the remains were at the same stratigraphical horizon. Radiocarbon dating now enables us to put a date in years on the bones themselves and also on the lake-muds in which the bones are entombed; a bone from Ballybetagh was dated to 10,600 years ago, a mud from Knocknacran was given an age of 11,300 years and a mud from Shortalstown was dated to 12,150 years ago, all of which are compatible with the Woodgrange Interstadial.

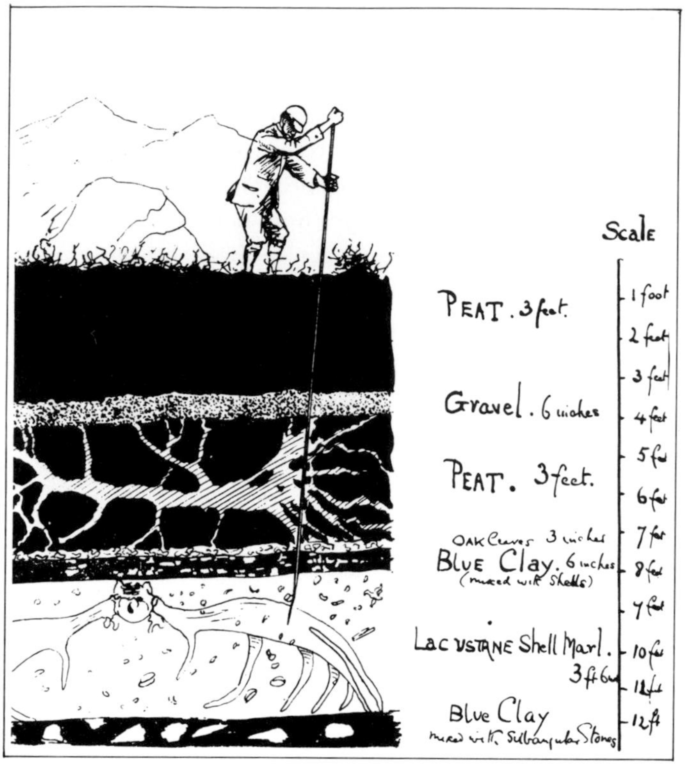

Illus. 63
Finding bones of the giant deer.

What is the record of the giant deer outside Ireland? Its ancestors appear in early Ice Age deposits in western Eurasia, but a related form appears as far away as China. In the later Ice Age, the giant deer was widely spread through Europe, northern Asia and northern Africa. In western Europe, as in Ireland, it seems to have become extinct about 10,000 years ago, but there are suggestions that it survived in Syria and southern Russia almost until the birth of Christ. It was present in England in interglacial time and was also there when the giant deer was undergoing its final expansion in Ireland, though numbers in England appear to have remained very much smaller. A Swedish find was dated to 11,330 years ago (*Illus. 64*).

As far as western Europe is concerned, we can picture the giant deer as a restless wanderer throughout much of the Ice Age; unable to go north to the tundras because of insufficient nourishment, or south to the forests because the spread of the antlers would impede movement. Giant deer, therefore, lived on the intervening grasslands which became poorer to the north and interspersed with

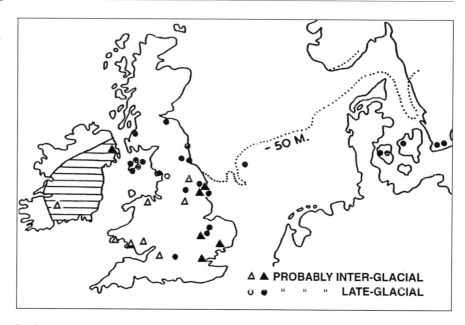

Illus. 64
Map to indicate some districts where remains of the giant deer (Megaloceros) have been found in north-west Europe. The open symbols indicate occurence in a cave deposit, the closed symbols occurrence in a superficial deposit. The shaded area in Ireland shows the area where it is commonly found in superficial deposits. On the floor of the North Sea an approximate −50m contour is shown: it may indicate the northern limit of submerged peats in the North Sea and thus give some indication of the late-glacial shoreline.

bushes to the south. With every climatic shift, these belts of vegetation would be correspondingly displaced and as the grasslands wandered, so the giant deer had to wander also. They were in the Blackwater valley at Castlepook about 34,000 years ago, were then expelled by Midlandian ice and returned for the last time in the Woodgrange Interstadial.

What did the giant deer look like? It was a splendid creature, standing about 2m high at the shoulders and over 3m to the tips of the antlers (*Illus. 65*). Only the male carried antlers and these could have a span of almost 3m and a dry weight of about 30kg. The antlers were shed annually and had to be grown again to a still larger size each spring. The necessity to produce so much bone tissue so rapidly must have placed a tremendous physiological strain on the animal and necessitated the consumption of large amounts of nutritious vegetable matter rich in calcium. Though heavy in weight and impressive in appearance, the antlers were structurally very weak with elongated points mounted on the edge of a thin curved plate. They would have been useless in combat and their only function can have been to impress. Like the Monarch of the Glen, the master stag of the herd would stand on some hillock in full view of the younger males and slowly raise and lower his magnificent antlers and trust that at least on that occasion his status would go unchallenged. What did he want? Two things; rich and abundant food and freedom from predators. The soils of Ireland in the Woodgrange Interstadial were rich in fresh and unweathered mineral matter, especially calcium carbonate and the plant cover must have been equally rich, at least for a short time, until the nutrient minerals had either been absorbed by the plants or washed out of the soil by weathering. In the warmer part of the interstadial, there would have been an abundance of bushes and grass – good food for the giant deer – but it seems to have been the later rich prairie grasslands, largely uninterrupted by trees and bushes, that nourished the large herds (*Col. 15*).

Illus. 65
An artist's impression
of the giant deer in
life. Though huge,
the antlers were frail
and for show rather
than combat. The
stag would take his
stand on a hillock
and slowly move the
antlers up and down
in order to display
them fully and
discourage rivals.

A distribution map of the remains makes this relationship with fertile soils quite plain (*Illus. 66*), even when we allow for the selective nature of such records. If animal fossil remains are to survive, the animal must die in circumstances that will make preservation possible.

Those whose remains were dragged into caves by wolves or foxes, or who died near lakes or ponds provide fossil material. In Ireland, caves are in limestone areas, and lakes tend to be on the lowlands and this must influence the pattern of fossil distribution. But the map (*Illus. 66*) does make abundantly clear the fact that finds are concentrated in the Limerick region; today Limerick is still noted for the richness of its grasslands which make it one of the centres of the dairy industry. Records are also abundant in Co. Down which today carries extensive milk production and in Co. Meath, now an important region for fattening cattle. By contrast the mountainous regions of Donegal, Mayo and Kerry with their poor and acid soils are empty of records. The blanks in the midlands are probably due not to the lack of fossils, but to the fact that thick accumulations of peat have buried the remains beyond reach of casual discovery. Lowland areas with rich grasslands were frequented by the giant deer, while the infertile parts of the country were avoided.

Ponds and lakes have provided many records as some animals were drowned. The lake margin will have been floored by soft muds and clays concealed beneath a floating mat of succulent water plants. An animal might come down to drink or to feed and find one foot becoming embedded in the mud. The struggle to extricate the trapped foot might lead to the others becoming enmired and occasionally the desperate trampings are recorded by disturbances in the muds immediately below the skeleton. For the males, the heavy antlers would have made balance especially precarious and once the animal went down, it would have found it hard to regain its feet and death would quickly follow.

Male skulls with antlers are much more frequently reported than female skulls which lack antlers. One explanation is that female skulls are mistaken for those of horses or cattle and are neglected by the finder, whereas an antlered skull immediately attracts attention. Another suggestion was that males with heavy antlers were more likely to be trapped and drowned than females. Dissatisfied with these explanations, Tony Barnosky of the Carnegie Museum in Pittsburg returned to Ballybetagh, which in the past had only yielded male skulls, although the excavators were competent zoologists looking for remains of both sexes. The valley with the lake at Ballybetagh runs north/south with a sheltered slope on its western side. Barnosky excavated here and found quantities of damaged bones and antlers and some antlered skulls which showed that death had taken place between late autumn and early spring. All remains that could be sexed were male. In the lifestyles of many modern forms of deer, the males and females only consort together in the rutting season. In winter, females and young tend to wander in open country, while the males group together in sheltered valley bottoms, just as we have at Ballybetagh. Winter mortality is higher among males than females because the males have exhausted themselves during the rut and enter the winter in poorer condition than the females. Barnosky pictures the carcasses being trampled and stamped on by other deer and so finds explanation for the damaged and scattered state of the bones he excavated. A giant deer jaw-bone that was found at the level where the mud of the grass zone was giving way to the sandier deposits above had a radiocarbon age of 10,600 years.

Although records of its remains are very much less common, the reindeer (*Rangifer tarandus*) was also in Ireland at this time and its distribution is generally similar to that of the giant deer (*Illus. 66*). There are two radiocarbon dates. The first one is of 12,500 years ago when there were scanty meadows of grass and *Artemisia* (sage or mugwort). Today *Artemisia* is a herbaceous plant of steppes and prairies and goes to 75°N in Novaya Zemblya. The second radiocarbon date is 10,700 years ago when tundra prevailed.

Predators offered little threat. There is no record of the lion (*Felis leo*) from Ireland and this animal had probably disappeared from England long before this late interstadial began. There would have been wolves, but while these would have preyed on old animals and sickly calves it is unlikely that they will have offered much threat to the herds. The red deer and brown bear, also recorded from this phase, went their own ways and did not disturb the giant deer.

Man was still absent from Ireland and there were no bands of specialised hunters like those who followed the reindeer herds in northern Europe. The giant deer must have found conditions in Ireland almost idyllic and proceeded to expand in numbers accordingly. Conditions in England must have been very similar and it is not easy to see why the giant deer should be so common in Ireland when it was so rare in Britain although numerous finds have been made in the Isle of Man.

Except for one old and tantalising account from Co. Monaghan, there are no records of other mammals from open country in the interstadial. Records from caves are now being ^{14}C dated. The account is in the *1715 Transactions of the Royal Society of London*. A flax mill was being built at Drumurcher near Newbliss in Co. Monaghan and beneath sand and gravel the excavations revealed a mass of vegetable debris including hazelnuts and part of the skeleton of a woolly mammoth and the molar teeth. Intrigued by this account, an investigation was carried out in 1940 when Tony Farrington took part. A series of holes showed that below the vegetable debris there were muddy silts with many remains of cold-loving plants and beetles, but no elephant. At that time the radiocarbon method of dating was unknown.

Russell Coope was impressed by the rich variety of the beetle remains and the site was again visited in 1975 to collect more material and get a sample for ^{14}C dating. The beetle story is told on page 95, and the date was 10,500 years ago. It was thought that by this time the woolly mammoth had been long extinct and that the original find must have been at a greater depth elsewhere.

However, in 1986 a sand-pit in Shropshire produced bones of an adult and, more remarkably, three infant woolly mammoths with an age of 12,700 years, showing that mammoths were still around 5000 years after they were supposed to have

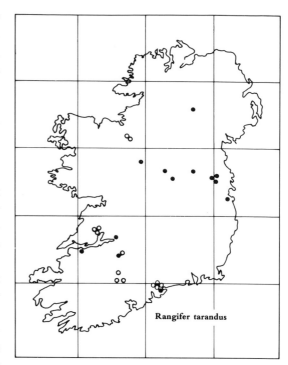

Illus. 66
*Localities where remains of reindeer (*Rangifer tarandus)* and giant deer (*Megaloceros giganteus)* have been found in Ireland.*

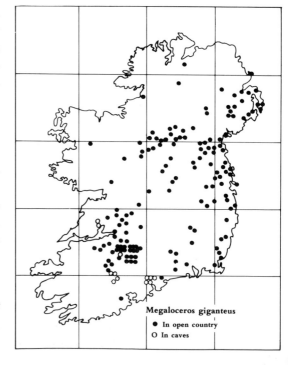

become extinct. If they were in Shropshire at such a late date, they could well have been in Ireland also. An extensive excavation at Drumurcher might produce more pieces of mammoth bone.

Only very occasional fish vertebrae have been found in the lake-muds, which is in marked contrast to the position in Denmark where muds of similar age contain abundant fish scales and bones. Some lake-muds were rich in shells of freshwater molluscs, others were completely lacking in such shells and the late glacial migration routes of these animals are still very obscure.

The Nahanagan Stadial 10,600 to 10,000 Years Ago

It has long been known that the uninterrupted return of warmth that marked the opening of the Postglacial or Littletonian Warm Stage – in which we live – was immediately preceded by a short spell of final cold, but until recently it was not known just how short it was or how cold. Radiocarbon dating has shown that the cold spell began about 10,600 years ago and that it ended about 10,000 years ago; it therefore had a duration of not more than 600 years. The North Atlantic Ocean, which by about 13,000 years ago had become warm, began to cool about 12,000 years ago and the rate of cooling steepened very rapidly about 10,600 years ago. Polar water, probably carrying winter ice pack and icebergs, reappeared briefly off the west coast of Ireland and onshore winds swept severe cooling air across the Atlantic coastline. This floating ice dropped a thin layer of sand and pebbles to the sea floor which has recently been dated to 10,800 years ago. Minor icecaps were created on high ground in Scotland, Wales and Ireland with permafrost on the lowlands.

Lough Nahanagan is a corrie lake at about 400m in the Wicklow Mountains, near Glendalough. It lies at the head of Glendasan, a valley that has been glaciated on more than one occasion. Late in the Ice Age, about 15,000 years ago, the corrie was occupied by a substantial ice mass and a big moraine was thrown across its mouth. The lake that was trapped behind the moraine has been incorporated into a pumped storage electric generating system and during the course of construction it was necessary to drain the lake temporarily. As the water level fell, it revealed a series of very small moraines banked against the hillside. These were studied in detail by the late Francis Synge of the Irish Geological Survey and Eric Colhoun who found that the moraines had lumps of organic mud embedded in them. The mud had a radiocarbon age of 11,500 years; it also had a pollen picture that suggested the transition from the juniper phase to the grass phase and macroscopic remains of arctic alpine plants. Clearly, the mud had formed in the Woodgrange Interstadial in an earlier lake held up by the main moraines and had been ploughed up by the ice of a smaller glacier that re-occupied part of the pre-existing corrie and formed the small inner moraines. As this was the first site to demonstrate that the cold spell was severe enough for glacier ice to form in Ireland, the cold phase has been named the Nahanagan Stadial. In Scotland, a small icecap formed on high ground at this time; its ice advanced as far south as Loch Lomond. Corrie glaciers formed in the mountains of Wales. However, the volume of ice formed was small and it is unlikely that the continuing upward rise of the land by isostatic recovery and of the level of the sea by eustatic release of melt-water was seriously interrupted.

Other evidence also points to severe cold. Ice re-occupied the great valley at Glenmalure in Wicklow (*Col. 11*) and a photograph of a modern ice-filled valley in Antarctica (*Col. 10*) shows an uncanny parallel. A jagged valley running down the east slope of Brandon was re-gutted by ice (*Illus. 67*). Both at Howth in Co. Dublin and at Old Head near Louisburg in Co. Mayo, solifluction moved till downslope where it buried organic deposits of Woodgrange age. There may even have been permafrost; Late Midlandian outwash gravels in Co. Londonderry are penetrated by ice-wedge-casts which can only have formed after the gravels had been deposited (*Illus. 26*). They may have formed in the Nahanagan Stadial and if so they indicate a mean annual temperature of less than 5°C. Pingos may have formed in Wexford at this time; near Camaross it was difficult to locate any early sediments in the pingo basins, but in one basin, deposits had only started to form late in the Nahanagan Stadial. Pingos in Wales tell the same story. Again very severe cold is indicated.

Illus. 67
Corrie lakes on
Mount Brandon at
600m.

The fossil evidence is similar. The basin at Drumurcher in Co. Monaghan lies between Midlandian drumlins. A muddy silt, dated to 10,500 years ago, yielded the first seed so far found in Ireland of the Arctic poppy (*Papaver radicatums* sl.); today the distribution of this plant is strictly arctic circumpolar. Great Britain, too, has only produced one fossil seed of this plant from a deposit of comparable age in Berwickshire.

Illus. 68
Distribution of the
beetle Diacheila
arctica.

Diacheila arctica **Gyll.**
▲ **Glacial and Interstadial sites**
● **Lateglacial cold sites**

Modern European Distribution

Many of the beetles indicated an arctic or sub-arctic regime such as occurs today in the lower alpine regions of the mountains of Scandinavia or the tundra regions of the far north. Recent re-examination of some material of this age at sea level near Waterville in Co. Kerry – as far into the Gulf Stream as it is possible to get today in Ireland – added *Diacheila arctica* (*Illus. 68*) to the local list. Another addition was *Boreaphilus henningianus* (*Illus. 69*), also confined in Europe today to the high north.

In western Ireland, arctic-alpine plants were also growing at low levels near Waterville, around Killarney and at modern sea level at Roundstone in Co. Galway and on Achill Island in Co. Mayo. At Ashleam Bay in Achill, the deposit had clearly originated in a snow patch, as sheets of least willow leaves were protruding from a sandy silt. The age was 11,170 years ago, subject to a marginal variation of 120 years either way. The snow patch had formed as the final Woodgrange temperature was falling rapidly. All this points to the build-up of the very severe conditions of the Nahanagan Stadial. On the mountains we have small glaciers in corries, on the lowlands the deposits are predominantly inorganic and may contain stones. Leaves of least willow are often abundant. Solifluction and snow patches are clearly indicated. The plant remains suggest an incomplete plant cover largely composed of arctic species.

Pollen of sage (*Artemisia*) is common; sorrel (dock) and members of the great family Caryophyllaceae – such as campions, pinks and chickweeds – were present in considerable variety (*Col. 16*). The very small arctic mammals, the lemmings, are popularly pictured as rushing in hordes down steep slopes and plunging into the lake below. Bones of two forms, the Arctic lemming (*Dicrostonyx torquatus*) and the Norwegian lemming (*Lemmus lemmus*) are known from deposits of Midlandian age in Ireland. Bones of Arctic lemming from a cave in Co. Clare were given a ^{14}C age of 10,000 years, so these little creatures survived in Ireland until the end of the Nahanagan Stadial.

With the disappearance of the grasslands, the giant deer disappeared also. It is not known if the reindeer survived the Nahanagan Stadial in Ireland, but they certainly survived it somewhere, perhaps far south in Europe and from there, as the postglacial forests re-advanced inexorably northwards driving the tundras before them, the reindeer kept pace with the tundra till they stabilised themselves in northern latitudes. The reindeer still survive there today if only by the courtesy of the Lapps and Eskimos who have learned that it is better to manage your meat supply than to exterminate it.

It is only very recently that we have come to realise exactly how severe conditions were during the Nahanagan Stadial and we have not yet realised the implications of that severity for many forms of animal and plant life. If we ask the question: Could there have been nearby refuges where some life could have survived when the Midlandian and the Munsterian ice masses were at their maxima, we must also ask what forms could have survived the last episode of cold. The answer is probably: 'Very few indeed.'

4. RESPONSE TO WARM CONDITIONS

10,000 TO 5,100 YEARS AGO

It is generally agreed that under present climatic conditions (i.e. those of a warm stage) and without interference from man, much of Europe would be covered by deciduous woodland. The period now under review shows that such a transformation of the European scene from open tundra to closed woodland did take place and that forests reigned supreme for about 4000 years.

However, about 3900 BC, natural disease and farming activities brought that supremacy to an end. At about that date, a large number of radiocarbon dates converge to reveal that the amount of pollen produced by elm trees showed a drastic, if brief, fall. The cause of the fall has been much argued over, but we agree with those who see this fall as the result of a wave of disease which spread rapidly throughout western Europe. In recent years, we have witnessed another such wave, which brought about a decimation of the elm population. The modern 'Dutch' elm disease is caused by a bark beetle and traces of a similar attack have been found in fossil elm trees dated to about 5000 years old. The dramatic drop in values of elm pollen 5100 years ago gives us a most valuable dating horizon.

How did the present population of plants and animals in Ireland arise? Several arguments have been put forward.

Refuges: *Despite the general cold, there will have been some sheltered localities on or off the west coast where some forms of life could have survived the rigours of the Ice Age.*

During the final cold snap we had tundra with arctic beetles at modern sea level near Waterville in Co. Kerry and snow patches at the same level in Achill Island in Co. Mayo. Sea level was lower then and there would have been an offshore coastal strip, but as the temperature of the sea was very low with floating icebergs, it is difficult to see how forms of life which were not extremely hardy could have survived in Ireland. The strawberry tree (*Arbutus*) is a native of the Mediterranean, but does grow around Killarney and in other places in western Ireland today; it could not have survived the last cold snap in or near Ireland.

Land-bridges: *It is strenuously claimed by some that the rapid rise in postglacial sea level would quickly have overwhelmed any possible bridges across the Irish Sea immediately after the decay of the ice sheets and that there was no possibility for temperate plants and animals to enter by such a route.*

However, we know that there were oaks growing in the south of Ireland 9000 years ago, the wild boar was near Coleraine in the north about the same time and the red deer was in the midlands near Tullamore 8400 years ago. Therefore, we prefer to picture organised woods advancing up a dry coastal strip, carrying those forest animals – the red deer and the wild boar – along with them, rather than to imagine the occasional acorn floating across the sea or being carried by a pigeon across the North Channel, while groups of pigs and deer were swimming across tidal channels. The ecological conditions that allowed these trees to migrate and then establish stable communities would also have allowed a myriad of other organisms – plants and animals, large and small – to do the same. How long did the land-bridges remain available as entry routes into Ireland? We would picture that from some time after 13,000 years ago until about 10,000 years ago, Ireland initially had a coastal path along the shore of the Atlantic and later a very remarkable type of automatic trackway across the Irish Sea. It was remarkable in that it not only allowed organisms to migrate from east to west, but was itself sliding laterally northwards at the same time, sinking in level and narrowing as it did so, until about 10,000 years ago, when it disappeared below the Irish Sea.

Casual Introductions: *There was never a land-bridge and plants crossed the Irish Sea by being carried by the wind or by birds, or by floating either unassisted or on a log; these agencies were also available to some forms of animal life, while others were able to swim or fly.*

Just as a team of monkeys banging away at random will eventually produce a faultless typescript of the plays of Shakespeare, so – given a long enough time – chance will introduce almost anything into Ireland. But with the aid of our pollen-diagrams, radiocarbon dates and dendrochronological diagrams, a credible ecological development of the Irish flora can be traced. Could this be done if the times of the various arrivals were dictated entirely by chance?

Introduction by man: *After man had arrived in Ireland about 9000 years ago, he introduced new plants and animals, some by design and some by accident.*

Man only reached Ireland about 9000 years ago and so was not concerned with anything that was already in Ireland by that date. However, these first intruders were aboriginal hunters and fishermen and can only have made a small number of introductions. But there is no doubt that when the first farmers arrived, bringing in crop plants and their associated weeds, domestic animals, vermin and garden plants, they greatly altered the balance of the modern Irish flora and fauna. It is difficult at times to draw a line between what has been introduced and what is truly indigenous.

SEA LEVEL

Between 10,000 and 9000 years ago, the temperature in north-west Europe reached a limit that enabled closed woodland to develop. The temperature continued to rise and probably passed the present level, for there is some evidence that about 6000 or 7000 years ago the average July temperatures were 1° or 2°C warmer than today. Evidence from Lough Neagh and other lakes suggests that lake levels were lower than at present and the climate may have been rather drier and boreal. This period has been referred to as the *postglacial climatic optimum*, and credit for its discovery is often given to Robert Lloyd Praeger, who towards the end of the last century noted that the estuarine clays and raised beaches formed in the north of Ireland at this time contained a molluscan fauna with species that do not live so far to the north today.

Robert Lloyd Praeger (1865-1953) (*Illus. 70*) was one of Ireland's most distinguished naturalists, who during a long working life made many important discoveries and substantially increased our knowledge of field botany in Ireland. However, he did not discover and never claimed to have discovered the climatic optimum. The attribution arose from the fact that W B Wright had, like many others, a great admiration for Praeger and when in 1936 he published the second edition of his book, *The Quaternary Ice Age*, he dedicated it to 'Praeger – the Discoverer of the Climatic Optimum'. The discovery had, in fact, been made as long ago as 1865 by T F Jamieson when he was studying the molluscan fauna of the estuarine clays of central Scotland.

Illus. 70
Robert Lloyd Praeger,
c.1940.

Praeger refers to Jamieson's work in his own paper and would, were he alive today, be most anxious to see that honour is given where honour is due. We do not make this correction with any intent to lessen Praeger's standing. Born with a love for natural history in his blood, he qualified as an engineer and one of his first jobs was on the excavations for dock construction in Belfast. These excavations gave a wonderful opportunity for molluscan studies and Praeger made the most of it, publishing a series of brilliant papers. However, botany called more strongly than geology and most of his subsequent work was primarily botanical. But he never overlooked the importance of fossil evidence and he realised that Ireland's bogs and lakes must hold great quantities of seeds and other plant parts, whose identification would throw much light on the history of Irish vegetation. Therefore, he made and lodged in the National Herbarium a collection of the seeds of all the plants regarded as native in Ireland. This was done long before organised studies of Quaternary fossil material were even thought of and it must have given Praeger enormous satisfaction when in the thirties, together with Tony Farrington and Adolph Mahr, he organised Knud Jessen's visits to Ireland and was able to see Jessen making full use of the collections of reference material he had put together many years before.

From this optimal level the temperature then appears to have fallen back and the climate became more Atlantic, or oceanic. It is not easy to document the change in Ireland, but in Sweden hazel could no longer grow as far north as it had previously done. Decreases of a degree or two in both summer and winter temperatures have been suggested.

CLIMATE

Since man arrived in Ireland about 9000 years ago, there have been minor changes in climate and in some of these it seems likely that significant temperature changes were involved. In Europe, there was a warmer period around 1200 AD which was followed by a decline that continued till about 1600 AD, when very cold conditions caused the *Little Ice Age*. The temperature then started to climb again and today, due to man's activities, it is threatening to rise still higher. Considerable research work is in progress, endeavouring to track down and evaluate these minor changes and the evidence so far assembled will be discussed when the narrative of this book reaches the appropriate point.

Temperature is only one parameter of climate. What are we to say about the other features of the Irish climate? Some would hold that there is no such thing as climate in Ireland, but only an irregular sequence of different weather patterns with the emphasis on frontal systems bringing wind and rain. Ireland is an outpost in the Atlantic Ocean and maritime influences predominate. Harsh frosts are rare; only the very centre of the country will know more than one day in the year when the temperature will not rise above freezing point throughout the twenty-four hours. High summer temperatures are also rare; 33°C is the highest temperature ever recorded. The annual range is only 9°C in the south-west and 10°C in the east.

The great frequency of winds of moderate to severe intensity is a notable feature especially in the west of the country and days of calm are almost unknown. The air being blown along is usually humid and the disagreeableness of the wind strength is rarely compensated for by good drying conditions.

The amount of rainfall is not excessive, 1400mm in the south-west and 700mm in the east, but the number of days on which it falls is very high. A map showing the number of rain days per annum will almost also serve, in a crude way, as a rainfall map except that it under-represents the rainfall along the south and south-east coasts (*Illus. 71a*). Depressions move along the south coast and up into the south Irish Sea, bringing occasional days of heavy rain although the number of rain days in this area is not high. Continued droughts are rare. Numerous rain days and infrequent droughts mean that humidity is high and evaporation low; another map (*Illus. 71b*) shows the saturation deficit for July, the month when the most favourable values are recorded. The saturation deficit indicates the potential

Illus. 71
Some Irish climatic features:
a number of rain days per annum;
b saturation deficit for the month of July when the drying property of the air is greatest;
c accumulated temperatures in day degrees per annum.

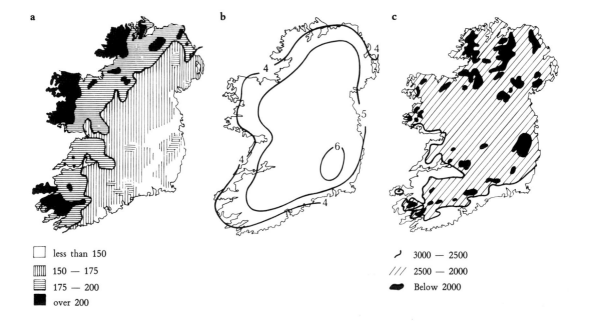

a

b

c

less than 150

150 — 175

175 — 200

over 200

3000 — 2500

2500 — 2000

Below 2000

capacity of the air to absorb more moisture and so gives an indication of drying conditions. In England, only the eastern shores of the Irish Sea show such low saturation-deficits; over the rest of that country the power of the air to absorb more moisture is very much higher. English visitors to the west coast of Ireland often comment unfavourably on the late hour at which the local farmers begin their hay-making operations. They overlook the fact that noon on the clock in Greenwich is eleven o'clock by the sun in Connaught and noon summer time is ten o'clock by the western sun. Several hours of morning sunshine are necessary before the local poor drying conditions can bring the grass into a condition in which it can be safely cut or turned.

The high humidity in Ireland brings about extensive cloud cover and a poor sunshine record. Plants such as primrose and wood sorrel, that grow in England in woods and shady places, find in the west of Ireland that the clouds provide an adequate sunscreen and so they grow on open and treeless hillsides. People living in Ireland are not exposed to strong sunlight and if they migrate to Australia or other areas with high sunshine records, they are very prone to skin cancers and other forms of skin irritation.

Irish emigrants often contrast the harshness of the Australian light with the softer colours of the Irish landscape. Australian air is almost free both from water vapour and industrial smog and it is these two elements that give to Irish air that slightest of haziness that appeals to the Irish eye. Winds from the east increase the haziness and mute the landscape colours; winds from the north-west bring clearer air with sunshine and drifting clouds and at once the landscape springs to brilliance. Variations in wind and cloud come rapidly in Ireland and the never-ending change in the strength of the light and the value of the colour tones brings delight to the eye – and despair to the brush – of many an artist.

The cloud cover cuts down the amount of sunshine that can actually reach and warm the soil and growth is correspondingly slowed. The actual quantity of heat that reaches the ground can be evaluated and represented cartographically on a map (*Illus. 71c*). Such a map shows a strip along the south and south-west coast that is relatively favoured, though only to the same modest degree as the extreme west coast of England; the other parts of England are much warmer. The rest of the lowlands of Ireland receive less heat and anywhere the ground rises, the amount of heat received drops again. Growth conditions in Ireland for many plants, therefore, are always slow and difficult.

While we can make some effort to trace the course of temperature in Ireland in the past, it is not so easy to pin down the other climatic features in the same way, but maritime influences would have prevailed.

SOIL DEVELOPMENT

If this were a textbook on Irish geography, we would have a map at this point which presented an outline of the soils of Ireland. But at the time about which we are speaking, 10,000 years ago, most of the soils which we know today and which the soil surveyors can record and enter up on their field map were not yet developed, the numerous lake-basins left behind by the ice were not yet overgrown by fens and there was no formation of peat. Therefore, we can only indicate the trend of soil development on different parent materials as time went by.

We have seen that the effect of cold was to refresh the soil parent material, either by the deposition of rock debris freshly crushed by ice action or by freeze-thaw disturbance and sludging bringing subsoil to the surface where it replaced, or at least diluted, the materials that had been deeply weathered during the preceding warm stage. At the opening of the Littletonian Warm Stage, the replacement of a dry cold climate by a moist warm one meant: first that water was now free to bring about chemical changes, second that the high humidity reduced evaporation, and third that vigorous plant growth – both by its foliage above ground and by the humus that its decaying debris was contributing to the upper layers of the soil below ground – checked water from flowing away along the surface and encouraged it to sink down into the ground instead.

Soil formation is a very complex process, or series of processes, in which leaching (or washing out), enrichment, redeposition and transformation all play a part. In Ireland, where the principal movement of water is downwards, leaching predominates in the surface layers, which tend to grow more acid with time. The application of lime to the surface halts or reverses this tendency and at least for the past 750 years, farmers have been engaged in this process. Shelly sand was collected on the shore or calcareous clays or marls were dug from pits and spread on the land. Limestone was roasted in kilns, slaked with water and spread; the abandoned limekiln is one of the characteristic features of the Irish countryside. Today, mechanically-crushed limestone flour is widely spread. Farmyard manure and seaweed were used extensively to replace lost organic material; today, macerated manure or *slurry* and chemical fertilisers are dominant. As a result of all these activities, man has profoundly altered the soil in many places.

The course that the soil-forming process takes is influenced by texture, by primary base status and by organic activity. As the water moves down from the surface, it carries readily-soluble substances (including humus) in solution and the very fine insoluble clay particles in suspension and so leaches material from the surface layers, giving rise to the leached or *A-horizon* of the pedologist. The materials carried down from above tend to be deposited below in an enriched, or *B-horizon*, while the as yet unaltered material below is styled the *C-horizon*. In this way, the three main soil horizons began to appear.

Initially, everything was C-horizon and in some areas there was little change, particularly if the parent material was rich in clay particles. Bodies of water that had been dammed up by ice often filled up with finely divided clays and such glacial-lake clays are not uncommon in Ireland. The upper Carboniferous shales of north Kerry, Clare and Kilkenny and the tills derived from them are very rich in clay; in Leitrim, the drumlins are built up of stiff clayey till; on the south-east coast, Midlandian ice which was active in the basin of the Irish Sea incorporated large quantities of marine clay in its deposits.

Because the spaces between the clay particles are very small, movement of ground water through such materials is extremely slow and so there is little apparent development of soil horizons; a wet waterlogged soil, known as a *gley*, results irrespective of the chemical composition of the parent materials. In fact, there are two different types of gley in Ireland, the *surface-water gley* which occurs on heavy-textured slowly permeable parent materials and the *ground-water gley* which is associated with a high water table, and occurs in low-lying areas. Decomposing plant material may accumulate on the surface of the soil; if the plant layer remains thin, i.e. does not thicken into peat, then the soil is described as a *peaty gley*.

By means of a map, we can attempt to indicate the initial distribution about 10,000 years ago of poorly drained and well-drained soils and also the much greater extent of lakes at this time, because they had not yet been overgrown by fens and bogs (*Illus. 72*).

If the parent material was poorer in clay and coarser in texture, water could move downwards and a well-drained soil, more favourable to plant root systems, could gradually develop. As the Littletonian Warm Stage proceeded, trees returned to the country and gradually a high forest of deciduous trees built up climax woodland where the parent soil materials allowed such development. If there were open-textured parent materials on limestone, the establishment of the forest went hand-in-hand with the development of a *brown forest* soil. The surface layers of such a soil consisted of an intimate mixture of well-decomposed humus and mineral matter. But because of the way man subsequently interfered with the woodlands, there are no virgin brown forest soils in Ireland today.

If interference has only been slight, the surface humus will have disappeared and the soil will have become a fertile *brown earth*, which in Ireland is often shallow.

Where the parent glacial material was non-calcareous, the chemical action of the ground water was more marked and there was a tendency for substances to be leached out of the top layer or the A-horizon and carried away in the ground water, or deposited lower down the profile in the B-horizon; such soils are commonly known as *acid brown earths* and occur widely in Co. Wexford. When the leaching was much more intensive, in the higher rainfall areas of south-west Ireland, the A-horizon tended to be bleached to a paler, ashy colour, a feature described as *podzolic*, while the B-horizon, because of enrichment with humus and iron there, took on a strong brown or yellowish-red

Illus. 72
Map to show areas where the very high primary clay content causes the soil to remain poorly drained and wet at all times. At the opening of the Littletonian Warm Stage, the lakes on the lowlands were much larger than they are today; the map endeavours to indicate the extent of these lakes before they were reduced in size by the growth of fens and bogs.

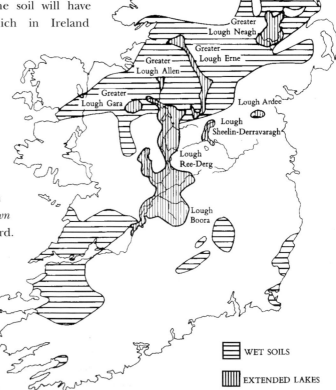

Greater Lough Neagh
Greater Lough Erne
Greater Lough Allen
Greater Lough Gara
Lough Ardee
Lough Sheelin-Derravaragh
Lough Ree-Derg
Lough Boora

▦ WET SOILS

▥ EXTENDED LAKES

colour called *brown podzolic*. The word podzol is based on the Russian words *pod* meaning under and *zola* meaning ash.

At higher elevations where the climate was colder and wetter, a thin layer of plant debris accumulated on the surface leading to the initial development of a *peaty podzol*. Peaty podzols have a very special importance in the history of the Irish landscape because they provided the substratum on which blanket bogs later developed. Subsequent climatic deterioration enabled bog to develop on lower ground. Later, the downward movement of iron in the underlying mineral material led to a concentration of iron in a thin wavy *iron pan* which is often impermeable.

Even in areas of relatively low rainfall, as in the south-east of Ireland, where the parent material was non-calcareous and rich in sand, marked leaching took place and iron, aluminium and humus were removed from the A-horizon which then became very pale in colour and was left in a highly acid condition. Because of the strongly bleached appearance, the soil is called a *podzol*. The materials leached from the A-horizon were precipitated in the B-horizon where the iron and humus often formed two distinct horizons to give the soils known as *humus-iron-podzols*.

In many parts of Europe where the parent material was calcareous and had some content of clay or of minerals that would break down into clay on weathering, the movement or flow of ground water down the profile over a long period of time gradually carried clay particles down out of the A-horizon and deposited them in the B-horizon which then became progressively enriched in clay. This resulted in the soil called *grey-brown podzolic*, so-called on account of its colour, bleached above and deeper below, because in addition to the movement of clay, other substances including iron have been lost from the A-horizon, but in fact its diagnostic criterion is the added clay in the B-horizon. Studies of fossil soils buried beneath raised bogs in Ireland show that the accumulation of clay has increased with the passage of time. Today, grey-brown podzolic soils are widely developed on the calcareous deposits of the last glaciation in the midlands, where they form very fertile soils. Ten thousand years ago, the movement of clay was only beginning and the soils must then have had a rather different character.

But we also have in Ireland another type of soil which is very rich in clay, some little distance down from the surface, which is called *pseudo grey-brown podzolic*. The quantity of clay present seems much too great to have arisen from the translocation of clays from the surface A-horizon and may be a feature inherited from the glacial material on which the soil had developed. Alternatively, in situ clay formation may have taken place.

Base status and texture are not the only factors affecting soil development. Topography including altitude, slope and aspect is also very important. In low-lying areas, rivers are sluggish and there may be lakes of varying sizes. On higher ground, temperature is lower and winds are stronger and these factors influence plant growth, especially tree growth. In many parts of the temperate world, trees grow at heights much higher than the highest Irish mountaintop and the absence of trees from higher ground today is partly due to the activities of man and partly due to the spread of blanket bog. We can picture three main landscape regions:

(1)   the lowlands, which are given an arbitrary upper limit of 150m (approximately 500ft), the height above which tillage is rarely practised in Ireland today;

(2)   the uplands above 150m (often today covered by blanket bog);

(3)   what can be conveniently called the 'wetlands', which include rivers, lakes, fens, raised bogs and extensive areas of gley soils on the lowlands. These three landscape regions had different patterns of vegetation, and their later uses by man differed widely; wherever it is appropriate they will be discussed separately. However we must remember that the differences between them are not fixed and immutable. If climate improved, tillage might have moved higher up the mountain slopes; if climate deteriorated and blanket bog spread, fertile lowland areas might have been turned into infertile wetlands.

We can now retrace our steps to about 10,000 years ago and ask ourselves what will happen when the Littletonian thermostat is given a vigorous upward turn? In the Nahanagan Stadial, there was a limited number of plants and animals requiring open habitats, but capable of surviving relatively adverse climatic conditions. Now they faced rising temperature and strong competition; some survived the change and held their own, others became extinct in Ireland and a few found refuge on cliffs or on mountain-tops. Where were their competitors? We can picture them strung out across continental Europe, as well as down the Atlantic coast of France, standing in their places like starters in a handicapped gold rush. When the 'off' was given, they sprang into action, each determined to stake out his claim. And this was a race against the clock, because there was only a very short time to go before a water-barrier would have to be crossed if they were to reach Ireland, the *Outpost of Europe*, as Grenville Cole, former Director of the Irish Geological Survey, called it many years ago.

Professor David Webb of Trinity College, whose death in 1994 robbed us of a great deal of knowledge of the flora of Europe as well as that of Ireland, discussed the flora of Ireland in its European context and the account which follows draws heavily on his work. Professor Webb placed his main emphasis on land-bridges, but he also called on survival to explain why some plants which occur in Ireland are absent from Britain.

Professor Webb drew up a table of the number of wild plants in the countries of north-west Europe as follows:

COUNTRY	NUMBER
France	3500
Belgium	1140
Ireland	815
Britain	1172
Denmark	1030
Isle of Man	576

Table 3

The poverty of plant life in Ireland is immediately apparent, as is the richness in France. But France is in a different league to the other countries; it is almost a subcontinent, ranging from the English Channel to the Mediterranean and varying in elevation from sea level to almost 5000m. Belgium and Denmark show that low-lying land on the European side of the English Channel can muster about 1100 wild plants.

Britain is much larger than Belgium, Holland and Denmark put together; it has a large area of high ground as compared with the Ardennes in Belgium and it has a much wider climatic range. East Anglia is akin to the continent, while the west coast is markedly oceanic. We should expect a much larger plant-life tally for Britain and so must regard its flora as impoverished also, though not to the same degree as that of Ireland.

Only the early wave of returning plants was able to reach Ireland before it was cut off; the Isle of Man, with its very restricted range of habitats, was up a side-road; later waves got to Britain. After Britain was severed from the continent, northern Europe continued to receive stragglers who might have reached the British Isles had they been quicker off the mark.

We can picture the process as a steeplechase (*Illus. 73*). Those continental plants that did reach Ireland presumably used the Channel land-bridge. They met their first 'fence' at a line between Tyneside and Exeter, drawn many years ago by the distinguished Welsh archaeologist, Sir Cyril Fox. This line separates Lowland Britain with its soft rocks, base-rich soils and low rainfall from Highland Britain with its harder rocks, less fertile soils and higher rainfall. Seventy-five of the plants that

Illus. 73 The Littletonian plant steeplechase.

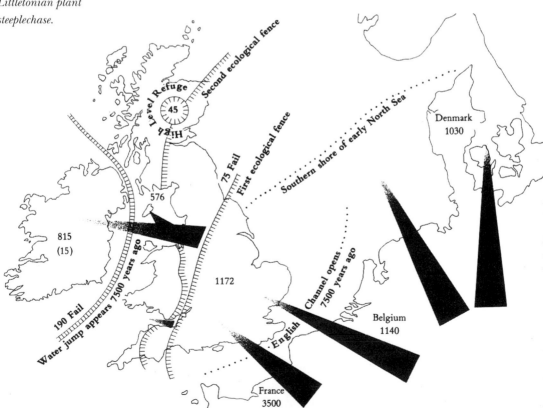

did reach Britain did not advance across this line and so had no opportunity to reach Ireland.

Still farther west, these highland factors become more extreme and even less attractive to incoming plants. An interrupted 'fence' was erected here, but through its gaps the fertile lowlands around the Bristol Channel and on the Cheshire coast could be reached. From here the Lake District hills could be skirted and then it was across the floor of the Solway Firth to the final land-bridge to the west. There would have been an advance party of plants of open country, but the trees quickly followed. And with the trees came the shrubs, lianes and herbs which tolerate and sometimes require the cover of deciduous trees, together with the mammals and other animals of the woods.

Freshwater molluscs appear to have accompanied them. Not far west of Dublin, near Newlands Cross, there is an extensive deposit of tufa (calcium carbonate deposited from the lime water) containing freshwater molluscs. These have been studied by Richard Preece of Cambridge with most exciting results. He also studied a comparable deposit in Wales and this deposit not only has the same age of about 7750 years ago, but also has an almost identical faunal sequence. The molluscs must have invaded Britain first and then reached Ireland before the land-bridge was finally cut. They then spread throughout the countryside, moving on from pond to pond as successive ecological groups and not at random on the feet of birds or other transporting agency. When washing the Irish material to separate the shells from the matrix of the tufa, a flint flake and teeth of a fieldmouse (*Apodemus sylvaticus*) were also discovered.

However, if the molluscs made the crossing successfully, freshwater fish did not, as it is generally agreed that non-migratory freshwater fish, such as pike, perch and bream, were introduced into Ireland by man. It is thought that during the last glaciation, all freshwater fish disappeared from Britain and Ireland. When the rivers of south-east England were still part of the Rhine system, they were re-colonised from Europe, but by this time Ireland was already cut off from Britain.

The migratory fish, salmon, trout and eel, returned to the Irish river systems early in postglacial time. The migratory habit is related to water temperature and becomes more pronounced under cold conditions. The pollan (*Coregonus autumnalis*) of Lough Neagh, the shad (*Alosa fallax killarniensis*) of the Killarney lakes and the char (*Salvelinus alpinus*) of several lakes probably used to come and go, but were trapped in inland waters when conditions changed.

However, we must return to the plant steeplechase. For the late-comers, the breaching of the Irish Sea bridge had introduced a water-jump, and there were many casualties here. Professor Webb reckoned their number at about one hundred and ninety, that is plants whose distribution in Britain suggests that there is no apparent reason why they should not have succeeded in Ireland had they managed to reach it.

Webb also excluded another group, about forty-five in all, that would have had nowhere to go had they reached Ireland. These were the plants of the high mountains of Scotland, a refuge habitat which has no equivalent in Ireland. This group is a little tricky because it includes some northern plants which were present in both Britain and Ireland in late-glacial time, but have since become extinct in Ireland. The habitat they require has disappeared from Ireland, though it still survives in highland Scotland. The dwarf birch (*Betula nana*) is such a plant. In Britain, these plants may thus be late-glacial survivors rather than early postglacial immigrants.

For Webb there was also another very problematical group, that is some fifteen plants that have restricted distributions in Ireland, but do not occur in Britain. Of the fifteen, eight occur in the north-west of the Iberian peninsula. We have already noted three heathers: St Dabeoc's heath (*Daboecia cantabrica*) occurring in Connemara and also in outlying stations not far from the French west coast, Mackay's heath (*Erica mackaiana*) in Connemara and Donegal, and Mediterranean heath (*Erica erigena*) in Connemara, with one outlying station near Bordeaux.

Two more plants are saxifrages, London pride (*S. spathularis*) and its close relative (*S. hirsuta*) found chiefly in the south-west. The sixth plant is the large-flowered pinguicula (*P. grandiflora*), found only in the south-west. The seventh, the strawberry tree (*Arbutus unedo*), also of the heather family, is Mediterranean and has an outlying station in Brittany; in Ireland it is confined to the west. The eighth is the Irish orchid (*Neotinea intacta*), found chiefly in Clare and Galway; an outlying station has recently been found in the Isle of Man.

There is also one animal, the spotted slug (*Geomalachus maculosus*) (*Illus. 74*), which is restricted to the south-west of Ireland, where it is quite conspicuous on wet rocks after rain.

Illus. 74
Kerry slug
(Geomalachus
maculosus).

While the absence of these species from Britain is hard to explain, we cannot feel that this group either survived off western Ireland or made its way from north-west Iberia to Ireland entirely by chance. As outlined already, we believe there was a west European coastal strip along which the group made its way to Ireland. Some stragglers were left behind, indicating the route. A convincing demonstration is the modern distribution of a shore-living bug, *Aepophilus bonnairei* (*Illus. 75*). The modern headquarters of this insect, which lives in rock-crevices near the low-tide mark and can neither swim nor fly, are on the Atlantic coast from Morocco to Portugal. It could not have survived the cold of the Nahanagan Stadial in the British Isles and when warmth returned at the beginning of the Littletonian Warm Stage, it marched north up the French coast, skirted the embayments of the Celtic Sea that then occupied the English Channel and the south of the Irish Sea and made its way on to the Atlantic coast of Ireland. The Irish orchid (*Neotinea intacta*), found only in the Isle of Man and in western Ireland, hints at the same route.

Recent detailed pollen studies by Fraser Mitchell and others enable us to see not only the time at which the various trees reached Ireland, but also the rate and direction of their migration. Pine, oak and alder followed the route postulated above for *Aepophilus*, moving north across the Bay of Biscay and the Celtic Sea. Elm and ash took a different path, migrating in a north-westerly direction across Britain from continental Europe and then on into Ireland.

Today, we can only study the variety and distribution of the Irish flora and fauna as we see them before us, but we must always remember that since plants and animals first arrived in Ireland they have been influenced by changing climate, pushed aside by expanding bogs and grossly interfered with by man.

Naias is an inconspicuous, totally submerged water plant. A small form, *N. flexilis*, still lives, though it is rare, in lakes in western Ireland and Scotland, with one outlying station in the English Lake District. However, about 6000 years ago, when summer temperatures were slightly higher than they are today, it was widely distributed in Scotland; in Scandinavia it extended further to the north than it does today. The larger form, *N. marina*, today survives in the British Isles only in the Norfolk Broads, but it was widely distributed in Britain and Ireland around

● AEPOPHILUS BONNAIREI

0   80   160
KM

Illus. 75
The modern distribution of Aepophilus bonnairei, *a shore-dwelling bug, which is most likely to have reached Ireland in early Littletonian time by moving along a continuous coastline that stretched from the Atlantic coast of France to Ireland.*

Illus. 76
Lough Mask, Co. Mayo. Stumps and trunks of pine, perhaps about 4000 years old, have been exposed by peat cutting. Such 'bog-deal' was formerly valued both for fuel and for building.

6000 years ago. On today's distribution we might think that *Naias* had reached Ireland by an Atlantic route; the fossil record lets us see that both forms are probably of north European origin.

The Scots pine (*Pinus sylvestris*) (*Col. 20*) probably died out in Ireland in the early centuries of the Christian era. Six thousand years ago it must have been widespread in Ireland, because in many places where peat has been cut, we can see a sheet of pine stumps at the base of the bog (*Illus. 76*). It was probably the wetter conditions that enabled the bog to invade the pine forest. If another change brought about a drier bog surface, then the pine could have invaded the bog and produced still another distribution pattern.

Man has been the chief disturber of natural distributions. He has introduced new plants and animals to compete with the indigenous forms and has brought about further gross change by cutting down forests, draining wetland and removing peat mechanically. When there were primeval woods in Ireland, there were woodpeckers here also, as shown by bones found in Clare caves; when the woods vanished, the woodpeckers also vanished.

The different animal groups also show deficiencies, as great as or greater than those of the plants.

Table 4

THE LAND MAMMALS OF IRELAND AND GREAT BRITAIN COMPARED	
Species native to Ireland	
Extinct	3
Native in Britain also	11
Naturalised in Britain	0
Absent from Britain	0
Total:	14
Species native to Britain	
Extinct	4
Native in Ireland also	11
Naturalised in Ireland	3
Absent from Ireland	14
Total:	32

Similar shortfalls are recorded among the birds (Ireland 354; Britain 456), the reptiles (Ireland 1; Britain 4) and the amphibians (Ireland 2; Britain 6).

Professor Webb's figures show that Ireland contains about 70% of the plants that occur in Britain. The same comparison has recently been made for groups of insects and other invertebrates occurring in terrestrial and freshwater habitats. Ireland has about 65% of the British number. It would seem therefore that the barriers which impeded access to Ireland operated with rather similar force on a wide range of plants and animals.

The current Littletonian Warm Stage is, we believe, merely another interregnum in a continuing cold and we can follow its development – as far as it has proceeded – in the same way as we followed earlier warm stages. *Illus. 77* shows

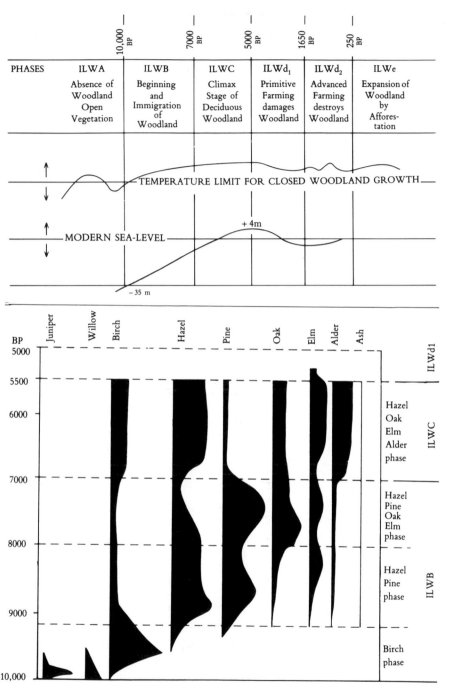

Illus. 77
Phases of woodland
development in the
Littletonian Warm
Stage in Ireland.

Illus. 78
Schematic pollen-
diagram to illustrate
the early development
of the Littletonian
woodlands in
Ireland.

the phases of woodland development into which it can be divided and also two very
tentative curves; one to indicate the movement of temperature and the second to
indicate the movement of sea level.

We can also draw a schematic pollen-diagram (*Illus. 78*) to indicate the order
in which the trees arrived in Ireland and give some indication of their relative

importances, as shown by the amounts of pollen they produced. The amounts indicated are 'raw' figures, that is to say they are the numbers counted; they ignore the fact that some trees are much more lavish producers of pollen than others, which might give the impression that they were more important in the woodlands than their counts warrant. Corrections can be made to allow for the relative pollen productions of the different trees, but they have not been done in this simple diagram.

As we have already seen, the Littletonian Warm Stage opens at 10,000 years ago when rising warmth brought the Nahanagan Stadial to an end. The beetles of the Nahanagan Stadial suggest an average July temperature of only 10°C, similar to that found in the Scandinavian Mountains today; they are then rapidly replaced by relatively thermophilous beetles which indicate an average July temperature of 15°C, which is similar to that of today. Temperature, therefore, was not a limit on the movement of plants and animals and immense migratory movements must have begun.

The first response of the flora to warming was a development of rich meadows with grasses, docks and meadowsweet. The meadows were quickly invaded by juniper and within 250 years, juniper scrub had replaced the meadows over wide regions. About 9500 years ago, tree willows began to overshadow the juniper scrub and these in turn gave way to tree birches and Littletonian Ireland had its first woodlands. Aspen (*Populus tremula*) was also present and – at least in the Burren – guelder rose (*Viburnum opulus*).

Therefore, we have a birch phase which lasted till about 9250 years ago, by which time pollen of hazel appeared in the pollen counts, indicating the arrival of this bush or small tree. The expansion of hazel was rapid and complete in some areas and slower and less overwhelming in others and differences in soil and in aspect must have had considerable influence. In some areas, the lake muds have been found to be full not only of hazel pollen, but also of fragments of hazelnuts and there must have been dense hazel-woods in these areas.

The pine moved into Ireland at about the same time as the hazel and its spread also seems to have been irregular. Following the coastal route, it appeared early in the south-west and only reached Donegal about 1000 years later. Soil differences may have kept the hazel-woods and the pine-woods apart from one another, but they both produced pollen abundantly and we have a hazel-pine phase from about 9000 to about 8500 years ago. Alder (*Alnus*) appeared about 7000 years ago, but its expansion was not synchronous.

THE FIRST APPEARANCE OF MAN C.9000 YEARS AGO

Just south of Coleraine in north-east Ireland, high bluffs dominate the lower reaches of the River Bann at Mount Sandel. This very strategic site has been occupied by man throughout the millennia and Peter Woodman has shown that it is here that we find the earliest detailed record of man in Ireland, in campsites that may go back as far as 9000 years ago (*Illus. 79*). The site appears to have been occupied by people who used small flint points or microliths (*Illus. 80*) and small axes struck from flint pebbles or from flakes off such pebbles. The microliths were

Illus. 79
Mount Sandel,
Coleraine, Co. Derry.
This Mesolithic site
dated to about 8650
years ago, gives us
our oldest record of
man in Ireland; it
produced hearths,
sites of huts,
microliths, axes and
bones of birds and
fish.

probably set as barbs in a harpoon-like implement. These people had no knowledge of agriculture and so they must have lived by hunting and fishing; they had no knowledge of the art of making pottery and so they had not attained the level of Neolithic culture. By the time they reached Ireland, the country had been re-smothered in trees and they were unable to range wide prairies in search of herds of big game, as the Palaeolithic hunters of Europe had done. They seem to have had axe-like implements of chipped or roughly-ground stone, but they either could not or did not use these for large-scale forest clearance, as the later Neolithic people were to do using their hafted polished stone axes to open up extensive cultivation-patches in the woodlands. They were hunters and fishers of Mesolithic (between Palaeolithic and Neolithic) status,

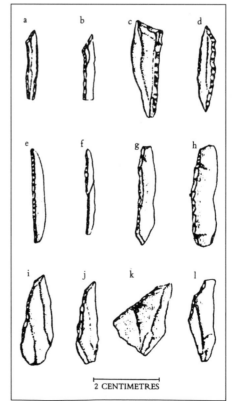

2 CENTIMETRES

Illus. 80
Twelve microliths, the
commonest form of
flint artifact at
Mount Sandel, are
seen here close to their
actual size. They fall
into three categories.
Scalene triangles
(a-d) were arrow-tips
or the barbs and
cutting edges of
composite implements.
Rods (e-h) may have
been used in food
preparation.
Obliquely trimmed
blades (i-l) could
have been small
knives.

restricted by their inability to clear large areas to roaming along the shores of lakes and rivers and along the coasts, hunting small game, catching fish and collecting nuts and seeds as seasonal opportunity offered.

Wild pigs seem to have been the largest animals they captured and they probably had dogs to assist the chase. They took salmon, trout and eels from the river and nearer its mouth, sea bass and flounders. Of birds there were four prime food forms: pigeon, duck, grouse and capercaillie and one bird of prey, the goshawk. The capercaillie is a bird of pine forests and it may then have been common in the early Irish pine-woods; it became extinct in the eighteenth century. The goshawk, now also extinct, was never a common bird and it is curious that its bones have been found not only at Mount Sandel, but at a later Mesolithic site on Dalkey Island in Co. Dublin and at the Early Bronze Age site of Newgrange in Co. Meath. Could it have been used in falconry, rather than killed as a bird of prey?

The Mount Sandel site was rich in hazelnuts, which must have been freely available in the neighbouring woods. There were also charred seeds of the white water-lily (*Nymphaea alba*). These seeds were eaten by Mesolithic man. Charred seeds of the yellow water-lily (*Nuphar lutea*) were found on a late Mesolithic site on Lough Derravaragh in Co. Westmeath.

Mount Sandel came to be noticed because archaeological debris was lying on its flanks. Then a second site appeared without warning and was excavated by the National Museum. It is in a large area of raised bog, known as Boora Bog near Tullamore in Co. Offaly, which is being developed by Bord na Móna. Usually, the basal layers of the peat are left in position so as to assist eventual reclamation. At one point, where a lake had formerly existed, all the peat was removed in order to create a settling pond for finely-divided peat debris. A gravel ridge carrying an early Mesolithic site and a massive beach were exposed. Here was proof that there had been large lakes in early postglacial Ireland (*Illus. 72*). The original Lough Boora would have been broad enough for strong winds to whip up considerable waves. When the waves reached the shore, they built up a substantial storm beach. There would have been a lagoon between the beach and the ridge and obviously the top of the ridge overlooking the lagoon would have been a very attractive site for Mesolithic fishers.

In north-east Ireland, where deposits of chalk still survive, *flint* – a siliceous concretion, usually pale in colour, which develops in chalk – was freely available as raw material for implements. There was no flint at Lough Boora, but the local limestone had siliceous concretions, which were black and are known as *chert*. From this chert, microliths very like those at Mount Sandel were worked and there were also ground axeheads of slate. The ^{14}C dates on these tools centre on 8400 years ago, a similar age to Mount Sandel.

Food debris was also similar to that at Mount Sandel, but in addition to pig, there were also red deer and hare. There were bones from ducks and small fish and again hazelnuts. The whole settlement was then swallowed up as bog vegetation developed and grew upwards, gradually blocking the local drainage system. The original Lough Boora shrank in area as continual bog growth constricted it.

However, its level was raised and the final remnant was left
perched high above its first level.

Similar microliths have also been picked up along the
River Blackwater, chiefly in the vicinity of Cappoquin,
but excavation failed to produce any organised traces
of a settlement. The microliths can be taken as the
signature tune of the first wave of
Mesolithic people and a distribution
map shows where such implements
have been found in Ireland (*Illus.
81*). We call these first inhabitants
the *Sandelians* from their best known
site (so far) at Mount Sandel. Where
did these first Irishmen come from?
Microliths and axes are found in
Mesolithic sites in Denmark. We
cannot, therefore, overlook Denmark in our
search for the original home of the first
men to reach Ireland. There is also an
early Danish Mesolithic and this spills
over into eastern England, where it
perhaps finds its finest flowering
at Star Carr, occupied about 9500
years ago. This wonderful site,
discovered by John Moore and
excavated by Grahame Clark, was on
the margin of a lake which was then at a
rather lower level and the damp conditions

Illus. 81
Known Sandelian
material.

created by a later rise in the water table had enabled bone and wood to survive.
Here was what we have yet to find in Ireland, a Mesolithic dwelling-site with all its
appurtenances. There were antler harpoons, both finished and unfinished and as if
this was not enough, carefully cut antler headdresses, which were used either as
stalking aids in actual hunting, or in ceremonies intended to promote success in the
chase. There were also containers made out of birch bark.

The Star Carr folk had an impressive range of implements of flint and stone.
Both axes and adzes were made from pebbles, not flakes; in addition to variously
trimmed flakes and microliths, they also had the burin, a chisel-like and invaluable
tool especially for the cutting and working of bone. Stone hatchets if mounted with
the cutting edge in line with the shaft were axes used for cutting wood; if mounted
with the cutting edge at right angles to the shaft, they became a digging tool.

In Denmark, lavish Mesolithic burials have been found; rows of shells in the
graves suggest that the bodies were buried in garments richly embroidered with
patterns of shells.

In Britain, many Mesolithic sites occur on the uplands of the Pennines, placed
perhaps where the lower forests were thinning out. This type of site has not yet been

found in Ireland. An upland site at Filpoke Beacon in Co. Durham, dated to about 8750 years ago, has microliths very similar to the Irish ones. Microliths and other implements with Pennine affinities also occur in the Isle of Man.

FURTHER WOODLAND DEVELOPMENT 8500 TO 7000 YEARS AGO

By 8500 years ago, the oak and the elm were beginning to overshadow the hazel on the heavier soils and the amount of hazel pollen fell. The pine may have been forced back onto the sandier and drier soils, but it continued to produce substantial amounts of pollen, which tended to increase in quantity. At this time, the climate in general may have been rather dry.

Under these circumstances, the alder, a tree of wet soils, may have been restricted to the margins of lakes and rivers and this may be why at first its pollen makes only a trifling appearance in the pollen record before 6500 BP. It expanded in Connemara a little later, but did not reach the upland areas of north-east Ireland before 5200 BP.

Ash was present, but was perhaps confined to dry limestone soils, a habitat which was not sufficiently extensive to enable it to make an effective contribution to the pollen rain. The yew was also present, but its pollen is relatively fragile and difficult to recognise in fossil form and was overlooked for a long time. Recent studies show that it was much more important in Ireland than was at first supposed.

Therefore, we picture Ireland as having been in a state of vegetational turmoil for some 3000 years. The drama began when the pioneer trees, juniper, willow and birch, invaded the open meadows. The taller hazels and pines then overshadowed the earlier trees. Hazel in turn had to give way to the forest-size oaks and elms, while pine was displaced from the better soils. The establishment of the high forest brought about a position of some stability, which lasted for about 1500 years until alder began to carve out an ecological niche for itself.

A visitor to Ireland at this time would have seen endless sheets of trees interrupted only by the water of lakes and river-channels. Such countryside has almost totally vanished today, though some fragments do survive in the Geeragh in the valley of the Lee, near Macroom (*Illus. 82*); much more is now submerged beneath the waters of the local hydroelectric scheme. Even the karstic areas of limestone were invaded by coniferous and deciduous trees and we can still see such forests in the former Czechoslovakia today.

While these trees did reach Ireland, what others fell by the wayside? It is difficult to understand why the small-leaved lime (*Tilia cordata*) failed to reach Ireland, as it accompanied the oak and elm in their advance as far as south Wales; and Ireland had plenty of limestone soils on which to receive it. The hornbeam (*Carpinus*) and the field maple (*Acer campestre*) did not advance seriously beyond south-east England. The beech (*Fagus sylvatica*) is more of a problem; after introduction by man in the eighteenth century, it spread widely throughout Ireland where it found the moist conditions very much to its taste. It had reached south-east England before 7000 years ago and its continued advance ought to have been rapid. Even if there was a water-barrier between Britain and Ireland, beech capsules can float and birds feed eagerly on its small edible nuts.

Did other trees arrive, and then fail to survive? It is commonly pictured that the climate at the opening of the Littletonian Warm Stage was relatively continental and boreal and that this may have meant that killing-frosts occurred later in spring than they do today. Within the range of plants that a botanist recognises as a single species, there will be forms or ecotypes that have different ranges of tolerance for various factors and it may have been that only those tree ecotypes that were sufficiently frost-hardy were able to hold a permanent position in the Irish woodlands.

It is one of the paradoxes of the modern Irish spring that some introduced trees, such as the horse chestnut (*Aesculus hippocastanum*) and the sycamore (*Acer pseudoplatanus*), which today are natives of more southern lands, put out their young leaves earlier than the native oak and ash and so are taking advantage of the sunshine while the Irish trees are still in bud. It may be that the modern Irish trees are the descendants of ecotypes that held back their leaves until the late killing-frosts were over, while other ecotypes that put out their leaves earlier were eliminated. In the more oceanic Irish climate of today, the horse chestnut and the sycamore escape killing-frosts and are able to flourish.

Illus. 82
The Geeragh near Macroom, Co.Cork, now drowned beneath a reservoir. Here the Lee expanded into a network of streams and wooded islets, uninvaded by grazing animals. Much of lowland Ireland looked like this before fens and bogs clogged the waterways and man and his animals damaged the woodlands.

THE SECOND WAVE OF HUMAN OCCUPATION C.8000 YEARS AGO

About 8150 years ago, the Irish Mesolithic implements altered completely. Microliths almost disappeared and heavy blades struck from large pieces of flint or cores appeared (*Illus. 83*). The edges of the microliths had been carefully reworked, but the sharp cutting edges of the blades were used without any modification. Did the earlier group of people, the Sandelians, disappear and were their successors, whom for reasons shortly to become clear we call the *Larnians*, of an entirely different stock? The problem is compounded because, just as we find it hard to find ancestors for the Sandelians, the Larnians stand in equal isolation; we cannot find a source for them either. In addition, the difference between the implements is so

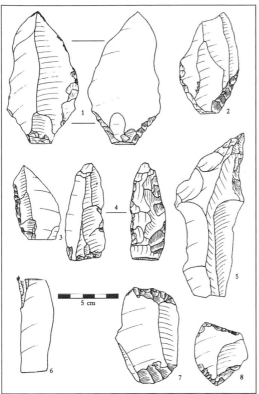

great that we cannot see the Larnian style as having developed from the Sandelian. Larnian sites are common on the west shore of the Irish Sea (*Illus. 84*) and this suggests that the Larnians were good coastal navigators.

We see the newcomers first at the north-west corner of Lough Neagh – where the Lower Bann makes its exit towards the sea – and a little later at Cushendun on the east Antrim coast. The oldest charcoal from Peter Woodman's excavations at Newferry on the Bann is 8150 years old. Many years ago, Hallam Movius excavated implements from estuarine gravels and silts in the raised beach at Cushendun (*Illus. 85*); charcoal and wood, collected at the same time, have now been dated by radiocarbon to an age of 7500 years. The sites provide a well-defined if restricted range of implements among

Illus. 83
Larnian implements from
Lough Kinale.

  1,2 Leaf-shaped flake
    3 Backed knife
    4 Blade
    5 Pick or borer
    6 Burin
  7,8 Scrapers

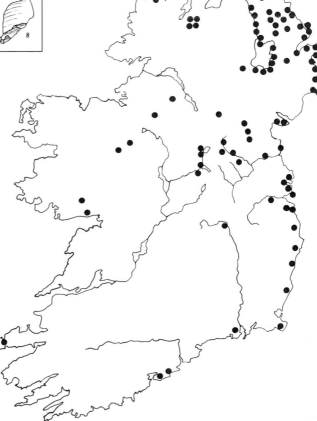

Illus. 84
Known Larnian material.

which the microlith, so common at
Mount Sandel, is very rare. Typical
implements of the newcomers are
common in the raised beach gravels at
Larne in Co. Antrim, where they have
long been collected and studied and it
is from this town that the name
Larnian comes.

   We get a tantalising Mesolithic
glimpse at Newlands Cross, west of
Dublin. About 8000 years ago, springs
were trickling from the local limestone, pond snails lived in the water,
and a thick deposit of shells and tufa
was formed. When collecting shells
for study, Dr Richard Preece of
Cambridge, as has already been
noted, dug up a worked piece of flint;
seeds at the same level had an age of
7700 years. Although the flint is not a typical Larnian implement, it shows that
Mesolithic man was here at the same time as the Larnians were.

Illus. 85
Raised beach at
Cushendun,
Co. Antrim, which
contains Mesolithic
flint implements in
Larnian style. This
beach has been
isostatically uplifted
to 8.5m above
modern sea level.

   We can picture parts of the Larnian way of life, but not as yet the full
sequence. Lough Neagh was then at a lower level and there were sandbanks and
bars both at Toome Bay where Lough Beg is cut off from the main lake and at
Newferry where the Lower Bann flows out of Lough Beg. Fishing parties taking
seasonally running salmon and eels occupied the sandbanks and almost certainly
smoked fish there. After about 7000 years ago, the Bann became more prone to
seasonal flooding and each year the water-meadows which flanked the river
accumulated thin sheets of diatom-frustules which gradually built up into a thick
layer of diatomite (*Illus. 86*). In places, the diatomite contains large spreads of ash

Illus. 86
Harvard excavation
of diatomite in the
Bann Valley,
Northern Ireland,
1934.

Col. 1
Benbane head,
Co. Antrim.
On the north coast
the horizontal sheets
of basalt (which
poured out as liquid
lava sixty million
years ago) are cliffed
by the sea. Halfway
down the cliff we see
a red band of tropical
soil formed during a
lull in volcanic
activity.

1

Col. 2
Boulder-strewn slope
of Clogher Head in
Co. Kerry running
down to an etch-
plain. Sybil Head
rises in the
background.

2

3

Col. 3
Near Aghavannagh,
Co. Wicklow.
Granite
characteristically
weathers to such
rounded slopes. The
blanket bog in the
foreground is planted
with young conifers.
Other older
plantations are also
seen.

4

Col. 4
Looking north across
the Mitchelstown
valley to the Galty
Mountains.
Hercynide thrusting
created east/west
structures here.
Limestone remains in
the valley but has
been stripped off the
mountain ridge where
more resistant Old
Red Sandstone
stands up.

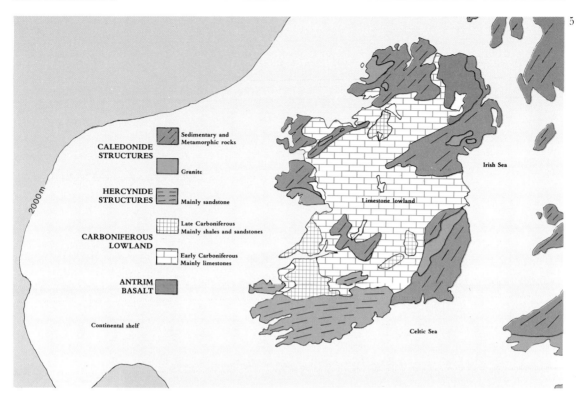

Col. 5
Outline geological
map of Ireland.

Col. 6
Opencast gypsum
mine near
Carrickmacross,
Co. Monaghan.

7

8

Col. 7
Portmagee, Co Kerry.
The cliff edge in the
foreground is slowly
collapsing seawards
as wave attack
undermines the cliff
face.

Col. 8
Giant's Causeway,
Co Antrim. As the
molten lava cooled,
shrinkage-cracks
arranged in a
hexagonal pattern
gradually developed.
Wave attack is now
exposing the
columnar structure.

9

Col. 9

The Burren, Co. Clare.

Limestone, laid down in layers on the sea-floor, was later raised in this area without much lateral disturbance as almost horizontal strata of rock. Ice later moved over it, stripping away any projections and leaving bare, rounded surfaces. In places the ice did deposit some of the rock debris which it had been transporting; on the lower right of the picture we see some dark-coloured remnants of such debris which has been gullied by rain water.

10

Col. 10,11

(Above)   *In the Queen Maud Mountains in Antarctica today, the Bowman glacier, following a pre-existing valley, is cutting away the flanks of the valley and deepening its floor.*

(Opposite)   *In the Wicklow Mountains about 15,000 years ago, a similar glacier carried out almost the same functions and created the U-shaped valley that we see today. The valley has been partly filled by later river gravel which gives it an inner flat floor. On the gravel in the centre of the picture we see the ruins of an army barracks at Drumgoff built in the late eighteenth century. At that time, just as in Scotland, military roads and barracks were built in upland areas to prevent rebellious forces assembling there.*

11

12

Col. 12
Tanga, Tanzania.
In tropical Africa the
dissolving away of
limestone by rain has
gone on
uninterruptedly for
millions of years
resulting in a deeply
fretted terrain; a man
shows the scale of the
erosion. In the mine
at Tynagh in
Co. Galway, where
the limestone had
been protected from
glacial action by an
overlying layer of
weathered ore, the
limestone was
similarly fretted.

13

Col. 13
Breidamerkurjokull,
Iceland.
The picture looks to
the melting edge of a
small ice cap. The ice
is thin and
mountains can be
seen standing up
through it as
nunataks. Central
Ireland looked like
this 15,000 years
ago.

14

Col. 14
Woolly mammoth and wild horses. More than 40,000 years ago we could have seen these animals near Dungarvan in Co. Waterford grazing on open tundra.

Col. 15
Abisko in Sweden.
This upland country,
with bushes growing
where a hollow gives
some protection from
the wind, seen in
Lapland today, gives
an impression of
Ireland 12,000 years
ago when the giant
deer and reindeer
were here.

Col. 16
Black Head,
Co. Clare.
Here the limestone
pavement of the
Burren sweeps down
to sea level. Plants
grow in the crevices
and we see mossy
saxifrage and sea-
pink. Both of these
plants were in
Ireland 12,000 years
ago.

17

Col. 17

An extreme version of the karstic landscape of the Burren, Co. Clare. Recent research suggests that some of its appearance may be due to farming by prehistoric people. Soil particles set free by agriculture may have been washed down the crevices by rain.

18

19

20
21

22

Col. 18
Abisko in Sweden.
In winter a deep patch of snow fills this hollow. As spring advances, a pond gradually replaces the snow. The green leaves of the least willow (Salix herbacea) cover the edge of the pond; this plant, which is now confined to some mountain tops, grew all over Ireland during the last cold snap 10,500 years ago.

Col. 19
Ballynafogh, Co. Kildare. This fen is artificial as the fen plants are invading a canal reservoir. However, it does give an impression of the Irish lowlands 9500 years ago when wide expanses of open water had not yet been obliterated by the development of fen-peat.

Col. 20
Ross Island, Killarney, Co. Kerry. These coniferous trees have been planted, but they do give an impression of the pine woods that spread widely in Ireland about 9000 years ago. There is only a narrow band of fen vegetation round the pond.

Col. 21
Derrycunnihy, Killarney, Co. Kerry. This oak-wood was probably planted, but there were also oak-woods around Killarney 8000 years ago.

Col. 22
Central African lakeside village. This is the sort of fishing village we saw on the banks of the River Bann 9000 years ago. (See also Illus. 79)

23

Col. 23

Muckish, Co Donegal . Blanket bog covers the ground except where slopes are steep as on the rocky ground across the centre of the picture and on the mountain's upper slopes..

Col. 24
*Bog of Allen,
Co. Kildare.
Ling (Calluna)
grows densely on
the surface of
the raised bog.
We can picture
the growing bog
as a glacier
slowly spreading
over the
surrounding
green
countryside.*

24

*Col. 25
Camderry,
Co. Galway.
On this raised bog we
see a hummock of bog
moss (Sphagnum
imbricatum) on the
right and a pool on
the left. Cross-leaved
heather (E. tetralix)
and bog asphodel
(Narthecium
ossifragum) grow on
the hummock. The
insect-eating sundew
(Drosera
intermedia) and
white beak sedge
(Rhynchospora
alba) grow round the
margin of the pool.
In the pool there are
another moss
(S. cuspidatum)
and bog-bean
(Menyanthes
trifoliata).*

*Col. 26
Near Knocknagapple, Co. Kerry.
Blanket-bog peat has been extensively cut here
and only a small pyramid of peat remains.*

*Col. 27
Abrupt change in
peat stratification at
Corstown West bog in
Co. Meath. Fresh
Sphagnum-peat
dated to 1100 ± 80
BP (light brown) is
resting
uncomformably on
humified
Sphagnum-peat
dated to 1920 ± 80
BP (dark grey).*

Col. 28
Lambay Island axe
production site,
Co. Dublin.
Excavation showing
worked face of
porphyritic andesite
and working floor
with debitage.

28

Col. 29
Behy, Co. Mayo.
Blanket bog overlying
the partly collapsed
wall of a cairn which
contained a
megalithic tomb.

29

30

Col. 30
Corlea, Co. Longford. This bog trackway was built with timbers felled late in 148 BC or early in 147 BC. It runs for about 1km between dry land at Corlea and an island in the bog at Derryadd.

and some of these produced clusters of leaf-shaped flakes which the excavator, Hallam Movius, suggested might have been hafted together to form some sort of multi-pronged fishing implement similar to one which today is all too frequently (and illegally) employed in many parts of Ireland.

Flint was very valuable for the manufacture of implements and this was easily obtained on the Antrim coast, where not only are there outcrops of chalk, but the glacial deposits and beach gravels are full of derived flint nodules. Larnian groups would have visited these shores and given a preliminary dressing to suitable flint blocks, leaving sheets of debris behind them. Sea level was still rising and the knapping-floors were overwhelmed by the waves and the scattered debris was embedded in inter-tidal spits which are now raised above modern sea level. Curran Point in Larne Harbour, which has been extensively built over, is such a spit and has long been famous for its content of man-worked flints. Excavating here in 1935, Hallam Movius opened up a pit 5m square and 5m deep and from it he obtained over 15,000 pieces of humanly-struck flint, but unfortunately relatively few finished implements.

Sustenance was easy on the seashore because both fish and shellfish were readily available; where the campsites were high enough to escape destruction by the sea, kitchen-middens of oyster, limpet, periwinkle and other shells have survived. It would have been impossible to cure shellfish, crabs and lobsters, but sea fish could have been salted and dried in a manner that continues today in Iceland and Newfoundland (*Illus. 87*). In these two countries, great areas of wooden fish racks are employed in the drying and smoking of cod and other fish and a substantial trade is carried on in the export of such preserved fish to Nigeria and other African countries where there is a shortage of protein. Porpoises and small whales would occasionally have been stranded or might under favourable circumstances have been driven ashore; after they had provided an immediate feast to the Larnians the rest of the flesh could be smoked, as mutton is smoked in Iceland today.

Illus. 87
Drying fish in
Newfoundland.

*Illus. 88
Aborigines spearing
fish and diving for
crayfish as depicted
in a painting of
aboriginal life in
New South Wales,
c.1820.*

*Illus. 89
Aran Islands,
Co. Galway.
The currach, which
still survives along
the western seaboard,
must have an
ancestry going back
through thousands of
years in Ireland.*

This was how the coastal Aborigines of Australia were living when white folk first arrived there. We are fortunate to have some paintings from which, if we ignore the difference in climate, we can form some impression of the Larnian way of life (*Illus. 88*). Most early peoples had light boats; today, in the currachs of the Atlantic coast of Ireland, we can imagine the descendants of Ireland's first boats (*Illus. 89*).

A knowledge at least of simple carpentry is needed to build boats and the Larnians must also have had implements of wood, bone and antler, but of these almost nothing has survived. At Toome Bay on Lough Neagh, some pieces of worked wood had got broken and were then used as firewood, but of the charred scraps it was only possible to say that they clearly had been worked for some special purpose. A kitchen-midden on the shore of Dundalk Bay produced two small bone points, which were probably used as fish gorges; a cord was attached to the point, not in the centre but towards one end. The point would have been baited and lowered into the water; an approaching fish would then be given full opportunity to draw the bait well into its mouth; a quick jerk would then be given to the cord in the hope that the gorge would turn at right angles and its ends would jam in the sides of the fish's mouth enabling the fish to be drawn from the water.

Most implements were made by a flaking process (*Illus. 83*). Suitable rounded pebbles of flint would be collected on the seashore or from glacial gravels; one end would be struck off and a flat surface produced. By striking blows at the perimeter of this surface, elongated flakes would be detached. Two forms of these were most sought after, parallel-sided blades or knives and leaf-shaped flakes, to be used as pointed knives or mounted in a shaft to serve as arrowheads or spearheads.

The Larnians were aware that a thin edge of flint could be strengthened by removing small flakes at right angles to the edge by the so-called retouching or reworking technique; in this way, flakes were turned into scrapers and borers. In the same way, one edge of a flake could be blunted, so producing a backed knife. Core-axes were occasionally made, by striking flakes off a chosen pebble until it was reduced to the desired shape. Flat pebbles, either elongated or rounded, were used for pounding or scraping with the result that the edges either flaked away or became faceted.

The Larnians appear to have made small clearings in the woodlands and the axes may have been of use here. If we make very detailed pollen-counts at critical levels in deposits associated with Mesolithic activities, we can see small irregular movements in some values which suggest that some artificial interference with the woodlands was taking place. A seasonal campsite may have been semi-permanently fenced and a stockade would have been necessary to keep wolves, foxes and an occasional wandering bear at bay. Such a campsite would be abandoned from time to time and the Larnians would soon note that deer came to browse on the young trees and bushes that started to recolonise the site. Deer haunt the margins rather than the depths of the forests and it would have been quickly realised that an artificial clearing would attract deer into positions where they could be easily trapped or shot.

Dependent as they were on hunting and collecting for their proteins and their carbohydrates, the Larnians must have led a semi-nomadic existence as the seasonal pattern of abundance of various foodstuffs led them on from one location to another. Such a pattern of life dominated the Maoris of the extreme south of New Zealand at the time when they first came in contact with white settlers. The Maoris had a wider range of implements than the Larnians, but like them they were essentially food collectors. For carbohydrates, they depended largely on bracken rhizomes and on the starchy roots and young stems of the cordyline (still known in New Zealand as the cabbage tree). They had a permanent village site, from which foraging parties travelled to places where they could live comfortably for several weeks, gathering and preserving seasonally abundant foods. For one such group the following yearly pattern in search of protein has been recorded: September and October, up to Tuturau for lampreys at the Mataura Falls; November, on to the Waimea Plains to get eels; December, back to Tuturau to dry food; January, to the coast to catch fish and collect seaweed; February, making seaweed bags; March, to the offshore islands; April, catching and smoking seabirds; May, return from the islands; June, bringing presents of smoked seabirds to friends and relatives; July and August, catching forest birds.

At a later Larnian stage, about 5400 years ago, the same type of activity was taking place throughout Ireland, both inland and on the coast. In Westmeath, on the shores of Lough Derravaragh, just where the Inny enters the lake, there were extensive fens which were visited by people living in Larnian fashion. Chert outcrops on the shores of the lake and this was used for the manufacture of implements.

There were open channels in the fen through which the river entered the lake and water-lilies grew in the open water beyond the edge of the fen. Excavation showed that in the fen-peat there were the ashes and charcoal of numerous isolated fires and associated with these were chert flakes, hazelnut shells and charred and uncharred seeds of the yellow water-lily (*Nuphar luteum*). We can picture parties of Larnian folk coming here in Maori style in early autumn, setting traps for fish in the fen-channels, collecting and perhaps parching water-lily seeds, gathering hazelnuts and giving a preliminary dressing to blocks of chert, carrying away the semi-worked pieces to be finished elsewhere.

The coast was similarly frequented. At Ferriter's Cove, near Ballyferriter in the Dingle Peninsula in Co. Kerry, a rock platform cut by earlier waves afforded a campsite and worksite between 6000 and 5200 years ago. Small hearths with charcoal, bone, shells and implements were scattered over the platform where they had been preserved under wind-blown sand (*Illus. 90*). A small number of cattle bones and a cache of polished stone axes suggested contact with an Early Neolithic group. Pig was the only common food bone; bird bones were virtually

Illus. 90
Implements from Ferriter's Cove, Dingle peninsula, Co. Kerry.
1,2 greenstone blades;
  3 greenstone Bann flake;
4,5 greenstone leaf-shaped flakes;
  6 spear-like implement (slate?);
  7 core borer (rhyolite).

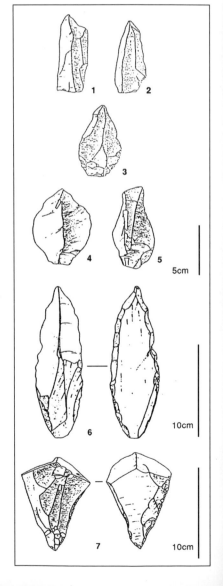

absent; both shore and open-sea fish were represented. A cluster of twenty ear-bones of the whiting suggests a simultaneous catch of a small shoal, perhaps taken on a long line or in a net. Small limpet shells predominated.

Ferriter's Cove lies only 3km north of Clogher Head where a suite of fine-grained acid volcanic rocks, including rhyolites and featureless greenstones, occurs. Blocks of these were common on the local beaches and were shaped into implements. The flint implements found are more puzzling; blocks of flint are excessively rare on the local beaches and the Ballyferriter flint must have come from some more distant source.

As usual on Larnian sites, rough flakes, struck off in the course of implement-shaping, far outnumber finished tools. But there are base-trimmed, leaf-shaped flakes that would be at home on the Bann and also a core-borer and a spear-like point (*Illus. 90*). On Valencia Island, also in Co. Kerry, a wooden platform embedded in a bog was dated to 6500 BP; no artefacts were found.

As already noted, we urgently need to find residential sites, where we might find the tools with which sophisticated objects in wood and bone were fabricated, and not just the waste stone fragments which were discarded by the thousand. And we need wet sites, where organic materials and objects fashioned from them will have survived, together with food debris and other potentially-informative rubbish.

One swallow does not make a summer and one worked flint does not make an archaeological site, but the flint from Newlands Cross is the only one, so far, to have come from a wet site of this age in Ireland and even a limited excavation there to see if there is an occupation site nearby would be of the greatest importance.

CLIMAX PHASE OF WOODLAND 7000 TO 5900 YEARS AGO

In organic deposits which were accumulating about 7000 years ago, the pollen counts show a dramatic change which must reflect a radical alteration in the woodlands. Alder rises from the meagre values it has hitherto shown and pine falls back to a much lower level. Related changes can be traced throughout north-west Europe and it may be that the climate had become more Atlantic and wetter, enabling alder to form fen-woods on the damper soils and forcing pine more exclusively onto the poorer soils. Temperatures remained high, with July temperatures perhaps 1° or 2°C warmer than at present.

Dense tall, deciduous woodland dominated by alder, oak and elm occupied the richer lowland soils, with birch and pine still probably holding their own on the uplands. The oak-woods were especially impressive and we can get some impression of them from later mature stands of planted oak. Near Rostrevor in Co. Down, we can look down on a continuous leaf canopy while Charlemont Forest, outside Tullamore in Co. Offaly, shows magnificent mature trunks.

The Climax phase of woodland stability – a hazel-oak-elm-alder phase – became established and then persisted for about 2000 years until it was dramatically altered by a wave of elm disease, just like the wave that recently swept western Europe and apparently due to the same cause, that is attack by a bark-beetle giving entry to a fungus.

Our evidence for a severe attack by disease is given by an important reduction

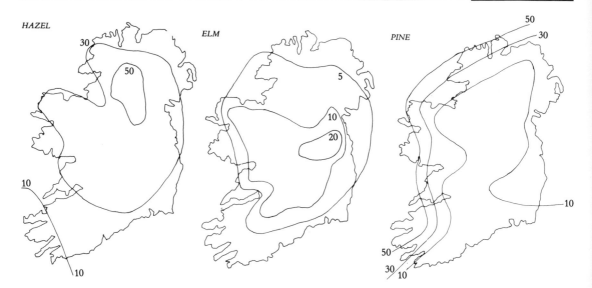

in the amount of elm pollen reaching lakes and bogs; after the fall, pollen values rise again, sometimes to their former value. The cause of this oscillation was a matter of acute controversy. Neolithic farmers started to reach Ireland shortly before 6000 years ago. Armed with polished stone axes with good cutting edges mounted in wooden handles, they undoubtedly opened up clearings in the woodlands where cereals, grasses and herbs then replaced the trees. Local pollen production was thus disturbed and we can see this disturbance in our pollen counts.

Elm trees grow on good soils and it was natural that the first farmers should be attracted to these soils and therefore clear away the trees. For many, this was the reason for the fall in pollen values. Others claimed that the first farmers must have been limited in numbers and could not possibly have removed enough elm trees to cause the fall in pollen values. Young leaves make succulent fodder for cattle and many primitive farming people cut leafy twigs off the trees and fed them to their stock. It was claimed that if such pruning of elm trees was severe, then the trees would fail to produce pollen. But again the question of farmer numbers arises.

Climate was considered as a possible explanation. If the temperature was falling, then the elms would not do so well and their pollen production would fall. But after the fall, we see the values for elm pollen rise again and so it seems that climatic deterioration cannot be the cause.

However, while the debate was raging, the number of radiocarbon datings for the elm-fall was steadily increasing. The fall is now not only the most dated pollen horizon in postglacial Britain and Ireland, but also, within the limits of the radiocarbon method, the most synchronous; 5900 years ago (3900 BC) can be accepted as a mean value.

We cannot overlook the fact that natural soil development must have been a factor in the establishment of the climax woodlands. However, when we try to trace out the history of soil development in Ireland, we come up against the problem that man himself has been interfering with the soils for at least half the time that has been available for soil development; it was about 6000 years ago that the natural

Illus. 91
Relative pollen abundances of elm, pine and hazel in Ireland 5900 years ago.

Hazel: *Common in centre, most common in north centre.*

Elm: *Common in centre, most common in east centre.*

Pine: *Rare in centre, most common along western seaboard.*

progression was broken by man starting to clear trees away in order to create clearings for farming operations.

The opening 5000 years of the Littletonian Warm Stage must have seen a hand-in-hand development of the forests and of the soils on which they grew. The early shallow-rooted birches were progressively displaced by bigger and bigger forest trees with deeper and deeper rooting-systems and deep soils would have formed. It was a very intimate relationship because if, on the one hand, the more deeply penetrating roots and their accompanying microflora and fauna promoted soil development, on the other hand the inherent texture and base status of the soil in turn affected the competitive powers of the different tree genera and thus influenced the composition of the woodlands. Due to the variety of Ireland's basic rock structure, and to the different flow paths followed by different ice masses, the parent material of the soils that developed on glacial deposits varied widely and so the forest pattern could not be monotonously uniform – as our pollen-diagrams often suggest – but rather presented a mosaic of different ecological systems, each in response to the local factors

Illus. 92
Map of Ireland
showing Littletonian
Regions (IRLa,
IRLb, IRLc).

With the increased amount of information on Irish forest history now available, Fraser Mitchell and a number of other Irish workers have recently come together and divided Ireland into three basic regions founded mainly on geological and edaphic features, but also on past forest history and contemporary phytogeographical considerations (*Illus. 92*).

(1) The Atlantic Fringe (IRLa): Climate strongly oceanic (200 rain days); much hill ground of mainly acid rocks; glacial drift on lower ground; peaty podzols and gleys; much blanket bog; land use difficult.

(2) North-east Ireland (IRLb): Climate oceanic (160 rain days); many varied rock types; much drift on lower ground with extensive spreads of sand and gravel; blanket bog peats and peaty podzols on hills, gleys and acid brown earths on lowlands; important dairy farming.

(3) Central and south-east Ireland (IRLc): Climate oceanic (160 rain days); much limestone on lowlands through which ridges of acid rocks

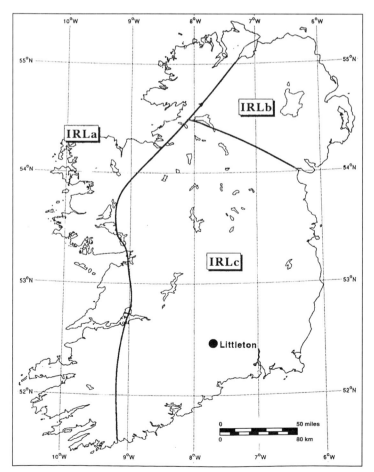

rise; thick mantle of limestone-derived tills sands and gravels on lowlands; acid brown earths in south and east, gleys and podzols in west; cereals in south-east, dairying in south-west, livestock in centre.

Most of the factors on which this three-fold division of the Irish landscape is based will have made their influences felt throughout postglacial time and brought about regional differences in the distribution of plants and animals. Therefore, while all areas had substantial forest cover, elm flourished on the calcareous soils of central Ireland, while pine was common in the more acid west.

When we look at the Irish countryside today, still almost treeless despite much hasty and ill-considered planting of conifers in recent years, it is hard for us to picture the majesty and silence of those primeval woods, which stretched from Ireland far across northern Europe. We are accustomed to an absence of trees, and if we do find some scraps of 'native' woodland, we are disappointed by the quality of the trees. For thousands of years, man has been roving the Irish woodlands seeking 'good' timber for houses, ships and other uses. As a result, all the well-grown good quality trees have long since disappeared and what are left are the progeny of 'bad' trees, rejected by earlier carpenters. If we visit the National Museum, we can see a dug-out canoe, 18m in length and 1.5m in width. Today in Ireland, we would find it hard to find an oak tree from which such a large canoe could be hewn. Similar fossil oaks are revealed from time to time in the English fenlands; they have straight trunks up to 27m without side branches, indicating a forest height far greater than in today's British woodlands. In relict natural woodland in Poland, oaks with long unbranched trunks and small crowns still stand to a height of 26m. In the National Museum, we can also see a wooden shield-mould, 45cm in diameter, worked from a slice taken from the trunk of a well-grown forest alder. It would be impossible in Ireland today to find a single alder tree capable of supplying a blank for such a shield. Only in some remote parts of Europe can we recapture something of the vanished dignity of the Irish forests.

FIRST DEVELOPMENT OF PEAT C.9000 YEARS AGO

Throughout the period of the Beginning phase (lLWB), from 10,000 to 7000 years ago, the great stretches of open water that were established after the cold conditions had ended were being progressively reduced in area by the growth of marginal fens and marshes. This was the first link in a chain of development that led to the building-up of raised bogs (*Illus. 93*).

Free-floating algae were probably the first plants to invade the water. Humus derived from their decay provided food for small planktonic animals and these arrived in great variety. Their faeces added to the detritus-mud accumulating on the lake floor. If the water contained some amount of calcium – and most early waters did – then the submerged stoneworts (*Chara/Nitella*) were abundant. Their leaves were encrusted with particles of lime and their debris accumulated on the lake floor as a yellow-brown mud or marl. Aquatic molluscs fed off the stonewort and other debris and the mud became rich in their small coiled shells. Thick deposits of shell-mud accumulated.

The build-up of shell-marl made the lake margins sufficiently shallow for

Illus. 93

Four stages in the development of a typical Irish raised bog:

a An open-water lake lies in morainic country which is covered by forest; an island of moraine rises in the lake, on whose floor open-water mud is accumulating.

b Fen plants, originally growing round the lake edge, whose decaying debris builds up fen-peat, extend in two directions; out into the lake as accumulating mud makes its margins shallow, and inland into the forest burying the tree-stumps with its peat.

c The same process continues and as the fen-peat thickens, its surface becomes less rich in nutrients and is invaded by the acid bog community dominated by Sphagnum moss. Nourished only by rainwater, the bog community slowly builds up a dome-like mass of highly humified Sphagnum-peat. As the bog grows, the local water table rises and the fen-peat creeps still higher up the surrounding slopes, killing more trees as it advances. The flanks of the dome of peat are relatively dry and some trees can grow there.

d Some change in conditions allows the Sphagnum-peat to form more quickly and the dome, now composed of fresh Sphagnum-peat, grows up still higher. The trees on the flanks of the older raised bog die and are buried by peat. The island, which had been getting smaller and smaller as bog growth continued, is finally overwhelmed by peat and its trees disappear.

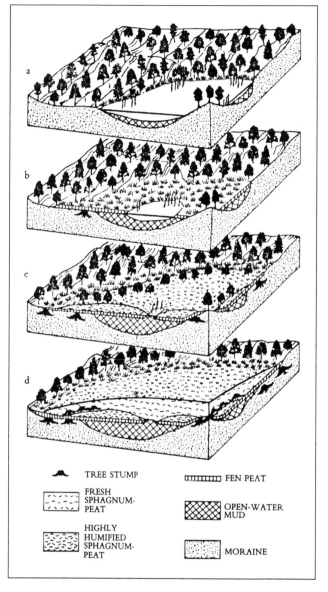

TREE STUMP

FRESH SPHAGNUM-PEAT

HIGHLY HUMIFIED SPHAGNUM-PEAT

FEN PEAT

OPEN-WATER MUD

MORAINE

higher plants with floating or sub-aerial leaves, such as the bur-reed (*Sparganium*) and the water-lily (*Nuphar*), to colonise the margins. Soon the margins were invaded by the reed-swamp plants, the bulrush (*Scirpus lacustris*), the reed (*Phragmites communis*) and many others. The accumulating vegetable debris gradually consolidated into fen-peat, which built up to water level and replaced the open water with a fen (*Illus. 94*). Sometimes, there were extensive stretches of reeds (*Col. 19*); at other times the margin was quickly invaded by water-tolerant trees, such as the willow and the alder; larger trees followed as the surface of the fen-peat grew firmer.

In the fen, species of *Carex* (sedges) and of grass were dominant and there were flowering plants, such as marsh cinquefoil (*Potentilla palustris*), marsh marigold (*Caltha palustris*), cuckoo-flower (*Cardamine pratensis*) and meadowsweet

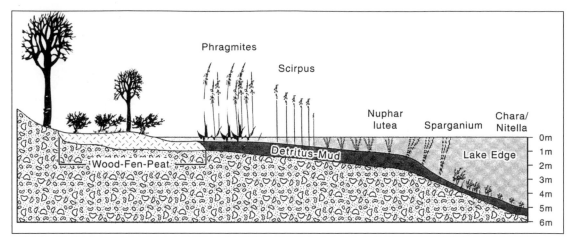

Phragmites

Scirpus

Nuphar lutea   Sparganium   Chara/ Nitella

Detritus-Mud

Wood-Fen-Peat

Lake Edge

0m
1m
2m
3m
4m
5m
6m

(*Filipendula ulmaria*). At Ballyscullion Bog in Co. Antrim, first investigated by Jessen and later re-investigated with the aid of radiocarbon dating by Alan Smith, such fen-peat was forming at least 9000 years ago (*Illus. 95b*).

If the level of the water table remained constant, willows and birches invaded the margin of the fen and as peat rich in sedge and wood debris began to build up, the wooded area extended. Other trees such as pine would have invaded the drier surfaces and gradually a thick layer of wood-peat was formed. Such a development took place at Ballyscullion Bog, as is shown in the cross-section drawn up by Jessen (*Illus. 95b*).

If the level of the water table rose, the drainage of the surrounding slopes worsened and the fens and fen-woods would have crept up the surrounding slopes beyond the limits of the primary basal fen. Bob Hammond of Bord na Móna examined such a situation in the Bog of Allen, one of the great areas of bog that now occupy much of the central lowlands of Ireland; a sketch-section summarises his results (*Illus. 95a*). There had been an early lake over a wide area and the open-water lake-mud is seen at the base of the section. On the right-hand side of the section, wet fen-wood is seen growing directly on the local glacial deposits 8500 years ago. When the lake margin was invaded by fen vegetation, the fen spread in both directions building fen-peat out over the lake-muds on the one hand and up the slope on top of the wood-fen-peat on the other hand. On the left-hand side of the section, where the slope is steeper, the wood-fen-peat took a longer time to extend upwards and its base is correspondingly younger, having only started to form about 5000 years ago.

This development was also recorded in the lake, fen and raised bog complex at Corstown near Drumcondra in Co. Meath, where the record ran from the late-glacial to the present day (*Illus. 96*). At each end of the section we see a ridge of glacial moraine. When the cold conditions disappeared about 10,000 years ago, a lake formed between the ridges and fine glacial clays were deposited on its floor. The water became warm enough for life to invade and debris from tiny animals and plants created a layer of detritus-mud. Molluscs flourished in the water and a layer of calcareous mud (marl) rich in shell debris was formed. The margins were now

Illus. 94
Transect from lake margin to bog (not to scale).

Illus. 95
Sections through three Irish bogs.
a Schematic cross-sections of large raised bog complex in the Irish midlands to illustrate its progressive expansion as time elapsed. (Based on work by R. Hammond)
b Cross-section of the raised bog at Ballyscullion, Co. Antrim, (Knud Jessen, with added radiocarbon datings by Alan Smith)
c Cross-section through blanket bog at Emlaghlea, Co. Kerry (Knud Jessen). All dates are years before present (BP). (not to scale).

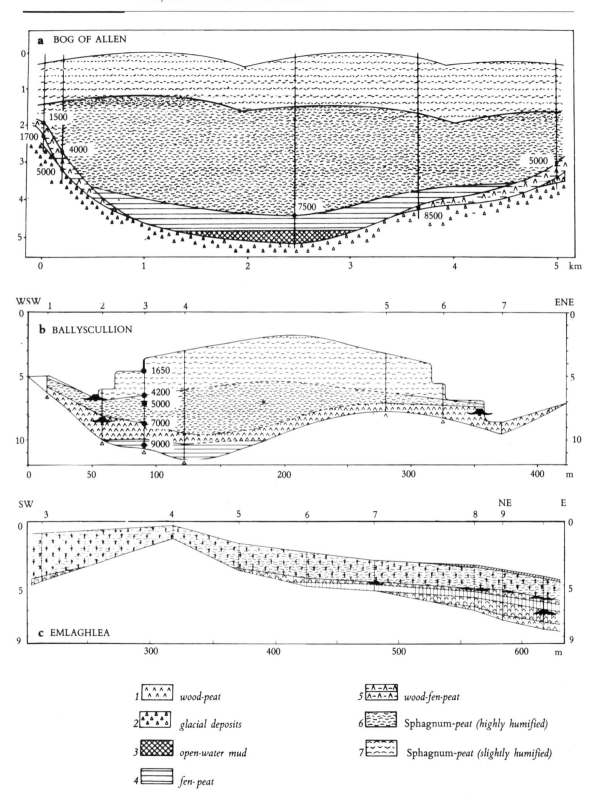

1 ⌃⌃⌃⌃ *wood-peat*

2 ▲▲▲ *glacial deposits*

3 ▨ *open-water mud*

4 ▤ *fen-peat*

5 ⋀–⋀–⋀ *wood-fen-peat*

6 ≋ *Sphagnum-peat (highly humified)*

7 ≈ *Sphagnum-peat (slightly humified)*

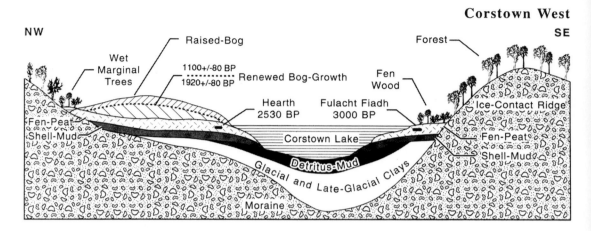

Illus. 96
Section of bog deposits in Corstown Lough Great, Co. Meath (not to scale).

shallow enough for fen plants to grow and debris from these plants built up fen-peat. This formation took place in the Bronze age and cooking fires were occasionally built in the fen-wood. On the north side of the lake the fen-peat became thick enough for its surface to become depleted in nutrients and plants of the raised bog community came in. Gradually, their debris began to rise into a dome. Growth was probably interrupted on many occasions; one such interruption occurred perhaps about 500 AD.

Lakes continued to shrink as fens and fen-woods extended. As the fen-peat thickened, as at Corstown, the surface plants found it more and more difficult to maintain a supply of inorganic material from the underlying mineral soil and the way was open for plants that could thrive on minimal amounts of inorganic nutrients to colonise the surface of the peat.

GROWTH OF RAISED BOGS

The moss *Sphagnum* was ideally suited for this purpose; it can grow vigorously when nourished only by rain and by the very small amount of nutrient material contained in the rain. *Sphagnum* has a remarkable capacity for capturing and storing rainwater. Many of its leaf-cells are like small hollow 'traps' with an aperture through which water can enter; it is then held in the trap until needed for further growth. We can picture that the fen surface was irregular and that rainfall was increasing. Pools would have formed in the fen hollows and vigorously growing *Sphagnum* species, such as S. *fuscum*, drew on the water and built themselves up into a small mound or hummock. There is a limit to the height of the hummock, whose top becomes very sensitive to periods of dryness. As soon as the top became reasonably dry, it was invaded by lichens and by ling (*Calluna vulgaris*). As the rain continued, the hummocks themselves now provided the high points between which water was trapped and shallow pools formed between them. Aquatic *Sphagnum* species that grow submerged, such as S. *cuspidatum*, invaded the pools and built up a muddy layer which shallowed the pools. Deer-grass (*Trichophorum caspitosum*), cotton-grass (*Eriophorum angustifolium*), white beak-sedge (*Rhynchospora alba*) and sundews (*Drosera* spp.) – which supplement their nutrient supply by catching insects – would have come in round the margin of the pond until the hummock-building *Sphagnum* species took over and a new hummock rose over the former pool; meanwhile, the tops of the old hummocks awaited flooding to form the next generation of pools. As the hummocks and pools scattered over the bog-surface replaced one another cyclically, capillarity carried the water table up with them and the *Sphagnum*-peat rose into a dome or raised bog nourished only by rainwater, forming the so-called ombrogenous bog (*Col. 24, 25*).

Such is the hummock/pool theory of raised bog growth although the picture is probably an over-simplification. Other studies suggest that the *Calluna*-occupied hummocks may have persisted and maintained a vertical growth creating a considerable thickness of peat, while the pools between them fluctuated in size. In some bogs, the pools have a linear arrangement, lying at right angles to the slope of the bog surface; if the bog had expanded due to the uptake of additional water, the pools might lie in tears in its surface. Given a constant climate, would the bog dome attain a certain degree of convexity and then come into a still-stand phase?

A bog can only grow when the rate of accumulation of vegetable debris exceeds the rate of decay. There is some initial decay in the top 20cm, because the debris there is relatively dry and open in texture. Below that level, conditions quickly become waterlogged, anaerobic and acid, with the result that only a few decomposing processes can operate. If debris accumulates quickly, much vegetable tissue survives in a remarkably undamaged condition as fresh or slightly humified peat. If growth is slow, plant tissues disintegrate or *humify* producing brown degradation products which culminate in jelly-like or liquid humic acids. Such peat is described as being highly humified. Efforts are made to correlate the degree of decay or humification with climate; strong *humification* being equated with relatively warm, dry conditions and weak humification with relatively cool, wet conditions.

If the climate moves towards warmth and dryness, the pools dry up, growth slows down, trees invade the bog margins, humification proceeds and a rind of well-decayed peat covers the bog. If cold and wet conditions return, the bog surface is flooded, the trees are killed and their stumps buried, as fresh unhumified peat starts to build up (*Illus. 76*). The horizon at which growth is renewed is described as a *recurrence-surface*.

If a high peat-face has been cut in a bog, a recurrence-surface may be seen running across it. Below this surface, the peat is highly humified and dark in colour, while above the surface the peat is fresh and light in colour. Changes of climate do affect the rate of bog growth and formerly it was thought that these recurrence-surfaces would be synchronous on a regional scale and that correlations of age might be made. Today, realising that the peat domes in an individual bog can migrate as the bog expands over uneven ground and so change the surface wetness from place to place without any change in climate, it is recognised that these recurrence-surfaces have little regional significance and only record changes in the movement of surface water on the bog.

One very dramatic recurrence-surface was seen in the Corstown West section of the Ardee Bog in Co. Louth. A bog cutting had advanced southwards in a series of vertical faces connected by bog-sections at right angles to one another. The most dramatic face was 6m long and 1.5m high (*Col. 27*). The surface of the lower highly humified *Sphagnum*-peat had been dissected by deep gullies, leaving upstanding ridges of peat between; the ridges could be traced into the adjoining peat-faces. The effect was so marked that at one stage it was thought that these might be old man-made peat diggings; but the point could not be proved, though similar but not so dramatic features could be seen in other old cuts in the vicinity. At all events, at a time when the bog-surface was relatively dry, its surface was dissected into ridges and hollows, most probably by natural surface erosion. Wetter conditions then returned and surface water lodged in ponds in the hollows. Here the leaves and stems of aquatic *Sphagnum* species lay in matted sheets. When the pond filled up, other less water-bound species came in, together with cotton-grass and ling, and the formation of fresh peat began and proceeded to build up a dome of raised bog (now almost completely cut away).

In an attempt to date the phenomenon, two samples were taken for ^{14}C dating, one below and the other above the recurrence-surface. The lower sample of highly humified peat came from the top of an upstanding ridge; it had an age of 1920 ± 80 BP (say 80 AD). The upper sample of aquatic peat came not from the basal layers in the former pool, but a little higher up, to lessen the possibility that crumbs of older eroded peat might have been washed into these layers; it had an age of 1100 ± 80 BP (say 900 AD). Therefore, this peat, which was formed at the beginning of the Christian Era, was flooded by water some 800 years later. People were living in ring-forts in the area by 400 AD and they could have created this wide gap when cutting peat for fuel.

Raised bogs, which were building up highly humified *Sphagnum*-peat, had certainly started to form both in the midlands and in the north of Ireland not less than 7000 years ago. At about the same time, alder started to expand in the Irish woodlands and both phenomena may be due to increased wetness, which enabled water tables to rise and allowed the fens to expand and the alder to establish fen-woods. Because the *Sphagnum* community can flourish when nurtured only by rain, it is tempting to think that increased wetness meant increased rain and that this was the factor that triggered off the growth of the ombrogenous raised bog. However, the inhibiting factor that prevents the development of the *Sphagnum* community may not be rainfall below a certain level, but rather the inability of the *Sphagnum* community to oust other communities, as long as the latter are continuing to receive at least the minimum amount of inorganic nutrients necessary for their growth. In other words, it was the thickening of the fen-peat, to the point where the roots of the fen-plants could no longer draw sufficient inorganic nutrient to make healthy growth possible, that gave the *Sphagnum* community its opportunity.

Two lines of evidence point in this direction. Raised bog peat seems to find it impossible to start forming directly on inorganic soil; there must always be an insulating layer of fen-peat, which has in many cases a peaty podzol soil at its base. Therefore, a peripheral band of fen-vegetation always lies between the plants of the mineral soil and the plants of the raised bog community and unless the band advances secreting the insulating layer beneath itself, then the raised bog cannot expand laterally, although it can grow upwards into a dome. The fens that lay in the poorly-drained ground between drumlins often provided nuclei for raised bog

Illus. 97
Derryadd raised bog
near Lanesborough,
Co. Longford, now
being developed
mechanically. Here
the intact bog surface
formerly showed
many open pools.
The ribbon of fen that
once separated the
dome of the bog from
the mineral soil of the
drumlin island has
been damaged by
local peat cutting,
but the broad band of
pale vegetation
between the fields and
the bog indicates its
former position. The
island is now treeless,
but the prefix Derry
in the name of the bog
shows that the region
was once covered by
oak-woods. Corlea
can be seen in the top
right-hand corner.
A wooden trackway
runs from Corlea to
the drumlin island.

growth and from such nuclei the surface of the bog would rise like a rising tide to surround and eventually engulf the drumlins. But at all times a ribbon of fen, whose plants drew their nourishment from the drainage water in the mineral soil of the drumlin, lay between the slopes of the drumlin and the rising dome of the bog (*Illus. 97*).

Today, we have the impression that raised bogs are very rare or absent near the east and south-east coasts of Ireland and that this reflects the dryness of these regions (*Illus. 98*). However, even in these areas we can find the townland name 'Redbog', usually associated with low-lying ground, where there were once raised bogs which were cut away for fuel in the days when the population was much higher than it is today. There are also sites that on superficial inspection suggest that they form admirable bases for raised bog growth. Examples include a site near Dunshaughlin in Co. Meath, where east of the village a large basin – 3km long, at about 85m OD and 25km from the east coast – is filled to the level of natural overflow by deep late and postglacial lacustrine deposits, but there is no evidence of a former raised bog. However, we have seen that west of Ardee in Co. Meath, a large basin – 6km long, at 40m OD and 15km from the east coast – is filled with lacustrine deposits and did develop large raised bogs on top of lake-muds. It is hard to understand why raised bogs should develop at some points and not at others.

The connection with rainfall is equally mysterious. Few parts of Ireland have an annual rainfall of less than 750mm; an area of the midlands between Athlone and Birr has no more rain than this, but it is an area that is buried beneath some of the largest and deepest raised bogs in Ireland.

The raised bog system, once its growth had been initiated, may have been more or less self-perpetuating. It could trap water directly from the air and build its own water table up above that of the surrounding countryside. As it expanded, it could build up a natural dam across valleys which had previously been free to discharge surface water. The raised bog can be likened to an enormous bag of water and while we have little knowledge of the degree to which there is a slow circulation of water within the bag – whether water leaks out of the bag into the surrounding countryside, or whether ground water from below is fed up into the base of the bog – it is obvious that such a mass of saturated material may well have important effects on the water regime in the surrounding area. The drainage of the neighbouring

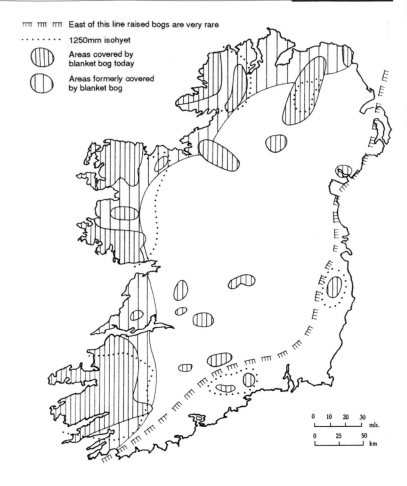

ⅢⅢ ⅢⅢ ⅢⅢ East of this line raised bogs are very rare

········ 1250mm isohyet

Areas covered by blanket bog today

Areas formerly covered by blanket bog

woodland areas could have been further impeded and the ground made still wetter.

Sometimes a depression appears in the bog surface and a *soak-away* allows water to sink down into the bog. Sometimes a spring appears on the bog surface; plants growing here now receive not static but actively flowing water and more nutrient is thus available. Rushes (*Juncus*) grow prolifically in what is termed a *flush*. Such springs are small scale; larger streams can also arise.

The large raised bog that formerly existed at Clonsast, north of Portarlington in Co. Offaly – 7km long, at 80m OD, 4km broad and with a dome 7m high – rested on a morainic landscape with ridges and isolated kames and little standing water. Before peat formation started, the area was wooded, as tree-stumps lay on the moraine. The surface then grew wetter, perhaps due to other bogs developing in the area and blocking the surface drainage. There does not seem to have been open water at any time. Fen plants invaded the woodland and after more than one metre of fen-peat had built up, the *Sphagnum* community invaded the fen and raised bog development started.

At the north end of the bog (*Illus. 99*), a natural channel in the moraine drained eastwards. As the bog developed, it respected the course of the river, gently lifting it up as it grew. Today the river is known as the North River.

Illus. 98
Distribution of bog in Ireland.

*Illus. 99
Contour map of
Clonsast Bog,
Co. Offaly.*

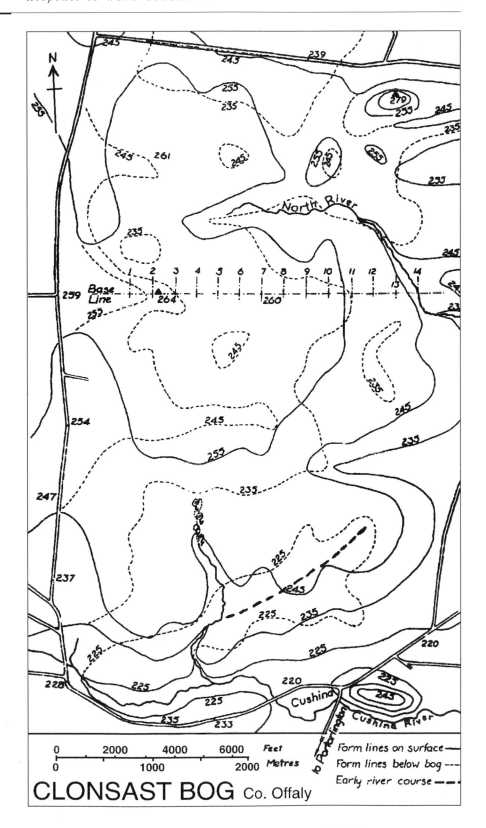

CLONSAST BOG Co. Offaly

At the south end of the bog, where there was also a channel, development was completely different. This channel ran north-east/south-west until, as a tributary, it met a larger channel running west/east. This channel defined the south end of the bog, and today it flows west/east as the Cushina River. But growth of the bog forced the tributary to back northwards, pushing it out of its original channel and up onto the bog surface, where it maintained a channel of its own. As it moved north, the stream-channel deepened and narrowed and became overshadowed by willow bushes, below which it emerged as a large spring.

The great mass of water in a bog may put the water that is in the materials below the bog under hydrostatic pressure. As a result, these materials may tend to rise into the base of the bog. Below parts of Clonsast Bog there had been karstic limestone covered with yew trees. Water rising through vents in the karst might first have flowed away as a surface stream. Continued growth of peat might have formed a roof over the stream which thus became an internal river.

If the ground water carried iron in solution, as may well have been the case, then the iron may have been precipitated in the peat as the hydroxide, or bog-iron-ore. Though no longer of commercial importance today, in the early part of this century bog-iron-ore was much in demand to purify the raw gas produced in municipal gasworks, and as such was extensively worked. The water that emerges in surface flushes is often stained by traces of iron.

If we picture the raised bog as a water-filled bag, we can immediately see that damage to any part of the bag can cause irreparable damage to the whole bog structure. Conservationists find it extremely difficult to convey this concept to those who would 'develop' a bog, whether on a small or a large scale. One cannot develop one half of a bog and conserve the other. Small hand-cutting at the edge of a bog allows large quantities of water to escape; the bog margin drops in level and becomes drier; the local pools disappear and the bog surface becomes heather-clad and incapable of growth. The large-scale developer wants to cut deep drains to get the water out of the bog. One such drain will inevitably separate what is to be developed from what is to be conserved and the developer cannot see that the drain will start a haemorrhage which will seriously damage the part to be conserved. Continued drainage will drop the whole bog surface by several metres.

Whatever may be the complicated factors that initiated bog growth, domes of highly humified *Sphagnum*-peat had started to develop at least 7000 years ago. Climate was still relatively warm and dry and bog growth was slow. This type of accumulation continued till at least 5000 years ago.

In the next chapter, we shall see how the first farmers affected the woodlands when they arrived in Ireland a little before 6000 years ago (about 4200 BC). But the acme of the Irish forests had probably passed with the climatic optimum. On the lowlands, the expanding bogs were starting to engulf the forest like an inexorable tide. On the uplands, increased exposure was probably enforcing a retreat of forest growth to lower levels.

5. THE FIRST FARMERS
c.4200 BC - 300 AD

A TIME OF CHANGE

Around 4200 BC, a great change took place in Ireland. From many different parts of the country the evidence of fossil pollens preserved in bogs and lake muds reveals an attack on the climax woodlands. The pollen rain, which falls from plants in spring and summer and gives those of us allergic to it the misery of hay fever, is a blessing in disguise for the student of environmental history.

As pollen sequences are fairly well-understood and are also distinctive, the method of pollen counting was used for many years as a way of dating archaeological sites and objects found in bogs, by relating them to phases in environmental history defined by the pollens with which they occurred. The true value of pollen studies is to tell us what was happening to the flora in a particular locality at a given time, while simultaneously recording fainter echoes of changes taking place at a distance. We can in a way think of the pollen record like a tape-recorder at a noisy party. It sits in the background registering the changes in the general volume of conversation, the occasional loud words, where conditions are favourable and picking up conversations close at hand with great fidelity. The pollen 'recorder' has been running for thousands of years and it is still running.

A second 'recorder' is also running. The annual growth rings of trees are in effect a record of change in climate. As we have seen, if growing conditions are poor, the tree rings will be narrower than those formed in good years. Professor Mike Baillie has developed a chronology of growth rings of oaks covering the last 5000 years. He has identified a number of short periods when the rings formed by the trees were exceptionally narrow showing that they were under great stress. Similar episodes have been noted in tree rings throughout the northern hemisphere and so the cause is likely to have been massive interference with normal weather patterns.

The most likely cause seems to have been volcanic eruptions on a scale perhaps even greater than the modern ones at Krakatoa, Mount St. Helens and Mount Pinatubo. Deposits of tiny spicules of volcanic glass – *tephra* – we have seen are found in bogs in Ireland in levels which coincide with the changes in the weather pattern. Because the sequence of tree rings gives accurate calendrical dates, events related to prehistoric Ireland have been noted at 4370 BC, 3195 BC, 2345 BC, 1628 BC, 1150 BC and 208 BC. These events usually lasted for a number of years showing that the weather remained appreciably wetter and colder before recovering to previous levels. This would have caused poor growing conditions and severely disimproved the ripening of corn and impaired its storage potential. The capacity of uplands to carry crops would have been reduced. Bog growth where it had begun would have been encouraged by the poorer drainage. It has been speculated that these short-term climatic events may have triggered significant social change by increasing the competition for diminished resources. But we do not know how well communities coped with protracted periods of poorer weather. The deterioration in climate may have been a matter of a drop of a degree or two in mean temperature and increased rainfall and while unwelcome, these conditions would still have been within normal ranges for Ireland. There may indeed have been local pressures but there were also certain competitive advantages for the stronger and fitter. Where there was a disimprovement in diet, the vulnerable – the old, the sick and the young – would have shortened life-expectancies while the stronger would have benefited. The paradoxical outcome of this is that the archaeological record might give the appearance of enrichment as resources were concentrated in fewer hands. There is a tendency as we approach the millennium (noted at the last one also) to propose catastrophe as the motor of change at the expense of obvious continuities and complexities. One of the events noted by Baillie occurs at about 4370 BC which coincides with the *advance* of agricultural societies into westernmost Europe. Long-term climatic change did, however, take place and this is very much a factor in the development of the landscape and human behaviour was undoubtedly modified as a result of it.

THE NEOLITHIC WAY OF LIFE

Mankind has only recently become a food *producer* – for most of our existence we have been collectors, scavengers, hunters and fishers. The development of systems of selecting and breeding plants to grow intensively at the expense of others was neither an obvious nor a straightforward matter; nor was the gradual domestication of animals, but this is precisely what did happen independently at a number of periods and places in the Old and the New World. For our purposes, the crucial developments took place in the Near East 10,000 to 12,000 years ago, where the wild ancestors of many of the cereals (wheat, barley) and animals (cattle, sheep, pig) which formed the basis of early farming in Europe were available. The gradual development of food production had a revolutionary effect and it was once fashionable to refer to the Neolithic (New Stone Age) Revolution by analogy with the Industrial Revolution because of the fundamental redirection of human history which it brought about. Without that change, none of the advanced technologies of urban civilisation on which we rely so much, would have been possible. The production of surpluses, the need to sow and tend crops, to harvest and process them and to manage animals promoted a sedentary lifestyle. In time, this led to settled villages and towns in the Near East. The surplus provided security, improved diet and health and probably encouraged population growth. Specialised new crafts developed and in time, elaborate new forms of social organisation emerged.

The success of the Neolithic economy can be seen in its rapid spread. It reached south-east Europe and expanded quickly, reaching the Low Countries by the sixth millennium BC and Britain and Ireland shortly afterwards. Early agriculture was wasteful by modern standards; the clearance of forest produced fertile soils for simple garden-style cultivation. Abandoned clearances in time developed a grass cover and created the pastures which are often thought of as the mainstay of much Neolithic farming. When the fertility of the cultivated areas had been exhausted by continuous cropping, new land was taken into cultivation. If not heavily grazed, the forest would recover in the older clearings; the trees, drawing nutrients from deeper levels, would deposit a rich compost of their leaves on the woodland floor and refresh the fertility of the soil. A renewed phase of clearance could be initiated and this seems to have happened in many regions although the local explanations for it may differ in detail from the broad picture presented here. Gradually, permanent grasslands were developed where once there had been forest.

How and when the Mesolithic peoples came to participate in the new way of life is unclear – it probably happened in different ways at different times in different places and involved peaceful accommodation as well as competition and violence. There is a happy myth that early farming communities were universally peaceable egalitarian societies and while land for settlement seemed limitless, there may indeed have been little stress and relatively little inter-communal aggression. However, as the landscape filled up and as clearances became impoverished and wasteland became precious as a fresh agricultural resource, strains may have begun to show themselves within farming communities as well as with external groups such as relict Mesolithic populations. The maturing of the Neolithic lifestyle in Western and adjacent parts of Central Europe saw the emergence of a series of regional cultures which had certain basic similarities – the building of rectangular houses, the disposal of some of their dead in long mounds or cairns, the use of a range of round-based pottery and the quasi-industrial organisation of the exploitation of certain raw materials such as the flint or stone for axeheads.

THE FOREST CLEARANCES

The Danish scholar Johannes Iversen was the first to recognise that an increase in grass pollen and the appearance of herbs associated with disturbance – ribwort plantain (*Plantago lanceolata*), dock (*Rumex*) and nettle (*Urtica*) – indicated forest clearance followed by farming. He gave the name *Landnam* to this process using the Old Norse word for settlement. Landnam phases are often succeeded by a period of forest regeneration. These changes coincided roughly with the massive drop in the pollen of elm throughout Europe and this was taken to be significant, as the elms grew on good soils especially congenial to early farming and would have suffered particularly in the clearances, it was also thought that elm leaves may have been used as cattle-fodder as they are very nutritious. It has now become clear that the elm destruction was probably the result of a variety of factors. A pandemic elm disease like the one which appeared in the 1980s is now thought to have occurred around the time that farming was beginning to reach western Europe. It is unlikely that the first farmers could have effected a synchronous destruction of a single type of tree across the whole continent. We now know for example that the beetle *Scolytus scolytus* was present in pre-elm decline deposits in Britain. This is one of two insect carriers of the fungal pathogen, *Ceratocystis ulmi*, which caused such destruction to the elm in modern times. It is also now becoming clear that agricultural activity had begun to appear before the destruction of elms happened. If the trees died off rapidly as a result of disease, the early farmers would have capitalised on the free clearances.

As the first farmers began to clear forest for the cultivation of crops, a number of parallel trends can be seen in the pollen of the period. The amount of tree pollen decreased due to forest clearances. The cleared areas allowed grasses to flourish and this grassland was encouraged for the grazing of animals; the amount of grass pollen increased significantly together with that of plants which naturally flourish in disturbed and open conditions. There are now so many sites at which the effects of the earliest Neolithic farming clearances can be detected, that it is better to try to sketch a broad picture of what appears to have happened to the woodlands throughout Ireland between about 4200 and 3000 BC. The Landnam phases seem to have occurred throughout Ireland at about the same time; they have not been demonstrated to be exactly synchronous as our dating methods are not sensitive enough to establish that. Better land – but not heavy lowland soils – would have been colonised first; the poorer and more upland locations would perhaps not have been settled until the growth of population made it necessary to take in new land. The pattern is not a settled one. Not all clearings were permanent and the record shows that forest often regenerated and clearances were later resumed. The second growth forest frequently differed from the primeval woodlands. Elm for example did not recover as quickly as oak because of increased competition from trees such as ash (*Fraxinus*) and yew (*Taxus*) which were favoured by the opening of the woodland canopy. On some sites, we know that there were a number of successive phases of clearance followed by agriculture or pasture or both. The pattern is very detailed and reflects in some cases very local changes, in others, perhaps, a more regional picture. The broad pattern which can be appreciated only by playing back the recorder very quickly, is of diminishing forests over the first thousand or fifteen hundred years and of the development of extensive grassland and heathland, with a significant regeneration of secondary woodland in places at about 3500 BC. The grasslands were probably a permanent feature of the landscape by the middle of the Neolithic.

Pollen studies at many locations throughout the island tell essentially the same story. In some cases, radiocarbon dates anchor the points, in others pollen diagrams are linked together because the phases are especially distinctive and can, with care, be correlated. Palaeobotanists have detected the decline in elm as a marker at many sites at about 3900 BC. Agriculture before the elm decline seems to be attested in a number of locations – Lough Sheeauns in Connemara in Co. Galway, Cashelkeelty in Co. Kerry, Leigh (Littleton Bog) in Co. Tipperary and Ballygawley Lough, Co. Sligo. Arable farming is not always noted because it is difficult to distinguish between the rare grains of pollen that might be from cultivated cereals and those from certain wild grasses. The weeds that flourish in disturbances were mostly present around woodland margins before the Neolithic and need not be considered specific to cultivation. The pattern recorded at Fallahogy in Co. Derry was one of the first to be dated by radiocarbon (*Illus. 100*). There, the high forest was attacked around the time of the elm decline, leading

	Birch	Hazel	Pine	Alder	Oak	Elm	Bracken	Plantain	Grasses	Dock	Nettle	YEARS AGO	WOODLAND PHASES
RENEWED CLEARANCE												2550	
SECONDARY WOODLAND												3000	$ILWd_1$
RE-GENERATION													
FARMING CLEARANCE												3900	
HIGH FOREST													ILWC

Scale in units of 10%

Illus. 100
Schematic pollen-diagram from Fallahogy, Co. Derry, to illustrate a cycle of Neolithic land clearance (approximate dates BC).

initially to an increase in oak pollen, as competition by elm was reduced. The hazel, an abundant pollen producer, also declines while there are fluctuations in the values for alder which prefers a slightly wetter soil. The values for pine, presumably growing on bog surfaces, hold steady throughout. After about a century and a half, oak too is reduced. Shortly afterwards, the pollens of grasses peak and substantial amounts of plantain, dock and nettle are recorded. Bracken grows abundantly at about this time. After about 350 years, the forest begins to expand again with oak recovering rapidly and elm not restored to its former levels until sometime later. After the restoration of the forest, the process is repeated in a renewed cycle of clearing at an advanced stage in the Neolithic.

A slightly different picture representing local conditions emerges at Red Bog in Co. Louth. Before the clearances, hazel dominates the spectrum and elm reaches its highest values. Pine is common in the locality presumably growing on the bog surface together with alder and birch. It seems that arable agriculture was limited in the area – the clearances were for pasture. Cereal pollen is rare and the weeds growing in the cleared areas are considered to have been unspecialised and could have grown in grassland – nipplewort (*Lapsana communis*) common nowadays in woodland and hedges, ribwort plantain and fat hen or white goosefoot (*Chenopodium album*) still common today on tilled ground and wasteland and once eaten as a spinach-like vegetable. The single grains of poppy and knotgrass (*Polygonum aviculare*) noted at Essexford Lough nearby could have been associated either with cultivation or with other disturbed circumstances.

On the west coast, even the larger islands were cloaked in forest. Pine was strongly represented in the tree cover before c.4000 BC and dominated after the elm decline in a pollen study on Clare Island. Afterwards, pine was also reduced and birch, oak and alder became dominant and open heathland formed in the vicinity. A little lake – Church Lough – on Inishbofin has yielded a long record of activity. While the elm decline and the rise in the representation of alder are not clear, at about 4000 BC yew increased – a rise which was noted also in a study at

Lough Namackanbeg, near Spiddal in Co. Galway. Slightly later, there is abundant evidence for the further opening of the landscape with the occurrence of heather, ferns and ribwort plantain with heathland forming locally. Broadly similar clearances are recorded at a number of sites along the western seaboard. At Mullaghmore in the Burren, pine was growing abundantly until about the time of the fall in elm when it too declined; at that point, yew began to flourish. There is an especially clear early attack on the forest at Cashelkeelty in Co. Kerry where the woodlands were disturbed shortly after 4000 BC. Traces of cereal pollen were found. Forest had re-established itself in the region by the end of the Neolithic Period but pine, once very common, had declined to insignificance in the record. Valencia Island, too, has produced evidence of a number of Neolithic clearances.

How were the clearances accomplished? Modern experiments have shown that the polished stone axeheads of the Neolithic were very efficient at cutting down substantial trees. Oaks of less than 35cm in diameter could be felled in thirty minutes. Small pines and spruce of 15cm in diameter could be dealt with in a matter of seven minutes each. Forest was also probably cleared by ring-barking. Trees that have been girdled by a deep cut will die and once their leaf cover has been removed, crops can be put in around the standing boles. Given that cultivation was by hand, there was no need for the kind of fields necessary for ploughing. A small number of axeheads may have been mounted with their cutting edges at right angles to their hafts or handles as adzes for specialised woodworking and as mattocks to cut through the tough sod of developed grassland. Scrub could have been cleared by fire. While it is common for charcoal to be noted in pollen studies, it is by no means agreed that fire was used to clear woodland; it is impossible to distinguish between natural and man-made burning, but the first farmers may be deemed guilty by association. The growth of some open species of plant for example bracken (*Pteridium*) is favoured by burning.

The clearances would have had many indirect effects – increased grassland would have provided improved grazing for deer and the removal of tree cover would have placed other wildlife under pressure. More widespread effects would have been a greatly increased run-off of rainwater from the formerly forested lands and in some areas a raising of the water table and long-term changes in soil chemistry.

THE EARLIEST IRISH NEOLITHIC CULTURE

We know that a variety of the western European form of Neolithic culture was established in Ireland by about 4000-3800 BC, but how this came about has been disputed. The pollen record suggests that the first clearances were taking place before the earliest dated Neolithic sites and monuments that we have been able to identify. This can be interpreted in a number of ways. Perhaps there was a phase of the Irish Neolithic which differed greatly from what came later and left little trace other than the effect seen in pollen diagrams – possibly a largely pastoral phase with impermanent settlements. Alternatively, there may have been a prolonged period of consolidation before structures of substance could be afforded by the new settlers. Could the native Mesolithic hunter-gatherers have gradually adopted the

Neolithic lifestyle through contacts with Britain and the continent – is the Irish Neolithic the result of many small scale contacts leading to the incremental growth of its distinctive economy? While we can probably be sure that they did in time adopt the Neolithic way of life, the evidence from the predominantly Mesolithic middens at Sutton and Dalkey Island in Co. Dublin, suggests that a mixed lifestyle was practised by the inhabitants in Neolithic times; the Irish Mesolithic seems to have been a period of isolation rather than of contact. The simplest explanation is that we have failed so far to identify the *archaeological* traces of the earliest Neolithic in Ireland and our methods of dating are probably too imprecise to discriminate between a very early and a slightly later Neolithic settlement. However, we can identify with confidence a full-blown Neolithic culture in Ireland shortly after 4000 BC which had many points of similarity with that in Britain and western Europe. The evidence of pollen analysis suggests that the first farmers had already spread fairly rapidly throughout the island.

Migration

The introduction of certain plants and animals, the techniques of their management as well as the same sort of cultural traits in architecture and domestic crafts as those of the inhabitants of Britain seem to imply colonisation from there. It is likely that the earliest farming settlers came via the shortest sea-routes which would have provided the safest crossings at the right season. The fact that Ireland can be seen from parts of Britain, especially from across the St. George's Channel, would have encouraged exploration by the more adventurous. Former arguments about the origins of the first Irish farmers were based on a theory about the development and distribution of megalithic tombs; changes in the form of the monuments over time were used to suggest either an eastern landfall of settlers from Britain or a western entry by farming colonists from north-western France. The arguments do not seem to be relevant any longer. The developments in the architecture of the tombs were pictured as taking place over a much shorter period of time than we now know the Neolithic to have lasted. The time from the arrival of the first farmers to the end of the Neolithic lasted about as long as the time from the birth of Christ to our own day, and so the development of tomb architecture requires new explanations.

The motivation to move a community of farming people must have been very compelling. Migrating to an island is especially difficult because of the problems of shipping animals as well as people, tools and seed. Humphrey Case has speculated that skin boats up to 10m long might have been used. These could have carried up to about a tonne of cargo plus a crew. Animals would have been shipped trussed in the bottom of the boat – much as cattle were carried until recently in currachs to and from islands on the western seaboard. Unless the voyage was short, the animals would have become distressed through lack of water and progressively more and more unmanageable. The boats would have carried litter and fodder and with the litter would have come the seeds of new plants, insects and perhaps even small mammals. We do not know where the first farmers landed – we have to conceive of the first Neolithic settlement as a process not as a single event – many groups over a period of time may have arrived at points widely scattered along the east coast. Advance parties may have established what amounted to base-camps and started to clear woodland and put in a crop before the main parties arrived. If the many groups originated in different areas in Britain, differences would already have been inherent in their culture. If some encountered larger Mesolithic bands, perhaps even living a sedentary existence near a major food source, while others entered areas without many indigenous inhabitants, local differences would have been further emphasised and regional trends established. However, the broad similarities of material culture among the first farming communities in Ireland seem to be more striking than the differences.

Neolithic Farming

The directing force of a colonisation must have been some form of strong discipline – to protect the seed and breeding stock from short-term needs for example. The first harvests would have been rationed. If immature cattle had been carried in the boats to minimise risks on the voyage, the wait to build up herds sufficiently large for culling may have been protracted. It may have been necessary in the earliest stages to depend on hunting, fishing and collecting to supplement the food supply. The first farmers must have found Ireland especially suitable to their way of life – the climate was reaching the so-called optimum and seems to have been a couple of degrees warmer on average than it is today. The better temperatures would have enabled cereals to be cultivated on higher land than is now possible and the range of potential settlement areas for arable farmers would have been greater. The moist Atlantic climate with relatively little frost and abundant rainfall would have been excellent for crops and for the development of grasslands once the forest clearings had been made. Forage in the woodlands would have been available and pigs would have thrived on the acorns. Cattle would probably have grazed on the developing grasslands all year round but we have no information on how stock was managed. The balance of probability is that cultivated plant food provided the mainstay of the diet but this is not reflected in the pollen diagrams. The forests provided building materials, fencing and fuel and remained throughout prehistoric times, indeed until modern times, an important resource, but the cultivation plots were vital to the support of the earliest Neolithic population.

Farming in the Early Neolithic was carried on in an environment which remained significantly wooded and where abandoned farm clearances were re-colonised rapidly by forest. We can only guess at the appearance of the earliest farms – the cultivated plots may have been small – we may imagine them as being not unlike the garden farming carried on by the Woodlands Indians of North America at the time of the European invasions of the seventeenth century. Many of the hillsides and heavier lowland soils would have been covered by trees; the upland summer pasturages, used so much in medieval Ireland, had not yet developed. One reconstruction visualises the appearance of the earliest Neolithic clearings; settlements were tucked away in the forest. Between the cleared area and the woods was a surrounding of mantle and outskirt vegetation. On the richer soils, the mantle vegetation would have consisted of hawthorn, wild rose, bramble, varieties of *Prunus*, with trails of woodbine and ivy. On the open side, the outskirt vegetation would have consisted of various herb species, including for example, the wild strawberry. In time, the mantle would have developed as an impenetrable barrier between the cleared plots and the woodlands and would have deterred wild animals from invading the clearings. A source of edible berries would have been created near the settlements and there is little doubt that collected wild plant food was an important supplement to the diet. On poorer soils, the mantle would have been mainly of furze and bramble. Abandoned clearances on good land would have been recolonised by forest within about fifty years, somewhat longer on poorer land.

Forest Clearance and Society

The earliest farming was probably a communal venture of a number of nuclear families acting together. Circumstances would have encouraged the population to be segmented into small groups and in time they would almost certainly have developed distinct identities. Settlement was indeed dispersed and the houses of the farming families tended to occur singly in the landscape adjacent to the fields being cultivated and within a manageable distance of the resources of the forest, waterways or seashore. Such an organisation of society may have had many consequences which are not visible archaeologically – one of these is linguistic. New Guinea has experienced agriculture in a forest environment for perhaps many thousands of years. With only a tiny fraction of the world's population, about 15% of the world's languages have been recorded there. Some of these are spoken by groups of a thousand or more but there are distinct languages which are known only to tiny societies of as few as twenty people. Groups living close at hand may often be mutually unintelligible. Some linguistic differentiation probably developed in Neolithic Ireland and this might have posed problems when higher levels of social organisation began to form. Prehistoric archaeology by definition can say nothing of these aspects of communication and identity, but we must allow for the importance of all these intangible aspects of human behaviour.

In time, with increasing population and enlarged herds of grazing animals, clearings coalesced and wider tracts of land began to open up. How did this affect social organisation? The opening of the landscape would have tended to even out differences between small social groups as communication between them improved. Within a few hundred years of the arrival of the first farmers, Ireland had seen the emergence of increasingly sophisticated megalithic architecture, the appearance and in places re-clearance of second growth forest and, it seems also, the growth of a substantial population managing arable as well as extensive pasture land in organised fenced fields. The evidence also allows us to assume that complex and regionally-varied social systems had emerged, some of which may have wielded an authority of some kind over wide areas. Monuments once built in an intimate landscape might have become visible for longer and longer distances. The preoccupation of some megalithic tomb builders with commanding views and high visibility would have been pointless if the hills on which they were sited were clad in dense forest and the clearings below hedged about with tall stands of timber obscuring their cairns. The very purpose of rituals and ceremonial architecture may have been reordered to reflect the aspirations of emergent regional polities.

We can see clearly that some of the monuments of the Neolithic period were invested with a deep significance which transcended any purely utilitarian purposes – they were intended to make a mark on the minds of contemporaries but also no doubt on those of all succeeding generations. Humans occupy a real landscape but they also invest it with abstract ideas which are often obscure to us and which occasionally foster a behaviour which we might not regard as strictly practical. It is not until we enter the historical period that we can see in placenames and in legend something of the symbolic and even spiritual overlays projected by the human mind onto nature. Difficult as they are to understand, the very physical relics of these thought processes are evident in the landscape today. It has become fashionable lately for archaeologists to speak in terms of 'ritual landscapes'. This badly-defined term seems to be used to denote complexes of monuments which had been built for ceremony – tombs, arenas and the like – in an area reserved especially for the purpose. The boundaries of these so-called ritual landscapes cannot be established with much precision. A place which seems at first sight to be exclusively devoted to one purpose may merely have been defined by the visible monuments only – major settlement and everyday use of the land around about may be difficult to detect but may nevertheless have been significant. The nature of prehistoric ritual from the simple and privately improvised to the elaborate ceremonial, both public and secret, is poorly understood. In the case of monuments constructed at least in part as tombs, we shall see that there was often an intimate association with the settlement landscape. Even great ceremonial centres require an infrastructure of food producers and labourers, and we cannot divorce these requirements from the everyday world.

MEGALITHIC TOMBS

The construction of megalithic (great stone) tombs was the most lasting monumental achievement of the Neolithic inhabitants of Ireland. Almost thirteen hundred and fifty tombs have been identified, most of which belong to the Neolithic period with one type – the Wedge tomb – beginning in the later Neolithic and continuing to be built and used well into the Bronze Age. The erection of a monument such as a tomb creates a virtually indestructible kind of claim to the possession of the land validated by the preservation within it of the bones of the ancestors; the frequent location of tombs on abandoned habitations testifies eloquently to the intimate relationship of the living and the dead. The creation of a monument also forms a special place for events such as rituals and assemblies. We cannot know what spiritual or imaginative protocols governed the siting of megalithic tombs; for example, we do not know if they lay in the centre of a settlement as its heart, or on the periphery as a statement aimed at neighbours. While many tombs are located on good land and the living kept company with the dead, others lie on marginal soils. The theories about megalithic tombs are virtually unlimited but we cannot look on them any longer as simply repositories of the dead. Even allowing that some tombs were sited on acid soils which would have

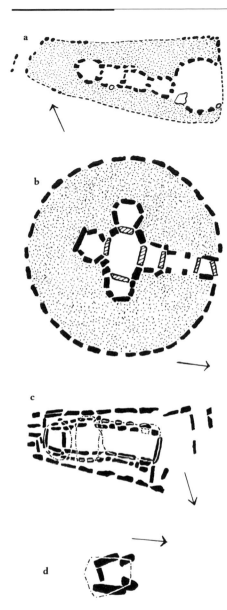

preserved bones poorly, it seems that relatively few people qualified for a tomb burial. However, there are exceptions. Large numbers of cremated burials were found in passage tombs at Tara and at Fourknocks in Co. Meath. Eligibility was a matter of selection and the basis of that selection might have been hierarchical, strictly familial or ritual in some sense not now easy to reconstruct.

The megalithic tombs of Ireland are normally divided on the basis of their form and details of construction into four major types (*Illus.101*) which still hold good for descriptive and some analytical purposes. The groups are the court tomb, portal tomb, passage tomb and wedge tomb. (Readers of older texts will encounter variant terms such as court grave/cairn, portal dolmen, passage grave and wedge-shaped gallery grave; these should be converted into the tidier terminology in use today.) A fifth type – a form of sealed megalithic chamber known as a Linkardstown Cist after a site in Co. Carlow – must now be added to the list. Since Irish archaeology is still in an age of discovery, new varieties may emerge as hitherto unclassifiable mounds are excavated and give up their secrets.

Court Tombs

The earliest type of megalithic tomb in Ireland is the court tomb of which almost four hundred examples survive. They are predominantly in the northern third of the country, but there are examples along the western seaboard as far south as Co. Clare and there is one in Co. Waterford (*Illus. 102*). They are generally found on light soils which would have been very suitable for early agriculture and as the tombs occur singly in the landscape they have long been regarded as a good indicator of the settlement pattern of their builders. Gabriel Cooney has shown that the megaliths of Leitrim are almost all sited on small pockets of good land associated with outcrops of rock in what would otherwise have been an area of poor

Illus. 101
Types of megalithic tomb found in Ireland:
a Court tomb,
   Browndod,
   Co. Antrim;
b Passage tomb,
   Carrowkeel, Co. Sligo;
c Wedge tomb,
   Labbacallee, Co. Cork;
d Portal tomb,
   Kilfeaghan, Co. Down.

settlement potential in Neolithic times. They are found both in lowlands and uplands and their siting can occasionally be prominent. Court tombs are characterised by a burial gallery built of massive stones entered from an open forecourt set normally in the broader, often eastern, end of a long cairn which is frequently trapezoidal in shape. Cairns are typically 20-30m long and are edged with a kerb of substantial stones sometimes combined with drystone masonry. The gallery which may consist of two, three or four chambers defined by jamb- and sill-stones is roofed by corbels but the forecourt is not. The courts may be roughly semicircular or u-shaped or completely enclosed in the cairns. They are defined by large upright stones (*orthostats* in archaeologists' jargon) sometimes also filled-in with drystone walling. The burials, usually cremations, occurred in the chambers. They were often accompanied by pottery and flint artefacts including arrowheads and scrapers and polished stone axeheads. The same sort of material is found on contemporary settlements, although the domestic pottery tends to be less ornate.

As a general rule, court tombs do not occur in clusters although they may be sited close to other examples; notable concentrations have been recorded in Mayo, Sligo and south-west Donegal. It is these concentrations which have led in the past to the argument that court tombs are the monuments of the first Neolithic settlers in Ireland who reached the west coast directly from the continent. Their density in an area may however be explained by the carrying capacity of the land in Neolithic times or by other factors such as competition between groups expressed in the form of monument building. Radiocarbon dating suggests that court tombs were in use throughout the period from shortly after 4000 to 3000 BC.

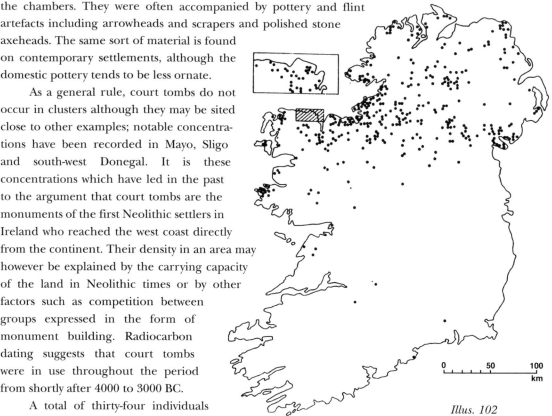

Illus. 102
Distribution of court tombs in Ireland.

A total of thirty-four individuals were buried in the court tomb at Audleystown in Co. Down. The court tomb at Creggandevesky in Co. Tyrone (*Illus. 103*) contained the cremated remains of twenty-one individuals of which five males, seven females and one adolescent were identified with certainty and the presence of eight other persons inferred from the fragmentary remains. The excavator, Claire Foley, thought that the presence of flint artefacts without obvious accompanying bones in the second chamber opened the possibility that unburned burials (now destroyed by the acid conditions of the site) had existed there at one time. Creggandevesky produced an important range of flint arrowheads, a javelin head, the remains of seven round-bottomed pottery bowls and one-hundred and twelve stone beads. The yield of burial remains from other excavated court tombs is very much less. The picture is clear however – the individuals buried in the tombs must represent a fraction of even our most modest estimates of contemporary population.

Each court tomb represented a considerable outlay of effort for a small community. The raising of the stones by manpower, the accumulation of the cairn, the planning and layout all required organisation, but perhaps we should not exaggerate the scale of the corporate effort. At a guess, a group of about a dozen or so nuclear families of about five individuals each might have furnished a workforce sufficient to erect a simple tomb fairly quickly especially if field clearance provided the stones for the cairn and glacial erratics could be used for the main structural elements. Some careful selection and transport of more regular stones may have

Illus. 103
Court tomb,
Creggandevesky,
Co. Tyrone. A well-
preserved court tomb
with its distinctive
cairn (8m long).
Perhaps as many as
twenty-nine
individuals were
interred in the tomb.
Earlier Neolithic
Period.

been necessary, but in general the court tombs were built from local materials. Clearly many more people may have been involved in their creation and this would change our calculations. Territories of tomb builders have been proposed by drawing lines on the map equidistant from each tomb. A network of polygonal shapes of varying sizes is thus created and where the tombs are most dense, these are small and could be interpreted as the home regions of the sort of small autonomous groups which we have discussed. It is on the whole a convincing picture except that one should not stress the relative isolation of the court tomb builders too much as the very architecture and contents of the graves suggest contact and communication outside the immediate locale.

Portal Tombs

Closely related to the court tomb is the portal tomb. Examples are seen in many places in the spectacular form which used to be called a dolmen. This is a megalithic chamber created by raising a large capstone on top of a number of upright stones. Portal tombs are so called because their capstones are pitched at their highest over a pair of upright stones which form an entrance or portal. The rear of the capstone usually rests on a single backstone. As we see them now, with their immense capstones balanced on three uprights they seem to be spectacular architectural *jeux d'esprit*. However, they are denuded remains which were once covered or partly covered by long mounds or cairns similar to those of the court tombs. The feat of erecting the capstones was impressive and to manoeuvre these great boulders into position and set them so that even when the cairn is removed, they continued to stand, took great engineering skill and organised effort. The capstone of the portal tomb in Kernanstown in Co. Carlow has been estimated to weigh about 100 tonnes, that of Brennanstown in Co. Dublin cannot be much less. The placing of the great roofing stones was probably achieved by building a ramp and using log rollers, levers and muscle power. Our knowledge of Neolithic livestock manage-ment is poor but it is theoretically possible that bullocks (castrated male cattle) could have been trained as draught animals and might have worked in harness to help in the movement and positioning of stones. Smaller rocks could have been drawn on sledges. We cannot prove the presence of draught oxen in the Irish Neolithic but we should not exclude the possibility when speculating about the construction of megalithic tombs. About one hundred and seventy portal tombs survive and their distribution is similar to the court tombs but with a significant scatter in the south-east extending from the neighbourhood of Dublin south-westwards to Waterford (*Illus. 104*). A number of portal tombs occur across the Irish Sea in Wales. Their siting

0   50   100
km

Illus. 104
Distribution of portal tombs in Ireland.

Illus. 105
Portal tomb, Goward, Co. Down. There are three burial chambers in this monument instead of the more usual two or four. A number of stones near the entrance suggest a facade like those of the related court tombs. Earlier Neolithic Period.

matches that of court tombs and some were built on the slopes of river valleys; the inclines may have been useful when moving the great capstones into position.

Excavated portal tombs yield the same kind of burial evidence as court tombs. The pottery is similar but with an even greater tendency for highly decorated pots to occur. Cremation is the commonest form of burial but there are examples of inhumation. The dolmen at Ballykeel in Co. Armagh (*Illus. 106*) produced no bones but the level of phosphates in the soil of the chamber suggested that bodies had been deposited in the tomb along with two spectacular pottery vessels. Anne Lynch excavated the Poulnabrone portal tomb on the Burren in Co. Clare and uncovered a well-preserved burial deposit and especially valuable evidence for the landscape history of the region in Neolithic times between about 3800-3200 BC. In the chamber were preserved the disarticulated unburned remains of up to thirty-three individuals – of these seventeen were adults and sixteen were children. Life expectancy was poor by modern standards – the majority of the adults had died by the age of about thirty – and the wear and tear on the vertebrae suggested that they had experienced a lifetime of hard physical labour, while their teeth indicated that they had survived on a diet of coarse, occasionally abrasive food. The tip of a chert or flint arrowhead was embedded in the ilium of what was probably a male. The bones are unlikely to have been in their original positions. As they were completely disarticulated and some had been pushed into the fissures in the limestone bedrock on which the tomb stood, they may have been buried or exposed elsewhere until their flesh had decomposed before transfer to the tomb. It may be that we have at Poulnabrone an example of a particular local tradition of burial. At the cairn of Poulawack, also in the Burren, which was built during the same general period, a chamber of the Linkardstown Cist type also contained disarticulated remains of a number of individuals whose bones had been defleshed elsewhere before final deposition in their tomb. Excavation of the cairn at Poulnabrone revealed that at

Illus. 106
Portal tomb,
Ballykeel,
Co. Armagh. This
dolmen with its
characteristic large
capstone is set in a
cairn 30m in length.
Excavation of the
chamber produced
both plain and
distinctively
decorated pottery and
flint implements.
Earlier Neolithic
Period.

the time it was built there had been a soil cover 10-12cm deep. It was a friable brown earth mixed with shells and stones but there was no trace of pollen preserved in it. The cairn at Poulawack by contrast was erected on the bare bedrock about 3350 BC.

Passage Tombs

The third major Neolithic category of Irish megalith is the passage tomb. At its most basic, the passage tomb consists of a burial chamber entered by means of a distinct passage which leads from the edge of a round covering mound or cairn. This is defined and revetted by a kerb of large stones set on edge and running around the full circumference. The tombs are remarkable for the variety and complexity of their architecture. Simple examples exist where a small polygonal chamber, roofed dolmen-fashion with a single stone, stands within a cairn but lacks the connecting passage to the perimeter. Examples of this form can be found in the Carrowmore cemetery in Co. Sligo and elsewhere. Some such as Newgrange (*Col. 31*), Dowth and Knowth in Co. Meath have long passages leading to elaborate chambers with corbelled roofs. Others have a simple passage which expands slightly at the inner end but which lacks a definite chamber – the so-called 'undifferentiated' type: still others have very complex plans. A very distinctive form is the cruciform, where the principal chamber has two added side-chambers and an end-chamber giving a pronounced cross-shaped ground plan. Newgrange is an example and there are many fine representatives of the cruciform type at Loughcrew and Carrowkeel (*Illus. 107*). A number of tombs may be covered by a single cairn. At Baltinglass Hill, a two-period cairn covers a sequence of three chambers. At Knowth there are two massive tombs back to back, one undifferentiated and one cruciform, under a huge mound which is the focus of a cluster of much smaller tombs one of which underlies the main tumulus. The nearby great mound at Dowth also covers two

Illus. 107
In the background, a cairn in the passage tomb cemetery of Carrowkeel, Co. Sligo, rises from the thin covering of blanket bog. The cairn has slumped since it was built; originally it would have been retained by its kerb of stones. In the foreground, the rectilinear chamber of a ruined megalithic tomb is also partly clothed in peat growth. Earlier Neolithic Period.

tombs. Passage tombs sometimes carry a distinctive art of spirals, angular designs, lozenges, meanders, circles; these are pocked or incised onto the surfaces of their passage, chamber or kerbstones. This abstract art sometimes, as at Newgrange, carved on stones where it would have been invisible after the construction of the tomb, clearly had a deep symbolic significance which is now lost to us. Massive kerbstones at the entrance to the passage of Newgrange and one of those at Knowth are exceptionally decorated and clearly were intended to be imposing markers. People have seen stylised faces, ships, trees, sun symbols and star maps in the art of the passage tombs but without carrying much conviction. One pattern on a kerbstone at Knowth does look remarkably like a sundial. On the whole however, the art of the passage tombs is abstract and its significance is elusive.

Newgrange was planned and built so that at sunrise in midwinter, the sun appearing above the local horizon would send a beam through the 'roof-box', an aperture constructed on the roof of the passage, to illuminate the rear chamber of the tomb (*Col. 32*). This was obviously planned carefully because the passage and chamber (combined length 24m) are built on a slope and the interior of the chamber is about on the level of the roof-box. The tombs at Knowth are orientated east to west and it has been speculated that they are turned towards sunrise and sunset at the equinoxes although there is no evidence for the penetration of the passages by the sun's rays. Speculation about the purpose of the arrangement at Newgrange has included the mystical and symbolic, with the sun signalling that the longer days were approaching, giving a kind of comfort to the dead entombed within; it has been suggested that the tomb was built to observe the phenomenon and so provide later generations with a reference point by which the year could be divided. It is clear that whoever planned Newgrange already knew how to make calculations about sunrise and could develop a system of survey points to lay out the site for construction. The speculation often made that farmers needed great calendrical precision to judge when to sow their crops is unconvincing; the decision on when to plant is much more empirical and based on length of day, weather and soil conditions. We can say that a skilled person or group of persons possessing arcane knowledge existed in the Boyne Valley. This individual or elite could command or influence the population to construct great monuments on carefully-planned and sophisticated principles. The landscape round about was organised to convey to the living, perhaps to the dead and certainly to the future generations, some deeply-felt statement. We may not be able to read the statement in more than the haziest approximation, but the power of the tombs is compelling and no one who witnesses it at Newgrange can remain unmoved by the sight of the first rays of the midwinter sun striking through the profound darkness at the heart of the great mound.

Passage tombs are often clustered together in 'cemeteries' and many are sited in conspicuous locations sometimes on hill- or ridge-tops. Because of this prominent siting, the impression may be created that passage tombs occur in extreme upland areas inhospitable to early farming, but prominence can often be achieved in a lowland setting – over 58% of all passage tombs occur below 150m OD and the majority of those on the uplands lie between 150 and 300m OD. Some do lie at extreme heights, for example on some of the Dublin mountains, just below the crests, on Slieve Gullion in Co. Armagh and most dramatically Maeve's Cairn (Miosgan Maedhbha) on top of Knocknarea in Co. Sligo overlooking the large cemetery-cluster of Carrowmore. (Although as it has not been excavated, we can only surmise that Maeve's Cairn is a passage tomb.) The visibility of the monuments was important in some way – about 16% of passage tombs are located above 300m OD; one example on Slieve Donard in Co. Down lies at 852m. Even where they have been sited in lowland areas, an effort has often been made to place them so that they dominate the local landscape. The three great mounds of the Boyne Valley tombs – Dowth, Knowth and Newgrange – impose themselves on the landscape. There can be little doubt that their siting and high visibility were carefully planned and had some meaning – spiritual, social or political – which may also be reflected in the enormous scale of some of the passage tombs. One such meaning may have been domination by an elite. The enormous work required to build a Newgrange suggests a strong social control. Some writers have seen the larger tombs as the outcome of processes of conflict resolution. They see these great achievements as an expression of some new-found communal feeling. Conflict resolution, as we know, can be achieved by domination. The mound at Newgrange contains a great deal of quartz which seems to have been collected from the fringes of the Wicklow mountains. At both Newgrange and Knowth, large cobbles of Mourne granite and other stones of northern origin occur. These were almost certainly collected from beach deposits along the Carlingford peninsula. Have we, in the collection of cairn material from distant places visible from the mounds, tokens of some kind of hegemony or of a sense of shared possession of the great monuments by a large and dispersed community?

About 50% of the two hundred and twenty-nine recorded passage tombs occur in the great cemeteries of the Boyne Valley, Lough Crew on the Slieve na Calliagh hills, near Oldbridge in Co. Meath, at Carrowkeel on the Bricklieve Mountains in Co. Sligo and at Carrowmore. The general distribution (*Illus. 108*) is not unlike that of the portal tomb. In other words, leaving aside the examples sited at extreme elevations, there is as much reason to regard the passage tomb locations as reflecting the settlement pattern of their builders as any other kind of megalithic tomb. The tombs of Carrowkeel are placed on the limestone terraces of the Bricklieve Mountains and are partly covered by bog which has grown after their construction (*Illus. 107*). At first sight, they

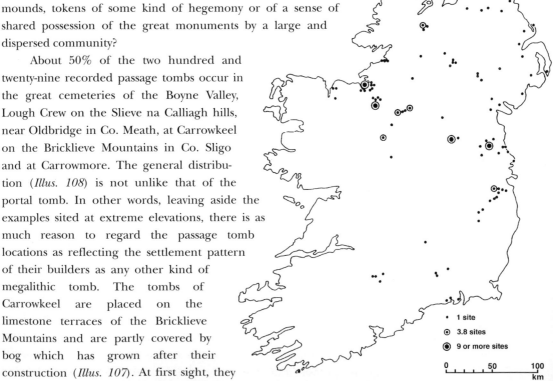

*Illus. 108
Distribution of
passage tombs in
Ireland.*

• 1 site
◉ 3.8 sites
◉ 9 or more sites

0   50   100
km

seem to be in an inhospitable situation but the area round about would have been congenial to farming at the time they were built. There would have been substantial forests of elm around the base of the mountains at the beginning of the Neolithic period and clearance began there about 3900-3800 BC. The area was perfectly capable of supporting a sizeable population. At Mullaghfarna just north-east of the passage tombs, there is a cluster of hut-sites, some of them partly covered by blanket bog. Whether these were the dwellings of the builders of the tombs at Carrowkeel is debatable; they are at least evidence that a settlement of considerable size existed in the neighbourhood at some stage in prehistoric times.

Illus. 109
Knowth, Co. Meath.
The macehead is
quite small, about the
size of a clenched fist.
It was found in dark
earth in the right-
hand side-chamber of
the east tomb. It is of
flint and must have
been cut and polished
using slivers of
quartz and sand; its
fabrication must have
been a very lengthy
process. When
completed it was
precious and
important and was
probably paraded on
ceremonial occasions.

Some simple passage tombs were being built by about 3400-3500 BC. (Claims that some Carrowmore tombs may have been constructed as early as 4200 BC are implausible.) It has been argued that the simplest passage tombs are the earliest and that there is a sequence of development within Ireland which culminates in large and complex examples. There may well be some truth in this – the great tombs at Knowth were not the earliest on site. Maeve's Cairn on Knocknarea, if it indeed covers a passage tomb, seems to have succeeded earlier structures. Thus the argument runs that increasing skill in construction, perhaps enhanced by contact with other architectural traditions outside Ireland and social change which may have brought about the sort of hierarchy to command such imposing structures, accelerated the development towards massive and sophisticated monument building. Each cemetery may represent the outcome of competitive emulation between the populations of substantial territories. This would have occurred over a period of time and it is likely therefore that the tombs in a cemetery represent a local sequence of development. The two great Boyne tombs which have been excavated, despite their differences, are to all intents and purposes contemporary – both Newgrange and Knowth seem to have been built around 3200 BC.

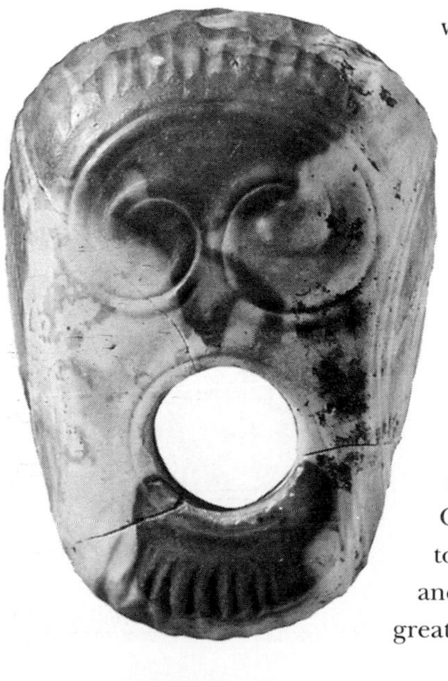

An older theory sees the Irish passage tombs as the works of new settlers arriving after the initial Neolithic colonisation, probably from Brittany where similar passage tombs exist. In this view, simple and complex forms were part of the package of architectural traits which were available from the start. Varieties of passage tomb occur along the Atlantic seaboard of Europe from southern Iberia to Scandinavia and particularly close comparisons to the Irish tombs occur in north Wales, Scotland and Brittany. There are suggestions of foreign contact in the ornament of the tombs and in the occasional occurrence of portable objects which resemble similar artefacts elsewhere. A stone idol from Knowth is similar to ritual objects found in Iberian tombs, and a remarkable decorated macehead of polished flint, also from Knowth, probably imported from northern Britain, indicates contact with the rich passage tomb culture of the Orkneys (*Illus. 109*). The resemblances between the Irish passage tombs and those overseas can only be accounted for by substantial and continuing contact. One cannot look at the structure of the great passage tomb mounds of the Boyne Valley without being convinced that they are the culmination in their tradition of building technology and of organisation. To what extent some of this development took place outside Ireland and was imported must remain a matter for debate.

The material culture of the passage tomb builders was essentially the same as that of the court tomb and portal tomb people. If the habitations in the Boyne Valley are any guide, the domestic pottery was part of the same range, similar flint implements were used and the domestic economy was pretty much the same. The tombs are then very particular, ritual and other expressions of what seem to be fundamentally the same people. Only in the passage tombs is found a particular kind of simple hemispherical bowl of coarse pottery, sometimes decorated with markings made by pushing and dragging a stick or bone into the soft clay before firing; arranged in loops or arcs, these patterns create a simple, but pleasing effect. Called Carrowkeel Ware after finds made in the cemetery in Co. Sligo, it has long been considered one of the distinctive facets of passage tomb material equipment. It is tempting to think of this pottery as specialised funerary ware, but examples of it have cropped up in domestic sites. A complete bowl was found in a bog at Bracklin in Co. Westmeath. It was caked with carbonised deposits and so may have been used as a cooking pot. Another example, one of two vessels, was found in the nineteenth century in a hearth on the mineral soil under a raised bog at Lislea, near Clones in

Illus. 110
Knowth, Co. Meath.
This magnificently
decorated stone basin,
more than 1m in
diameter, lies in the
chamber in which the
macehead was found.
The back stone of the
chamber is decorated
with typical symbols.

Co. Monaghan, along with two greenstone axeheads. The other vessel is now regrettably lost. Neither find was made in an area associated with passage tombs. Examples of Carrowkeel Ware pots used to contain burials have been found at the small tomb, 'The Mound of the Hostages', at Tara and within a Later Neolithic enclosure at Monknewtown, Co. Meath, close to the great Boyne tombs. Bone pins and stone pendants – often in the form of a hammer – represent the more striking finds from the burial deposits. Intermediate between the smaller artefacts and the tomb architecture are the stone basins which occur in some passage tombs. These are found in passage tombs in the east; there are four at Newgrange, three at Knowth and one at Dowth. Usually placed in the side chambers of cruciform tombs, they are large boulders hollowed on top which may have been used as temporary repositories for the cremated burials

which are more usually placed on the floors of the side-chambers. They seem to be a peculiarly Irish phenomenon occurring nowhere else in European passage tombs. The large cruciform tomb at Knowth contained a remarkable decorated example of a stone basin in its right-hand recess (*Illus. 110*). It was placed there during the construction of the chamber and cannot be removed.

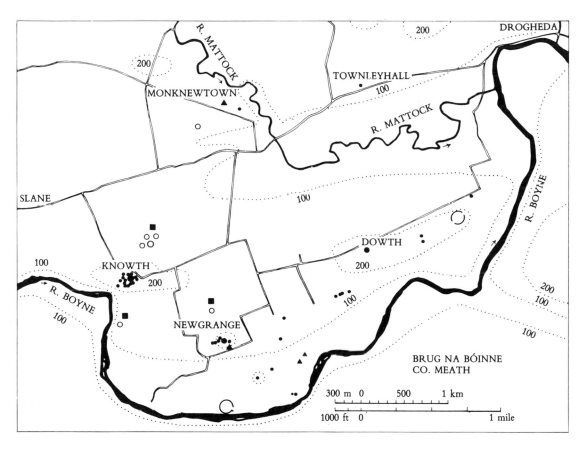

Illus. 111

● *The great mounds of Brug na Bóinne, the House on the Boyne*

▲ *Early Bronze Age sites*

■ *Early historic sites*

... *Form lines*

The Boyne Valley and Passage Tombs

The Boyne Valley tombs are amongst the most imposing prehistoric monuments in Europe (*Illus. 111*). The scale of the three major mounds of Newgrange, Knowth and Dowth is stupendous, but they are only the most visible evidence of this ancient man-made landscape. Around Knowth there is a cluster of satellite tombs focused on the main tumulus. Newgrange, too, has three identified satellites. In all, the region has about forty tombs together with the Neolithic habitations identified at Townleyhall and Knowth. Newgrange measures 79 x 85m in diameter and, before excavation, it varied between about 11m and about 13.5m in height. Dowth is about 85m in diameter but much of its mound was quarried away for road metal in the nineteenth century. Knowth measures 80 x 95m (*Illus. 112*).

The late Professor Brian (MJ) O'Kelly of University College Cork and excavator of Newgrange described the building of Newgrange in detail. The great mound stands on a ridge overlooking the Boyne at 61m OD. The mound of

*Illus. 112
The great passage
tomb mound with its
surrounding
kerbstones at Knowth,
Co. Meath (under
excavation). Smaller
satellite tombs with
surrounding kerbs lie
nearby; these too
would have had
mounds and two
reconstructed mounds
can be seen at the top
right. A black circle
in the lower right-
hand sector covers a
reconstructed
souterrain; from here
a passage, in which
coins struck in
Winchester about
950 AD were found,
leads down the side of
the mound. Scattered
masonry blocks on the
top of the mound
come from an Anglo-
Norman building.*

Newgrange was defined by ninety-seven kerbstones each weighing a tonne or more. A further four hundred and fifty slabs formed the tomb structure and all but two are greywacke and seem to have been glacial erratics collected for the purpose. None has been quarried; they are weathered and carry the striae caused by glacial scouring. These erratics were located in the area, partly concealed in scrub forest, partly buried and requiring to be dug out and dragged up the hill to the building site. About 200,000 tonnes of stone form the cairn, much of it loose water-rolled cobbles. A large figure-of-eight shaped pond on the lowest terrace of the river about 750m away from the tomb and 46m below it seemed to O'Kelly to be the likeliest source for much of the cairn material. This may well have been so but the feature seems to have been deliberately lined with clay as Pete Coxon discovered when he attempted to take a core from the pools for pollen analysis. The possibility exists that the pool was created for some purpose entirely unrelated to the building of megalithic tombs. Substantial quantities of quartz were incorporated into the cairn about the entrance area and this is now reconstructed in a form which has proved controversial.

We feel that the topographical basin in which Newgrange stands, about 50 sq km in extent, could have supported about two hundred farmsteads of about 25ha – a population not much different from today's. The farms may have supported families of an average of six (grandparent, two parents and three children) and each could have spared two able-bodied people for non-agricultural work. Estimating the quarrying of materials nearby (about 400m from the tomb) and that

Illus. 113
Cutting to show the
complex construction
of the mound at
Knowth, Co. Meath.
The lowest layer is of
field sods, the second
is of small stones and
the third is of black
shale, the local rock.
Similar layering is
repeated throughout
the mound.

the cairn might have been assembled by a workforce of four hundred people in about four years with about another year for the assembly of the structure of the passage and chamber, the whole tomb might have been built by this small community of about twelve hundred people in about five years. This now seems to have been an underestimate. The cairn is much bigger – four times bigger – than calculated and if the pond was the source of the materials, then the work of accumulation would have been much slower. There is evidence that construction of the cairn had stopped in places on at least three occasions long enough for a thin cover of vegetation to form. This suggests that raising it may have occupied a longer time, perhaps on similar calculations up to thirty years or so. Naturally, these figures are simply guesses. With animal power pulling sledges or slide-carts, the time may have been much less, or if workers were drafted in from a greater area, this too would have speeded up the work.

Whatever theory is proposed, the fundamental insight remains convincing that the surrounding area of the Boyne Valley was a settled farming landscape at the time the tombs were built. The mounds of the great tombs were carefully laid down; they are not random heaps of material. They play an important part in stabilising the tomb structures underneath and their layered construction helps to shed rainwater. Both the mounds of Newgrange and of Knowth contain substantial amounts of sod carefully cut and laid (*Illus. 113*). These were taken from mature grasslands which perhaps had passed their best and the tombs were themselves built on grassy sites. Pollen samples taken from the sod layers of Newgrange confirm that open conditions prevailed as a result of generations of agricultural activity. The familiar weeds associated with disturbance or pasture – plantain and docks – were present. Turves were taken from wet pastures close to the river where alder and willow were growing with ferns in the undergrowth. Pine, oak and elm grew on the higher parts of the river valley, with hazel growing on the margins. Pollen of both wheat and barley were identified from the mound and so crops were probably growing in plots nearby. Seeds of blackberry and crab apple together with buttercups, nettles, dandelions, sedge, knotgrass, stitchwort and chickweed were found confirming that for the most part the turves came from a weedy, moist meadow. We thus have clear evidence that the tombs of the Boyne Valley were built in the middle of a landscape where mixed farming was the mainstay of the population. It is something of a paradox therefore that another of the closely-dated, short-lived, climatic downturns should have taken place around 3195 BC, just about the time when these magnificent monuments were being raised. Is this an example where stress in society facilitated the emergence of a hierarchy able to direct the building of great monuments or is it merely a coincidence?

Linkardstown Cists

In recent years, chance discoveries together with the reassessment of old finds have brought to light a new form of megalithic tomb – the Linkardstown Cist – named after a site in Co. Carlow. (The term 'cist', pronounced *kist*, which we will meet a great deal from now on, is used by archaeologists to describe a sealed rectangular or polygonal slab-lined grave built on or in the ground.) The majority of these tombs have been found in the south-east usually when an unidentified round mound is being removed. Examples have been excavated in counties Carlow, Kildare, Wexford, Wicklow and Kilkenny. Some are more widely distributed, including one at Ardcrony in Co. Tipperary and another at Poulawack in Co. Clare which we have already seen. The cists are substantial polygonal chambers built on the old ground surface by leaning a series of slabs together to enclose an irregular space. To secure the slabs, others were leaned against the outside of the chamber stones to prop them up before the mound was raised. The little tombs thus created were roofed with a number of capstones and finally sealed by the building of a circular covering mound. Unlike the other tombs we have seen, the Linkardstown cists invariably contain unburned remains. One example had some cremated bone deposited with an unburned skeleton. Many contain a single male burial. Two cists contained pairs of skeletons – Knockmaree, Phoenix Park in Dublin (accompanied by a necklace of *Nerita littoralis* shells) and Ardcrony in Co. Tipperary. Linkardstown cists seem to have had a preponderance of male burials and while they have been described, often inaccurately, as 'single' burials, they are by no means always so. Nevertheless, they show a clear interest on the part of their builders in the interment of a very restricted category of individuals probably people of high status, normally males. Highly decorated pots from the graves have their closest analogues in examples from portal tombs and from a small number of pit-burials of the same period. Radiocarbon dating has now established beyond doubt that Linkardstown cists were being built between c.3500 and 3300 BC. Clearly the burial practices of the Irish

Neolithic varied from period to period and from region to region. The other major category of megalithic tomb – the wedge tomb – we shall consider later.

SETTLEMENTS

Few Neolithic houses have been found. Many were built of wood and so all that survives in the soil are the ghost impressions of the wooden posts which supported their walls and roofs, the foundation trenches in which the walls were set, traces of hearths, refuse or storage pits and scatters of artefacts. Many ploughed fields in the eastern part of Ireland and especially the north-east have yielded collections of flint artefacts and the debitage of their manufacture. In some cases, these may be the markers of now vanished settlements but some could conceivably have been the relics of midden scatters spread on early fields to fertilise them or of specialised or seasonal encampments. While Neolithic settlement was very widespread, indicators are much less in areas where arable agriculture is not common and where the extensive growth of bog since the Neolithic has buried the ancient landscape.

At Ballynagilly in Co. Tyrone in the 1960s, Arthur ApSimon excavated a rectangular Neolithic house. It lay between 180 and 215m OD, about five miles west of Cookstown, in a region rich in Neolithic monuments. It overlooked a small valley bog – once a lake – which preserved evidence of forest clearances of pine and elm associated with pine charcoal in the peat. A slightly earlier clearance of oak was noted nearby. Settlement extended over about 950 sq m and took the form of pits, post- and stake-holes and occupation debris. Some isolated pits were located up to 50m from the house. The house measured 6.5 x 6m and showed as a pair of parallel foundation trenches 30-40cm wide and 20-30cm deep. In one of the trenches, there was a sheet of standing charcoal which preserved a vertical grain. Careful excavation showed that this was the remains of a series of wooden planks placed side by side vertically in the trench to form the wall. The planks were made by radially-splitting an oak trunk lengthwise, using wedges to prise the wood apart. The planks had been packed in the foundation trench with stones and the post-holes of timbers which supported the roof were clearly identified. Inside were two hearths, post-holes and pits. Fragments of typical Neolithic pottery and three leaf-shaped arrowheads of flint were found in the house. The Ballynagilly house was probably the home of a single nuclear family living in an upland area about 3800 BC.

At Tankardstown in Co. Limerick, two Neolithic houses were found about 20m apart. Both rectangular, they had been built on a southwest-facing slope overlooking a small river. The site had been so heavily ploughed that only the features dug deeply into the subsoil were traceable; there was absolutely no visible surface indication. One house measured 7.4m x 6.4m. Like the Ballynagilly house, it too had been built of split-oak planks set vertically in a foundation trench. Post-holes occurred at the corners and midway along the walls and suggested that the interior may have been divided in two. The entrance was to the north-east. A patch of oxidised clay may mark the site of a hearth. Inside the house area, an arrowhead of flint, a flint blade and some sherds of Neolithic pottery were found. The other house was much bigger, 15.75m long and 7.5m wide. It was divided into three parts by two cross-walls which defined a central room of about the same size as the first house. Perhaps the space was divided to accommodate different functions, with the central room devoted to living and one of the smaller end spaces used for stalling animals. A similar house at Ballyglass in Co. Mayo was demolished to make way for the building of a large court tomb.

Also in Co. Limerick, at Knockadoon – a rocky promontory projecting into Lough Gur – there was at an advanced stage in the Neolithic, a cluster of round and rectangular houses. There seems to have been no broad chronological distinction between the two types. They shared the same general techniques of construction and produced the same kind of finds. The rectangular house at Site A was 12.2m long and 7.6m wide and was built of a double wall of posts on either side of a low inner wall of stone. The walls were carried up by means of wattle screens plastered with daub. The roof was hipped. Some of the Lough Gur houses were sited in small stone-walled enclosures. Round houses were found at Slieve Breagh in Co. Meath which might have been Neolithic. Round Neolithic huts have been excavated on the slopes of Knocknarea in Co. Sligo where they may have been associated with specialised activities. Two of these huts yielded exceptional numbers of hollow scrapers – a distinctive Irish type of flint implement with a crescentic working edge. The huts were demarcated by low banks and ditches or gullies and their posts may have supported hide tents. An early Neolithic rectangular house was excavated at Knowth in Co. Meath and it dated to about 3700 BC. At the same site, a habitation constructed of stakes, consisting of more than one dwelling renewed over time, preceded the construction of the great megalithic tomb. Nearby, a dwelling of the same type at Townleyhall in Co. Louth was succeeded by a simple passage tomb. The site is called Townleyhall II to distinguish it from another Neolithic encampment excavated nearby. Habitation traces were found under court tombs at Ballymarlagh in Co. Antrim and Ballybriest in Co. Derry and beneath the passage tomb on Baltinglass Hill in Co. Wicklow. This association between dwellings for the˙ living and burial places may reflect the very complex thinking which evidently lay behind the construction of megalithic tombs.

Smaller structures of Neolithic date – perhaps some form of shed – were also found at Lough Gur in Co. Limerick (*Illus. 114*). At Ballyglass in Co. Mayo, one was excavated under a court tomb which covered the rectangular house. These structures may have been used as stores and even byres, but our knowledge of ancillary buildings is limited. The Neolithic houses, however, do give us a view of something of the domestic arrangements of a family of farmers in that remote period. The occurrence of arrowheads is not necessarily suggestive of hunting as they would have armed efficient weapons for fighting. We have a very good picture from Tankardstown of the plants which formed part of the diet of the inhabitants. Emmer wheat (*Triticum dicoccum*), hazelnuts and crab apple *(Malus sylvestris)*, which seems to have been dried to preserve it, were noted. The seeds of both the dock and goosefoot families were found also and while their occurrence was probably accidental, they provide valuable evidence of open conditions nearby. Emmer was found at both Townleyhall II in Co. Louth and Baltinglass Hill in Co. Wicklow – both habitations which preceded passage tombs – and at Site 17 at Knowth. There was an emmer impression and also one of einkorn (*Triticum monoccum*), a robust

FT. 0   4   8   12

FT.   0   5   10   15   20

*Illus. 114
Reconstructions of
types of Neolithic
houses excavated by
S P Ó Ríordáin at
Lough Gur,
Co. Limerick.*

form of domesticated wheat, on pottery from Ballymackaldrack court tomb in Co. Antrim, while the tomb of Creggandevesky in Co. Tyrone produced pottery with impressions of naked and hulled barley. The animal bones from Tankardstown – all burnt fragments raked from hearths – included cattle, sheep, sheep/goat and pig and a fragment of red deer. The minimal importance of wild animals in the diet compared with cattle is reflected in the animal bones from Lough Gur which have been analysed. This is odd in a way because the increased clearances of the Neolithic would have encouraged an expansion in the deer population and one might have expected it to figure more prominently in the diet. However the greater productivity of managed cattle herds on grassland provided a more reliable source of food.

The charcoal from cooking fires on domestic sites sometimes survives well enough to be identified. At Lough Gur, hazel, ash, whitebeam, holly, oak, hawthorn, cherry and pine were noted; much of this would have come from the mantle vegetation described above or from scrub around the shore of the lake. Charcoal from megalithic tombs in Leinster included hazel, willow, poplar, oak, whitebeam, hawthorn, birch, alder, ash, ivy, elm and elder.

ENCLOSURES AND DEFENCES

At Knowth, after the rectangular house phase, a stout palisade enclosing an area perhaps 85m in diameter was constructed. This may have been a yard or perhaps a defence of some kind. At Lyles Hill in Co. Antrim, overlooking the valley of the Six Mile Water, a hilltop measuring 385 x 210m was enclosed by two successive palisades erected in the Neolithic; one about 3000 BC and a second outer one built between two hundred and six hundred years later. There was much occupation debris at Lyles Hill and at some stage a small cairn was erected within the enclosure. Not far away, also overlooking the same valley, Donegore Hill was enclosed by a gapped series of banks and ditches encompassing an area about 200m x 150m. These ditches were dug into tough glacial till and basalt without the benefit of metal tools; experiment suggests that using antler picks, a work team might have needed about 18,000 man-hours to excavate the two ditches at Donegore, something which might have been accomplished over a number of seasons by a work force of about thirty.

The ditches at Donegore varied between 1 and 2m deep and were up to 3m across. The gaps between sections of ditch have been compared to the similarly gapped or causewayed camps of the southern British Neolithic. Within its enclosure were traces of houses and substantial amounts of occupation material including pottery and flint. Lived in between about 3000 and 2700 BC, the occupation at Donegore must have overlapped with that of Lyles Hill; Jim Mallory has also suggested that the sites may have been in opposition to one another at a time of increasing stress. Traces of a palisaded enclosure were found under the passage tomb, 'The Mound of the Hostages' at Tara in Co. Meath. This was perhaps the first defence to be erected on this site which was to assume immense symbolic importance in later prehistoric and historic times. The older notion that the first farmers were egalitarian pacifists is certainly losing ground.

Where monuments have a defensive character it is logical to attribute their construction to stress of some kind. There is a clear connection between the nature of the structure and one of the symptoms of stress – the threat of violence. A defensive structure embodies the need to exercise control in order to manage whatever crisis may have emerged. The building of great ceremonial structures as the settings for ritual have also been explained as the products of processes of stress-resolution in society. There may well be some truth in this, but human behaviour being what it is, there are likely to be other explanations also. One of these may well be the accumulation of wealth and general stability, factors which have been seen as encouraging monument building in some modern societies. In all monument building we cannot rule out coercion as a driving force and some ambitious projects may be testimony of resolution in the form of domination and conquest.

CRAFTS, EXCHANGE AND TRADE

We have mentioned some of the characteristic artefacts of the Neolithic in passing – pottery for example, found in both houses and tombs, is an innovation. Studies show that the typical Neolithic pottery of Ireland was made generally of local clays and built-up by hand in coils or rings of rolled-out clay (*Illus. 115a,b*). Afterwards the surface of the pot was smoothed with a fine stone and left to dry before firing, probably in batches, in a bonfire. The clay was usually mixed with some coarser material – grit, broken shell, broken pottery and the like – to make it more plastic and thus easier to work. The burnishing process often produced a remarkably smooth surface which in some cases, frequently on funerary pots, carried fine decoration incised or impressed in the wet clay before firing. The commonest Neolithic pottery is plain, round-bottomed either hemispherical or with a pronounced shoulder and a neck-feature with a simple rolled rim. As a rule, it is thought that the practice of decorating the pottery became more common with the passing of time. In the manufacture of pottery we have clear evidence of a domestic craft.

Although the sheep/goat was known in Neolithic Ireland, we have no evidence for textiles of any kind and we must assume that skin clothing was worn and the preparation of hides must have formed part of the activities of the settlements.

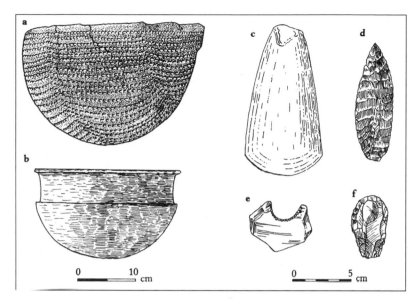

Illus. 115

Some typical Neolithic objects:

a decorated round-bottomed bowl, Mound of the Hostages, Tara, Co. Meath;

b plain-shouldered bowl, Browndod, Co. Antrim;

c polished axe, stone, Dunloy, Co. Antrim;

d javelin-head, flint, Bann Valley;

e hollow scraper, flint, Tamnyrankin, Co. Derry;

f end-scraper, flint, Ballynagard, Co. Antrim.

The polished stone axehead, mounted in a perforated shaft of wood, seems to have been the multi-purpose tool of the Neolithic; over eighteen thousand have been documented (*Illus. 115c*). The process of manufacture was simple and theoretically any suitable pebble could have been polished on a rubbing stone to shape it for use. This doubtless happened on many occasions but we know that in Ireland as in Britain, fine, hard igneous or metamorphic rocks which could take and keep an edge were favoured for the manufacture of axeheads. On the slopes of Tievebulliagh Mountain in Co. Antrim and at Brockley on Rathlin Island there are small outcrops of porcellanite which was especially favoured for axehead manufacture – almost 54% of Irish axeheads studied are of porcellanite. So-called factories using the stone existed and their products were distributed widely throughout Ireland and even in parts of Britain where a number of similar factories were in production at this period. A handful of axeheads from the factory of Great Langdale in Cumbria has turned up in Ireland. Other exotic axeheads included examples from western and south-western Britain. It is likely that fires were set at the outcrops to splinter the stone so that pieces of suitable size could be obtained. These were then chipped into approximately axehead-shaped forms on site (so-called 'rough-outs') which were then taken away and finished elsewhere. A rubbing stone and five partially polished axeheads were found at Culbane in Co. Derry. Axeheads of porcellanite have been found both as stray finds and amongst the objects deposited in megalithic tombs. Some are quite small, others are large and intended for serious tree-felling. A few are of exceptional size and could not have been used in a practical way and may have been made for a ritual purpose such as those found together in a hoard at Malone in Belfast. The wide distribution of these distinctive products in Ireland requires a reassessment of trade and exchange in Neolithic Ireland (*Illus. 116*). Gabriel Cooney has been documenting the axe factory on the island of Lambay off the coast of north Co. Dublin (*Col. 36*). There, outcrops of porphyry were quarried for polishing into axeheads which in their finished form have a particularly beautiful appearance. His excavations have produced pottery and flint artefacts associated with the quarrying activity.

Flint which occurs in nodules in the chalk around the edges of the Antrim plateau was also exploited. It is no accident that in the north-east we have vast collections of fine quality flint artefacts and many sites where there is good evidence

of manufacture. Where fresh flint in situ was unavailable even
through trade, then the Neolithic flint-knapper was
obliged to depend on pebbles from beaches or glacial
deposits. This material because it had been subjected to
all the processes of water or glacial transport, was
often full of hairline cracks and other flaws and
more dificult to work or to find in
pieces sufficiently large for making
certain artefacts. At a late stage in
the Neolithic, there is evidence
for the trade in flint as hoards of
flint implements have been found
in a number of places. The
techniques of Neolithic flint-
working are much more sophisticated than those of the Mesolithic
(*Illus. 115d,e,f*). The quality and variety
of Neolithic flint-work is very high with
some pieces, especially the javelin
heads, attaining a quality of finish
and aesthetic appeal which
is remarkable in such func-
tional objects. The organised
exploitation of flint in the
Neolithic is well-known. Extensive flint mines in southern
Britain, France and Belgium
have been studied. No mines have
been found in Ireland and it is likely that the flint was taken from cliff exposures,
especially along the Antrim coast. Some sites, such as Goodland in Co. Antrim, have
been tentatively identified as the settlements where specialised exploitation of flint
resources was the intention of the occupants.

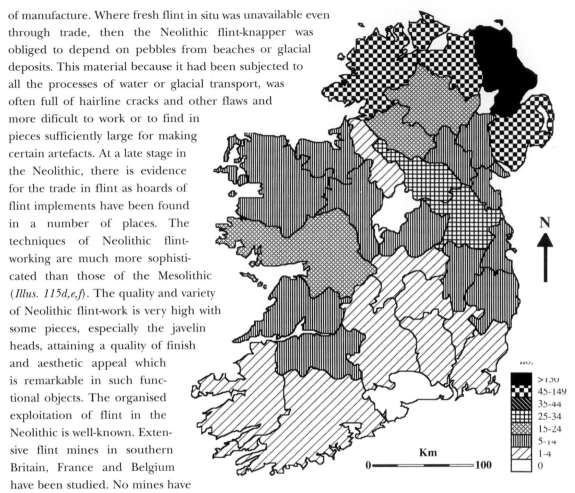

	>150
	45-149
	35-44
	25-34
	15-24
	5-14
	1-4
	0

*Illus. 116
Distribution of
porcellanite axes in
Ireland by county.
This map illustrates
that porcellanite axes
are common
throughout Ireland
and are particularly
abundant in the
north-east close to the
source areas.*

MANAGING THE LANDSCAPE

We have taken the story of the first farmers from the earliest clearances to the
heyday of the Boyne passage tombs – a period of at least a thousand years. In that
time we have seen regrowth of forest and renewed clearances and we have
suggested that the more favourable areas of the country were occupied by a
substantial population of farming families who may have developed wider social
groupings which in turn may have become more and more *organised* as the
landscape began to fill up and as competition for resources emerged. Competition
between groups, contacts outside Ireland, quasi-industrial exploitation of raw
materials and long-distance trade and exchange of goods would have emerged. All
these can be argued and the evidence of our pollen recorder of events near and far
confirms the taming of the landscape. One strand of evidence which we have yet to

look at concerns the field systems. From an advanced stage in the Neolithic period, we have surviving patterns of field boundaries which show that in part at any rate our surmise of a settled, organised landscape over large tracts of the countryside is likely to be right.

The bleak boglands of north Mayo conceal a more ancient landscape of field walls, megalithic tombs and settlements which show that the region once supported farming communities who had organised the land to manage it, probably for their livestock. Séamus Caulfield has spent many years surveying these pre-bog stone walls, first noticed by his late father. In the Behy/Glenulra area, now generally referred to as the Céide Fields, turf-cutting and later programmes of survey using probes, together with some excavation, have enabled him to trace extensive field systems defined by stone walls and occasionally by banks of earth thrown up from flanking ditches dug on the uphill side (*Illus. 117*). About a square kilometre has been studied in the area. Agriculture probably began in the area around 3600 BC, and the court tombs to be found there are probably associated with this. It appears to have been predominantly pastoral with some arable agriculture. This phase lasted for about a thousand years, towards the latter part of which the field systems appear to have been built. The stone walls were constructed on the mineral soil

Illus. 117
Old field system being revealed as blanket bog is cut away at Behy, Co. Mayo.
▲ *Tomb*
■ *Enclosure*

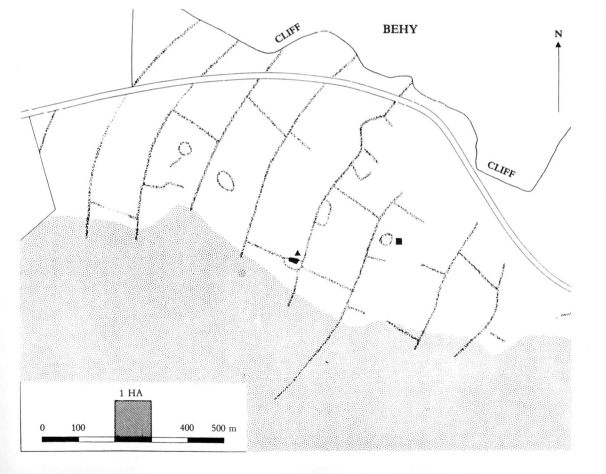

before the bog began to grow around 2500BC. Long parallel walls divided the land into strips about 150m wide which were then sub-divided into fields by offset cross-walls. The remarkable thing about the Behy/Glenulra system is that the fields were planned as a single system and either a community or an individual, with powers of persuasion or command organised the work. The walls – especially if topped by a thorn reinforcement – would have prevented cattle from straying but would not have formed a significant barrier for sheep or deer. Caulfield is convinced that the fields were intended for the management of herds of cattle which would have thrived on the pasture within the enclosures. The growing season for grass in Mayo at present is about nine to ten months depending on winter temperatures and in the slightly warmer conditions of 3000-2000 BC, it may well have been even longer. Haymaking for winter fodder was unnecessary. Allowing for lesser yields than in modern herds and assuming that the Neolithic cattle in Ireland were somewhat larger than has been thought, Caulfield thought that the Céide Fields could have supported about five family farms of about 25-30ha, each hectare producing about 100kg of beef per annum. Based on figures for the cattle of the Late Neolithic settlement at Newgrange, he has postulated that herds of fifty animals grazing about 30 hectares may have been the norm. The harvest would have been the three-year old beasts and the older cows past the productive stage. The slaughter of a beast, however, would have presented problems. If, say, an animal of about 500kg was killed, about 300kg of meat would be produced and unless the beef could be preserved by drying, salting or smoking, the neighbours would have to have co-operated in the consumption of the kill and in the rational staggering of the slaughter times to ensure a continuous supply. Such co-operation is implicit in the walls and organised landscape. The harvest from the early cattle economy, if the figures are right, would in Caulfield's opinion have supported two hundred to two hundred and fifty families in the 50 sq km which would have been required to feed one equivalent hunter-gatherer family. On present evidence, the creation of the field systems seems to date to the final stages of the Neolithic. They were extensively used in the Bronze Age and we shall return to this later.

The fences of the Céide Fields are by no means the only pre-bog field systems to have come to light. Caulfield has traced similar fields at many locations elsewhere in north Mayo. Pre-bog field fences are now reported from many other parts of the western seaboard from Donegal to Kerry, but as yet the dating of many of them is unknown. On Valencia Island, around the Imlagh Basin, the remains of a substantial system of stone field walls emerges from peat and one of these has been dated by radiocarbon to the Later Bronze Age. The bogs elsewhere preserve the evidence of Later Bronze Age land management also.

Fences of Neolithic age are only haphazardly known from other parts of the country, preserved by accident. The palisade at Knowth and the enclosures at Tara, Lyle's Hill and Donegore, while probably built for other purposes could also have been used for the protection of stock. Small enclosures were associated with the settlement of Lough Gur which was never inundated by bog. We have no evidence for Neolithic enclosures for most of the island despite all the other traces of Neolithic settlement. An unusual long megalithic cist at Millin Bay in Co. Down had

Illus. 118
Millin Bay,
Co. Down.
A long burial cist in
a kerbed mound
fortuitously preserved
a section of an earlier
Neolithic boundary
wall.

been constructed so as to preserve within its cairn part of the line of an earlier stone wall (*Illus. 118*). Field boundaries of probable Neolithic age at the site of Beaghmore in Co. Tyrone were partly overlain by an Earlier Bronze Age complex of stone circles and alignments. We can only conclude that the earthen banks, hedgerows and wooden fences which probably existed were obliterated by regrowth of forest and by later ploughing and reorganisation of the landscape. Only in areas where conditions prevented the re-establishment of forest and where bog had grown up to cover the walls, did circumstances favour their preservation. Nowadays, only the very substantial monuments stand out in the countryside to mark the former presence of the first farmers.

THE LATER NEOLITHIC AND THE BEGINNINGS OF METALLURGY

About 2800-2000 BC

The Boyne passage tombs do not appear to have been used for more than perhaps three or four centuries, but it seems that their importance continued to be recognised because their location attracted continued interest. It has been argued that at some stage in the later Neolithic there was significant change in ritual practice which now became something of a public performance rather than the private rites which it has been speculated took place in the darkness of megalithic tombs. Large earthen embanked enclosures were built in the Boyne Valley and aerial photography is beginning to reveal more elsewhere. Many of these are internally ditched and resemble the henges of Britain. They may have been the settings for ceremonies or games which could have been viewed by large numbers. Thirteen have been identified in Co. Meath close to passage tombs. Indeed, the passage tomb connection of the examples excavated so far is emphasised by the finds and is especially noteworthy. One lies on the terrace below Newgrange. The enclosures are defined by flat-topped banks encompassing circular or oval spaces with entrances facing either east or west. They are frequently sited on slopes or in a couple of cases on the bottoms of river valleys; their builders contrived to give them a prominent siting within their immediate settings. They range in diameter from 106m to 275m, the smaller examples tend to be circular in plan while the four largest ones are elliptical. Some enclose mounds or other features and there is strong evidence to suggest that the banks were formed not by the upcast from an encircling ditch but by scraping the interior. At one of them, Micknanstown in Co. Meath, near the passage tomb of Fourknocks, geophysical survey indicates that the enclosure succeeded an earlier ditched monument of some kind and this may also have been true at the site of Balrath in Co. Meath. We may conclude that the sites were like the passage tombs, the foci of continuing interest. At Micknanstown beside the enclosure is a fine well-preserved tumulus. Monknewtown in Co. Meath lies on the bank of the Mattock, a tributary of the Boyne, close to the passage tombs of Newgrange, Knowth and Dowth. Originally about 107m in diameter, excavation revealed a number of pits containing cremation burials and a Carrowkeel Ware pot which contained cremated bone lying on the old ground surface. A ring-ditch surrounding a pit-burial and a house site associated with a new type of ceramic,

*Illus. 119
Knockadoobrusna,
Co. Roscommon.
An Earlier Bronze
Age landscape
survives dominated
by ritual sites:
earthen embanked
enclosures, mounds
and barrows.*

Beaker pottery, which clearly placed it in the final Neolithic, occurred in the south-eastern part of the site.

Other sites which share the characteristics of the enclosures near the Boyne Valley have been identified in counties Roscommon, Sligo, Clare, Limerick, Laois, Waterford, Wicklow and Down. The Giant's Ring at Ballynahatty in Co. Down is an oval enclosure with a bank about 19m wide and almost 4m high enclosing a circular area about 200m in diameter prominently sited in the Lagan Valley at the edge of a steep slope. It seems to have been centred on a partly destroyed passage tomb which was badly disturbed in modern times. Recent work at the site has shown that Ballynahatty is the centre of a complex of ritual structures not unlike those at Newgrange and Knowth. The complex includes a large oval double-palisaded enclosure of post-pits 70m x 90m in extent containing a smaller enclosure within. Large numbers of burials of the Later Neolithic and Earlier Bronze Age have been identified at the site. Other examples of enclosures of this time include Castleruddery in Co. Wicklow which is about 35m in diameter and is lined with stones along its inner face; a pair of quartz boulders mark the entrance. The Grange stone circle at Lough Gur in Co. Limerick is a much larger version of the Castleruddery monument. It is about 65m in diameter and the area enclosed by the banks is about 45m across; it has a stone-lined entrance. Standing stones line the inner face of the bank which is about 10m wide. The levelling of the interior provided the material for the bank. The excavations by Seán P Ó Ríordáin produced substantial quantities of Neolithic and Beaker pottery and stone and flint tools. These composite stone and earthen examples introduce us to another new class of monument; the stone circles which appear about this time are widely distributed in Ireland and in Britain and excite more speculation than most prehistoric monuments in these islands.

Stone Circles

About two hundred and forty stone circles – rings of upright stones (*Illus. 120, 121*) – exist in Ireland, the vast majority of which occur in two areas: one hundred and ten sites in mid-Ulster (counties Tyrone, Fermanagh and Derry) and one hundred and seven sites in south-west Munster (counties Cork and Kerry). A small number is scattered around the rest of the country, but they are lacking in many regions. The circles occasionally enclose other monuments within their circuits. The classic example is Newgrange where a massive circle was erected around the already ancient passage tomb mound. They are often associated with alignments of standing stones, cairns and, in Cork and Kerry, with a particular form of massive tomb constructed dolmen-fashion from large irregular boulders. At Beaghmore near Cookstown in Co. Tyrone, a group of monuments now covered by bog occurs. Clearance of the bog has revealed three pairs of circles, stone rows and cairns which succeeded a series of Neolithic field walls. Although some Neolithic material was found on the site, radiocarbon evidence indicates that the monuments were erected between about 1500 and 700 BC. The Cork/Kerry stone circles have been studied in detail by Seán Ó Nualláin and consist of examples with circuits of five stones to others with circuits of from seven to nineteen stones. The latter range in size from

Illus. 120
Stone circle known as
'The Piper's Stones',
Athgreany,
Co. Wicklow. Later
Neolithic or Earlier
Bronze age.

4m to 17m in diameter. They have distinct entrances consisting of two uprights taller than the other stones. Diametrically opposite is the 'axial' stone; this is a stone laid down with its long axis along the line of the circumference. They also have a distinct orientation and viewed from the entrance, the axial stone lies in the arc from south-west to north-west with a distinct preference for the south-west. Some examples excavated have produced evidence of burial; there was a pit in the centre of the fine circle at Drombeg in Co. Cork which contained a burial in a coarse pot. Radiocarbon dating suggests that stone circles in Cork and Kerry may have been built as late as about 700 BC – well into the Later Bronze Age. Despite their long survival in Ireland, the stone circles clearly owe their origins to the henges and stone circles of Late Neolithic Britain and Ireland. Examples which combine standing stones with earthen banks (as we have seen at Castleruddery and Grange and also at Nymphsfield near Cong in Co. Mayo) are a link to that tradition. (The classic example, Stonehenge, began as a banked enclosure.) The orientation issue has prompted a good deal of research into the astronomical alignment of the circles

Illus. 121
Boleycarrigeen stone
circle, Co. Wicklow,
framing a view of the
Brusselstown Ring
hill-fort in the
background. The site
of the circle is now
completely concealed
within a forestry
plantation.

and given the consistent interest in orientation shown by the builders of megalithic tombs, this is potentially a fruitful area of enquiry. The question of the alignment on critical points of the heavens must depend to a great extent on the local topography because the siting of some circles is such as to preclude uniformity of orientation. This point cannot be emphasised too much; each site lies in a particular part of the landscape and it is only by inspection on the ground that the relationship of a monument to its topographical setting can be properly appreciated. Prominent landmarks, rather than celestial bodies, may lie behind a particular orientation.

Cursus

Another form of monument with what may be a ritual function is the cursus. These are pairs of parallel banks often closed at the ends, sometimes flanked by ditches, which may have formed processional ways of some kind. A good example at Tara was formerly identified as a banqueting hall in medieval Irish tradition (*Col. 34*). Aerial photography is revealing them in increasing numbers at sites where complexes of Neolithic and later ritual monuments occur. There is at least one in the Boyne Valley at Newgrange and another at Loughcrew in Co. Meath, but a map of Irish cursus monuments will take some time to compile. Examples have also come to light at Knockainey in Co. Limerick – a site rich in mythological associations – at Kiltierney in Co. Fermanagh and at Blank Banks Hill on the Blackstairs Mountains in Co. Carlow. Like the henge, the cursus occurs in Britain where notable examples in the vicinity of Stonehenge have been identified. The progress of field survey is revealing that the Neolithic and Earlier Bronze Age saw a profusion of ritual monuments, many of them on a large scale, and until we have a great deal more data, we can only speculate about how they interrelate.

New Ritual Structures and Pottery Styles

At Newgrange and at Knowth, pottery with grooved decoration makes its appearance in the later Neolithic. The closest comparisons for it are to be found in Later Neolithic contexts in Britain and it hints at the importance of continuing contact between the two islands. At Knowth, Grooved Ware was found to succeed habitation of round stake-built huts of the passage tomb builders but to predate a concentration of Beaker pottery. There, George Eogan and Helen Roche recently found a ritual structure similar to one identified at Newgrange. Located about 12m from the entrance to the eastern tomb in the great mound, it was defined by a circle of thirty-three post-pits which had contained thirty-five posts. Inside were four large pits defining a rectangle which almost filled the circle. The entrance faced east. The pits were generally either cylindrical or tapered, 50-80cm in diameter and 66cm-1.18m deep. The post-pits at the entrance and in the interior were larger. The pits were carefully backfilled after the posts which they had held were positioned. First sterile material was placed in the pit but in the immediate area of the posts, packing-stones along with earth and artefacts were put in in such a way as to be clearly segregated from the outer fill. The excavators speculated that bark may have been used to keep the inner and outer fill apart. The upper part of the pits was filled with a random mixture of earth, packing stones and habitation refuse. The unusual care taken with the filling enabled the builders to place the artefacts of the inner fill neatly and systematically about the posts in a manner which suggested that they were votive deposits. Additional deposits, also ritual, took place at the four internal post pits; they each had small extensions added on to contain flints, rounded stones, potsherds and in one instance a porcellanite axehead. Like the axehead, the good quality flint looks as if it had been imported from Co. Antrim. Animal bones among the votive material included cattle and pig. The excavators were tempted to compare the site with another near the Giant's Ring at Ballynahatty. Grooved Ware has been found at Lough Gur and at Longstone in Co. Tipperary, where a phase of Beaker and Grooved Ware succeeded a habitation level which contained Carrowkeel pottery.

Around the entrance to Newgrange and at Knowth, settlements with quantities of Beaker pottery were established. The Beaker phase was well underway by about 2500 BC. At Newgrange a remarkable series of ritual developments similar to the Grooved Ware structure at Knowth took place after the passage tomb had lapsed into disuse. Sometime, probably between about 2500 and 2300 BC, a great circle of posts was erected south east of the entrance (*Illus. 122*). It was 90m in diameter and defined by up to six concentric rows of pits. The outer circle had contained posts. Inside this was an arc of pits up to 1m deep and 1m wide which were lined with a daub of sterile clay. They had had fires lit within them in which animal bones were burnt; after this they had been back-filled. A second inner row of pits had contained a mixture of clay-lined examples and others which, despite their large size had contained posts. Finally there were three arcs of smaller pits

Illus. 122
An artist's impression of the great post-circle monument at Newgrange, Co. Meath. The Neolithic mound is in the foreground on the right.

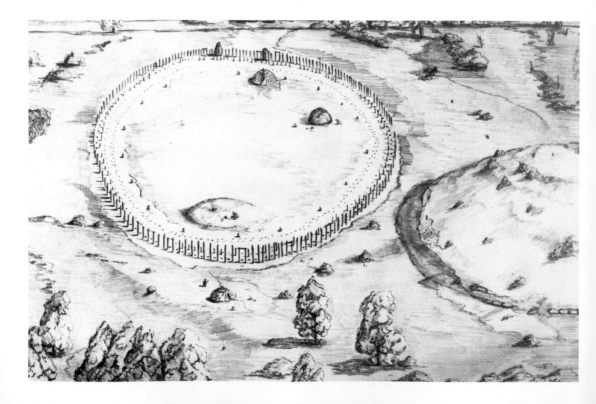

Illus. 123

Some typical Beaker objects:

a *beaker, Dalkey Island, Co. Dublin;*

b *wrist-bracer, stone, Carrowkeel, Co. Sligo (found below 2.5m of blanket bog peat);*

c *pointed knife, flint, Dalkey Island, Co. Dublin;*

d *barbed and tanged arrowhead, flint, Dalkey Island, Co. Dublin;*

e *hollow-based arrowhead, flint, Dalkey Island, Co. Dublin.*

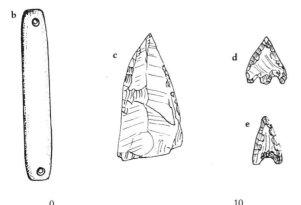

containing cremated animal bone. Within the circle was a habitation marked by stake-holes and flint-working associated with Grooved Ware and Beaker pottery; it seems to have been a temporary occupation site. It was clearly a ritual site and parallels may be found in Later Neolithic Britain where circles of pits have been identified as early features often succeeded by more permanent structures. The Newgrange pit-circle was succeeded by a stone circle, but not one superimposed on it. David Sweetman who excavated the site was able to establish that the great stone circle which was built around the passage tomb of Newgrange was the final major ritual construction there and probably dated to about 2000 BC. The burnt animal bone was difficult to identify but the presence of cattle, deer, pig, dog and sheep/goat were established. A larger and a smaller breed of dog were present. The identifiable charcoal from the site included hazel and ash, a piece of willow/poplar and also what may have been birch.

Some distance away, about 50m west of the passage tomb, Sweetman found another ritual site associated with Beaker pottery. This consisted of an arc of pits probably about 20m in diameter, succeeded by a post-built structure which may have been roofed. There was some Beaker pottery and flint associated with the site and a fragment of a stone bowl, but the excavator did not interpret it as a habitation. The post-built structure may have been a ritual site or assembly place. The fragmentary animal bones from the pits were mainly of pig with cattle present only in the material from one pit. At Knowth there were also Beaker burials in two of the satellite tombs.

Beaker Pottery

We have mentioned Beaker pottery a great deal already and it is time to explain a little about it. Around about 2500 BC this type of pottery appeared in Europe with vessels known from Poland to Iberia (*Illus. 123*). They are unmistakable in their shape: thin-rimmed, flat-bottomed, often with a sinuous profile and they are noticeably better made than much of the indigenous pottery with which they are often found. Over much of Europe, they occur in burials with a distinctive assemblage which includes tablets of finely-polished stone perforated for attachment to the wrist as an archer's bracer or guard against the blow of the bowstring when an arrow is released.

Accompanying these are flint barbed-and-tanged arrowheads and a particular form of button which suggests that a distinctive costume was associated with the assemblage. Occasionally, copper knife-daggers or trinkets are found. The classic burial is a single one. It was once thought that the Beaker folk constituted a distinctive group of essentially itinerant metalworkers who disseminated the ideas of metallurgy throughout the west.

This tends to be discounted nowadays and the pottery is thought to be a fashion adopted by the cosmopolitan rich and powerful everywhere. Beaker traits are thus an overlay on essentially continuing native traditions and Ireland may be a good example of this because the classic Beaker burial does not occur here. Instead, Beaker pottery occurs in a variety of contexts side by side with material of indigenous character and sometimes, as at Knowth in Co. Meath, a Beaker burial is placed inside an existing monument, in this case a small passage tomb. Mike Baillie has identified another period of successive seasons of poor growth in the oaks of the period at 2345 BC, a date which coincides roughly with a critical period of change and, despite healthy modern scepticism, the appearance of Beaker pottery does coincide roughly with those changes. (Incidentally, tephra has been found in Irish bog deposits, implicating a massive eruption of the volcano Hekla in Iceland in the cause of the climatic downturn.) The formation of bog on the uplands which begins to be a problem for settlement thereafter would have been encouraged by a period of more than usually wetter conditions but the trend to bog formation must have been longer-term and not sudden.

Animal Husbandry

At Newgrange and Dalkey Island there were settlements with Beaker pottery. At Newgrange there seems to have been a cluster of huts and while some of the occupation post-dated the circle of pits, it is likely that the users of Beaker pottery were associated also with the building of the ritual structures. Their settlement produced a significant corpus of animal bones which were studied in detail by Louise van Wijngaarden-Bakker of the University of Amsterdam to cast valuable light on the economy of the settlement. They also provide us with one of the first records of the domesticated horse, introduced into Ireland towards the end of the Neolithic. Cattle comprised 56.5% of the bones from the settlement and they were a fairly large breed, the cows standing 120-130cm at the shoulder – somewhat larger than those of Lough Gur which stood only 106-118cm. A bull or steer was estimated to stand about 137cm. The cattle were raised primarily for meat and not for dairying or traction. 55% reached the age of two-and-a half years and 20% reached the age of three years. Most beasts were slaughtered between two and three years old, the classic pattern of beef farming. The pig was significant also, represented by about 40% of the bones. Most were slaughtered at about two to two-and-a-half years of age and clearly made a significant contribution to the diet. About 3.5% of the bones were of sheep/goat. Dog bones indicated that some of the animals were quite old when they died which suggests that they were kept for guarding and herding duty and even as pets. There were at least five horses at Newgrange, three adult and two young animals. As the bones of horse do not occur in early Neolithic sites we have to conclude that their introduction is an example of yet another luxury import at this time. These were the first in a long line of noble animals which were to figure so greatly in Irish myth and legend down to the present day. Red deer were hunted but made only a minor contribution to the diet. It seems therefore that the grasslands which were in existence when the passage tomb was built perhaps five to seven hundred years before, remained the mainstay of the economy at Newgrange. The pigs were also important in the diet and might have grubbed for their food in the surviving areas of woodland. It has recently been argued by Charles Mount that the bone assemblage from Newgrange may not be typical of the pastoral economy of the time. He believes that the material may have been, in part, ritually deposited and thus be unrepresentative. The very high proportion of pig bones at later sites has been attributed to feasting. Whatever the interpretation, it is clear that the economy of the time was capable of providing the food and other animals present at the site. George Eogan believes that the various phases of activity in the Boyne Valley from the earliest Neolithic, through the passage tomb phase and the Beaker period were essentially exclusive – they represent episodes of successive and not necessarily related activity. However, the landscape seems not to have changed significantly in the locality since the tombs were built and this argues for stability of settlement and land management rather than dramatic change. Bronze Age burials are found just south of the Neolithic tombs along the south bank of the Boyne and the region must have been continuously occupied and farmed.

Wedge Tombs

In one area of activity, we can see strong continuity with older traditions. Some time in the later Neolithic, a new type of megalithic tomb developed – the wedge tomb. This is by far the most numerous type of tomb in Ireland. About four hundred and sixty five wedge tombs have been identified and their siting *(Illus. 124)* is very similar to the other megaliths which we have discussed. They occur singly in the landscape and there is little doubt that they reflect the settlement pattern of their builders. They

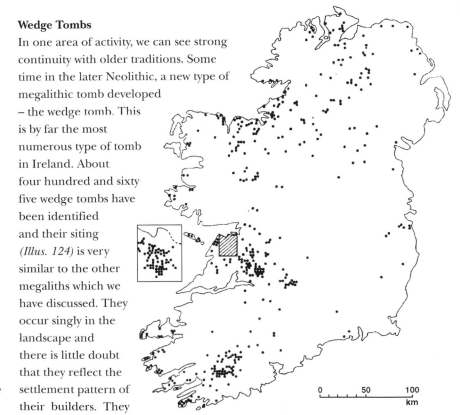

*Illus. 124
Distribution of wedge
tombs in Ireland.*

are fairly evenly distributed from the lowlands to heights of about 300m OD and apart from notable clusters which we shall see below, they are often found near other types of megalith. One such pairing is to be seen at Proleek near Dundalk in Co. Louth where the famous dolmen has a wedge tomb as its close neighbour. It does not follow that the two were in use at the same time, indeed it is unlikely to have been so. Wedge tombs are generally simple constructions consisting of a long burial gallery which tapers in plan from front to back. They tend to be higher at the front and the chamber is often paralleled by settings of stones set outside it in the cairn. The chambers are generally made of upright stones and roofed by lintels and normally contain cremations but unburned burials are occasionally found. A common form of cairn is roughly D-shaped with the entrance opening off the flat side but round mounds are also known. A number of examples have an antechamber. Of the twenty or so wedge tombs which have been excavated, eight have produced Beaker pottery and a couple have yielded finds which suggest that they continued in use well into the Bronze Age, arguably as late as about 1400-1200 BC.

Comparisons have been made between wedge tombs and a particular form of megalithic tomb in Brittany and it has been suggested that they represent an introduction from there, if not actually a new settlement of people from north-western France. This is now discounted. The origin of wedge tombs can be plausibly traced in the Irish megalithic tradition and it is unnecessary to canvass the idea of a further influx of new people to account for their appearance. The material found in the tombs is essentially that which we find on other sites. Wedge tombs are widely distributed along the western seaboard with a scatter in Ulster and a small number along the east coast. There are notable concentrations in West Cork, the uplands of west Tipperary and the shore of Donegal Bay – an area rich in megaliths since the appearance of the court tomb. An exceptional concentration occurs in the Burren in Co. Clare on what is now bare limestone pavement. There can be little doubt that the area once supported a substantial population which the late Ruaidhri de Valera thought might have been pastoralists exploiting the winter grazing; this is still a feature of the Burren today despite its forbidding appearance at first sight. We have already seen that a covering of soil existed under the cairn of the Poulnabrone portal tomb in the Neolithic, and there is some tentative evidence that a type of ancient field boundary termed 'mound walls' may date back to the period when the Burren wedge tombs were being built. These consist mainly of large slabs laid horizontally which preserve beneath them some of the ancient soil cover which may in part have been heaped up to form a low embankment on which the walls were built. The fences stand on pedestals of limestone less weathered than in the surrounding areas because they were protected by the wall and its soil base and this suggests that they are very ancient. In the western Burren at Ballyelly and Coolmeen at heights of up to 274m OD, walls of this type have been shown to predate later field enclosures which cross them. The wedge tombs of the Burren are distinctive because their construction is simplified by the easy availability of flat limestone slabs which enabled the builders to erect chambers with single stones forming the sides and roofs. It seems that the builders quarried and used the slabs right way up to judge from the weathering patterns on them.

THE FIRST METALLURGY

The wedge tombs of Cork and Kerry share a distribution pattern with the distinctive stone circles of the region. Ó Nualláin has argued that here the settlers who built the tombs and circles may have had a strong interest in the copper deposits of the area which were extensively mined in the Earlier Bronze Age. In recent excavations at the Toormore wedge tomb, a decorated copper axe and two pieces of copper were found at the entrance. The settlement at Newgrange also produced an axehead of copper and we can see that with the appearance of the Beaker pottery in Ireland as elsewhere, we are on the threshold of a metal-using society. We must consider what effect the changes in technology had on the landscape and what, if any, changes in population were ushered in during the period between the first tentative importation of copper trinkets and implements and the emergence of a full metal-using society that had mastered the suite of technologies of prospecting, mining and smelting ore as well as manufacturing and distributing the products.

Our understanding of this has been enriched by the discoveries made by Dr Billy O'Brien who has made a special study of early mining in Ireland. At Ross Island on Lough Leane near Killarney in Co. Kerry, there is a substantial stratum of Lower Carboniferous limestone rich in copper ore. This was mined in the eighteenth century and again on a large scale in the nineteenth century. Early accounts of the mining refer to 'Danes' mines' being found. These were thought to have been destroyed but happily some have been relocated and have proved to date to between about 2400 and 2000 BC. A significant deposit of spoil from the mines and an encampment where the ore was concentrated have also been found. Concentration of the ore was by 'cobbing' – that is hammering the rock to break it so as to separate the richer ore and discard the parent material. Slabs of stone used as anvils and stone hammers as well as crushed limestone were found there. Small pit furnaces in which the ore was smelted occurred on the site. The miners lived in post-built wooden huts; the bones of domestic animals, the refuse of their food, indicate that they were supported by an agricultural community. Beaker pottery – so far the remains of about twenty drinking cups – has been found within the campsite in clear association with the mining activity. The mines were worked by fire-setting to break up the rock which was further detached by hammering with mauls. These were large round stones collected from river beds nearby. A groove was carefully pecked around their girth to enable a twisted withy handle to be wound around them. Spoil was shovelled with ox shoulderblades, a form of tool used widely in Neolithic Europe. The Ross Island excavations, still in progress, have given us the first unequivocal association of Beaker pottery with very early mining activity and they have also provided us with a remarkable insight into the whole range of mining processes and into the social and economic infrastructure which supported it.

LITTLETON BOG, Co. TIPPERARY

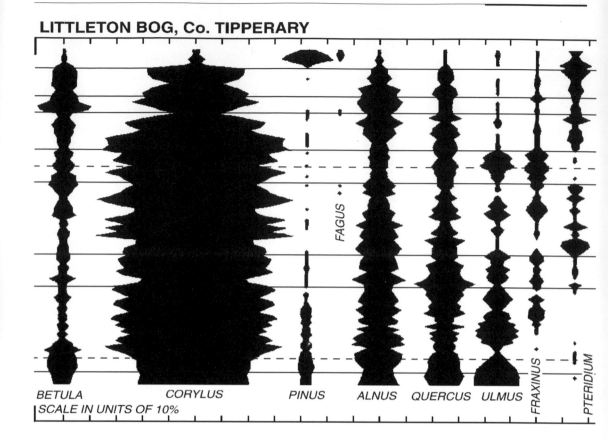

BETULA   CORYLUS   PINUS   ALNUS   QUERCUS   ULMUS   FRAXINUS   PTERIDIUM

FAGUS

SCALE IN UNITS OF 10%

A Record of Woodland Interference from Neolithic Times to the Present Day
Some thirty years ago Hilda Parkes (whose recent death was a great loss for pollen studies in Ireland) and author Frank Mitchell made a boring 8m deep in a raised bog near Littleton in Co. Tipperary; detailed pollen counts were made from the samples taken (*Illus. 125*). The pollens of heathers and rushes – which would have been growing on the bog surface – were omitted from the counts. The pollen diagram showed that the bog held a continuous record from the Woodgrange Interstadial 12,000 years ago until almost the present day and the bog was subsequently chosen as the type-site for the current warm stage, which is thus in Ireland called the Littletonian Warm Stage. The bog lies in a fertile area and its *Sphagnum*-peats provided a splendid record of the waxing and waning of agricultural activities in the vicinity of the bog.

Unfortunately the bulk of the fieldwork had been done before radiocarbon datings became generally available and the diagram was rather put aside. But in the succeeding thirty years a great number of radiocarbon datings have been produced, with dendrochronological studies becoming available to give a check on the dates. It has recently been recognised that wind currents carry volcanic ashes over long distances and that very thin sheets of ash were deposited on bog surfaces. The *ejecta* from different eruptions vary

*Illus. 125
Pollen-diagram from
Littleton Bog,
Co. Tipperary
showing a record of
vegetational
developments through
the past 6000 years
(5900 BP=elm
decline=3900 BC).*

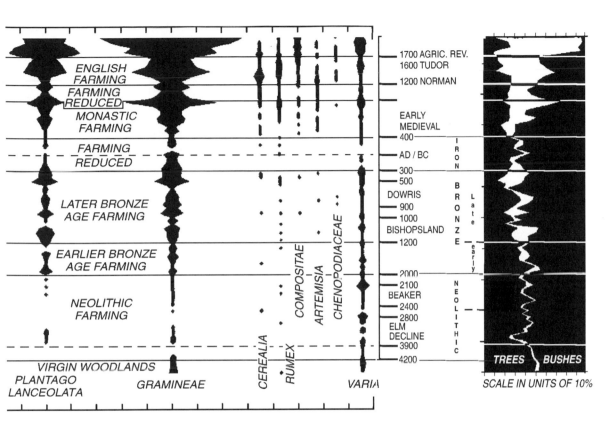

ENGLISH FARMING

FARMING REDUCED

MONASTIC FARMING

FARMING REDUCED

LATER BRONZE AGE FARMING

EARLIER BRONZE AGE FARMING

NEOLITHIC FARMING

VIRGIN WOODLANDS

PLANTAGO LANCEOLATA

GRAMINEAE

CEREALIA

RUMEX

COMPOSITAE

ARTEMISIA

CHENOPODIACEAE

VARIA

1700 AGRIC. REV.
1600 TUDOR
1200 NORMAN

EARLY MEDIEVAL
400
AD / BC
300
500
DOWRIS
900
1000
BISHOPSLAND
1200

2000
2100
BEAKER
2400
2800
ELM DECLINE
3900
4200

IRON

BRONZE (Late / early)

NEOLITHIC

TREES   BUSHES

SCALE IN UNITS OF 10%

slightly in chemical composition and it should be possible to trace ash layers in Irish raised bogs back to specific dated Iceland eruptions.

In recent years, many workers have switched their attention from peat to lake muds, which record rather a different picture. If farmers used fire as part of their clearance rotation, some charcoal will have blown onto the surface of the bogs. But a great deal of it may be washed by rain into rivers and so into lakes, or be carried by soil erosion directly into lakes. We can see that soil erosion took place, because often at a level where the pollen-record shows that there has been woodland clearance, the rate at which sediment accumulates in the lake shows an increase due to washed-in debris. A palaeomagnetic survey will also help to date the inflow. These features are interpreted as indicating that man's activities are disturbing the local vegetation.

Pollen studies have grown in numbers and precision and their palaeo-ecological interpretation becomes increasingly sophisticated. It has become clear that before man's disturbance of the woodlands began there was not a uniform tree cover over the whole of Ireland, but that there was considerable regional variation. The original native woodlands of Ireland reflected their location, the nature of the soil, exposure and many other factors. It is now also possible to trace patterns of farm activity indicating the ebb and flow of agricultural clearances and woodland regeneration. Thus it becomes possible, with reasonable certainty, to insert in the Littleton diagram interpretative information and, in particular, calendrical dates obtained at other sites.

The many diagrams available cannot be discussed here and rather than give numerous examples, Littleton Bog alone is discussed because of its very long record and its relatively central location in south-east Ireland.

Littleton Bog is (or was) a large raised bog complex, about 11km east of Thurles, at an altitude of 450m; the underlying rock is carboniferous limestone, the glacial deposits are calcareous till and the soils are grey brown podzolics with a wide range of uses. Mostly these formations are buried by bog. Bord na Móna began its exploitation for fuel in 1950, our visits were in 1954 and today the bog has virtually disappeared. The Board's officers kept an eye out for antiquities, but as the vast majority were brought to light by mechanical diggers, there was little reliable stratigraphical evidence. There were bronze implements, a wooden weaving-sword and a well preserved corpse, still fully clad. Numerous wooden trackways were intersected, some of which connected with farm laneways still in use.

The surrounding country has small stone castles (c.1450 AD), a Cistercian abbey (1183 AD), two small churches (c.1000 AD), a rich hoard of church treasure (deposited c.925 AD) and several raths (c.300-1000 AD). Down the ages the area has been densely settled. Before the farmers arrived, the area was covered by high forest of oak, elm and alder, with thickets of hazel and birch; some pine trees were scattered here and there and there was virtually no grassland. A short-lived phase of Neolithic clearance and farming had started in the vicinity, perhaps as early as 4200 BC, as in the north of the country; grass and bracken are recorded. The white channel up the centre of the right-hand column of the diagram (*Illus. 125*) shows the way the area of farming clearances oscillated with that of trees and bushes. Neolithic farming was of an alternating nature. At times elm returned in force, oak and alder regained ground and the clearance patches were overgrown.

About 2400 BC metal-using farmers settled at Littleton. We have already seen evidence of them at Fallahogy (p.158-159) when sickles first appeared. Farming later declined once more and elm and ash made some recovery. Then, at about 900 BC, there was a marked phase of renewal. Elm and ash were cleared away and evidence of farming rose to a higher level than ever before, as the Dowris phase of the Late Bronze Age opened (see p.221). As we shall see later, this was probably the time at which the plough, or at least a primitive type of it, the ard (*Illus. 136*) and more efficient socketed bronze tools were introduced into Ireland and much more effective tillage became possible.

Agriculture centred on grassland on the one hand and tillage on the other. Can these be separated in the pollen records? High values for grass, plantain and bracken are thought to indicate grassland; high values for cereals and for weeds associated with arable land in Ireland such as dock (*Rumex*), thistles (*Compositae*), sage (*Artemisia*) and goosefoot (*Chenopodiaceae*) are thought to indicate tillage. Thus in the diagram, do the sharp but short-lived rises in grass, plantain and bracken at about 900 BC indicate a sudden swing to grassland? Or does it merely mean that a new meadow was established quite close to and upwind from the point on the bog where the samples were taken? Similar sudden rises in these pollen types can be seen in other Irish pollen diagrams, but efforts to interpret the pollen record in agricultural terms can easily be carried too far.

We then see a definite revival in agriculture at about 500 BC and this probably indicates the arrival of new ideas; about this time we see some traces of influences from the Early Iron Age (Hallstatt) in the archaeological record. The most important Irish site, a crannog, is at Rathtinaun in Lough Gara (see p.230-231).

Gradually farming ebbed away and elm and ash bounced up once more. Pollen which may indicate arable land virtually disappeared and grass and its associates fell back to low levels. It is not easy to interpret the picture, but a falling-away of farming and expansion of secondary woodland is clearly indicated.

A new clearance, at about 300 BC announces the Iron Age as influences from the European La Tène Iron Age flooded into Ireland (see p.237-238). Iron begins to displace bronze as the metal in most common use and curvelinear designs appear in many different media. This remains one of the more obscure periods in Irish prehistory. It seems to have been a time of political disturbance, which interrupted farming activities.

A dramatic phase of woodland regeneration follows and this can be traced in almost every Irish pollen diagram that covers this period. It is possible that the climate may have worsened and that there was a drop in population numbers.

A new phase of intensive farming opens about 400 AD. The diagram shows a devastating clearing away of elm and ash, a removal from which they never seriously recover; hazel scrub is also attacked. Tillage is resumed and grasslands expand.

Though the Romans never invaded Ireland, knowledge of their way of life and of their agricultural techniques certainly penetrated the country and gave rise to intensification. It was probably at this time that ploughs armed with iron coulters (*Illus. 138*) came into Ireland and that tillage became both easier and more rewarding. The spread of Christianity in Ireland and the establishment of large monasteries with their own farmlands will have hastened the rise in agricultural efficiency.

A continuous record of pollen of sage (*Artemisia*) appears about 400 AD, and the increase of this weed may be associated with different agricultural practices. It made a similar appearance in the Burren area about 800 AD. The first pictorial representation of a plough fitted with a mouldboard is in a continental manuscript dated to about 650 AD. Use of this type of plough may have favoured sage.

However, this activity runs out of steam and alder, birch and hazel expand. Anglo-Norman farmers reached the area in the twelfth century and their tillage activities are shown by the rise in pollen of grass, arable weeds and cereals. This appears to have been a short Golden Age in Irish climate when cereals flourished.

This situation is then reversed and alder and hazel rise, though elm and ash have been reduced to a level so low that they cannot expand and indeed never do so again. It is tempting to correlate this reversal with the fall of temperature that is thought to have taken place early in the fourteenth century (*Illus. 154*). At the very end of the phase we see a further major clearance of the Irish woodlands, which set in with the initiation of Plantation schemes and see how even the hazel scrub that had for so long dominated the Irish countryside was seriously reduced at this time.

About 1700 AD the Agricultural revolution, which eliminated periods of fallow from the crop rotation cycle, reached Ireland and further wide clearance took place; even the hazel which had seen many ups and downs was swept away. The top samples with their traces of pine and beech, mark the end of the millennial periods of woodland reduction and the reversal can be attributed to the foundation of the Dublin Society (later the Royal Dublin Society) in 1730. The Society was largely composed of the wealthy estate-holders who emerged as the Agricultural Revolution (see p.328) developed. The Society offered *premia* for general tree-planting, though beech and other exotic trees had begun to be planted on large estates about 1700 AD. The pine which had been almost extinct in Ireland for thousands of years was planted widely.

FURTHER BOG DEVELOPMENT 5500 YEARS AGO

On the lowlands, reed-swamp and fen continued to invade and to obliterate open-water and where raised bogs had been established, they continued their slow growth both upwards and outwards, building up a *Sphagnum*-peat that was in general highly humified. Hammond's radiocarbon dates from the bogs of the Central Plain enable us to follow the lateral expansion (*Illus. 95a*). On the right-hand side of the figure we can see that before 3000 BC the *Sphagnum* community was beginning to develop on top of wood-fen-peat which, as waterlogging increased, had been creeping up the sloping surface of the underlying glacial deposit. At the left-hand side of the diagram, we see wood-fen-peat beginning to form at a still higher level about the same time. Here after 1000 years had gone by and about 50cm of this type of peat had been built up, its surface became too poor in nutrients to allow this kind of vegetation to continue to grow, and the *Sphagnum* community moved in and started to form highly humified peat. Thus throughout the Neolithic period, raised bogs surrounded by a rim of waterlogged fen-woods were invading and engulfing areas of low-lying forest.

When about 2500 BC at the end of the Neolithic we move on into the Bronze Age, such bog growth was continuing. The raised bogs were now creating an obstacle to man's wanderings in the countryside and trackways were constructed across them at strategic points. A trackway in a raised bog at Corlona in Co. Leitrim was examined by Dr van Zeist and one of its timbers was dated to 1450 BC which places it early in the Bronze Age. It lay in peat of varying composition and humification, but it was not possible to find positive evidence that the bog surface had got wetter (and softer) at the time it was constructed. For many years, the study and particularly the radiocarbon dating of early trackways in Ireland lagged much behind work in England, where Godwin and later Coles and others have done detailed work in the Somerset Levels. But as the continuing cutting-away of Irish boglands by Bord na Móna proceeded and many trackways were exposed and destroyed, in 1990 the Office of Public Works set up a Wetland Unit in University College, Dublin. So far the Unit has operated in only 20% of the area worked by Bord na Móna but it has recorded eleven hundred trackways or *toghers* of various methods of construction and other sites. Most of the trackways are of Bronze Age date, as later examples would have already been cut away. In the coming years, most discoveries will be Neolithic in age.

At Ballyscullion Bog (*Illus. 95b*), about 2250 BC, peat of varying humification, such as that in which the Corlona trackway lay, began to form. This was in contrast to the peat of uniformly high humification that had preceded it; a similar change at Fallahogy Bog was dated to about 2500 BC. Corresponding changes can be seen in other raised bogs and it is possible that this more rapid growth was due to a climatic deterioration causing an increase in wetness or a decrease in temperature or both.

At about the same time, profound changes were taking place on the uplands. The end-result was that over thousands of hectares which originally would have had a relatively well-drained soil with woodland and which in many areas would have been extensively cultivated by early farmers, the soils first degraded to peaty podzols and then became buried below thick layers of peat. Upland peat would certainly have started to form before 2000 BC and its invasion of new areas appears to have continued into the present millennium.

This changeover from mineral soil to peat can be well demonstrated at Goodland in Co. Antrim, where at an altitude of about 250m the bedrock is chalk. About 1m of sandy glacial material rested on the chalk and when first deposited this material must have had some content of calcium carbonate; today all traces of calcium carbonate have been removed by long-continued leaching. Early Littletonian woodlands developed in the area and as the soil formed under forest, there was some modest movement of iron downwards so that a layer about 50cm below the surface became enriched in iron giving rise to a brown podzolic soil. Sometime after 4000 BC, Neolithic farmers arrived in the area, cleared away the trees and proceeded to scratch the surface of the ground, initiating as they did so a new cycle of soil formation; Early Bronze Age folk continued the farming activities. Then, either because of continued disturbance of the ground encouraging leaching or because of deterioration in climate, podzolisation took place. Waterlogging of the soil followed and about eight hundred years later the wetter parts of the area had been smothered by invading rushes (*Juncus*). The sward of rushes gradually built up a thin layer of black amorphous vegetable debris or peat full of *Juncus* seeds and often crowded with charcoal fragments. Such a layer frequently develops where the soil has been cultivated and is known as *mor*; it is perhaps a version of a peaty podzol.

Mor is a very puzzling deposit and appears to develop at the level, immaterial of age, where agricultural land is giving way to blanket bog. Thus on Valencia Island, it formed in Neolithic times on the top of Bray.Head at 150m, where heathy grassland full of weeds was being overwhelmed by blanket bog about 5000 years ago. It formed again in the Late Bronze Age near St. Brendan's Well on the north side of the island at 30m, where grassland was giving way to heather-rich blanket bog about 2500 years ago. A detailed study of mor formation is long overdue as it must contain information about early agriculture and also about climatic change.

The surface of this peat was very low in inorganic nutrients and it was invaded, just as the lowland fen-peats had been invaded earlier, by the *Sphagnum* community which started to form a highly humified peat. As waterlogging enabled the rushes to spread, so the formation of peaty podzol expanded and gradually the ground became buried beneath a layer of peat which covered it like a blanket, initiating the formation of the so-called blanket bog which is now so widespread in Ireland (*Col. 23*).

The locations at which the ground first became sufficiently waterlogged to enable peaty podzol and then peat to form would have depended on the local topography. Therefore, just as with the raised bogs, peat formation would have expanded outwards from initial foci. There was no moment in time at which peat started to form everywhere the basal peaty podzols may be of very different ages at different points. There is no reason why basal layers younger than 1000 AD should not be found because if the blanket bogs had not been interfered with by man, it is quite possible that they might still be thickening and expanding at the present day. At St Brendan's Well on Valencia Island, crosses were erected perhaps around this time; their bases were presumably inserted into solid ground. During the ensuing nine hundred years peat has grown up around them to a thickness of 75cm (*Illus. 126*).

*Illus. 126
Peat-buried cross,
Valencia Island,
Co. Kerry.
Here, a knoll of rock
has become
progressively buried
by bog, graphically
illustrating the
continuing growth of
peat. A well and
crosses were set up
here in honour of St.
Brendan, possibly
about 800 AD. Since
then 75cm of peat has
grown up around the
cross in the
foreground. The
highest point on the
knoll lies behind the
cross and another
slab stands there. All
the rock is now
covered by heath
vegetation.*

However, for thousands of years man has grazed his animals on the blanket bogs, has burned the vegetation to stimulate growth and has cut the peat for fuel or dug it away to reclaim agricultural land. We can show that the thickness of some blanket bog has been built up by 10cm during the last 250 years, but we have no record of how the margins have behaved.

We can say 'thousands of years' because of the work that is being done by Seamus Caulfield in north-west Mayo, where blanket bog has a very wide extent at the present day. In early Littletonian time, forest development in this area seems to have paralleled that in the rest of the country, except that elm was rarer. A pine stump at Bellonaboy, rooted in mineral soil and dated to 5150 BC, goes back to the time when the climax woodlands were developing.

Neolithic man appears to have been established before 3000 BC in the Behy area, to judge by the presence of court tombs. Some of the tombs and field walls were buried by blanket bog, but it is by no means clear that tombs and walls are contemporary (*Col. 29*). Similar walls, also sitting on mineral soil appear in the Belderg valley and here Caulfield has revealed a very complex series of features, all again buried by blanket bog. Neolithic pottery and flint implements are found on the mineral soil and there must have been some forest clearance. Blanket bog peat then started to form, but once a thin layer had been laid down, its surface was invaded by secondary woodland, with large trees of both oak and pine. A pine stump, whose roots were clearly separated from the mineral soil by a thin layer of peat, was dated to the end of the Neolithic Period and a similar oak was dated to shortly before 2000 BC. At Bellonaboy in Co. Mayo, a pine stump sitting on 20cm of basal peat was dated to before 2500 BC. The modern visitor to this now bleak and treeless area has to recognise that not only was it clothed in high virgin forests at 5000 BC, but that after those woods had been damaged by early Neolithic man, the climate was still good enough at 2000 BC for secondary woodland of tall well-grown pines and oaks to re-establish itself at the end of the Neolithic. If man's influence was removed, trees would return again to the areas where mineral soil is exposed although they would be slow to invade the bog surface.

Around 1400 BC, well into the Bronze Age, man returned to Belderg where blanket bog had now developed on an extensive scale, though the peat perhaps was not as yet very thick. There is a vein of copper ore in a nearby cliff and this may have been the lure that brought man back to a site that was by now much less attractive from the agricultural point of view. A house, 10m in diameter with a drystone wall and post-holes, produced saddle querns and rubbers; a charred block of wood within the house was dated to around 1400 BC. Nearby there were further stone walls; these started on mineral soil but continued on out into the blanket bog which surrounded the site where they rested on peat. Oak stakes built into the wall extended down into the peat and where the wall ended, a line of stakes continued into the bog; the stakes were dated to about the same time. Subsequently, the whole site had been deeply buried by peat and this had protected some remarkable features of the site: criss-crossing dark marks in the subsoil, interpreted as plough marks or marks of an ard, the more primitive fore-runner of the true plough (*Illus. 136*), and cultivation-ridges or lazy-beds. If the modern title is taken to imply lack of energy and enterprise on the part of the farmer who employs this system, it is a complete misnomer. The building-up of drier ridges separated by trenches to drain off the surface water gives an efficient method of cultivating soils with poor natural drainage. The Irish name *iomaire* emphasises the importance of the ridge.

The field evidence suggests that the house is younger than the cultivation ridges, and therefore the age of the latter may lie between the later Neolithic occupation of the site, starting perhaps at 2500 BC and the building of the house about 1400 BC. Whichever end of the range we favour, it is clear that this cultivation method is of high antiquity in Ireland. What of the plough marks? Ard marks on chalk soils in Wiltshire go back to more than 2880 BC and there is also evidence of early use of the ard in northern Europe. Therefore, there is no chronological reason why the ard should not have been in use in Mayo at an early date. However, the very stony nature of the soils there, with consequent constant damage to the share of the ard, would seem to make its use hardly worthwhile. It is of course possible that if the area to be worked by an ard was first dug over with spades and the large stones picked off by children, the ard would then run easily through the loosened soil.

As we have seen nearby at Ballyglass, a court tomb had been built on the site of a large rectangular wooden house dated to c. 3160 BC (recalibrated) and there can be no doubt that this area, which today is so desolate and so lacking in human inhabitants, had considerable settlement in Neolithic time.

At Bunnyconnellon, also in Co. Mayo, on the north-west slopes of the Ox Mountains, at an altitude of about 100m, Michael Herity has revealed extensive lazy-beds by digging away the overlying blanket peat. At this site, the base of the peat was dated to 1650 BC, although on the coast nearby bog formation had started much earlier. There was a concentration of lazy-beds on a nearby knoll and a pollen-diagram suggested that these were in use around 800 BC. The primary soil on the knoll gave clear indications of strong podzolisation which means that it cannot have had a high fertility. What compelled Bronze Age people to occupy an area of poor climate and poor soils requires some explanation. The date is around 100 years earlier than that taken for the general expansion of agriculture that accompanied the Dowris Period of Bronze Age prosperity, but population pressures may have been building up. Agricultural pollen declines in value in the pollen-diagram, but it rises strongly again at several higher levels. Looking at the barren blanket bog landscape today, it is hard to imagine why earlier people could have chosen to live there.

If we picture that the climatic optimum was a time of relatively continental climate with warmer summers and fewer rain days, then we can envisage any subsequent deterioration as involving falling temperatures, more rain days and lower evaporation rates generally. Where raised bogs already existed their rate of upward growth would have been speeded up and the soils generally would have become loaded with an increased content of water; raised bogs would have expanded still further laterally and the formation of blanket bogs would have been encouraged.

There is some evidence, as we have seen, that between 2550 BC and 2250 BC, the type of peat being formed in the raised bogs began to change, with a peat that was of uniformly high humification giving way to a peat of varying humification. In south-west Ireland, a pine stump was found rooted in mineral soil and buried by blanket bog on the slopes of Carrantoohill in Co. Kerry, at 250m, another in eastern Ireland was in a similar position on the slopes of Kippure in Co. Dublin at 730m and in the west, tree stumps were discovered on thin blanket peat at Belderg in Co. Mayo; all had ages between about 3000 and 2500 BC. All this evidence adds up to suggest that climate did alter in the centuries preceding 2000 BC and that the change enabled raised bogs to grow more quickly and blanket bogs to start to form throughout the country. As these bogs spread, they gradually covered great areas that had been farmed by prehistoric peoples. There is circumstantial evidence that some blanket bogs may have been established in Mayo before Neolithic man arrived there. We have tombs on the north coast between Downpatrick Head and Belderg and again on the east shores of Broad Haven, but in between there is a blank. Was this area already covered by bog?

It is tempting to think that there was a deterioration of climate which led inevitably to the development of blanket bog wherever a critical threshold was passed and that the part that man played was only a secondary one in that his agricultural activities had made the soil particularly susceptible to podzolisation and waterlogging. It would be nice to know whether man had abandoned the former farm areas after exhausting the soil before peat had started to form, or whether he was forcibly driven out when the soil became waterlogged to the point that it was impossible to cultivate it. Michael Conry, who has been studying the soils of Ireland for many years, has shown that iron-pan formation followed directly as a result of peat growth and he suggests that blanket-peat development was initiated as a result of climatic changes rather than waterlogging caused by pre-existing iron-pan. He further suggests that after the growth of peat had begun, reducing conditions in the mineral layer mobilised the iron and deposited it lower down as a thin wavy pan enriched in iron.

Whatever happened, the upland soils changed drastically as agricultural areas gave way to blanket bog. When work, still to be done, enables us to draw a map of the soils of Neolithic Ireland, it will differ substantially both from the sketch-map of the first Irish soils (*Illus. 72*) and from the sketch-map of Irish soils today (*Illus. 155*). As far as prehistoric man was concerned, great areas of agricultural land on the uplands in the east and at low levels in the west must have been abandoned, while farming continued in other areas.

If we take two limestone areas which were intensively occupied in Neolithic and Early Bronze Age times, lying in the same longitude but at different elevations, we can see this exemplified. The low hills (alt. 120m) around Lough Gur in Co. Limerick were not buried by peat; the outlines of the Neolithic houses there can still be seen above ground, the sod layer is full of prehistoric pottery and agriculture still goes on. The higher hills (alt. 250m) at Carrowkeel in Co. Sligo were covered by peat which has built up to a depth of 250cm and partly buries the cairns of the passage tomb cemetery. Today, men cut the peat for fuel and sheep graze on the blanket bog, but that is all. People must have moved from the higher land to the lowlands, but the archaeological story is not yet able to tell us whether the refugees endeavoured to take farmland by force from those already occupying the better land or whether they contented themselves by clearing further woodland and scrub.

Today, blanket bog is extensively developed wherever annual rainfall in excess of 1250mm per annum causes waterlogging of the ground (*Illus. 71*). Therefore, in much of the west of Ireland the blanket bog runs down to sea level, and even below it, giving great stretches of country buried by peat. This is interrupted only where slopes are steep and, as we have seen, below much of the peat there is a layer of tree stumps to indicate the former extent of forest (*Illus. 76*). Away from the west coast, it is only on higher ground that rainfall rises to 1250mm and the blanket bog is confined to hill-tops and upper slopes.

The blanket bog areas give an impression of dreary uniformity covered by a sheet of bog vegetation pierced only by occasional rocky outcrops or lakes. But the underlying substratum has its own minor relief, rising into elevations and sinking into hollows. In many of the hollows, sediment had accumulated since the opening of the Littletonian Warm Stage and this was the case at Emlaghlea in Co. Kerry. This site was examined by Professor Jessen during his programme of work in Ireland and part of Jessen's section is reproduced in Illus. 95c. The early peat, which was a wood-fen-peat, can be seen at the base of the right-hand end of the section.

The fen surface in its final stages seems to have become relatively dry because pine and birch were able to grow freely on it. Up to this point, the formation of the peat had been controlled by surface water and by ground water and the ridge of higher ground to the left had been bare of peat and perhaps under cultivation. Then some change took place and the oligotrophic plants of the bog community – which need to be nourished only by rainwater – invaded the whole area and began to bury it below blanket bog. At Slieve Gallion in Co. Tyrone, a similar change was dated to 2665 BC.

Today, we tend to draw an arbitrary distinction between raised bog on the one hand and blanket bog on the other, but the plants of which both are composed are essentially the same though the proportions they occupy in the various communities are rather different. Typical raised bog is found where the topography of the ground can bring about waterlogging even though the rainfall is below 1250mm per annum (and can be as low as 750mm p.a.). The additional water is provided either by ground water filling a closed basin or by drainage water being concentrated by a slope. Fen vegetation flourishes and the raised bog plants come in as soon as the fen-peat has blanketed off the soil nutrients. The raised bog, therefore is always surrounded by a rim of fen where the necessary waterlogging of the ground is taking place. If the lateral advance of the fen is slow, then lateral growth of the raised bog must be slow. But there is no corresponding limitation on upward growth and the bog centre grows upwards into a domed form which is dominated by *Sphagnum*.

In the blanket bog regions with rainfall above 1250mm (*Col. 23*), the ground is of necessity waterlogged – except on steep rocky slopes – and the ombrogenous vegetation can establish itself everywhere. Neither lateral nor upward growth is restricted and peat forms a layer of relatively uniform thickness. The surface vegetation carries some *Sphagnum* hummocks and there can also be pools, but on the whole the low-growing *Sphagnum* is largely concealed by the taller cotton-grass (*Eriophorum vaginatum*), purple moor-grass (*Molinia caerulea*), bog-rush (*Schoenus nigricans*) and white beak-sedge (*Rhynchospora alba*). Among the heathers, *Calluna vulgaris* and *Erica tetralix* are widely distributed, while in the west of the country some of the rarer heathers find their last refuge on the blanket peat.

Peat formed in this way is seen at Emlaghlea where the top of the bog is formed of almost 2m of blanket bog peat (*Illus. 95c*). The peat was dominated by remains of *Molinia* and fibres of both species of cotton-grass, *E. angustfolium* as well as *E. vaginatum*; twigs of *Calluna* and *Myrica gale* were also common. The bog-myrtle (*Myrica*) is widely distributed on the western blanket bogs and it alone of the bog plants can supplement its nitrogen intake by means of symbiotic nitrogen-capturing bacteria living in nodules on its roots, in just the way that clovers and other legumes do in grassland. Bog-myrtle has a rather less fortunate distinction in that its pollen is very like that of hazel and is often confused with it in pollen counts from such peats.

Where the surface of the ground below the blanket bog is undulating and there are some relatively level areas, there will be little lateral run-off. Here, the peat may thicken and the bog surface will rise into a dome, mimicking the dome of the raised bog.

Though its ash content will be higher than that of raised-bog peat, blanket bog also forms a useful fuel and was formerly extensively cut away. Where the underlying topography is irregular, outliers of peat may be left in precarious positions (*Col. 26*).

The human population was not the only one to be affected by the expansion of blanket bog; plants and animals also had to adjust. Today, the country between Roundstone and Clifden in Co. Galway carries a lake-studded area of blanket bog with relict stations for rare heathers, such as *Erica mackaiana* and *E. erigena*, with St. Dabeoc's heath (*Daboecia cantabrica*) growing on rocky outcrops protruding through the bog. At the end of the Ice Age, this was an area of ice-scoured rock with innumerable ponds in the hollows. In the early Littletonian Warm Stage, the area was wooded and the ponds gradually filled with mud and fen-peat containing seeds and pollen from the surrounding area. Professor Jessen did a lot of work here and was able to show that when the mud was forming, the surrounding countryside was wooded and that *E. mackaiana* was growing in the woods in the same way that it grows in its main centre of north-west Spain today. It seems almost incredible that this plant, which was presumably already struggling for existence at the limit of its ecological tolerance, should have been able to make the drastic change in habitat from shaded forest floor to open blanket bog and still survive as it does – barely – in Ireland today.

At first, the discharge of excessive rain from the vegetation of the blanket of peat seems to have been by sheet-flooding rather than by the development of drainage runnels. Like the peat in raised bogs, a section through blanket bog often shows highly humified peat below and fresher peat above. If the peat was developing on an undulating slope, the weight of the thickness of peat on a steep slope might overcome the strength of the peat; the vegetation-mat would tear, the lower peat would undergo a thixotropic reversal to the liquid state and would flow out from under the upper fibrous peat. Such a flow could become catastrophic and would rush downslope carrying floes of vegetation with it. Such bog-bursts can be massive, flowing for a long distance and causing damage to property. Many more are on a small scale, flowing no more than a short distance and leaving a minor gutter in their wake (*Illus. 127a, b*).

Illus. 127a
General view from the south, of a bog flow on the side of a Wicklow mountain.

After discharge, peat growth invades the stripped area and as time goes by the wound is healed, but usually a tell-tale scar remains. Scanning a peat covered hillside, it is often easy to see that bursting is probably a regular feature of peat development. If sections through the peat are inspected, clearly-defined layers may be seen where peat and mineral soil are closely intermixed (*Illus. 128*). Such layers indicate the former passage of a bog-burst.

However, in many upland areas, the blanket bog is being stripped away by channelling. If the peat became drier and could no longer liquify, then the excess run-off might be carried by erosion-channels Today, a complicated mosaic presents itself. In one place, deep channels are beginning to dissect a still continuous peat cover; in a second place, strips of mineral soil are separated by islands or haggs of peat; while in a third place, mineral soil is dominant, with its surface broken only by a few isolated mounds of surviving peat (*Illus. 129*).

Illus. 127b
View from the south-west, of the southern branch of this flow showing also marginal ridge and border of an earlier flow.

This natural erosion may have been due to some climatic drying. It seems unlikely that peat would continue to form after the bog surface had been broken. We have seen that around 1700 AD, pine was reintroduced and exotic trees were brought in for plantations. We find the pollen of these trees in the top layers of some blanket bogs, which must have continued to grow after that date. Traces of industrial soot also indicate late growth.

ridge
→

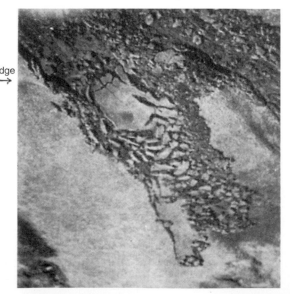

The recent dramatic and catastrophic acceleration of the erosion is entirely due to man. If this is not halted immediately, vast areas of western Ireland now covered by blanket bog, will be turned into rocky deserts. In many areas, grazing pressures have long been too high and the plant cover has struggled against repeated burnings; where the plant cover was broken, erosion of the peat began. In the mid 1980s, in a well-meaning effort to maintain a reasonable income for western hill-farmers, the European

Union introduced a system of headage-payments which effectively meant that the more grazing animals you had, the more money you got. Sheep numbers exploded. Before this, it was accepted that in winter to avoid over-grazing of the blanket bog surface, sheep had to be moved from the upland bogs to alternative lowland pastures. The pastures could not accommodate the increased numbers of sheep and so the farmers began to leave the sheep on the hills and carry feedstuffs up to them. This was the beginning of the calamity.

The plant cover was progressively destroyed, the sheep tramped the underlying peat into a greasy paste, vulnerable to erosion by rain, and soon bare rock began to appear (*Col. 52*). Streams and local water-supplies began to be contaminated by particles of peat and sheep-droppings. The point from which recovery is possible may already have been passed, but unless the overgrazing is halted immediately vast areas of the west will come to resemble the soilless areas of the Burren.

Illus. 128
Valencia Island,
Co. Kerry.
The lens of layered peat and sand at the top of the section behind the ranging rod was deposited from a surface flash-flow. The stone projecting from the peat face is part of a damaged Bronze Age trackway; a displaced stone lies on top of the peat.

Illus. 129
Tonelagee, Co. Wicklow. Blanket bog is being eroded away at an altitude of 530m.

THE EARLIER BRONZE AGE

Bronze Age Mining

The few copper objects in the Late Neolithic, because of their rarity, probably established an association between metal objects and prestige, but their appearance does not constitute the beginnings of what we might call the Bronze Age. It was not until metal was mined and fabricated on a substantial scale and we can begin to see the new material taking its place regularly in the tool kit, that we can speak of Ireland entering the new age. We must not however confuse the adoption of a technology with a population change of significance, although it is quite likely that there was some migration of specialists in the centuries between 2500 and 2000 BC, when the technology of mining metals was fully established in Ireland, as we have seen at the Ross Island mines. The Earlier Bronze Age saw the exploitation of the extensive copper deposits of the peninsulas of west Cork and Kerry which may well have produced a surplus of metal and so enabled trade in the commodity to take place. At Mount Gabriel near Schull in Co. Cork, over thirty small mines tunnel for short distances into the Old Red Sandstone. The fuel used in fire-setting at one of the mines included hazel (47.6%), oak (38.7%), ash (8.1%), alder (2.8%), willow (1.9%) and birch (0.7%). In addition, there were chips of pine probably used to make torches for lighting the interior. By weight, oak seems to have been the most important and the fuel may have been collected from scrub woodland growing in the vicinity of the mines. It was not possible to relate the phase of mining accurately to pollen analysis of deposits in a small peat basin nearby. However, it seems that open heathland and grassland prevailed with diminished mixed woodland nearby. The demand for fuel over the period of about 200 years when the mines seem to have been in use may have been as much as 15,000 tonnes; this potentially heavy attack on adjacent woodlands is not reflected in any marked decline in tree pollens. Could fuel have been hauled up the mountain to the mines? The Mount Gabriel mines were in production at the height of the Earlier Bronze Age industry between about 1700 and 1500 BC. After the mines fell into disuse, the area was covered by blanket bog.

Metalworking

Laurence Flanagan has calculated that about 2500 tonnes of dry fuel were needed to smelt a tonne of ore to produce usable metal. He thought this was about the equivalent of a hundred mature oaks which had to be felled, logged and converted to charcoal. For obvious practical reasons, therefore, the centres of smelting were at some distance from the mine in places where fuel was abundant. The first and most lasting effect on the landscape of the new metal technology was the consumption of woodlands by the smelting furnaces. The copper that was produced was converted into simple cakes or round ingots and was then available for casting in moulds. The earliest metal objects produced in Ireland were of copper and cast in open stone moulds. Some examples still show the bubbles which formed on their upper surfaces when the molten metal was cooling and it was a matter of chance if some naturally-occurring impurities hardened the metal. Axeheads were mounted like their stone counterparts in holes cut in wooden shafts. It was not until after 2000 BC that alloying the metal with tin to produce a true alloy – bronze – became common, giving rise to much more durable implements. While tin is occasionally found in alluvial deposits in Ireland in very small quantities, it is very likely that it was imported, almost certainly from Cornwall where it was mined throughout the last 4000 years.

The products of the foundries were widely distributed and Flanagan has painstakingly established patterns of distribution of axeheads cast in the same matrix. Many stone moulds of the period are known and others were inferred by the comparison of axe profiles. Even if we multiply many times over the surviving Earlier Bronze Age axeheads – about two thousand are known – to approximate the original total, production must have been modest and axeheads would have been owned by the few. Therefore, we cannot conceive of a renewed attack on the remaining forests led by woodsmen wielding efficient mass-produced bronze axeheads; many hundreds of years were to pass before metal implements became widespread throughout society and replaced stone as the material of everyday tools. Some axeheads were highly decorated and said much about the prestige of the owner. One axehead was found in a bog at Brockagh in Co. Kildare; it was in the leather scabbard provided for it when it was dismounted from its wooden haft.

Axeheads of the Earlier Bronze Age are widely distributed throughout Ireland and many have been found in hoards (caches of two or more artefacts, deliberately concealed) or in wetlands where they may have been ritually deposited. In this way, they are like the earliest gold ornaments of the Bronze Age – the gold *lunulae* (collars) and discs of sheet gold – many of which were concealed in hoards or, in the case of lunulae, deposited in watery places which subsequently became bogs. We may suspect that some climatic deterioration causing slightly wetter conditions combined with the troublesome expansion of bog on both the lowlands and highlands at this time encouraged an interest in rituals connected with lakes, marshes and rivers. The gold was probably obtained from placer deposits in streams of which the Goldmines River at Croghan Kinsella in Co. Wicklow was one identified source. A new programme of gold analysis holds out the hope that other Irish gold sources will be identified as contributing to the industries of the Earlier Bronze Age.

The growth of bogs to impede communications prompted the construction of wooden causeways already in Late Neolithic times and throughout the Bronze Age there is a considerable increase in bog-road building to keep connections open between useful areas of land. Mike Baillie has identified, using tree-ring dating, a peak of bog-causeway building and lakeside settlement at 1520-1480 BC. Barry Raftery has excavated an important series of trackways of packed brushwood and later tracks, towards 1200 BC, incorporating panels of woven hurdles on Corlea and Derryoghil bogs in Co. Longford (*Col. 30*). The deterioration of large tracts of upland once supporting a large population in Neolithic times will have increased the pressure on the available productive soils though the diminishing stock of good land and will have encouraged the taking-in of more and more wasteland and the clearance of woodland. But once again we cannot speak of a uniform advance of bog, as there were periods when the surface dried out sufficiently for oaks to grow on the peat. The climatic downturn, centred on the year 1628 BC, manifests itself in a sequence of poor growth rings in oaks and these may be attributable to increased rainfall and poor drainage on the bog surfaces affecting the trees which had managed to establish themselves there during more favourable periods.

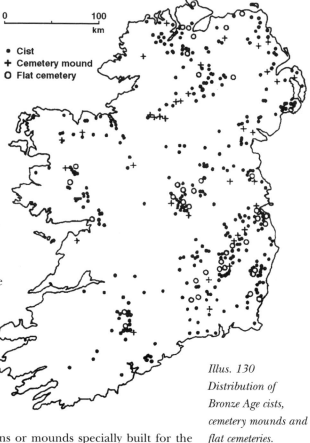

* Cist
+ Cemetery mound
O Flat cemetery

Burials

The wedge tomb and stone circle form part of the very rich pattern of Earlier Bronze Age ritual activity in the period from about 2000 to about 1200 BC. Single burials became common but the communal tradition of multiple burial was still represented not only by the continued use of wedge tombs but also by the interment of more than one individual in graves and by the clustering of their graves into small cemeteries. Burials were placed either in pits or in cists constructed in the ground and often grouped in flat cemeteries, in cairns or mounds specially built for the purpose or in the tumuli of pre-existing megalithic tombs (*Illus. 130*). Occasionally, a Bronze-Age burial was intruded into the chamber of a Neolithic tomb. There seems to have been some differentiation in the status of those buried; the construction of a large cist, the choice of accompanying goods placed with the dead

*Illus. 130
Distribution of
Bronze Age cists,
cemetery mounds and
flat cemeteries.*

*Illus. 131
A typical crouched
burial in a cist grave,
Clonickilvant,
Co. Westmeath.
A 'Food Vessel' is
placed in front of the
face. Earlier Bronze
Age.*

and perhaps even the position within the cemetery may mark the grave of a person of higher status. Cist graves, because of their structure, have been found in substantial numbers (*Illus. 131*); well over six hundred have come to light to date. Pit burials have been recorded in smaller numbers because they are most often only identified when some other discovery signals the presence of a cemetery. Even allowing for what may have been destroyed, the cemeteries so far documented do not account for the whole population and other forms of burial or disposal were practised which left little or no trace in the landscape.

Children are under-represented in Earlier Bronze Age cemeteries and adult males are probably present in numbers disproportionate to their composition of the population. This may be due to the higher visibility of the graves of those of high status. Gabriel Cooney and Eoin Grogan have argued that a youth buried in the Earlier Bronze Age cemetery raised on top of the passage tomb at Tara (*Illus. 132*) and accompanied by luxury objects including a necklace of faience beads, gained his status by heredity and hardly by his own adolescent achievements. A preoccupation with status seems to be reflected in the metal artefacts of the time A particular form of curved implement, the so-called *halberd*, may have been an emblem of rank of some kind and the gold ornaments which we have mentioned may also have been attributes of high status. Little of this metal finds its way into burials although daggers, elaborate stone battle-axes and, later, razors and knives are attributes of male burials in the period.

Cemetery cairns and reused tumuli mark some of the burial places in the landscape. Some Earlier Bronze Age graves were surrounded by ring-ditches, others were associated with standing stones. Wooden markers may have existed at some sites but this has not been demonstrated. In the midlands, prominent gravel ridges

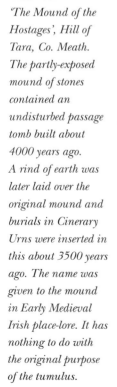

Illus. 132
'The Mound of the Hostages', Hill of Tara, Co. Meath. The partly-exposed mound of stones contained an undisturbed passage tomb built about 4000 years ago. A rind of earth was later laid over the original mound and burials in Cinerary Urns were inserted in this about 3500 years ago. The name was given to the mound in Early Medieval Irish place-lore. It has nothing to do with the original purpose of the tumulus.

were often the sites of Earlier Bronze Age burial. An apparently isolated cist grave near Bagenalstown at Sliguff in Co. Carlow, occurred in an area rich in small mounds, ring-ditches and the like visible only to aerial photography. What we have in the burial record, therefore, represents only a tiny fragment of the whole picture.

Burial Pottery and Other Grave Goods

Many graves contain pots often excavated intact. In very broad terms, we can trace a sequence where highly ornamented bowls accompanied crouched unburnt burials (from about 2000 to about 1600 BC). A related pot form of a more vase shape, became fashionable during this phase and often accompanied cremated bones. Other cremations were sometimes placed in enlarged pots (urns) which themselves show a number of changes of style. A new fashion of urn decorated with cordons or applied bands appears about 1400 BC. There is no generalised sequence from unburned burial to cremation; both rites occur side by side in the same cemeteries and both have been found within the one grave. Even urn-burials may contain the remains of more than a single individual. The bowls and vases which accompanied burials are still often referred to as Food Vessels on the assumption that they once held food or drink to sustain the deceased in afterlife. Both urns and Food Vessels share to some degree or another affinities with contemporary pottery styles in Britain (*Illus. 133*). Throughout much of the Bronze Age, Ireland and Britain remained largely in step in terms of burial practices, metalworking traditions and probably settlement types. We cannot be certain if the similarities are the result of continued close contact by way of trade or if they imply some migration to and from Britain. After about 1400 BC, the classic urn tradition appears to have died out and burials – often just token amounts of cremated bone – accompanied by coarse plain pottery, or sometimes contained in such vessels, seem to continue the earlier traditions in a modified form. The absence of significant accompanying artefacts has suggested to some that the ritual disposal of valuable tools and weapons in rivers and other wetlands may have replaced the burial of prestige goods with the departed of high social standing. It has been remarked that the number of hoards tends to increase in periods when the burial record becomes impoverished. These are significant issues which, as we shall see below, have an important bearing on landscape history.

Cemeteries of barrows or mounds containing burials are being documented in increasing numbers; Carrowjames in Co. Mayo and Cush in Co. Limerick are examples. Surveys are revealing remarkable concentrations of barrows and an important cluster has recently been identified at Mitchellsdown North in Co. Limerick. The siting of barrows on the flood plains of rivers in the north Munster region and the occasional placement of them on opposite banks suggests that they may belong to small territorial entities extending from the river banks. The archaeological survey of Co. Louth has revealed a rich variety of types of barrow; some have surrounding ditches, some have large tumuli and others are small. Siting of barrows varies greatly with some occurring in lowlands and others having prominent upland locations. A cluster of barrows at Summerhill in Co. Louth has, with the exception of a small cairn, been ploughed out. Aerial photography

Illus. 133
Some typical Food
Vessel objects and one
Cinerary Urn:
a *bowl-form vessel,*
Mount Stewart,
Co. Down;
b *Cinerary Urn,*
Burgage Mor,
Co. Wicklow;
c *Food Vesel of vase*
form, Ballon,
Co. Carlow;
d *battle-axe, stone,*
Bann Valley;
e *flat decorated axe,*
bronze, Scrabo
Hill, Co. Down;
f *flanged axe,*
bronze, no locality.

reveals a succession of smaller barrows and other larger ones in the vicinity. At Collon in Co. Louth, three different types of barrows form an alignment on a hilltop. The variation of type suggests that the site had been used for burial over a substantial period. Unclassified or unclassifiable round mounds and cairns are widespread throughout Ireland – about six thousand have been listed so far – and only with excavation will we be able to identify and date them. The abandonment of the practice of depositing metal artefacts in graves has the effect of making it difficult to relate changes in the wider archaeological record with the sequence of burials. The record from cemeteries, single graves, wedge tombs and later barrow clusters is sufficient to indicate a fairly general settlement of the island in the

Earlier Bronze Age – a surmise supported by the wide distribution of typical artefacts of the period.

Tools and Weapons

At an advanced stage in the Earlier Bronze Age, new weapons – the so-called rapier (a greatly elongated dagger) and the spearhead – make their appearance. The spear in theory is relatively cheap; a small investment in metal creates the business end of a long wooden shaft to produce a weapon which, in the form of the stabbing spear rather than the javelin for throwing, is most effective when used by bodies of warriors fighting in a disciplined manner. However, the earliest spearheads often represent a considerable investment for the time; they tend to be fairly large and their appearance coincides with the adoption of improved techniques in casting metal. Elaborate two-piece stone moulds replaced the earlier open moulds and enabled the craftsman to produce socketed spearheads which could be strongly hafted and rapiers which had stout and often beautiful mid-ribs for greater strength. Unquestionably these were the attributes of high status. The appearance of elaborate and expensive weaponry may reflect the tensions created by pressure on usable land; the Earlier Bronze Age in Ireland may have been a time of considerable conflict managed by an elite of warriors. The axehead too undergoes a sequence of development and in time smaller ones cast with a long crescentic cutting-edge appear. Fitted with high flanges and a stop-rib, they were mounted in L-shaped hafts with the shorter arm being split and the axehead bound tightly within and held by its edge flanges.

In addition to the growth of blanket bog, we have to reckon with the brief period around 1628 BC when climate became distinctly less favourable. If the general trend in Earlier Bronze Age artifacts seem to reflect a preoccupation with status and military equipment by the few, this may be a response to the competition brought about by the diminishing stock of agriculturally useful land.

The old material, stone, does not go out of use and flint remained important for small tools, knives, arrowheads, scrapers and the like. The carving of stone moulds eventually reached high standards of precision and finish. The preoccupation with status which we have seen in bronze weaponry is reflected also in a number of elegant artefacts such as stone ceremonial battle axes (*Illus. 133d*) which have been found with burials. These often have carefully bored shaft-holes and with the available technology they must have taken thousands of work-hours to manufacture. One example from Ballintubbrid in Co. Wexford was found burnt and broken in three pieces accompanying a cremated burial.

Bronze Age Houses

The pollen evidence shows clearances at a number of sites in the Earlier Bronze Age. At Ballynagilly there were two clearances, one associated with the Beaker settlement in the area and a later one. At Essexford Lough in Co. Louth, a clearance at this period also produced the first record of flax-growing in Ireland. There was some Earlier Bronze Age expansion of arable agriculture at Cashelkeelty in Co. Kerry. There was an increase of grasses accompanied by an increase in cereal pollen at Red Bog in Co. Louth around 1600 BC. We cannot generalise from these scattered records and although there is evidence for continued cereal growing and for open pastures, we are not yet in a position to estimate the relative importance of each. In Co. Mayo, between about 1700 and 1300 BC, there was renewed settlement with pastoral farming on the sites of the older fields at Céide. By this time they had already acquired extensive bog cover so there may have been either a brief tempting halt in the growth of bog or the local pressure on land required the bringing of the most marginal areas into production. A round house within an enclosure was found at Belderg. To the east at Carrownaglogh, a similar settlement was uncovered by Michael Herity. There, a stone field enclosure about 2.2 ha. in area contained traces of a round house and many cultivation-ridges of lazy-bed type all covered by a layer of blanket bog. The ridges may have been formed by about 1300 BC. Research by Michael O'Connell indicated that a woodland clearance with arable agriculture – both wheat and barley were cultivated – occurred about 1000-600 BC followed by woodland regeneration dominated by oak with hazel, ash and, later, yew represented at about 500 BC. The Carrownaglogh site brings us to the threshold of a major change in the Irish Bronze Age which we will consider later.

Lough Gur seems to have enjoyed continuously favourable conditions from Neolithic times and both round and rectangular houses were occupied there in the Earlier Bronze Age. At Coney Island on Lough Neagh, traces of rectangular sod-walled houses were associated with sherds of bowl pottery succeeded by a phase when urns were in use as domestic vessels. Two round houses at Downpatrick in Co. Down were occupied by the users of cordoned urn pottery showing, incidentally, that these vessels were domestic as well as funerary. One of the houses measured about 7m in diameter, the other about 4m. They had central hearths and roofs supported by posts. The settlement is likely to date to sometime around 1400 BC. Cordoned urn pottery found in a domestic context at Lough Enagh in Co. Derry, contained impressions of wheat, oats and barley. At Carrigillihy in Co. Cork, the earliest of two houses discovered was oval in plan and measured 10m x 6.7m in diameter. Its wall was stone and its roof was thatch and timber supported on posts. It was built within an oval wall which enclosed an area 24.4m x 21.3m. Radiocarbon dating suggests that the house was occupied about 1500-1200 BC. Carrigillihy is the earliest well-documented example of the enclosed isolated homestead which was to become characteristic of the Bronze Age and later settlement of Ireland. An oval banked enclosure with an outer and an inner ditch at Chancellorsland near Emly in Co. Tipperary has been partly excavated; it contained the burnt remains of at least one oval hut. A quantity of coarse pottery and remains of cattle, sheep and pig and the bones of at least one dog were recovered from it. Radiocarbon evidence suggests that the site belonged to the Bronze Age, arguably to the earlier part of the period, although the spread indicated by some of the dates is very wide. A wetlands version of the enclosed domestic settlement was excavated at Cullyhanna Lough in Co. Armagh during the 1950s. A wooden stockade of posts enclosed an area almost 17m in diameter in which there was an oval house of posts about 6.5m x 5.3m and a curved windbreak of light poles. It was built in 1526 BC. Another wetlands site which has come to light is on exposed peat in the Shannon estuary at Carrigdirty in

Co. Limerick. There, Aidan O'Sullivan has located an arc about 5m in diameter of round alder posts set vertically. The bark of the posts showed the marks of a metal axe. Inside the arc was the jawbone of a calf. Radiocarbon dating suggested the site belonged to the period between about 1678-1521 BC. Another similar structure with associated cattle bones exists nearby. It is conceivable that this was an area of periodically flooded woodland which offered occasional summer grazing and that the structures were the temporary huts of the cowherds.

Cooking Sites

The Earlier Bronze Age saw the appearance of a new and specialised type of monument – the cooking sites or burnt mounds known in the Irish tradition as *fulachta fiadh* (*Illus. 134*). These cooking places were attributed to the Fianna, the legendary militia led by Fionn Mac Cumhal. Their use was described by the seventeenth-century historian, Geoffrey Keating, who explained that food was cooked by heating stones in a fire and adding them to water in a trough or pit to bring it to the boil. Surprisingly, where there is evidence of date, the cooking places have almost all proved to belong to the Bronze Age; the earliest example dates to about 1800 BC. At least four thousand five hundred of these sites are known to exist and in areas of Waterford, Kilkenny and Tipperary there are very high densities of them. Over two thousand have been recorded in Co. Cork alone. Clearly they were not the haphazard campsites of wandering hunters. Such concentrations suggest that they must be related to settlement sites. Cooney and Grogan, in their study of prehistoric Irish society, see them as part of an integrated complex of settlements and burials in south Limerick. In west Cork, they occur in the areas of the stone circles, but in Kilkenny their distribution is complementary to that of what must be

Illus. 134
The reconstructed cooking site (fulacht fiadh) at Ballyvourney, Co. Cork, showing the water-filled pit in which heated stones were placed; within the hut a bench-like structure perhaps supported a butcher's block.

Bronze-Age burial sites identified in survey. The *fulachta fiadh* may have been used for communal cooking and perhaps also for heating water for bathing – late Irish literary tradition includes the bath as one of their purposes. An example in the Imlagh Basin on Valencia Island had a well-made stone trough and a well-defined hearth. Radiocarbon dating suggested that it was built about 1300 BC. In the absence of wood, the stems of ling were used as fuel. The *fulachta fiadh* are all located on wet sites and experiments conducted by Brian O'Kelly in a reconstructed example at Ballyvourney in Co. Cork showed how efficiently the cooking operation could be carried out; a 4.5kg leg of mutton wrapped in straw was cooked

in about four hours. The trough at Ballyvourney held about 450 litres of water and it was brought to the boil in about half-an-hour. Professor O'Kelly calculated that the trough at Ballyvourney had been used for about fifty such operations judging by the amount of discarded burnt stone in the mound. Substantial trees were cut down to provide the planks for many troughs. The makers of one example at Curraghtrasna in Co. Tipperary reused part of a dug-out wooden log-boat for the purpose; it dated to about 1150 BC. The cooking places acquired their characteristic appearance as the mound was gradually built up when stones that were raked out of the trough after each heating were thrown up in a heap, often kidney-shaped, around three sides, leaving one side open for access to the cooking area. The site of the trough is often marked by a depression. Much more work needs to be done on these intriguing monuments but their widespread distribution can, with care, be taken as an indication that bronze age settlement was intense in some areas.

THE LATER BRONZE AGE c.1200-600 BC

Sometime around 1200 BC, great changes took place across Europe and the Mediterranean world. North of the Alps, a series of rich new Bronze Age cultures emerged. We can begin to discern in them the lineaments of the Europe which was centuries later to become known to us through the works of the classical authors. Ireland was not immune to change and the period is seen as the great divide between the Earlier and Later Bronze Ages. Archaeologists have tended in the past to recognise this change largely through artefact studies. We need not concern ourselves in detail with the definitions entered into by scholars about when exactly we should begin the Later Bronze Age – a scheme of three phases proposed in 1964 by George Eogan still works quite well as a framework for the period. Eogan divided the period into three phases each named after a find of metal artifacts: the Bishopsland Phase (c.1200-1000 BC), the Roscommon Phase (c.1000-900 BC) and the Dowris Phase (c.900-650 BC). There is now some doubt as to the continuing usefulness of defining the middle phase, as the surviving artifactual remains attributable to it are so few.

The Bishopsland Phase

The appearance of new tools such as socketed axes and new metalworking techniques such as clay-mould casting together with a variety of new ornaments, especially gold *torcs* made of twisted metal, marks the opening of what Eogan called the Bishopsland Phase (c.1200-1000 BC). He named this phase after a hoard of tools (socketed axe, hammers, anvil, clamp-anvil, saw, sickle, chisels, flesh-hook and tweezers) found when cutting a channel for the Poulaphouca hydroelectric scheme on the borders of Co. Kildare and Co. Wicklow. The Bishopsland hoard was not so much the tool kit of a specialised craftsman but rather that of an individual practising a variety of technical skills, in much the same way that some modern farmers repair the full range of farm implements. We have in the hoard both wood-working and metal-working equipment as well as a sickle for harvesting cereals. The collars of the socketed axehead and of one of the hammers show a raised rope-moulding pattern. This was achieved by casting in clay moulds. This is novel in the Irish metal-working tradition and the introduction of clay-mould casting marks the adoption of a technique which was to remain in favour in Ireland for over two thousand years. The Bishopsland Phase is noteworthy for a range of important hoards of gold ornaments, some found in bogs like that from Derrinboy in Co. Offaly. The methods of production of the new and sumptuous gold ornaments, like the bronze tools, indicate that Irish craftsmen were adapting the designs and techniques of international metalworking traditions to their distinctive local technology.

Once again it is tempting to link the appearance of new tools, weapons and, as we shall see, fortifications, to a short-term climatic downturn which was severe enough to cause, between 1159 and 1141 BC, the narrowest sequence of growth rings in the whole Irish tree-ring record. This event may have been caused by another massive eruption at Hekla in Iceland. As the climatic event occurs close to the archaeologist's traditional date for the beginning of the Later Bronze Age in Ireland and the beginning of all the major changes that happened throughout Europe, there is a temptation to attribute the innovations to the consequences of the disimprovement in the pattern of the weather. This may have been so when the now familiar cycle of poor weather, diminishing harvests on the lowlands, severe limitations on settlement of the uplands and increased growth of bog began to have its effect. But things were probably much more complex and we should probably see the changes as the result of cumulative development, of which the climatic factor may just have been one cause. The opening of the period probably saw the continuance of farming on marginal land in Co. Mayo and the evidence of Carrownaglogh suggests continued agriculture on less favourable land throughout the phase. Does this imply that an increasing population placed pressure on the existing agricultural resources?

The Roscommon Phase

An apparent hiatus in the record follows the Bishopsland Phase for about a century or so. Eogan called this the Roscommon Phase after a poorly recorded hoard from that county. This interlude is chiefly marked for the appearance of the first true swords. It is also unaccountably distinguished by a gap in the tree-ring chronology of Irish oaks and there may be good reason to believe that oaks growing on bog surfaces had been coming under increasing pressure because of gradual climatic disimprovement. No Irish oak has yet been found which grew across the period centred on 948 BC and there is a significant increase in evidence for building of lakeside settlements and trackways just after this time – a cluster not unlike that noted between 1520 and 1480 BC. Whether it is useful anymore to distinguish a separate stage in the period is moot. The great changes which we see so marked in the next period of the Later Bronze Age are surely founded on what went before and represent the outcome of nearly three centuries of internal adjustment of society to local conditions combined with external contact.

The Dowris Phase

The final phase was the Dowris Phase (c.900-600 BC). This period was named after a large and probably votive wetland deposit from near Birr in Co. Offaly. It was something of a golden age when we encounter a massive increase in the number of surviving artefacts, many of them having analogues abroad in places as far afield as the Nordic region and the Mediterranean. Major technological changes are evident in complex castings such as large horns and in sheet-bronze work which appears for the first time in the form of buckets and cauldrons, shields and bucklers based on exotic models. The gold ornaments of the period, including sheet gold collars, cast and hammered dress-fasteners, bracelets, hair ornaments, pins and what seem to be ritual objects – boxes and amulets – present an astonishing range of high technical virtuosity. The sheer bulk of the gold from some finds is impressive. The Great Clare find, sadly mostly melted down after discovery, was found during the building

Illus. 135
Bronze tools of the
Dowris Period of the
Bronze Age:
1,2,3,4 socketed and
*   tanged knives;*
5   curved socketed
*   knife;*
6,7 socketed sickles;
8,9 socketed gouges;
10,11,12 socketed
*   chisels;*
13,14,15 tanged
*   chisels;*
16 socketed
*   hammerhead;*
17 razor.

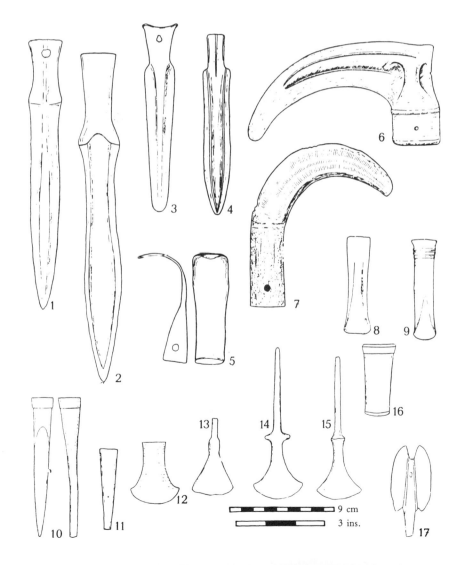

9 cm
3 ins.

of a railway near the trivallate hill-fort at Mooghaun in Co. Clare, and contained almost 150 ornaments. Some individual pieces from elsewhere are so heavy that their metal content alone is almost sufficient to have provided all the gold ornaments which survive from the Earlier Bronze Age. The dress fastener from Clones in Co. Monaghan weighs over a kilogram and clearly would have been difficult to wear; it may have been made for a ritual purpose.

The vast numbers of hoards of the period – over one hundred and fifty are known – contain tools (*Illus. 135*), weapons or personal ornaments. Relatively few of the hoards are mixed, although it is rare but not unknown for gold ornaments and tools to occur together. Some of these hoards are small, perhaps the personal possessions of an individual, while others are larger. Some hoards contain scrap metal and may have been the stock-in-trade of a metalsmith. An exceptionally high proportion are found in wetlands and may have been deposited ritually. The Dowris find, for example, contained over two hundred objects including bronze horns, 'crotals' (we do not know what they were used for – they are hollow cast bronze pointed-globular objects fitted with rings), a cauldron, axeheads, spearheads and tools. As varieties of artefact more usual in either northern or southern distributions were included together in Dowris, it may have been a kind of ritual central place located in the middle of Ireland, important as much for its geographical centrality as for anything else. It was not a hoard strictly-speaking, because as a votive deposit the material may have been cast into the lake over many years.

Only a scrap survives of the immense wealth of gold ornaments from the Bog of Cullen in Co. Tipperary found in the eighteenth century and consigned to the melting pot. Like Dowris, this site must have been a ritual place of deposition of great importance, used over a long period. Some hoards clearly had been personal possessions concealed for safety by someone at a time of danger. A small cache of amber beads, boars' tusks and rings of tin, bronze and of lead covered in gold foil had been buried in a wooden box in the floor of a lakeside dwelling at Rathtinaun, Lough Gara in Co. Sligo. The hiding place had been carefully marked by two discreet wooden pegs but the owner had never returned to retrieve the possessions. It is of special interest that this hoard had been deposited during a second occupation of the site when iron artefacts were already present there. Other hoards have been found cached under stones in circumstances which suggest concealment for safekeeping rather than votive offerings. The substantial group of sumptuous ornaments from Gorteenreagh in Co. Clare was hidden in this manner and to reinforce the impression of concealment, the major piece – an elaborate gold collar – had been taken apart.

The truly large numbers of spearheads and swords along with the shields of metal and bronze and fine scabbard fittings reveal a society in which parade of military trappings was important. This reflects the intensification of the trend which seems to have become firmly established during the Earlier Bronze Age. Spectacular hoards of gold have been found in a cluster around the lower Shannon basin. Another concentration occurs in the south-east in Co. Wexford, a part of the country which must always have been agriculturally very important. We may be seeing in the metalwork a reflection of a rich and confident local grouping which landscape archaeology has yet to flesh out with habitations and centres of significance – although the site of Rathgall in Co. Wicklow was an important settlement site in the general area. Across the wetlands of the midlands in the Shannon basin and northwards to mid-Ulster and to Co. Antrim, the finds of Dowris Phase metalwork extend in significant numbers and it has been suggested often that we can begin to see the regions, seen today as important in historic times, already emerging as significant centres of wealth and power at that time.

The presence of so much personal ornament in the record gives us some insight into the costume of the period. Dress is indicated in part by the gold dress-fasteners which functioned like giant cuff-links probably to fasten cloaks and by a range of cloak pins, but also by some surviving textiles. A small hoard of objects was found in a bog at Cromaghs near Armoy in Co. Antrim wrapped in two pieces of woollen cloth; among the objects were tassels of horsehair, perhaps part of a belt. Sheep were kept for their wool as well as for meat production. Flax was grown and no doubt a form of linen was manufactured. Leather working is well attested and a particular form of bronze implement with a splayed, curved blade is often found; it is almost certainly to be interpreted as a cobbler's knife. Among the warrior's equipment we find *chapes*; these are the fittings which fastened the ends of scabbards together. It is likely that the scabbards themselves were made of thin wooden boards covered with leather. We can assume that men of high status were sometimes clean-shaven, as razors already present in the previous period continued to be made.

We cannot assume that significant changes in high-quality metalwork and other portable objects along with the appearance of new techniques of manufacture signal a major change in the population. It is likely, although proving it is difficult, that the coarse pottery and the simplified burial practices that were developing towards the end of the Earlier Bronze Age are continued in the succeeding period. Change in luxury items is often the result of contact and communication between elites, and this may account for the production in Ireland of complex and expensive prestige metal goods, modelled on prototypes from abroad, which occur so much in this period. This emphasis on the exotic is perhaps often overstated. The vast bulk of the production of the Irish Later Bronze Age industry is utilitarian and the prominence to contemporary eyes of the exceptional objects has the effect of creating a false view of a population consisting mainly of warrior-plutocrats. As ever, elites are supported by a much larger population of hewers of wood and drawers of water whose traces in the archaeological record tend to be harder to find and more difficult to read. It is however clear that the wealth of the period – at least that controlled by the elite – was considerable and we must look to other evidence to see what the basis of this prosperity might have been.

Hill-top Enclosures

Recent excavation has shown that hill-top enclosures were built in this period and this, combined with our knowledge of other settlements, indicates a hierarchy among settlement types and hints at a social organisation which may have imposed

*Illus. 136a
Navan Fort (Emain
Macha) near
Armagh, one of
Ireland's most
important prehistoric
monuments,
nominated for
inclusion in
UNESCO's World
Heritage List, before
encroachment by
quarrying. A wooden
ritual structure was
erected on the hill at
the beginning of the
last century BC.*

*Illus. 136b
After a twenty-two
day public hearing in
1986, the Planning
Appeals Commission
sanctioned a further
expansion of
quarrying. This
decision was
overruled by the
Minister of the
Environment who
directed that all
quarrying must stop.*

itself on the landscape in a manner familiar from historical times. One of the great centres of the early legends set in the early centuries AD was Emain Macha in Co. Armagh (*Illus. 136a,b*). This is now plausibly identified with Navan Fort just to the west of Armagh city which is sited in an area of highly productive soils still valued today for their agricultural potential. Excavation has shown that Navan Fort – the military designation is probably a misnomer – was one of the later developments in a complex of earthwork sites. The story of this complex begins as much as a thousand years before the heyday of Emain Macha and a little over a kilometre to the west. There on a low hill called Haughey's Fort, three concentric ditches were dug probably between 1200 and 1000 BC during the Bishopsland Phase. The outermost ditch encloses an area about 340m in diameter. The ditches were V-shaped and about 4m wide at the top and about 2.5m deep; the upcast from them presumably formed concentric banks but these have entirely eroded away. Fortunately, the innermost ditch contained waterlogged deposits which preserved well the remains of wooden objects – a handle for an axe or pick and a wooden bung or stopper, a fragment of an alder wood vessel and a number of sharpened stakes of hazel. The bones of domestic animals included cattle (64%), pig (30.4%), sheep/goat (6.5%), dog and horse. Some of the cattle were of exceptional size and the skulls of two dogs were from a breed about the size of the modern alsatian. Red deer, fox and raven bones were also noted. Inside the enclosure were post-holes of what may have been a stockade. There were pits containing burnt stones, charcoal, potsherds and quantities of charred barley. The grain was fairly pure and free of contaminants which may suggest that it was gathered together at the fort from the places where it had been grown and threshed. In other words, Haughey's Fort may have been a place where quantities of grain were brought partly for consumption on site and partly for re-distribution.

Pollen analysis indicates substantial clearance and, for prehistoric Ireland, high values of cereal pollen in the vicinity during the period of occupation of the site and for about two hundred years before its construction. Seeds of chickweed, thistle, plantain, buttercup, dock, elder, water dropwort and nettle came from the ditch together with an intact apple. Wood from the site included *Prunus* (33%), hazel (6%), ash (4%), alder (2%) and hawthorn (1.7%) with values for oak, holly, willow and birch at less than 1%. A large presence of elder (*Sambucus*) at 51% may reflect the growth of that tree on the abandoned settlement after about 1000 BC. Saddle querns were found in the ditch which Jim Mallory has speculated was also used as a latrine by the inhabitants – a factor which may have added to its defensive properties. There was also evidence for the practice of goldworking. The coincidence of a substantial enclosure demanding a great effort to construct along with large breeds of animals and traces of luxury metal production all suggest that here at Haughey's Fort there was a centre of power of some kind. The site seems to have been abandoned about 1000 BC and Mallory was inclined to link this with an advance of forest recorded in pollen analysis about that time. Therefore, the basis of the wealth of the inhabitants was agriculture, both arable and pastoral.

Much remains to be done to investigate the later prehistoric enclosures of Ireland but the evidence of Haughey's Fort has given us a new insight into circumstances at the end of the second millennium BC. In addition to the single homesteads which we must imagine dotting the landscape, we may now add the defended enclosures of a powerful elite capable of mobilising a large workforce and controlling the production of prestige goods. These are the props of power of rulers and it may be that the stresses which we have hinted at, as usable or unoccupied land became more scarce, spurred competition which encouraged the emergence of a higher level of organisation than we have been able to deduce since the building of the Boyne Valley passage tombs. The standing of the occupants of Haughey's Fort may possibly be confirmed by the remarkable site below it called in local tradition 'The King's Stables'. This odd monument is a round hollow defined by a circular bank which impounds an artificial pool. It was excavated by Chris Lynn who found that it contained a deposit of fragments of clay-moulds for swords along with bones of animals: cattle, red deer, dog, pig and sheep. This was not domestic refuse; the bones of dog and the antlers of red deer were strikingly numerous and some of the bones seem to have belonged to animals thrown intact into the water. The facial bones of a young man, apparently deliberately cut off, were also found. This all seems to emphasise the sacrificial nature of the material. Radiocarbon dates suggest that 'The King's Stables' is contemporary with the occupation of Haughey's Fort. Here, we seem to have the conjunction of a high status occupation site and a ritual structure which embodies, in artificial form, the preoccupation with water which the countless deposits in wetland seem to imply; all the more odd in this instance as there is a small bog nearby which could notionally have served the purpose of votive deposition. Clearly by creating a place especially for ritual purposes, a particular emphasis was being placed on the rites whatever these may have been. Some message of control of the sacred may have been intended.

Later, in the Dowris Phase, we can continue to see the preoccupation with hilltop locations, arguably defended, where the practice of metalwork may have been carried on in protected or controlled circumstances. Discussion of them is bound up with the question of the hill-fort – a large fortified enclosure of one or more ramparts exploiting the natural defensive characteristics of the topography. These are often considered to be par excellence the monuments of Celtic peoples and their discussion in Ireland has been hampered by lack of excavation and dating evidence; there is now general acceptance that they originate in the Later Bronze Age. The hill-fort is a clearly defensive structure and should not be confused with another type of monument associated with Iron Age centres of importance. These are also massive hilltop enclosures which have as their principal characteristic the placing of their ramparts downslope of their ditches, an arrangement which does not seem to have been dictated by military considerations. As the principal examples of these monuments – Tara in Co. Meath, Emain Macha, Knockaulin in Co. Kildare – figure prominently in mythology and legend, there is good reason supported by archaeology for considering them to be ritual sites of the Iron Age. Like the hill-forts, there is evidence that they had acquired some importance in prehistoric times and at Tara and other examples, the incorporation of a prehistoric earlier burial mound or mounds within their enclosures seems to have been a significant consideration. We shall return to these later.

At Rathgall in Co. Wicklow, within the enclosure of a hill-fort there was intensive Later Bronze Age settlement with evidence for burial, coarse pottery and luxury products including elaborate stone beads and goldwork. Above all, the site was used for the manufacture of cast-bronze artefacts; thousands of fragments of clay moulds were found there in quantities not so far matched on any other site of the period. There was also a substantial circular house. We do not know for certain if the habitation of the period was associated with the system of defensive ramparts around the hill, but it is a strong possibility. The great stone fort of Dún Aengus on the largest of the Aran islands consists of a central citadel-like enclosure within a system of three other stone walls describing rough semi-circles with the precipitous sea-cliff as their base; one wall is simply a short stretch of masonry (*Col. 39*). A massive *chevaux-de-frise* of upright stones girdles the three inner walls. Long thought of as Iron Age, its history now appears much more complex. Claire Cotter has shown that there was a substantial period of Later Bronze Age occupation on the site represented by round huts and metalworking debris. She has identified two periods of occupation: one lasting from about 1300 to 1000 BC and a second from about 1000 to about 800 BC – essentially these seem to have been continuous. Her work is still continuing and has yet to establish whether or not the dwellings were enclosed. The central structure was built not in the prehistoric period, but much later when the stone-built cashels of the Early Medieval Period which it so much resembles were constructed. The central wall seems to overlie the Later Bronze Age habitation. The outer walls could conceivably be Iron Age or Later Bronze Age in date and it is to be hoped that sufficient soil deposits survive to enable the true relationship between the Later Bronze Age habitations and the enclosing walls to be established. The animal bones from the site are of great interest – sheep predominate at over 52% of recovered bone, cattle are somewhat less at 33.5% and pig at 12.4%; red deer was also noted. Finbar McCormick who is still examining them notes that most of the sheep were slaughtered at less than a year and that few of them – about 20% – lived to three-and-a-half years old. This suggests that they were reared for their meat rather than for wool production. He believes that the red deer bones represent imports from the mainland. There was activity also during this period at a hill-fort at Clogher in Co. Tyrone. Whether the Later Bronze Age occupation of the site was associated with the defensive enclosure there is still to be established beyond doubt. A connection between Dowris Phase activity near the sites of hill-forts is emphasised by the finding of Later Bronze Age hoards near or on them. At Downpatrick in Co. Down, there was Later Bronze Age habitation also and at Mooghaun in Co. Clare, where radiocarbon evidence now suggests that the outer rampart at least was constructed between about 1260 and 930 BC – about the same period as Haughey's Fort. Some time after the beginning of the Later Bronze Age, Lyle's Hill in Co. Antrim, defended by palisades in the Neolithic, was again enclosed, this time by a bank. Although not strictly a hill-fort in the military sense, a hoard of the Bishopsland Phase was said to have been found at Tara in Co. Meath.

At Navan Fort, long before its prominence as an Iron Age centre, a small Later Bronze Age farmstead on the hill was enclosed by a wattle fence and a ditch crossed by a causeway. The house had been renewed many times over the centuries and it is possible that here we had a settlement occupied throughout much of the final Bronze Age and perhaps even into the Iron Age. David Weir carried out pollen studies in the area which suggested that around 600 BC, there was an increase in grassland in the area indicating the possibility that pastoralism may have increased at the expense of both forest and arable land. Evidence is now accumulating that there were other structures on the hill at Navan – circular houses or enclosures identified by geophysical survey confirming the resemblance to Tara.

Later Bronze Age Houses

In earlier editions of this book, it seemed more important to advance explanations of why we knew so little of Later Bronze Age habitation other than on wetland sites which preserved a substantial record of human activity, but over time new discoveries are filling in the picture and we have less need to explain away the absences. At Curraghatoor in Co. Tipperary, there was an unenclosed cluster of round houses associated with fences and other structures. The inhabitants were farmers cultivating cereals. This exceptional site, discovered during gas-pipeline development, reminds us that many of our Bronze Age habitations leave no surface evidence and the existence of this cluster of houses, in effect a little farming village, makes it clear that a variety of forms of settlement existed. Enclosed homesteads may have occupied an intermediate place in the hierarchy between small nucleated settlements and larger fortified sites. A rectangular enclosure, also found in pipeline construction, at Ballyveelish in Co. Tipperary produced evidence of cereal production and animal husbandry; bones of cattle raised for meat were found there. At Ballyutoag in Co. Antrim, there was a house within an oval enclosure of the period. These dryland sites both enclosed and unenclosed remind us of the complexity of the settlement pattern of the period which is only slowly being revealed.

At Clonfinlough in Co. Offaly, an irregular palisade of ash posts defined an enclosure in which there were at least three wicker houses, each with a plank floor and a central hearth. Dendrochronological dates for the site establish its construction between 908 and 886 BC. It was built on the surface of the bog and beside a small lake. Two remarkable wooden paddles from the site indicate that the occupants used a boat of substantial size. The fact that it was built on the bog suggests that there was some drying-out of the surface at the time, an issue to which we will return later. A substantial number of lakeside habitations of the Dowris Phase have been excavated. They are often referred to as crannogs, a term derived from the Irish word *crann* meaning a tree and applied more accurately to the elaborate artificial island-dwellings of the Early Medieval Period. It is perhaps better to be more circumspect in the use of the term as the Later Bronze Age habitations tend to be much more varied in construction than the very regular and systematic massive structures of later times. Nevertheless, the Later Bronze Age wetland sites often represent considerable effort in building up a platform with dumped earth and stone and consolidating it with piles of timber and brushwood. A number of structures at Lough Eskragh in Co. Tyrone, produced coarse pottery, saddle querns and in one area, traces of the manufacture of cast bronze swords. One of them dates to the tenth century BC, others are later and fall within the floruit of the Dowris Phase. Two alder-wood vessels were found, one of them was in a dugout canoe or logboat. A second logboat was also found at Lough Eskragh. At Island MacHugh in Co. Tyrone, a small brushwood platform yielded occupation debris and a sword. Its Later Bronze Age occupation may have lasted from about 1200 to about 800 BC.

At Rathtinaun in Co. Sligo, a dwelling had been created on a slight rise in the lake bed by piling on it layers of timber and brushwood. On this were the remains of a large round house as well as seven hearths. It was later succeeded by a further structure after a term of abandonment and it may be that here, as at Navan Fort, we have a sequence of occupation from the Dowris Phase through to the Iron Age because iron implements, including a shaft-hole axe crudely forged from three billets of metal, occurred with objects entirely typical of the Later Bronze Age. The inhabitants grew naked and hulled barley and wheat. Flax was also grown in the vicinity. At Ballinderry crannog No. 2 in Co. Offaly (so-called to distinguish it from the neighbouring crannog No. 1 in Co. Westmeath), the earliest phase was a gravel island in the lake which was partly extended and consolidated. On this was built a massive structure of oaken timbers about 12m square. It consisted of parallel rows of beams, each about 1.5m apart, joined at the ends by crossbeams. The planks were provided with holes to support upright poles. Too narrow to have been the aisles of a building, the purpose of the structure must remain a matter for debate; perhaps the uprights were sufficiently strong to have supported a platform. (It is interesting to note that the timbers of some Later Bronze Age bog-roads are slotted or mortised and appear to have been recycled from substantial timber buildings. Sophisticated structures, therefore, were part of the Bronze Age builders' repertoire.) There were many red deer bones at the Ballinderry site, not all necessarily the result of hunting. The majority of the domesticated animal bones were of cattle (about 75%) with pig (about 10%) and sheep and horse also represented. A saddle quern for the grinding of corn was found. The charcoal of the domestic fires suggests that secondary woodland was growing nearby; the bulk of it consisted of alder, ash, hazel and willow. Hawthorn and yew were represented in the worked wood found on the site. At Knocknalappa in Co. Clare, a substantial platform in Rossroe Lake was occupied at this period; it too was the habitation of an essentially agricultural community. Animal bones at the site were dominated by cattle and sheep/goat, with pig and horse also represented. The firewood used at Knocknalappa was predominantly of hawthorn and hazel with much lesser quantities of oak, alder, willow/poplar, ash and holly mostly derived from secondary scrub woodlands. Oak, willow/poplar, alder and hazel were used for construction.

Bog Roads

New research is showing us just how important the construction of bog-causeways was in the Later Bronze Age. Many were built in that shadowy century occupied by the Roscommon Phase. We can argue that this was a response to wetter conditions but this now seems to be much too simplistic an explanation. The record of trackway construction dates back to at least 3500 BC in Ireland. Bog had also been invading land previously used productively for almost as long. There were episodes of relative dryness when trees recolonised the surfaces of the bogs and when man returned, as in Mayo, to re-use fields which had once been abandoned. Trackways may have been built both in wet periods and in drier ones. In Littleton Bog in Co. Tipperary, a number of wooden tracks were built to connect substantial areas of dry land. One of these was probably built around the mid-tenth century BC to connect higher land on the east with the extensive dry lands around Liathmore to the west. The road was subsequently repaired, probably about a hundred years later, and at some time someone hid a sword in the displaced timbers.

The trackways were important in keeping the maximum amount of usable land in production. They also represent a considerable investment in their construction and in the exploitation of woodlands where substantial trees, especially oaks, were cut down, trimmed and split into rough planks for road building. Where hurdles were used, it seems that the rods came from coppiced hazel. Large quantities of brushwood were cut to make underlayers. Barry Raftery investigated a track at Annaghcorrib in Garryduff Bog, Co. Galway, where the road bed rests on a substructure of logs, brushwood and occasional discarded planks and consisted of two layers of finely made oak planks often as little as 2-3cm thick. Mortise holes had been cut in the planks but these were only occasionally used for pegs to hold them in position. Perhaps they had been fashioned for some other structure and only later used for road building. The trackway has been traced for about 1.5km across the bog leading from dry land to the south towards shallows on the River Suck, perhaps a fording place. The road was built in 892 ± 9 BC. A track at Derryoghil in Co. Longford (no.1 in Barry Raftery's listing) was made of split roundwood and planks and dated to the years 938 ± 9 BC. The Wetlands Survey is uncovering very large numbers of trackways, mostly of Bronze Age date, on the raised bogs of the midlands.

One interesting structure found at Islandmagrath on mudflats on the upper Fergus estuary in Co. Clare may also have been connected with communications. There, Aidan O'Sullivan has mapped a linear wooden structure about 35m long and 2m wide running along the foreshore. Made of closely-spaced stout ash and alder roundwood posts with wattles interwoven, the interior is laid with horizontal panels of hurdles pegged in place. A piece of withy, perhaps a form of rope, was found. The structure is dated by radiocarbon to between about 800 and 550 BC. It may have been a trackway or perhaps a jetty.

The Economic Value of Woodlands

The scale of preservation in bogs and other wetlands enables us to grasp what must have been true in earlier periods – that wood was the primary raw material on which the very survival of people depended; for shelter, for tool-making, for fencing the land, for fuel and for communications. Vessels of wood have been found and wood is the ubiquitous fuel for domestic and industrial activities such as metalworking. Cremated burials are attested in the Later Bronze Age although few have been identified so far and this ritual requires a substantial investment of timber. Boats were fashioned from large logs. We have extensive evidence for the use of timber for fine work. The box for the Rathtinaun hoard is but one example, another from Killymoon in Co. Tyrone contained a gold dress-fastener. The metal shields of the Later Bronze Age were for parade. Experiment has shown that they would not have provided much protection. Shields of cowhide and of wood were used for fighting. The hide shields – an example from Clonbrin in Co. Longford, survives – were formed on wooden moulds carved from solid blocks of which at least two survive, from Kilmahamogue in Co. Antrim and Churchfield in Co. Mayo; both were bog finds. The Kilmahamogue example was about 45cm in diameter and was made of alder. The cutting of substantial trees and the working of wood posed no problems for the tool kit of the time. Our awareness of the importance of woodlands has been diminished in Ireland for centuries, but a visit to countries where forests are still extensive will quickly remind us what an adaptable and basic raw material timber is and how dependent on it we remain in so many ways. An important resource like woodlands needed protection. There is clear evidence, in the abundant roundwood used in building lakeside settlements and roads, that the woodlands were managed to produce the timber required for specialist purposes. In older secondary woodland and in areas where primeval forest may have survived, trees of much larger size than we are accustomed to seeing nowadays were growing.

Farming in the Later Bronze Age
The woodlands also contributed their quota of grazing for pigs and clearings for cattle. Rough grazing was available too on the surface of the bogs, especially at times of relative dryness. The habitation sites show clearly that the mainstay of the economy was farming and there is no doubt that tillage farming was important. Few sites fail to yield evidence of cereals and the forest must have provided the timber for the making of the most important technological innovation which we may infer at this period – the plough.

Pollen analysis from sites widely distributed throughout the island seem to indicate that there was a rise in arable farming from about 1400-1300 BC which reached a peak about 800 BC. The rise seems to have been sustained therefore for about five hundred years, and there is no doubt that grain-growing represented a considerable factor in the economy of the Later Bronze Age. David Weir has pointed out that the broad trend of pollen evidence throughout the Bronze Age suggests that grasslands were of relatively greater importance and we have argued that the clearances had probably created permanent grasslands even in Neolithic times. He has noticed an increase in grassland in the Navan area around the time that we conventionally end the Dowris Phase. An expansion of open conditions at Littleton Bog after the floruit of the Dowris Phase also suggests that in some areas there were occasional marked local variations from the general pattern. In the Burren in Co. Clare, pollen analysis indicates a later clearance phase where at Lios Larthin Mor, a sharp drop in tree pollen after about 800 BC and a significant expansion in open conditions marked by an abundance of *Plantago lanceolata* were observed. This was sustained for many centuries until a sharp but short-lived rise in local woodlands at about 1600 years ago. Cereal production generally in prehistoric Ireland never assumed the position in relation to grassland that it does in the pollen spectra from the Early Medieval period. This should not lead us to believe that cereals were unimportant. Weir argues that the low level of arable farming may have ensured for cereals an important economic position which may be distinguished from their actual contribution to subsistence.

We have no direct evidence to prove it, but it is likely by analogy with other countries that the Later Bronze Age saw the introduction of the plough to Ireland and we might attribute the increase in cereal production to its adoption. The plough of the time was the ard, examples of which have been found in Denmark and illustrated on the rock-carvings of the Bronze Age in Norway (*Illus. 138*). This was a simple device for drawing an oak point or *share* across the ground just beneath the surface. In so doing, it pushed the soil it was penetrating upwards and forwards. As it moved through the ground, some of the upper soil fell down into the cavity caused by the passage of the share. In this way, the soil was loosened and some of the lower soil richer in nutrients was brought to the surface. A second ploughing of the plot at right angles to the first was necessary to break up the ground and this had a tendency to encourage the formation of square fields. Ards were unable to tackle the tough sod of old grassland because they lacked the later innovation of a knife or *coulter* suspended in front of the share to cut the grass roots. It was necessary, therefore, for the sod to be chopped up by hoes or spades before the ard could be used. A further, much later introduction – probably in the seventh or eighth century AD – was the *mouldboard* which turned the surface layer over to form ridges and furrows (*Illus. 138*). At Belderg in Co. Mayo, as we have seen, Séamus Caulfield has discovered criss-cross markings which seem to be the traces of ard ploughing buried under bog and arguably of this period. The adoption of the plough was neither simple nor easy – like all new technologies, it required significant preparation before the benefits became obvious. We have seen the continuing need to break up grassland by hand but the hard manual labour does not end there.

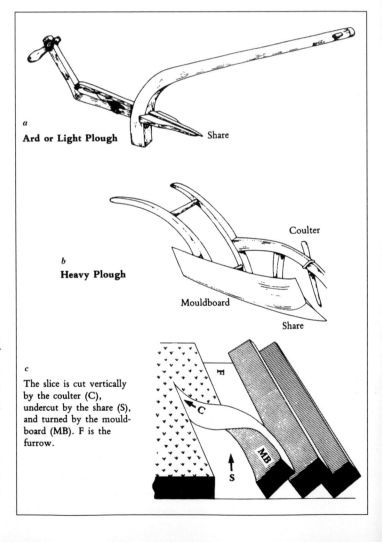

a
Ard or Light Plough   Share

b
Heavy Plough

Coulter

Mouldboard

Share

c
The slice is cut vertically by the coulter (C), undercut by the share (S), and turned by the mould-board (MB). F is the furrow.

F

C

MB

S

The ard is most effective in stone-free soil and so time will have been spent in clearing fields of the large obstructions which could then be most usefully used in creating field walls. Often, however, they were thrown up in a heap and a number of these clearance cairns, now covered by bog, have been found in Antrim and Mayo.

In order to pull the plough, oxen required training. First the young male animals were castrated and then followed a long period, perhaps of two or three years, during which the animals were trained to work together probably in pairs. This created a need to preserve trained oxen for longer than if they had been raised merely for meat, indeed the worth of a trained beast would have far exceeded its slaughter value.

The breaking of the sod and the turning up of the earth when constantly repeated would have enabled rainfall to leach the nutrients more readily from the fields, gradually creating an impoverished soil. Without careful crop rotation, manuring and fallow periods, the soil would eventually have become sour and acid, a process counteracted in modern farming by the spreading of lime (calcium carbonate) on the fields. With the available land already settled, the ploughlands could not revert to woodland and have their nutrients restored as seen earlier with the growth of secondary forest. The need to clear fields for the plough may have fixed the land devoted to cultivation exposing it to much longer-term use and degradation than before. The soils leached of nutrient and becoming increasingly acid would have been attractive for the development of heathland and it is possible that the introduction of the plough may be responsible for an expansion of heathers over land that was once capable of supporting mixed farming communities. The leaching effect would have been more severe on thinner lighter soils. Even quite modest increases in annual rainfall would have greatly accelerated the process.

We may attribute the worst episodes of soil deterioration in the Bronze Age to a combination of circumstances of which more intensive use of the land by man may have been particularly significant. A contraction of agriculture which seems to have followed the Dowris Phase may have been brought about by overuse of old areas of arable land. Without the technology needed to exploit the heavier soils of the lowlands, in time this alone would have placed society under severe strain. It was probably during the Later Bronze Age also that the first simple wheeled vehicles came into use in Ireland. A block-wheel from Doogarymore in Co. Roscommon – one of a pair – survives from the transition period between the Later Bronze and Iron Ages. It is likely that the carts of the time were pulled by oxen and this innovation may have gone hand-in-hand with the adoption of the plough. It seems likely, therefore, that the economy of the Later Bronze Age was grounded in agriculture in which cereal production was economically important. Cattle, pig and sheep were raised for meat with the cattle being grazed on grasslands that had been developed over many centuries.

Of other economic activities, we may probably assume the continued exploitation of copper deposits although the direct evidence for mining in Later Bronze Age Ireland is lacking. Tin probably continued to be imported but some copper-alloy manufacture at least was based on recycling of scrap metal. Lead,

Illus. 137
Plough types:
a The frame of the ard supports a basal projecting point, the share, which is either of wood or stone.
b A downward projecting metal knife, the coulter, is mounted on the frame in front of the share to cut plant roots. A curved board, the mouldboard, follows the share and inverts the cut sod.
c Twisting by the mouldboard inverts the severed sod.

probably imported, was alloyed extensively with copper and tin in the bronzes of the period; a small admixture improves the casting properties of the metal. The extensive lead-ore deposits of Ireland do not appear to have been exploited in prehistoric times. Research on the origins of the gold in Irish Bronze Age ornaments has been renewed and it is likely that placer deposits – that is dust and nuggets in alluvial deposits – in some areas were exploited for the industry of the time. The contacts which brought the metalworking influences which have been detected in Ireland also brought another import, amber, which occurs in large amounts in the form of necklaces of large beads. This almost certainly reached Ireland from Jutland or the Baltic coast.

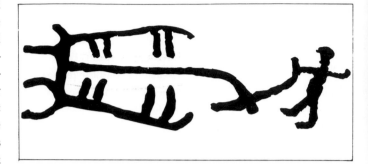

Significant areas of woodland survived but it seems unlikely that there were very large continuous tracts of forest unbroken by extensive clearances for pasture and tillage. The clearance of woodland would once more have favoured the deer population, but there is little evidence that hunting played a significant role in the diet of the people and it may even then have begun to be the preserve of those of higher status. The rivers would have been a fruitful source of food with runs of salmon and eel, but the archaeological evidence for this is

lacking despite the number of wetland sites excavated. In addition to the domestic pigs foraging in the woods, there were wild boar and, doubtless, feral domesticates. The wild cat and the wolf were present together with many species of bird now extinct in Ireland. We cannot estimate the human population of the time – settlement was widespread and varied from open village clusters, through single enclosed homesteads to larger centres of power and re-distribution of wealth. The final phase of the Bronze Age seems to mark a high point and the succeeding dark age with its hints at deteriorating climate – an apparent decline of agricultural production and an expansion of woodlands – marks a radical change which has

Illus. 138

Top:
Bronze Age ard-
plough.

Middle:
Medieval coulter-
plough.

Bottom:
Medieval
mouldboard-plough.
The boy should be
walking backwards
in front of the team;
the man sowing has
nothing to do with
the plough.

prompted Barry Raftery to write poignantly of the plight of the inhabitants contemplating 'waterlogged and ruined crops...rivers bursting their banks and weeks of leaden skies and unceasing rain. Ireland's Late Bronze Age farmers – soaked, cold and hungry – could have felt themselves on the brink of Armageddon.' We all know the feeling.

FROM BRONZE AGE TO IRON AGE c.600 BC-200 AD

The testimony of many of the pollen-diagrams which cover the period is that there was a decline in arable agriculture and a contraction in grasslands after the end of the Dowris Phase. Tillage continued although greatly reduced in scale and while it is clear that in some places – for example at Red Bog in Co. Louth – woodland advanced into areas previously cleared, the picture is not entirely uniform. In general, there was decline but not perhaps the catastrophic falling-off envisaged in some scenarios and much open country remained. There is some evidence also for a disimprovement in the climate at this period, certainly after about 500 BC. In addition, at 430 BC and at 208 BC, there are short-term episodes of narrow oak ring growth which seem to coincide with brief hemisphere-wide disruptions in normal weather patterns, possibly volcanic in origin. In the archaeological record, we have a few artefactual traces of the Hallstatt Culture (an Iron Age culture associated on the continent with people historically identified as Celtic); around 650 BC, some personal ornaments and a series of bronze versions of typical Hallstatt iron swords appear. These are the faint echoes of the rising Iron Age civilisation of mainland Europe and of Britain, but they seem to have represented no more than a continuation of the pattern of copying prestige objects from overseas which we have already seen in the Dowris Phase. We would probably be quite unjustified in postulating an invasion on the basis of these few weapons and trinkets but we might deduce that there was some turmoil towards the end of the Dowris Phase to account for the deposition of the majority of hoards which cannot be explained as votive. There is simply not enough evidence to decide if we are witnessing a fortuitous combination of minor events, internal stress manifesting itself as violence or the threat of violence, or some external danger. The changes in agriculture and land-use generally may have been the result of cumulative processes over many generations and may not have produced immediate and catastrophic distress until some critical point of imbalance was reached.

Barry Raftery has posed the problem neatly: at the opening of this dark age we have the Later Bronze Age culture in full flower and by about four hundred years later we have a fully-fledged La Tène Iron Age civilisation established in the northern half of the country and no apparent evidence of continuity between the two. (The La Tène culture named after a votive site on Lake Neuchatel in Switzerland is the term used for the rich Celtic culture of Later Iron Age Europe – it was well established in both Britain and Ireland during the Iron Age.) In the intervening period, iron was adopted as the metal most appropriate for tools and weapons. Bronze in the Iron Age became largely confined to ornamental pieces or utilitarian objects of high status – horse trappings, vessels, personal ornaments and the like. While some sites, Emain Macha and Rathtinaun for example, seem to show continued occupancy, we really lack a sequence of material, illustrating a gradual transition or revealing a point at which continuity was broken, around which we might construct a theory. Over much of the southern part of the country, there is little or no evidence of the La Tène culture.

What are we to make of this? Was the distinctive material culture of the La Tène carried by an aristocracy who imposed themselves on the populace in the northern half leaving the inhabitants of the south to continue relatively isolated and only gradually adopting the traits of iron-using and other technologies? The most striking thing about Ireland at the end of the Iron Age, say about 400 AD, is the uniformity of its economy and material culture. One explanation is perhaps that the civilisation of Later Bronze Age Ireland continued in isolation for a period and we cannot identify the moment of change because conservatism in the artefact tradition and in settlement and hoarding practice has ensured that the kind of evidence used by archaeologists to track change has been smoothed out. When the first La Tène style artefacts make their appearance, at about 300 BC, they can be dated approximately with reference to similar objects abroad. There is the tendency common in archaeological reasoning to polarise events around fixed points and thus to create the appearance, entirely misleading, of discontinuities – the appearance of the first La Tène decorated objects may be one such artificial polarity. Our pollen recorder takes no account of these artificial boundaries and there is even some evidence, probably highly localised, for additional clearance in places and certainly for continued agriculture, albeit reduced in scale, throughout the period. Eoin Grogan and Gabriel Cooney have rightly emphasised that patterns established in the Later Bronze Age of deposition of hoards are detectable again in the Iron Age and we have already seen how the centres of importance which emerged in the Later Bronze Age retained their significance in the Iron Age. There seems, therefore, to have been an essential continuity between the two periods.

THE IRON AGE c.400 BC-400 AD

At Aughinish Island in Co. Limerick, two small enclosed settlements may date to the dark age we have just discussed and while the basic economy and equipment may not be distinguished from that of the Later Bronze Age, an iron horse-bit was found which may be one of the earliest examples of the use of that metal in Ireland. The Aughinish sites fit comfortably with what we know of settlement patterns already established in the Later Bronze Age and we can see the occupants adopting iron technology without a major alteration of their way of life much as we have already noted at Rathtinaun. We probably have to reckon with the gradual adoption of iron for the manufacture of tools and weapons in the period between about 600 BC when the Dowris industries were still in existence and 300 BC when we know La Tène culture was established in Ireland.

Iron is a very common metal but working it was not straightforward. Some re-orientation of the metalworkers' skills was required. Iron ore was smelted, that is it was roasted in a furnace to produce a chemical reaction. The process caused impurities in the ore to melt and settle in the bottom of the furnace as slag. This left behind an impure spongy mass of iron which to be usable had to be heated and hammered before eventually being forged. Cast iron is a modern development. Iron ore is quite widely available in Ireland in various forms, but the most commonly worked was probably bog-iron, an oxide deposited in bogs. Because iron rusts easily, the archaeological record of early iron-working is very incomplete. We have a number of iron swords of the early Iron Age; they tend to be small – the largest are no more than about 45cm long. Spears were probably common in the period but paradoxically while we have few spearheads, many spear-butts survive because they were made of bronze. Indeed the principal evidence normally discussed for the period is the range of high-quality bronzes including personal ornaments and horse-trappings, a few of which – suites of paired snaffle-bits and Y-shaped leading-pieces – suggest that the chariot drawn by pairs of horses had been introduced. Cremated burials and the use of coarse pottery not unlike that of the Later Bronze Age is attested. We will not concern ourselves with the detail of the artefacts of the period but we badly need a great deal more evidence of economic activity and more excavation of domestic sites if these can be identified. Recent research has shown us that despite our suspicions of agricultural contraction, there were very significant, indeed massive, constructions in the early Iron Age which signal a highly organised society directed to achieving communal objectives which have left their mark on the landscape to the present day.

Fortifications

We have already looked at hill-forts and considered the probability that they may have had their beginnings earlier (*Col. 36*). They are commonly associated with Iron Age society in Britain and the continent and there is no question that they were in use in Ireland during the Iron Age and later times. Freestone Hill in Co. Kilkenny, produced Roman-period material and the site of Grianán Aileach at the base of the Inishowen peninsula was used as the inauguration site of the Northern Uí Neill in historic times (*Illus. 139*). Barry Raftery has noted the problem that the majority of the sixty or so hill-forts so far identified in Ireland lie in the south and south-west, that is in the areas where the La Tène Iron Age tradition seemingly made little or no impact. He has divided the hill-forts into a number of types based on whether they have one or a number of ramparts and he has also linked them with a series of what are described as inland promontory forts. These are fortifications created by throwing a rampart across the neck of a mountain spur or other feature with precipitous sides, so as to create a defensive enclosure. There are spectacular examples at Caherconree and Mount Brandon in Co. Kerry and at Lurigethan and Knockdhu in Co. Antrim.

The difference between univallate (single rampart) and multivallate hill-forts is difficult to clarify. A process of addition could account for turning one into the other. At a number of examples – Grianán Aileach, Dún Aengus and perhaps, Rathgall – the innermost defence is a citadel-like drystone structure in the tradition of the cashels of the end of the Iron Age and of the Early Medieval Period. It is difficult to decide if this is coincidence or the result of continuity of use of some kind, given that the earlier builders had chosen their sites well and later people recognised and exploited this. The history of the hill-fort is likely to be complex.

Illus. 139
Grianán Aileach,
Inishowen,
Co. Donegal – chief
centre of the kingdom
of the Northern
Uí Neill. The site
consists of a massive
Early Medieval cashel
(heavily restored in
the nineteenth
century) within an
earlier hill-fort.

Recent work by Tom Condit has not only been adding to the number of such sites in Ireland but also revealing the remarkable scale of some of them. Near Baltinglass in Co. Wicklow, there is a remarkable and well-known group of hill-forts in commanding positions overlooking the Slaney valley. On Baltinglass Hill are two forts, Rathcoran and Rathnagree, and on the west side of the river are three more. Condit has also discovered that an enormous stone rampart along the 300m contour encloses the great fort of Brusselstown Ring and Spinan's Hill to the north-west which also has traces of a hill-fort. The newly-discovered rampart, much of it doubled, can be traced for about 4km and encloses an area of over 130ha. This extraordinary structure is as yet undated and in the absence of carefully targeted excavation, its function is unknown. The encircling of the two hill-forts in an area rich in such monuments is unlikely to have been fortuitous and an association with the builders of the hill-forts is very likely. The scale of the newly-found enclosure is such that a truly remarkable investment in labour and organisation was called for – Spinan's Hill was not just a response to local needs, there must have been a centre of regional importance there. The concentration of hill-forts in the area reinforces this impression, although it must be admitted that they may not all be contemporary. Given that they occur in a cluster on either side of an important river valley, we may have here an example of groups locating important assembly or defensive centres on the frontiers between two tribal territories. The hill-forts may therefore be rival works inspired by competitive emulation between polities of some kind whose areas of influence bordered each other along the River Slaney. Alternatively, they may represent a shifting of the central place of a single tribal group from site to site within a small area over time – we have already seen that this may have happened at Navan Fort and its environs from the Bishopsland Phase to the Iron Age. We can conclude at least that hill-forts were centres of regional importance; they must have been the central places of substantial tribal societies and from the evidence seen so far, they are likely to have been of enduring significance well into the Iron Age if not in some cases actually built then.

Ritual Sites

We have already noted that some enclosures – Tara, Navan Fort, Knockaulin in Co. Kildare and others – were not defensive but ceremonial of some kind. Tara is a complex of a large variety of earthworks and other monuments partly excavated some years ago and it clearly had been a ceremonial centre for many centuries (*Col. 34, 35*). Parts of the hill are densely covered in burial mounds and other earthworks of various sizes, some clearly overlapping earlier ones and suggesting continuous resort to the site for ritual and other purposes. Its symbolic significance was retained in historic times; it was the inauguration place of one of the most prestigious kings, and like Navan Fort, it was the focus of a great cycle of myth and legend. Sophisticated survey techniques without further destructive excavation are now revealing that the hill is like a palimpsest manuscript, cleaned and overwritten constantly. The largest enclosure at Tara – Raith na Righ – seems to be a ritual site of a type which just conceivably might trace its origins to the Late Neolithic henge-like earthworks. It has its bank outside its surrounding ditch. Although probably not built originally for military purposes, a palisade was erected inside the line of the ditch, perhaps in late prehistoric times, to render it defensive.

Two other sites of this type have been extensively excavated, Navan Fort and Knockaulin. Navan Fort as we have seen was occupied from Later Bronze Age times. Inside its great enclosure, an enormous ritual structure was erected during the Early Iron Age on the site of the occupation already discussed. It consisted of four rings of upright posts, the outermost being over 37m in diameter and clad in horizontal planking. In the centre was a single upright post over 55cm in diameter; this was set in a deep post-hole. The central post may have been about 13m high and it was so large that a ramp 6m long was cut to enable it to be dragged into the hole at an angle before being raised to the vertical. Two rows of posts defined a kind of passageway towards the central upright. The stump survived and it has been dated dendrochronologically to 95-94 BC. It is uncertain whether the Navan structure had been roofed or not. Shortly after it was built, it was ritually destroyed – packed first with limestone blocks and then burnt. We know that the uprights were in position when this was done because the late Dudley Waterman who excavated the site, found the voids created by the decay of the posts in the cairn material. We can have little doubt that here was a temple of some kind however short-lived.

Knockaulin in Co. Kildare, plausibly identified with the Dún Ailinne of early legend, is a massive enclosure with an internal partly rock-cut ditch on a hill near Kilcullen. It was excavated by Bernard Wailes of the University of Pennsylvania, who found off-centre a series of successive round palisade trenches, the final phase of which was a concentric pair enclosing a circle of free-standing posts about 25m across. Inside this was a hut about 5m in diameter. This had not seen occupation although there was evidence of burning on its floor. Around the outer wall of the hut were radially-set pits. At some point, the structures were dismantled and thereafter there was a phase of sporadic use of the hill, perhaps for occasional feasting; scatters of animal bones and charcoal interleaved with narrow bands of humus perhaps resulting from growth of vegetation all suggested this interpretation. The radiocarbon evidence indicates use of the site between about 400 BC and 300 AD. There was no evidence for material of later date. Knockaulin was clearly a ritual site and while not identical with the structure at Navan, there can be little doubt of the relationship between its circle of posts and that at Emain Macha. The site yielded an iron sword, bronze safety-pin brooches of Roman type and an iron spearhead. The creation of large enclosures for ceremonial purposes and the erection of massive ritual buildings gives an impression of considerable organisation and social control in the hands of the ruling elites of the time. Barry Raftery lists other sites of this type – Carrowmably in Co. Sligo, Knockbrack in Co. Dublin, Cornashee near Lisnaskea in Co. Fermanagh, Raffin in Co. Meath and Glasbolie in Co. Donegal – and future survey may well increase the number significantly.

The Corlea Road

A massive bog-causeway of the period was excavated at Corlea in Co. Longford (*Col. 30*). Originally about 1km long, it connected with a small island of dry land beyond which was another road of essentially the same age continuing the route for about another kilometre. The timbers of the Corlea road were felled in the year 148 BC. Thousands of man hours must have been involved in the work. Wood from 200-300 large oaks, birch and some alders, elms, hazel and yew were used. The birches formed the substructure of runners and were trimmed on the bog; the branches were lopped off and thrown down for added support. Some of the logs were more than 10m long. Oak sleepers formed the road and were normally wedge-split from mature trees. They were 3-4m long and up to 65cm wide and 20cm thick. Some were adzed smooth. Where required they were pegged through adzed mortise holes to secure them. Some of the holes may have been cut to facilitate dragging the heavy timbers into position. Finds associated with the road included a wooden mallet, a wedge, fragments of wooden vessels and some fine pieces of boards, perhaps part of a cart. The scale of the road was exceptional and sets it apart from earlier trackways which may have served simple farming communities. This was a grandiose work which had conceivably been commanded by a potentate. There is evidence at one point that the road may have been deliberately damaged and it is possible that it became the object of the attentions of a rival group. Could it have connected important centres of power? Could it have been created to facilitate and thus control trade? Whatever interpretation is correct – and there are many possibilities – it remains one of the most massive and imposing prehistoric monuments in Ireland, now happily preserved in part for the future. The odd thing is that a rise in hazel pollen suggesting an invasion of open land by scrub woodland seems to have happened at Corlea at about the time the road was built.

Linear Earthworks

We can now can date some of the linear earthworks – that is, banks and ditches – which run often for long distances across country. The best known is the Black Pig's Dyke in south Ulster but there are others. In south Armagh there is the Dorsey (from the Irish *doirse* meaning doors) presumably because it straddled and thus controlled one of the passes into the interior of Ulster. At least one stretch of the Dane's Cast running north/south in Co. Armagh and Co. Down may relate to the frontier of the kingdom of Ulster when it had shrunk to the area east of the River Bann to which it was confined in Early Medieval times. There are important stretches of linear earthworks in counties Monaghan, Fermanagh, Longford, Leitrim and Roscommon. In Munster, the Claidh Dubh runs for about 22km across the Blackwater Valley between Castletownroche and Doneraile. The earthworks are not continuous; presumably in the past they linked naturally impassable areas created by bog or thick forest to form a defence, but one probably intended to keep cattle in, mark a frontier or control an important crossing rather than a continuously manned military position. They vary in construction – there are double banks and ditches, double banks with a single ditch between them or even single banks flanked by two ditches. Parts of the Black Pig's Dyke in Monaghan are up to 24m across, and a portion of it was found to have a palisade along the edge of the inner ditch. Radiocarbon dating suggested that it may have been built at that point between about 500 and 100 BC. The Dorsey in Co. Armagh seems to be an enclosure at first sight but it is really a pair of banks of slightly differing date, in all about 4km long. Where the rampart meets boggy ground, a palisade of posts continues its line. There is an entrance in the southernmost section of the banks. A dendrochronological date for a palisade that continued the line into the bog gave a felling date of 95 ± 9 BC, essentially the same date as the massive structure at Navan Fort. In Co. Roscommon, a huge earthwork, pierced by two entrances cuts off a peninsula formed by a loop of the Shannon between Drumsna and Jamestown. Some of its sections are 30m wide and 6m high. It was intended not to enclose the land within the loop but to control the crossing of the river along the shallows there – it may have been a toll-point. Wood from the base of the bank at Drumsna was felled in the mid-fourth century BC. The Claidh Dubh of Munster may have been constructed before 100 AD. Some linear earthworks may have been built in historic times; there is a legendary reference which implies that they were considered the boundaries between provinces.

Iron Age Farming

Among the animal bones at Knockaulin, cattle predominated at 53.9%, followed by pig at 36.3%, sheep/goat at 7.3% and horse at 2.5%. Wild animals seem not to have formed a significant part of the diet and cereals were not much in evidence at the site, although there were a few seeds of barley. The relatively high proportion of pig is appropriate to the interpretation of feasting at the site as these were par excellence the animals raised for meat. Pork is the meat of warriors in early legends. An especially high proportion of pig bones was noted at Navan Fort and here too feasting may have been related both to ritual and to the entertainment of those of high status. Among the animal bones found at Navan was the skull of a barbary ape imported from North Africa and once perhaps the epitome of luxury and conspicuous consumption. Since only the skull has been found we may have to be cautious about imagining the unfortunate ape shivering through its last days at Emain Macha. If a live ape had been imported it may have been a diplomatic gift or perhaps a present from a foreign merchant anxious to gain the favour of the powerful people who controlled the region. The cattle at Knockaulin seem to have been relatively small beasts standing from about 1.07 to 1.15m high at the withers. This is considerably smaller than the animals which were recorded from the Beaker settlement at Newgrange two and a half thousand years earlier and those from Haughey's Fort about a thousand years before. If large breeds of animal really are the hallmark of high status sites, then the beasts slaughtered at Knockaulin were not collected from the herds of an elite of prize cattle-breeders but perhaps from their dependants in the form of tribute. There is evidence of the cultivation of barley, rye and oats at Carrowmore in Co. Sligo around this time, but our direct evidence of the foodstuffs of the Iron Age is meagre.

We have in this period the first direct evidence for the ard. One of two ard points found at Gortnacartglebe in Co. Donegal was dated by radiocarbon to around the beginning of the Iron Age and a well-preserved point was found under the timbers of the Corlea road. The best archaeological evidence for the practice of tillage is indirect and dates to the first or second centuries AD. Sometime around then, a new implement for grinding corn was introduced – the rotary quern. This consists basically of a lower stone upon which an upper stone is turned on a pivot. Corn fed through a hopper-pipe or hole in the upper stone is ground between the two stones. One type in Ireland has a heavy, bun- or beehive-shaped upper stone and it occasionally carries decoration in the form of simplified La Tène-style motifs. About two hundred of these have been found, all of them in the northern half of the island and they complement the distribution of other La Tène material. Perhaps derived from Britain, they may be associated with an agricultural revival which is clearly marked in the pollen-diagrams around the third century of the Christian era, a period which we believe also saw the introduction of the plough with coulter. This phase of later Iron Age agricultural growth marks a fundamental change in the landscape with woodland giving way permanently to tillage and pasture and never again advancing significantly over farmland in times of stress.

Other Landscape Changes

We have looked until now at the changes effected by the activity of man and occasionally at issues of soil degradation which may have been partly triggered by human actions, but it is possible that there were other effects that altered the landscape in important ways in the period from about 4000 BC onwards. Coastal erosion and deposition is a constant process which accelerates and slows down from time to time. At the maximum transgression of the sea, features such as raised beaches and the tombolo linking Howth in Co. Dublin with the mainland were thrown up. Sand bars and the like are continuously built up at rivermouths and were presumably in constant formation then. The low clay cliffs of the mid-section of the east coast may have been under constant attack throughout the period. A pair of passage tombs seems to have fallen into the sea at Gormanston in Co. Meath and they are eloquent testimony to the loss of land to the sea since Neolithic times. A little further south at Barnageera in Co. Dublin, between Skerries and Balbriggan, a large stone carrying typical passage tomb art was found on the beach below a clay cliff; it may be the last recognisable element of a megalith now completely eroded away. A portal tomb at Rostellan on the east side of Cork Harbour now stands in the water. At Ringarogy Island in the estuary of the River Ilen, about 3km north-east of Baltimore in Co. Cork, a small passage tomb is almost completely covered at high tide. These are eloquent testimony to the changes in land and sea levels since Neolithic times in the drowned valleys of the coastline of the south-west. Inland it is possible that the flood plains of many rivers were being built up in relatively recent prehistoric times. This we might attribute to the increased run-off regime of streams and rivers caused by the removal of tree-cover. At Ballinvegga in Co. Wexford, at the southern tip of the Blackstairs mountain, a stream which is a tributary of the Barrow drains a shallow basin. It has an extensive flood plain which has been drained artificially. Its sands and gravels are about 1.5m thick and rest directly on glacial deposits; the sands and gravel contain a great deal of vegetable matter from oak trunks to hazelnuts. A radiocarbon date from the base of the deposit gave an age of about 1825 BC. It is possible, therefore, that the flood plain was forming from about 4000 years ago and was, in part, a consequence of local removal of forest. The sediments washed out by the increased run-off frequently contain ancient pollen and this is often deposited on top of younger material, thus inverting the record. Researchers must be vigilant, therefore, to ensure that they read it in the correct sequence.

6. THE BEGINNINGS OF HISTORY 300-840 AD

300-450 AD

Pollen studies from sites scattered throughout Ireland show that at about the end of the second century AD there was a dramatic increase in arable farming. Forest which had expanded during collapse of agriculture in the early Iron Age was cut back and the pollens of grasses, plantains and bracken increased. At Lough-na-shade beside Navan Fort, clearance continued steadily until levels of farming achieved their pre-collapse intensity by the end of the sixth century AD. At Navan, sampling intervals were close enough to pick up a slight hiatus in the later sixth century when scrub hazel seems to have re-colonised some of the newly-cleared land and this suggests a slight check in the expansion of farming there for reasons which are not clear. This new phase of clearance marks a decisive turning-point in the history of the Irish landscape: before, farming took place in an environment where there was considerable forest capable of renewing itself rapidly, but after the clearances begun in the later Iron Age, the destruction of the major woodlands began – a slow and unreversed process. From then on, forest survived in a landscape dominated as never before by agriculture and pastoralism. What brought this about?

The expansion in farming has suggested to some that a new population group entered the country, perhaps refugees from Roman conquests in Britain. There is some slight archaeological evidence in the first and second centuries for this. A cemetery was found at Lambay off the coast of north Co. Dublin. It included the grave of at least one personage of high status who was buried with personal equipment typical of first century AD Britain; other finds from the cemetery included copper-alloy brooches of Romano-British style and a local imitation of them. On the mainland opposite, at Drumanagh just south of the village of Loughshinney, is a large promontory fort which has recently gained some notoriety because of wildly inaccurate claims that it had been the site of a Roman fort. Over the years, some Roman material has been reported from the site after ploughing. In more recent times, an exceptional group of artefacts was collected illicitly from the fort by treasure hunters. It is clear from the material that an emporium of sorts existed at Drumanagh where the manufacture of high status objects – typical Irish Iron Age snaffle-bits in bronze and also in iron – took place. Substantial numbers of large copper ingots in the form of cakes of metal testify either to the importation of significant quantities of metal from Roman Britain where the distinctive ingot type is well-known, or to the exploitation of the deposits of copper ore available in the sea cliffs to the north between Loughshinney and Skerries. These were mined in the later eighteenth and nineteenth centuries and some of the workings are still visible today. An identical cake of copper from Damastown in Co. Dublin, some distance inland, suggests that there was an internal trade not only in finished pieces but also in raw material. Roman coins and Romano-British safety-pin brooches (*fibulae*) provide clear-cut evidence of overseas trade as well as welcome independent dating evidence, the value of which is unfortunately impaired by the unsatisfactory and undocumented nature of the recovery of material. Ploughing on the fort in the 1970s revealed a series of hut sites and a sherd of a late Roman two-handled wine storage vessel or *amphora* picked up at the time suggests that Drumanagh may have remained an important entrepôt until the beginning of the Christian era. At least one find at that time – a dome-headed bronze pin – belonged to the Early Medieval Period conceivably as late as the tenth or eleventh centuries AD and the promontory fort may have been the site of an Early Medieval nucleated settlement or village.

Promontory Forts

The promontory forts as their name suggests are a coastal phenomenon and many examples, large and small, are to be found on suitable headlands around the coast (*Col. 37*). Loughshinney has produced more early material than any other single site of Iron Age times but whether we can ascribe the building of the fort to the first couple of centuries AD or to an earlier period must await further research. The east coast, because it is much less indented than the west and north, has comparatively few forts but there are excellent examples on Lambay and at the Bailey in Howth. (There is an important early saga devoted to the siege of Howth.) Some promontory forts were occupied in the Early Medieval Period – Drumanagh, Larrybane in Co. Antrim and Dunbeg in Co. Kerry are examples. A few surveyed by T J Westropp at the turn of the nineteenth century seem to have features which indicate that they were modified in later times, conceivably in the Later Medieval Period as one excavated by Brian O'Kelly at Dooneendermotmore in Co. Cork had been. Prehistoric burial mounds cluster near two promontory forts in Co. Clare. Promontory forts provide interesting evidence of coastal erosion since Iron Age times. One stack – Dún Briste, the Broken Fort – off the Mayo coast was once a fortified promontory, and a stretch of sea cliff on Valencia Island in Co. Kerry, without any trace of promontory or fort, carries a number of placenames with the element *doon* as a reminiscence of features now swept away by coastal erosion.

Some placenames, such as Drumanagh or a few kilometres to the south, Inber Domnann (the estuary of the Broadmeadowwater in north Co. Dublin) and Bargy in Co. Wexford (containing reminiscences respectively of the Menapii, Dumnonii and Brigantes) are linked linguistically to Celtic tribal names known on the continent and in Britain. These together with a number of other somewhat garbled placenames and tribal names are recorded on a map of Ireland by the second-century geographer Ptolemy (he notes the Boyne and Shannon rivers and possibly Emain Macha), but opinion is divided on the significance of these and they are more likely to reflect a common linguistic heritage than specific invasions. Some early sagas make constant reference to external armies invading and Tacitus records that at least one disgruntled Irish king attempted – without success – to interest his father-in-law Agricola in an invasion of Ireland around 82 AD. A small scatter of Roman imports in the east and north-east including some late Roman coins and other objects deposited at Newgrange – perhaps as an offering to the local gods from merchants – suggest continuing contact by way of trade and exchange with Britain, but cumulatively, the archaeological evidence hardly supports an invasion theory.

New Farming Techniques

It is, therefore, doubtful if there was a substantial transfer of population to Ireland at this time. Small groups, or processes of exchange and trade, could have effected the technological changes which seem to have underpinned the agricultural expansion. Of these, improvements in the plough which we have already discussed were probably the most significant. Because the new plough failed to turn the sod over, cross-ploughing was still essential and so fields remained square. This technology was almost certainly borrowed from Britain where the coulter-plough was well known in Roman times; the introduction may have taken place at about the same time as the rotary quern which we have already considered. The improved plough opened up new land to cultivation – heavier soils could be tackled with the more efficient equipment, the food supply could be increased and a larger population could be supported. The increased number of mouths to feed would have created pressures to take ever more land into cultivation and so gradually at first, but increasing in tempo, the attack on the surviving forests and the reclamation of wasteland proceeded. There was nothing either irrevocable or inevitable about this – very little primeval forest remained undisturbed and most of the woodlands destroyed in the rise in agriculture was of secondary and even tertiary growth and many of them were managed to provide essential timber for building. It is worth considering the speed at which forest can re-colonise farmland. In the eighteenth and nineteenth centuries much of Massachusetts was farmed. Field systems of stone walls with their associated root cellars, abandoned within the last two hundred years, can be traced in many parts of western Massachusetts now deep in areas of mature forest.

There is some evidence to suggest that initially the climate in the later Iron Age was slightly warmer than at present. This will have meant that grain crops would have ripened better; in later times, it was necessary to dry corn in kilns before grinding it. The adoption of the new form of agriculture must have had considerable social consequences. The improved ploughs were not cheap – the amount of iron required for a coulter and a share was substantial – and the cost of ore, smelting and the labour of forging might well have been beyond the resources of a farmer of low to middling status. The iron in some surviving medieval coulters would have furnished the metal for perhaps four or five typical sword blades of the pre-Viking age. The new technology may have encouraged the development of complex co-operative farming to share costs and opened up the opportunity for a well-heeled elite to expand their influence by loans of equipment or capital to purchase the new ploughs. The capital cost, the relative openness of some areas to new influences, even the receptiveness of individuals and leaders to fresh ideas will have ensured that the new farming practices spread unevenly throughout the island. On the other hand, the opening up of new land reclaimed from forest gave opportunities for the more adventurous to gain a better living and to rise in status. The uneven distribution in time and space of the benefits of the new farming may well have effected the balance of political power among ruling elites and helped to trigger the extensive re-ordering of tribal politics in Ireland, which can be dimly discerned in our earliest historical sources as taking place around the time of the introduction of Christianity.

Finbar McCormick argues that a second revolution in farming took place somewhat later – the introduction of systematic dairying as distinct from the simple seasonal exploitation of milk. This was probably an innovation from Roman Britain and one which greatly increased the food potential of land devoted to pasture. Its adoption by the Irish left a profound stamp on the structure of their society. Dairying has certain clear advantages – a cow instead of providing an occasional calf, meat and a hide, produced milk and offspring regularly over a number of years before being herself slaughtered at the end of her productive life. Of the offspring, male and some female calves were slaughtered for meat in the autumn to avoid consuming scarce fodder unproductively over winter. Some castrated males were kept to maturity or near maturity, for meat, a few were selected for training as draught animals to work in plough teams. A much smaller number was reserved for breeding stock. An early law tract on status suggests that the free farmer known as the *bo-aire* may have had a herd with the ratio of about two bulls to twenty cows as well as six oxen for the plough team. Female calves were preserved to become in their turn milk- and calf-producers. The milking of the cows, the churning of butter, the production of curds and cheese all required a degree of specialisation which in turn would have reinforced tendencies towards social stratification. Milk and its products are nutritious and even allowing for the lower yields and lesser fat-content of pre-modern farming, a rich supply of fats and protein for immediate consumption and storage for winter use became available. A common find in bogs is so-called bog-butter, buried in the anaerobic conditions to preserve it for winter. Sometimes contained in a wooden vessel, often simply wrapped in bark; analysis has shown that it is indeed butter and not cheese as is sometimes commonly thought. The practice continued into early modern times.

New patterns of land management were encouraged. Summer grazing on hills and mountainsides became important to conserve pasture on the lowlands for winter, fallow land was grazed and penned animals provided a rich supply of manure for the fields. Ireland proved, then as now, to be an ideal place for the development of dairying; the long growing season for grass and mild climate meant that animals could be left out all year round. Grass was preserved as a standing crop and investment in haymaking was unnecessary. Fencing to protect growing grass and to pen stock for milking, breeding and other purposes was required. Some of this fencing could have been temporary but it is extremely likely that there was a significant increase in permanent field enclosure. The lower nutritional content of winter grass and occasional hard winters would have placed stress on the herds. The early annalists were very concerned with bad winters and with diseases of cattle which might have threatened the livelihood and even the survival of people.

The End of Prehistory

The pattern of dispersed settlement with some regional centres (represented by the hill-forts) which we have seen established in prehistoric times persisted into the later part of the Iron Age and into the Early Medieval Period, although the hill-forts may have become merely traditional rather than regularly-used places of importance. When much of Britain came under Roman rule, a complex settlement of cities, towns, military establishments, roads, mines and other industries along with sophisticated villas with their carefully-managed estates grew up there. Ireland remained largely unaffected by these developments despite some trading contacts and some initial Roman interest in conquering the island. In parts of Britain within the Roman colony and outside it, especially north of the frontier, an older Iron Age

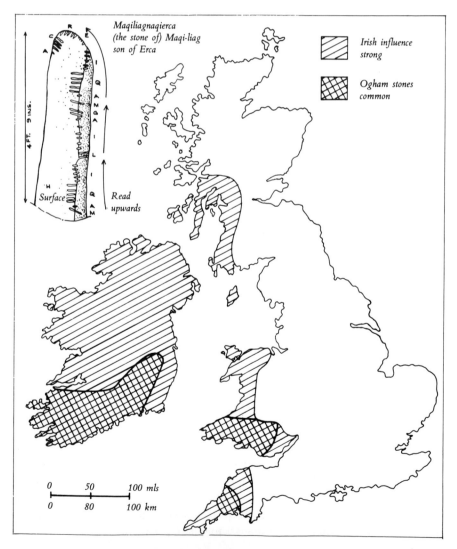

Illus. 140
Typical Ogham stone and distribution map to show areas where such stones are common and also areas in Western Britain into which there was migration to Ireland in the fourth century AD.

pattern of settlement and social organisation persisted. From the late third century onwards, but especially in the fourth, the Irish and the Picts of what is now Scotland began to raid the Roman colony. In the fourth century, Irish settlements were made in north and south Wales and perhaps in Cornwall. In the fifth century, the Dál Riata of Antrim established themselves as a ruling dynasty in Argyll. Contact with Roman culture in Wales may have been the gateway through which developments such as the agricultural improvements may have taken place and there was a considerable degree of borrowing of British words into the Irish language at about this time. The influence of Latin civilisation began to make itself felt also and Western Britain almost certainly acted as the conduit for this. Early Latin words crop up in Irish and writing in the ogham alphabet, derived from Roman script, makes its appearance. Ogham employs a series of strokes on either side of or across a stem to form letters. It seems to have been specially suitable for carving on the edges of stones and many pillarstones with ogham inscriptions survive in Ireland. The inscriptions run vertically up the side of a stone and, if necessary, across the top and down the opposite side. The inscriptions in an archaic form of Old Irish are simple commemorative formulas usually in the form of: 'A' son (or son of the son) of 'B'. One inscription at Ballineesteenig in Co. Kerry reads *Moinena maqi Olacon*: Moinena son of Olacu. Linguistic scholars have detected tribal names and personal names – even ones which may conceivably reflect service in the Roman army – embedded in the terse formulations of the ogham monuments. In Ireland, ogham stones occur in large numbers in counties Cork, Kerry and Waterford – regions associated with colonisation in south Wales (*Illus. 140*). A significant number occur in south-east Leinster and a small scatter exist in the midlands and west. Ogham stones are rare in Ulster. About 300 are known in all. In Wales, where oghams are also common and may be regarded as markers of Irish settlement, interesting variants occur where inscriptions in Latin script are found written vertically in the manner of oghams. The oghams, the first inscribed monuments in Ireland, bring us to the threshold of history and to the changes ushered-in by the arrival of Christianity.

EARLY CHRISTIANITY c.400-800 AD

The Irish colonies in western Britain, by way of intermarriage and the seizure or purchase of slaves, were probably the source of the first Christians to come to Ireland. In 431 AD, Prosper of Aquitaine recorded that Pope Celestine sent Palladius as the first bishop to the Irish believing in Christ. This was a momentous event – it was the first time in the western church that a bishop had been sent to a community outside the boundary of the Roman Empire. There is strong evidence that Palladius was most active in the east midlands and south-east of the country and that the earliest Christians in Ireland may have been established in those regions where ogham stones occur. We do not know much about the Palladian mission except what educated guesswork from placenames and some later hints in historical documents can give us. Perhaps those church sites that carry the placename element *domhnach* (angl. donagh) from the Latin *dominicum* (originally 'church building') mark the sites of some Palladian foundations. Charles Thomas has suggested that the introduction of the word *cella/cellula*, a monastic cell (later as cill, a church, to become a common placename element in Ireland), may date to the time of the earliest missions and reflect the likelihood that the very first missionaries were familiar with the monastic movement which had originated in Egypt and had begun to find favour in the west in the fourth century. The word *cella* had a specific monastic connotation in the early church.

We can picture that the missionaries slowly introduced new elements into the country – Latin learning and Latin script, books, literacy and the new architecture of churches and their associated cemeteries. Initially, there must have been many accommodations with native traditions. Converts may have continued to be buried in ancestral cemeteries; there is growing archaeological evidence for this. Land may not have been readily available for church building because the native practices of landholding would not have allowed for property to pass out of the ownership of the kin group. This may have restricted the foundation of churches to land that was the private property of an individual and some of this may have been reclaimed from woodland or other wasteland. At first therefore, the church may have established itself on more marginal land – a tradition which later became formalised by some in the search for monastic solitude. In the beginning, the liturgy may have been celebrated more often in private houses than in public places. Aspects of Christian teaching may have been especially difficult to accept – salvation for slaves and social inferiors on the same basis as for those of higher standing, for example – and the process of Christianisation may have been slow.

Other than ogham inscriptions, the earliest historical documents to have been written in Ireland are two by St. Patrick. A Briton of good family captured as a youth and enslaved in Ireland, Patrick returned after his escape from captivity and seems to have laboured amongst the northern and western Irish. His two writings: *Confession* and *Letter to the Soldiers of Coroticus*, provide a remarkable insight into the often dangerous life of a missionary working in a tribal society, negotiating the problems of dealing with local potentates, avoiding the social traps for the unwary in a highly stratified social system and constantly facing danger. An informal, almost experimental form of monasticism was known to Patrick – particularly among women – but essentially he introduced the form of Christianity into Ireland that he had known in Britain, in the same way that Palladius and his fellow-workers would have established the variety known to them in Gaul and perhaps Rome. Their ideal would have been a church ruled by bishops of territorial dioceses. A simplistic notion has grown up that a church of bishops and presbyters was planted in Ireland by the first missions and that this was superseded in the sixth century by a monastic organisation which essentially subsumed the earlier elements and provided for ecclesiastical rule by abbots. It used to be thought that an episcopal church which originated in cities of the Empire was unsuited to the rural and townless Ireland. We now know that this was not so. Bishops retained their significance and churches of importance maintained their ecclesiastical independence from abbatial rule despite the great influence of monastic foundations. Small churches, often family-owned, provided a network of pastoral care for the laity.

During the sixth century, monastic life became very popular in Ireland as a result of the example of great teachers. The impetus seems to have come from Britain but the germ of the movement seems already to have been present in the Irish church from the beginning. By the end of the century, not only had many monastic houses been founded in Ireland but Irish monks were themselves travelling abroad – St. Columba (Colmcille) to Iona, St. Columbanus, the first of many, to Europe – and the beginnings of important monastic federations can be detected. Monasteries were very often termed *civitas*, a city, in Latin. If not actually great centres of population, they were spiritual cities in a rural landscape where the proprieties of a full episcopal urban liturgy on the Roman model could be approximated. Clearly a great rapprochement between the church and secular society had been achieved by about 600 AD – in the monastic schools rules with an Irish flavour were being codified, developments in scholarship were taking place and a vernacular literature was being forged. The clear beginnings of royal interest in monasteries can be detected in the legends of the founding of Clonmacnoise by St. Ciaran with the help of the soon-to-be King of Tara, Diarmait mac Cerboll, or the foundation of monasteries by St. Columba, a scion of one of the great ruling houses of the north. His monastery at Iona (founded about 563 AD) and many of its associated houses were governed by his kinsmen over the following century. The church became a great driving force for change in Irish society and it had a deep influence on the system of land tenure. It was as Thomas Charles-Edwards pointed out the first *institution* in Ireland and unlike the individual it never died and so when it became property-holding it tended to accumulate land and goods in a manner that a secular lord could not and to transmit its wealth unimpaired though the generations. Secular rulers used to dividing inheritances must have envied the church.

The clerics gave us the first true native historical documents, initially almost entirely focused on ecclesiastical concerns but in time giving due weight to secular matters. The new writings included annals (laconic entries of the years' important events at first probably written into tables for reckoning the date of Easter) saints' lives – the first of them composed in the seventh century, along with secular and canon law and sagas. They all combine to tell us about the management of the landscape. Donncha Ó Corráin describes:

> the deep impress of the Christian church upon the toponymy of Ireland: it shaped and named the land to an extraordinary extent. It domesticated the landscape – mountains, islands, wells – and imposed thousands of its names and name-elements on the lands of settlement.

With the emergence of historical documents, the landscape began to be described and the enormous resource of placenames to be recorded. These often enshrine the memory of features now vanished, hinting at the preoccupations of the population and at how the land was managed. The appearance of native literature also marks a stage in the process of idealisation of the landscape – the eyes of the monastic solitary, or of the poet, see a different world from that of the farmer, warrior or ruler. We all construct landscapes in our imaginations, we all perceive them differently even while we accept that they may be measured, mapped and analysed.

SETTLEMENTS

Homesteads

The commonest monuments in the Irish countryside today are the circular enclosures known variously as *rath, lios, caher* or *cashel* and occasionally *dún*. Cashel and caher are normally applied to stone structures as is dún occasionally (*Illus. 141, 142*). Rath and lios are applied to examples made principally of piled earth, although many may have stone-faced banks (*Illus. 143*). The earthen examples are often referred to as ring-forts by archaeologists but this is a tendentious term as many seem never to have been intended as truly defensive. There is linguistic evidence to suggest that the terms rath and lios are not interchangeable – the word rath connotes digging and refers to the rampart and the surrounding ditch from which the upcast soil for the bank was dug. As a placename element, rath is very common in Leinster, less so in Munster and Connacht and relatively rare in Ulster. The word lios originally denoted the space enclosed by the rath but later became used loosely to indicate the entire enclosure. Extremely common in the west midlands and south Ulster and more rare but evenly distributed along the western

Illus. 141 Near Shrule, Co. Mayo. This hill-top cashel with a drystone wall lies almost on limestone bedrock. Part of its interior was cleared relatively recently, but bushes are re-invading it. The clearance revealed older cultivation-ridges; some are still buried by heavy scrub.

seaboard, the term is scarcely used in south Leinster. There may be both a chronological and an operative hierarchy in the placenames as names containing the elements rath and dún are referred to in saga and other ancient literature but lios names never. The term dún seems to connote prestige and is often the word for a king's residence. The stone cashels (the term preferred in the north west and in south-east Munster) or cahers (common in placenames in the mid-west and south-west) are rarely enclosed by ditches because they are often in rocky terrain and quarrying a ditch through rock was difficult (*Col. 40*). The word cashel, best known in the great Munster centre in Co. Tipperary, is derived from the Latin *castellum* meaning a fort.

Counts made from the Ordnance Survey maps of the last century suggest that 30,000-40,000 of these monuments existed but recent work indicates that this is an underestimate and the original total, adjusted by allowance for the rate at which aerial photography has revealed large numbers of hitherto unknown sites in many areas, may have been nearer fifty or sixty thousand. The vast numbers of placenames which include rath, lios, cashel and caher testify to the importance of these settlements. Of the many thousands of such monuments which exist today or which once existed, only about two hundred have been excavated and few of these have been totally examined. Once preserved by the superstitions surrounding them, they have been destroyed at an increasing rate in the latter part of the

Illus. 142
Staigue Fort,
Co. Kerry.
A massive cashel of
drystone masonry
with internal
chambers in the walls
and flights of stairs
leading to the tops of
the walls. It is
surrounded by a
ditch. Probably Early
Medieval Period.

twentieth century. In some areas near to urban and industrial developments, almost 60% of monuments have been removed since the Ordnance Survey began in the 1820s. But there are still areas of the country where the numbers surviving must be close to the original total and the opportunity of preserving and studying an ancient managed landscape cannot be missed.

The overwhelming trend of the evidence from excavations is that the majority of raths and their stone equivalents were built in the second half of the first millennium AD. Until recently only one, the Rath of the Synods at Tara, which was excavated by Sean P Ó Ríordáin in the 1950s, produced material which suggests that it might have been occupied as early as the second century AD, but now there is some reason to doubt that the site was truly a rath. Conor Newman who is surveying the monuments of Tara believes that it is more likely to be an assembly or ceremonial site like Tlachgta (the Hill of Ward in Co. Meath) an ancient place of formal gathering. Radiocarbon dates for houses within a rath partly levelled in the 1970s at Lislackagh near Swinford in Co. Mayo, suggested a dating range of between c.200 BC and 140 AD. While some raths were inhabited into the period after the Norman Invasion, there is as yet no compelling evidence that any were built so late. The great stone cashel of Cahermacnaghten in the Burren was the site of the O'Davorens' law school in the seventeenth century and a number of cashels in the west have added mortared architectural features which imply late occupation also. Of the vast number of sites, we can be sure that not all were lived in at the same time, some may have been built but never occupied. A substantial rath at Garryduff

Illus. 143 Cloncannon, Co. Tipperary. The rath or ring-fort, Ireland's commonest field monument, was built in the Early Medieval Period to give protection to a small settlement. Typically it is a circular area, about 30m in diameter, surrounded by an inner bank and outer ditch.

in Co. Cork excavated by Brian O'Kelly had never been used for human occupation while one nearby yielded rich evidence of occupation in the period of the seventh to eighth centuries. Some dispute exists as to whether the primary occupations were short-lived or not. At least one poem contrasts the brief lives of kings with the enduring importance of the rath of Rathangan in Co. Kildare:

> *The fort opposite the oakwood*
> *Once it was Bridget's, it was Cathal's*
> *It was Conaing's, it was Cuiline's*
> *And it was Maelduin's*
> *The fort remains after each in his turn,*
> *And the kings asleep in the ground*

Raths and cashels are not uniform and the commonest form is that of modest size with a single bank and ditch (univallate) or stone wall, typically enclosing a space of about 25-60m in diameter (about 30m is a common measurement), although examples enclosing a greater space are numerous in some areas. The bank is usually placed directly along the inner margin of the ditch and its collapse into the ditch must have been frequent although some were revetted with timber posts or stone. Some banks were crowned with a palisade – at Killyliss in Co. Tyrone, a fence of wattles woven around split oak posts had stood on the bank. The site was probably occupied from the eighth to the eleventh century AD.

An entrance in the form of a gap in the bank and a causeway across the ditch can often be seen: entrances tend to face in an easterly direction. Raths with a series of two and three banks and ditches are fairly common *(Illus. 145)* and the assumption from their imposing appearance and the obvious expenditure of effort in their construction that they were high status sites is confirmed by the indications in early Irish law that the rath of a king had a triple rampart. It is a very unsubtle statement of status; dependants were obliged to construct the raths of kings and nobles and what better way of showing off the number of your followers than the building of additional ramparts? In some cases, occupation continued at raths when the banks and ditches had fallen into disrepair and it may be that the act of digging the ditch and raising the bank was in many cases sufficient to demonstrate prestige. Maintenance, it seems, was not a requirement of status. At Seacash in Co. Antrim, the ditch had rapidly become overgrown with scrub and it became the dump for rubbish. It is rare for stone examples to have more than one enclosing wall; the demonstration of prestige may have been expressed by the massive size and finish of the masonry which almost certainly in the best examples was supervised by professionals.

Of one hundred and sixty-three raths or cashels in Co. Louth which could be analysed, the commonest, with sixty-nine examples, was univallate without a surrounding ditch and only six were bivallate and two trivallate. These were mainly recorded in the Carlingford peninsula where soil cover was thin and rock outcrop frequent. In Co. Louth, there was effectively no difference between the areas enclosed by the univallate sites and those with two or three ramparts, which seems to confirm the assertion of status as the purpose of the builders. The raths of the adjacent baronies of Ikerrin in Co. Tipperary and Clonlisk in Co. Offaly have been analysed in detail – 19% of the total of three hundred and fourteen were bivallate and interpreted as belonging to socially prominent occupants.

Status was also signalled by raising the interior of the rath in a high mound. A number of these have been excavated in Co. Down and Antrim. Some of them – now termed raised raths – show periods of occupation succeeded by the deposition of layers of soil to create fresh living surfaces thus building up the interiors. Others were constructed as platforms from the beginning. One platform rath, Dún na Sciath (The Fort of the Shields) on the shores of Lough Ennel in Co. Westmeath was associated with King Mael Shechnaill mac Domhnall, King of Mide and of Tara in the late tenth and early eleventh centuries AD. Just offshore is the great crannog of Cro-Inis also associated with him. At Knowth in Co. Meath, the passage tomb mound was used in the Early Medieval Period as a centre for a local dynasty. At one phase, two ditches were cut, one of them surrounded the mound just inside the kerb of the tomb, the second was dug around the top of the tumulus creating the effect on a grand scale of a platform rath with two ditches, with the kerb of massive stones perhaps conceived of as an outer bank. Among the raths of Co. Louth, there were nineteen raised and five platform, examples created by scarping a natural feature. In all, 19% of the Ikerrin/Clonlisk raths had their interiors raised above the level of the surrounding countryside, but the explanation there may be that they were built on low-lying and poorly-drained soils and so the interiors were raised to provide a drier and firmer living surface.

Some bivallate raths in the Ikerrin/Clonlisk region were associated, in upland regions, with groups of small univallate examples and also with clusters in disadvantaged lowland areas. Here the occupants of the more impressive sites may have been supervising or protecting those living in the less imposing raths. Could this be evidence of lordship preserved in the landscape? Another group, sited in lowlands, consisted of raths enclosing significantly larger areas than most in the region (their average diameter internally was almost 47m). A few of them showed traces of internal divisions. These seemed to be of intermediate status and they rarely occurred near more imposing sites. They may have fulfilled a variety of functions – as well as houses they may have accommodated cattle-pens. The presence of dung and of lice specific to livestock on the site of Deer Park Farms in Co. Antrim suggests that animals were penned there. However, Chris Lynn believes that the absence of trampled soil on many excavated raths argues strongly that beasts were not normally stalled within the enclosures. The evidence is equivocal – there are documentary hints to suggest that raths were used as pounds for animals seized in the course of distraint, and excavation on sites of higher status may not have revealed the full range of domestic and agricultural activities.

Matthew Stout also noticed a tendency for high status sites to be located near routes, ecclesiastical settlements or territorial boundaries. He believes that the evidence of location supports the schematised evaluation of land preserved in a law text where, among other factors which increased the value of land was proximity to a monastery or a recognised route. (Location, location and location, then as now, were the three guiding principles of house value.)

Some of the more imposing raths had elaborate entrances – Garranes in

Co. Cork had perhaps as many as five wooden gates. Some stone forts show similar elaboration – the much restored Grianán Aileach, overlooking Lough Swilly in Co. Donegal, has an elaborate entrance with mural guard-chambers defending it (*Illus. 139*). Many stone forts have finely-laid drystone masonry walls which present an imposing appearance. The central enclosure of Dún Aengus on the largest of the Aran islands, like Grianán Aileach, is set within a multivallate enclosure of prehistoric date (*Col. 39*). Despite its large size and D-shaped plan – it is sited above a sheer sea-cliff – the details of its construction suggest that here, too, we have an Early Medieval structure in the tradition of the cashels of the Burren. The presence on Aran of a number of exceptionally imposing stone forts which may all be of Early Medieval date reminds us that small island communities frequently create remarkable variants of mainland monumental traditions – for example, the Neolithic temples of Malta and its stupendous modern parish churches, or the imposing figures of Easter Island. Prestige and competitive emulation may conspire to produce the most surprising outcomes in relatively isolated communities.

Excavation evidence clearly shows that the occupants of raths and cashels were a predominantly agricultural people. Equipment for farming activities – occasional plough components, bill-hooks for reaping and perhaps hedging, shears perhaps for shearing sheep, and quernstones – are numbered among the finds. Domestic craft production – evidence of weaving and small-scale iron working, perhaps what was needed to make or repair the simpler agricultural tools – was also present. A few sites of high status, for example Garranes and Garryduff in Co. Cork, have yielded evidence of luxury craftworking, especially metalworking and occasionally of the importation of exotic materials from overseas; late Roman wine- and oil-container fragments and even tableware from the eastern Mediterranean and later from Gaul have been noted on a number of sites.

Houses

Traces of houses have been excavated within raths. There seems to have been a generalised sequence from round to rectangular houses. This is clearly indicated at the small stone cashel of Leacanabuaile in Co. Kerry where two clochan-like houses (drystone, corbelled structures) preceded a rectangular example. At Dressogagh in Co. Armagh, a round house, about 7m in diameter, was represented by rainwater gullies and traces of successive walls of wicker and spaced posts. A smaller, round house was annexed to it, referred to as a backhouse in the laws; it may have been the kitchen. These are also mentioned in literary sources and were found in Chris Lynn's remarkable excavation at Deer Park Farms. There uniquely in a rath, a succession of collapsed houses of wattles had been preserved through waterlogging and this enabled the excavator to throw a sharp light on the domestic arrangements of the period. The houses were circular and ranged from about 4m to about 7m in diameter. They had been built mainly of hazel rods woven basketry-fashion about close-set upright posts each about 1m high, taking care to keep all the sharp cut-ends pointing neatly inwards. When the weaving reached the height of the posts, new ones were simply driven down into the wall beside the lower uprights. The houses were double- or cavity-walled with an insulation of grassy material – moss, straw and heather – between the outer and the inner walls. Only the door frames were made of more substantial oak timbers. One complete, collapsed door frame survived and where they would have been inserted in the ground, the jambs preserved their bark; these gave a felling date of 648 AD for the tree from which they were made. The sides of the jambs were slotted to receive the wattles of the walls. The top of the lintel carried a row of holes to continue the weaving of the wicker across the top of the doorway. At one level there were three houses, two with backhouses. The houses had central hearths and beds arranged around the walls were filled with a litter of bedding. It was estimated that to build one house would take about 8km of hazel rods, surely requiring local coppiced woods. In all, the outlines of thirty houses were found at Deer Park Farms and it seems that three or four houses at a time may have stood within the rath. This may suggest that accommodation for an extended family and its dependants was provided there. The essentially agricultural occupation of the inhabitants was emphasised by the discovery on the site of the discarded paddle and hub of a horizontal mill-wheel, a bill-hook, pruning-hook, shears and a plough-sock. A drill bit testifies to carpentry and a wooden last to the making of shoes.

Social Theory and Raths

Raths are homesteads and indicative of a dispersed rather than a nucleated settlement pattern. Thus they represent a continuation of what seems to have been the dominant settlement pattern of prehistoric times. Elaborate theories have been constructed to explain their origin, but in essence raths are simple and could owe their development to the earlier enclosed sites becoming more formalised in their shape and construction over time. Some see them as a distinctive new phenomenon in the landscape, owing their appearance to similar enclosures of late prehistoric date in either Cornwall or perhaps Wales. Harold Mytum suggests that they are part of a package of external influences which included Christianity. The new religion with its emphasis on private salvation he believes placed a premium on individuality and encouraged the growth of personal property. He sees the developing dispersed settlement pattern in western Britain in late prehistory as evidence of the rise of individual as opposed to communal holding of property, imported later to Ireland through interaction with Irish settlers in Wales. Finbar McCormick argues that the adoption of dairying was a significant factor in the development of the rath, with the enclosure being used to pen and protect valuable cattle as well as to provide living space for humans. Neither approach is convincing. Dispersed settlement was a feature of prehistoric Ireland, not an exotic innovation (private property may thus have had remote prehistoric origins here too), and the ideological interpretation smacks more of twentieth-century wishful thinking than of early medieval reality. The stress placed by Mytum on a complex of factors is, however, important. Reliance on a single characteristic to explain the phenomenon of the rath and all it implies for social development and for complex and formalised social stratification is unwise. It is very likely that the rath originates in part in the simple enclosed settlements which we know existed in the Bronze Age and some at least of which were built and occupied in the Later Bronze Age-Iron Age transition. The new findings at Lislackagh strengthen the notion of some continuity. Other evidence might be that the royal site of Cruachan (Rathcroghan in Co. Roscommon) ancient centre of Connacht, is a complex cluster of raths and other enclosures and mounds. However, geophysical survey by University of Galway has now revealed a massive ritual enclosure, so perhaps we must think of it in the same terms as Tara and Navan Fort. Navan, which was probably finally abandoned as a major political centre in the fifth century, may well have enclosed a small rath within the circuit of its rampart. Tara, which symbolically at any rate continued to be politically significant in historic times, encloses two other rath-like enclosures within its principal circuit, Raith na Righ. Cashel, which seems to have been founded at the dawn of history and to have virtually no prehistoric occupation, was as its placename implies, a great stone fort whose occupants engaged in long-distance trade – exotic pottery has recently been found there.

CRANNOGS: LAKE DWELLINGS 500-1000 AD

Another form of dwelling the origins of which are contested is the crannog. Essentially crannogs are substantial artificial or partly artificial islands constructed in lakes as platforms for dwellings. It has been argued that they represent a continuation into the Iron Age and Early Medieval Period of the tradition of lakeside habitations of the Later Bronze Age. The crannog of the Early Medieval Period has certain formal characteristics which mark it out in a special way from the earlier lake dwellings – the structures are substantially artificial although some exploit a small natural island or a rise in the lake bed to economise on efforts of construction. The adjacent crannogs of Ballinderry 1 (in Co. Westmeath) and Ballinderry 2 (in Co. Offaly) show the contrast very well. Ballinderry 1 was a wholly artificial construction while Ballinderry 2 was built on a small island and the early medieval layers sealed the Later Bronze Age habitation. The basal levels of Ballinderry 1 were placed on a layer of nineteen massive split-oak balks pegged to the bottom while at Ballinderry 2, a substantial log-boat had been incorporated into the foundations. At Moynagh Lough in Co. Meath, John Bradley has found that the crannog was built on a site that had seen a succession of occupations as far back as the Mesolithic Period. The typical crannog is defined by a circular palisade of close-set piles driven into the lake bed. These revet the material – a mix of stone, brushwood and timbers – which forms the platform. In a number of cases, a palisade of stout posts with planks fitted into grooves in their sides was constructed. The latest in a series of three at Lagore Crannog in Co. Meath took this form and traces of another were identified at the royal crannog of Cro-Inis in Lough Ennel in Co. Westmeath. Some midlands crannogs seem to have been largely built of stone – massive stone-cores have been identified on sites in Lough Ennel. Cro-Inis is a massive cairn of stones within wooden palisades; a small castle-like structure was built on it in the Anglo-Norman period. In Donegal, there are crannogs composed largely of heaps of stone dumped on lake beds. These different approaches to building may have been governed by the scarcity or abundance of timber or to the degree of difficulty encountered in carrying stone as opposed to floating wooden building material to the construction site. There may be a chronological element however and the pattern of oak growth established by dendrochronology suggests that in the later first millennium, mature oak had become rare and management of woodlands to produce structural timbers of good size may have become important. Large crannogs composed almost wholly of wood may then have become uneconomic.

Crannogs were substantial undertakings and their builders must have made significant inroads into the local woodlands to provide the roundwood for piles and other structures, the split planks for palisades and the vast amounts of brushwood and wattles for the houses constructed on them. Most crannogs surveyed show gaps in the palisades – usually facing the shore – to accommodate the coming and going of boats. Some were reached by causeways and some have revealed evidence of elaborate entrances – there was a log pathway to the entrance at Moynagh Lough; one of its timbers gave a dendrochronological date of 625 AD. At Cuilmore Lough four massive posts at the entrance have prompted the suggestion that a gate-tower existed there. A succession of houses was excavated at Moynagh Lough where an earlier round house of about 7.5m diameter was replaced by one of 11m. At Lagore Crannog, a sequence of early dwellings on site seems to have been compressed by later building as earlier layers compacted and settled into the lake bed.

Illus. 144
Iron implements from
Lagore Crannog,
Co. Meath:
a ploughshare;
b plough-coulter;
b billhook;
b axe.

There may have been as many as two thousand crannogs and on the basis of recent dendrochronological dating of Ulster examples and of Moynagh Lough, it seems that the heyday of crannog building was the late sixth to early seventh century AD. We know that many had long occupations; some were modified in post-Norman times, and there is evidence in the occurrence of large quantities of Later Medieval cooking pottery on crannogs in Co. Fermanagh that lake sites there were occupied into the seventeenth century. An illustration on a map of Ulster shows a crannog under siege during the Nine Years' War (1594-1603). The early medieval deposits on crannogs show that their occupants were mainly farmers. Tools and occasionally weapons are found, but because the conditions for preservation are so good, a much greater range of organic evidence is available. Wooden vessels, leather, textiles, spinning and weaving equipment were found. A distaff was recovered at Lough Faughan in Co. Down and fragments of woollen cloth found at Lagore. Animal bones show the same pattern of food production as those from raths. Many crannogs yielded evidence of luxury production. At Moynagh Lough, for example, bronze-working was important; many hundreds of mould-fragments for the manufacture of trinkets were found. At Lagore, which we know from documentary sources was a royal residence, fine metalwork was produced also but perhaps there it was undertaken from time to time at the behest of the noble residents rather than as part of the day-to-day livelihood of the occupants. Although the range of evidence from the crannogs matches very closely that from the raths, we can

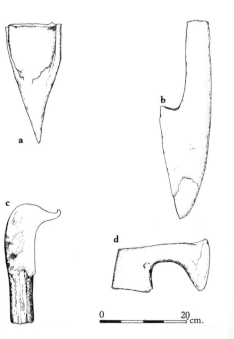

Illus. 145
This small lake at Lisleitrim in Co. Armagh contains a crannog. On the slope nearby is a massive rath, the ramparts of which signal that its occupant was of high social standing. The relationship of the crannog to the rath has not been demonstrated but they are likely to be roughly contemporary and they could conceivably have been the residences of a single important family. The crannog might have served as a refuge in a time of crisis.

be certain that in one respect they differ – it was extremely unlikely that animals were stalled on crannogs. The occupants lived by farming and dairying on shore or by the control of those who did (*Illus. 144*). The crannogs clearly had a defensive purpose, their occupants had valuables to protect and if they were rulers or important lords, their persons would have been valuable also. Some crannogs seem to have had on-shore sites associated with them. The platform rath of Dún na Sciath beside Cro-Inis on the shore of Lough Ennel is a case in point. Lisleitrim crannog in a small lake in Co. Armagh is overlooked by a splendid trivallate rath on the slope above the shore (*Illus. 145*).

Other habitations

Open habitations are difficult to locate but a few have been identified. At Craig Hill in Co. Antrim, a timber-framed rectangular house was built on a terrace on a slope. A souterrain was associated with it. Near Larne at Antiville, another rectangular house was set in marshy ground; it too had a souterrain. At Ballywee in Co. Antrim, a rectangular house with a souterrain was set beside a bank and close to outbuildings including what may have been a barn. Two more souterrains were found at the site. At Lough Gur in Co. Limerick, a site called 'The Spectacles' consisted of a series of little plots, one of which contained a round house about 4.5m in diameter.

At Knowth, in the tenth century, there were at least nine rectangular houses associated with a number of souterrains. On Beginish in Co. Kerry, a settlement of the Viking Age was represented by a number of houses associated with a pattern of fields.

Open settlements along the seashore, which occur frequently, pose a problem. Were their occupants seasonally exploiting the food resources of the sea or were they in a sense permanently confined to a strandlooping existence? At one site at Dooey in Co. Donegal there were burials and extensive evidence for craft-metalworking. This is odd because all the necessary materials and fuel had to be imported onto a remote location.

Promontory Forts

A number of promontory forts show use in this period. At Larrybane in Co. Antrim there was an intense period of occupation and the evidence of animal bones suggests that there was a particular interest in sheep-rearing. At Dunbeg on the Dingle peninsula, a complex of five ditches and a stone rampart defended the small promontory (*Col. 42*). A ^{14}C date from one of the ditches suggests that it was built in the later first millennium. The stone defences have an elaborate entrance with guard chambers in the wall. Inside was a stone house of clochan type with two phases of occupation dating roughly from the ninth to the thirteenth centuries AD.

Souterrains

One of the most enigmatic and numerous monuments of the period – with over two thousand known examples – is the souterrain (*Illus. 146*). Essentially these are underground passages, usually stone-built, leading to one or more chambers. Equipped with creepways which cause the person entering to bend or even crawl and often with changes of level, they were intended as a form of defence. They are associated with raths, promontory forts, monastic sites and some unenclosed houses. At Dunbeg, a souterrain ran from the house under the rampart to emerge along the causeway; clearly this could have functioned as a sallyport for defenders. Many have only a single entrance and some are equipped with air vents. They may have been suitable for temporary refuge during a raid but probably perilous for anything longer.

Col. 31
Newgrange and its setting on the bend of the River Boyne. In the centre right is the tomb with its reconstructed facade. To the left on the terraces of the river valley are smaller tombs, earthen embanked enclosures and other features. Immediately beside the tomb are the concreted markers indicating the site of the great ritual circle. Below the tomb are the traces of the parallel embankments of a cursus monument of the Later Neolithic period. The modern field system is probably no earlier than the eighteenth century. Trees and bushes are now confined to the field banks and river margin.

Illus. 146
Artist's impression of a souterrain. A feature of many of these are changes of level which oblige the person entering to crawl while those further in can stand comfortably.

32

Col. 32

*The interior of the passage
tomb of Newgrange,
Co. Meath.
This view taken from the
innermost recess of the
cruciform chamber looks
towards the passage.*

Col. 33

*Rathellin near Leighlinbridge,
Co. Carlow.
A crop mark of concentric banks
and ditches marks the site of a
ring barrow of probable Bronze
Age date. Aerial photography
regularly reveals the hidden
landscape as the disturbed soil
of ancient sites is reflected in
varying patterns of vegetation.*

33

34

Col. 34

Tara, Co. Meath, looking south. In the foreground is the 'Banqueting Hall', a linear earthwork, probably a processional way, perhaps a Later Neolithic cursus. In the middle of the picture is the multivallate 'Rath of the Synods', a monument of uncertain purpose. The circuit of the large enclosure, Raith na Righ, at the top of the picture encloses a pair of conjoint earthworks possibly of rath type and the passage grave and Earlier Bronze Age cemetery, 'The Mound of the Hostages'. The site of Tara was in use from Neolithic times and the surface of the hill bears a complex pattern of successive earthworks. In early Irish legend and history, Tara enjoyed immense prestige and the kingship of Tara was hotly contested by leading dynasties of the Early Medieval Period. Note the pattern of plough marks indicating the cultivation of the site in modern times.

35

36

Col. 35
Clóenfherta or 'The Sloping
Trenches' at Tara, Co. Meath.
A complex of earthworks to the west
of the 'Banqueting Hall' built on a
steep slope. These enigmatic
monuments are arguably either
burial mounds or habitations.
Legend tells that a king of Tara,
Lugaid Mac Con, gave false
judgement and as a consequence the
royal house collapsed thus
accounting for the features of the
site.

Col. 36
Knockadigeen hill-fort near Nenagh,
Co. Tipperary. A prehistoric
rampart surrounds the summit. The
ancient landscape is about to be
engulfed in forestry – the tracks and
furrows for the plantation can be
clearly seen in the picture.

Col. 37
Dundoilroe
promontory fort,
Co. Clare.
Prehistoric barrows
can be seen in the
vicinity of the fort.

37

Col. 38
Shanid,
Co. Limerick.
This splendid rath
has a high, platform-
like central area and
two protective banks
and ditches.

38

39

Col. 39

Dún Aengus on the largest of the Aran Islands, Co. Galway is a multivallate cliff-top fort. The inner wall is built in the same manner as many Early Medieval cashels. It is likely that the fort was built about that time on the site of an earlier, Bronze Age, occupation dating to the Bishopsland Phase. The fort is defended by a chevaux-de-frise of upright stones designed to deter assault on the walls.

Col. 40

Caherballykinvarga, Co. Clare. A palimpsest landscape of ancient fields and enclosures around a great stone cashel defended by a chevaux-de-frise. A modern rectilinear field pattern is superimposed on the earlier man-made landscape.

Col. 41

Rathlogan, Co. Kilkenny. Ancient landscape survives almost intact in the valley of a stream which has escaped the attention of land improvement schemes. Overlooked by a massive multivallate enclosure – probably a large ring-fort – the valley contains ancient field boundaries and, close to the stream, fulachta fiadh or cooking sites.

40

41

42

43

Col. 43

Clonmacnoise, Co. Offaly. Founded in the middle of the great system of raised bogs flanking the River Shannon, Clonmacnoise remains a centre of devotion to the present day. The complex of churches includes the early tenth century cathedral, a round tower, Romanesque and later medieval churches. Important sculptures include high crosses and hundreds of grave slabs. A medieval castle lies just south of the graveyard. What we see within the modern graveyard is simply the core of the monastic settlement. Originally enclosed within a much larger earthwork, Clonmacnoise held workshops and houses. Recent underwater investigations have revealed the former presence of a later medieval timber bridge across the River Shannon. In the background on the west bank commercial peat extraction is in progress. The impact of tourism is shown by the jetty for cruisers and by the visitor centre (the complex of round buildings to the left of the round tower).

44

Col. 44 The principal standing monuments of the monastery of Glendalough, Co. Wicklow. The larger church is the catherdral with the round tower nearby. On the left is the small church called St. Kevin's Kitchen. These buildings belong to the eleventh or twelfth centuries and are much later than the original foundation of the monastery. Much admired in the nineteenth centry for its image of romantic picturesque desolation, early prints and photographs show the valley as treeless (see Illus. 182).

45

Col. 45

A view of a cluster of monastic buildings – beehive huts, an oratory, a cemetery and terraced gardens – on the island of Skellig Michael, Co. Kerry. Early Medieval Period. Recent investigation has revealed the existence of another hermitage on the island.

46

Col. 46

Charles Fort, Kinsale, Co. Cork. Started in 1677 on the orders of the Duke of Ormond, this massive artillery fort in the contemporary European manner was intended to guard the prosperous port of Kinsale. It served as a military barracks until 1921.

47

Col. 47
Looking south-west to
Scariff and Deenish
Island, Co. Kerry.
The offshore islands
lost their population
a long time ago. The
small holdings on the
mainland slope are
difficult to access and
will find it hard to
remain viable.

48

Col. 48
Discarded car,
Valencia Island,
Co. Kerry.

49

Col. 49
Bellacorick, Co. Mayo.
Formerly covered by
blanket bog, a
considerable area is
now being harvested
mechanically to fuel
the small electricity
generating station.

Col. 50
The conveyor belt from
a small-scale peat
dredger spreads
macerated sods on the
bog surface, Co. Mayo.

50

51

52

Col. 51
Bellacorick wind farm, Co. Mayo. Conflict exists between the need for new renewable energy sources and concern that wind farms are unsightly and noisy.

Col. 52
A blanket bog breaking down into a sea of black mush, as a result of overgrazing, Co. Mayo.

Some souterrains were constructed in a large open trench and then back-filled. Others were cut into rock, still others were tunnelled into clay where the soil was suitable for this. Many are of drystone masonry with either round or rectangular chambers. In some cases, chambers are partly corbelled and then finally roofed with large slabs. The passages which may be very long – souterrains over 100m in length are known – are often lintel-roofed and may lead to a complex of chambers. A fine example at Kealduff Upper in Co. Kerry showed a combination of techniques of drystone work, lintelling and tunnelling through the unsupported clay. The entrance to one of the chambers was cut through a large slab. Brian Williams excavated a wooden example in waterlogged ground at Coolcran in Co. Fermanagh; a dendrochronological date of 822±9 AD was obtained for the timber. Another souterrain at Antiville in Co. Antrim was associated with a house on marshy ground so considerations of dryness may not always have been important. The high quality of the stonework and the scale of many examples suggests that there may have been specialist souterrain-builders. It is likely that souterrains were also used for storage as their cool, usually dry interiors would have been suitable for keeping dairy products. However, surprisingly little evidence of this has been found. Barrels may have been stored at Balrenny souterrain in Co. Meath. A souterrain at Marshes Upper in Co. Louth, seems to have been used as a farrowing pen; a high concentration of neonatal pig bones was found in it in circumstances which did not indicate that the bones had been from dumped carcasses. The souterrain – called *uaim* meaning a cave in Irish – seems to have been the subject of Viking attack. The caves of Dowth were plundered by the Norse in the ninth century. It is interesting that on this site a large souterrain intersects with the passage of the Neolithic tomb. Perhaps the plunder was captives – always a valuable commodity – who would later be sold into slavery.

There is some uncertainty about the date and origin of Irish souterrains; similar structures are found in Iron Age Scotland, in Cornwall and in Brittany. Despite occasional reports of Bronze Age and Roman Period material having been found in them, the evidence at present suggests that Irish souterrains belong to the period 500-1000 AD. Irish souterrains associated with houses always occur with rectangular structures and these appear later than round houses.

Economy and Society

Documentary evidence, especially the law tracts written down from the early eighth century onwards, throws light on how the landscape was organised. The jurists show a proper lawyerly regard for order which leads one to suspect that many of their formulations are ideals – things are described as they ought to be not as they were in the untidy reality of daily life. Tracts on status describe in detail the possessions appropriate to different grades in society and assess legal standing. There are laws of distraint, of compensation and of management of relations between neighbours. Texts reveal the nature of inheritance or assess the relative values of different classes of land and much more.

Land was generally held in common by a kindred (*fine*) but private land existed, which an individual could inherit or acquire and dispose of without reference to relatives. In the beginning, the operative kindred seems to have been the common male descendants of a great-grandfather (*deirbfine*) but as the period wore on, a simpler, closer kindred became the more usual. Private property may well have been becoming more and more important in parallel. The earliest record of an Irish land sale is recorded in the ninth-century Book of Armagh where silver forms part of the transaction. Balancing of relative land values was accomplished by occasional reallocation of the kin-land. The law tracts make it very clear that the farmers of Early Medieval Ireland were not pastoralists as has sometimes been stated, but practised arable agriculture as well as tending herds of cattle, pigs and sheep. The laws describe in great detail the ownership of ploughs and their teams and mills for grinding corn. However, there is no doubt that cattle were of immense importance so much so that idealised values were expressed in terms of milch cows, heifers or bullocks. The highest measure of value was the *cumal* or slave woman; a term also used confusingly as a measure of land. The honour price of each grade of free member of society was calculated in terms of the payment in cattle equivalents in compensation for death, injury or insult. The honour price also established the standing of an individual's testimony in a court. Relationships of dependency were reinforced by nobles who advanced a capital of cattle to clients who regularly had to pay over a hefty proportion of the increase of the herds. Society was broadly divided into the free and the unfree. Among the free were farmers, nobles and at the top, kings. Specialists of many kinds, learned men (jurists, poets, bards and, later, clergy), craftsmen (led by those working in iron and wood) were also free and some attained a very high standing. At the bottom were those who were tied to the land but were not slaves. Of the slaves we hear a great deal in literature and other sources but they are not the subject of much attention by the lawyers concerned with status.

It has often been remarked that Early Medieval Ireland had a plethora of kings and indeed estimates suggest that as many as one hundred and fifty petty kingdoms existed at one time. One explanation for this is that the desirability of being 'royal' encouraged each segment of a dynasty to hang on to royal status like grim death even if only in a small territory. Another view may be that the variety of small kingdoms is a survival of a very ancient segmented society and that the history of early Ireland is in part the course of rationalisation of this state of affairs through organisation into larger and more powerful polities as time went on. If society in early historic Ireland was segmentary, then we might conclude that it was of a relatively recent regrowth, as we have seen some evidence in prehistory for the emergence of regional groupings which built for themselves central places (hill-forts) of importance. If any value is to be placed on the legendary history and the earliest historical sources then we can see that some kind of regional powers were in existence around the arrival of Christianity and we may allow ourselves to speculate that this was an even more ancient dispensation. The nature of early Irish society as it is reflected in our earliest sources had complex origins and some features of it, the *dynastic* segmentation for example, may have been recent and might even be regarded as the outcome of a period of disorder. One effect which was seen to operate in Later Medieval Ireland was a tendency for the members of a ruling kindred within their territory to displace other free landowners who did not share their descent. This may well have been in operation in earlier times and the romantic fiction that each polity or tribe was a great family of kinsmen acting corporately – holding the land in common and sharing the same name – has given rise to a notion of the *clan* on the romantic Scottish model which is largely unsustainable in the record of early medieval Ireland. Romance had nothing to do with it – it was all strictly business.

Enclosure

The kindred sharing ownership of land acted together to manage ploughing and harvest, access to water for stock and to deal with fencing. The laws are very useful on the subject of fences. It was essential to keep these in good repair and a variety of types is recognised: the ditch (*clas*), stone fence (*cora*), the oak fence (*dairime*) and a fence of post-and-wattle (*felmad*). The laws specify the tools used for making the fences – a spade (*rama*) for a ditch, a ploughshare (*soc*) for a stone wall, an axe (*biail*) for an oak fence and a billhook (*fidba*) for a post-and-wattle fence. Donncha Ó Corráin has explained the use of the ploughshare for the stone fence as both marking the line and by turning away the topsoil, providing a better foundation on the subsoil. The ditch and stone fences were in the bare plain (*nochtmachaire*), possibly arable land, the oak fences were in the wood and the post-and-wattle fences were in the half-plain (*lethmachaire*) which Ó Corráin thought might have been pastureland which was occasionally tilled, but here the schematising hand of a legal commentator might have been at work. The laws prescribe that a ditch should be about 3 feet (1m) wide, 3 feet (1m) deep, and 1 foot (about 30cm) wide at the bottom, the upcast earth being used to form a bank. A stone fence should be about 3 feet (1m) wide at the base and about 6 feet (2m) high. The post-and-wattle fence should also be about 6 feet (2m) high with three courses of wattle and proof against large and small animals. It was crowned with an extra defence of blackthorn. The builder of a post-and-wattle fence was expected to make the top even – a rough fence could cause injury – and here we have an echo of the care taken at Deer Park Farms to ensure that all the sharp cut ends of the wattles were contained inside the cavity wall. It is likely that post-and-wattle fencing was impermanent – it could be erected quickly to protect a plot of crops or to fence a common summer pond for cattle. It could have been used to create small temporary pounds for animals and the like. The oak fence may simply have been a line of trees felled to create a barrier. The trees were not cut through and so the branches may have lived for a time afterwards – a technique known nowadays as plashing. The law of fences is an expression of the very clear notions of private property, trespass and the standards of appropriate boundary demarcation. This is further evidence, if any were needed, that here we have a sedentary farming society.

One of the most important questions to be answered about the landscape of Early Medieval Ireland is the degree to which it was cleared of forest and enclosed for ploughland and pasture. Do we imagine islands of agriculture separated by substantial tracts of forest which only gradually gave way to the expansion of farming? We have already seen that extensive tracts of permanent grassland had developed in prehistoric times and it is likely that these remained into historic times. Enclosure had been part of the structure of pastoralism in Ireland since the later Neolithic Period at least; clearly-defined fields for cultivation are well-attested at some locations in the Bronze Age so the practice is likely to have continued into the Iron Age but our evidence for this is slight at present. The ancient laws tell us of the value of woodland and some of this too was enclosed in early medieval times, no doubt to protect the hazel rods so necessary for house-building and fencing and to control access to the nuts and mast and the other fruits of the woodland which were so valuable as supplements of the diet and as feed for livestock. The expansion of agriculture and the heavy demands placed on the oak woods led in time to a shortage of timber. There is some evidence from dendrochronology to suggest that oaks suitable for building were rare in the eighth and ninth century and again in the eleventh and twelfth centuries. Management of woods for building timbers was therefore essential. Unfenced wooded uplands are mentioned in the law tracts. Woodland was not of course uniform throughout the island. In the drier uplands of the west, pine may have continued to grow into historical times and although mentioned in early sources as a structural timber of importance, it seems to have disappeared from the pollen-diagrams by the Early Medieval Period. Perhaps it did linger on in a few localities into medieval times and some of the pine trees growing in Ireland today may be of native rather than imported descent. In the east, woods may have been confined to river valleys not otherwise suitable for cultivation, to uplands and to managed stands in farmed regions. The early sagas speak of chariots being driven freely across the plains of Ireland (good tank country) unhindered by anything as mundane as fencing, and as the tales reflect the time at which they were written down, this may indicate two quite different views of the landscape – a romantic view of the past combined with the knowledge that the contemporary landscape had been largely cleared of trees. This is an area which would repay research.

Trees

The jurists of early Ireland with their emphasis on schematisation classified the tress and shrubs of the woodland and assigned them a value. A lost text of the seventh century dealt exclusively with tree judgements. Another surviving tract classifies trees as follows: *airig fedo* (nobles of the wood), *aithig fedo* (commoners of the wood), *fodla fedo* (lower divisions of the wood) and *losa fedo* (bushes of the wood). The ordering is based on the economic importance of the tree either for the production of timber or fruit – in the case of yew for its dense wood prized in high-quality carpentry (many shrines of the period are made of yew). Oak is accorded a high status because of its acorns and its timber: hazel likewise is highly-regarded. The preoccupation with the fruits of the forest is confirmed by the annals of the time which note years when acorns were plentiful. Ash was also considered noble because its timber was used in the making of spear shafts. Pine figures as noble also, despite its lack of representation in pollen-diagrams, because of its value for building purposes. Amongst the commoners of the wood were alder, willow, rowan and elm. The lower divisions included blackthorn, elder and arbutus. The presence of the latter suggests that the text was of Munster origin since the arbutus probably only survived in the warmer extreme south-west as it does today. Fines were imposed for damage to trees, so clearly the protection of an economic asset was a priority for the jurists and their preoccupation with trees may reflect the pressures which were being placed on woodlands by widespread exploitation and clearances. Some trees were sacred and the cutting of such a tree was a profound insult and a clear demonstration of domination by an invader. Sacred trees and bushes associated with early Christianity (perhaps inherited from pagan traditions) are also known and the sight of offerings of cloth tied to a bush near a holy well can be seen in the countryside even today. At least one sacred tree at Clonenagh in Co. Laois cannot be descended from the original as it is a sycamore, a species imported only in modern times. Poisoned by the offerings of coins hammered into its trunk, it has recently fallen. Trees feature prominently in placenames. A sacred tree (*bile*) occurs in the name Moville, for example, and oak (*dair*), ivy (*éidhean*) and yew (*iur*) are common elements in names of places.

Illus. 147
Kilshannig,
Co. Kerry. Old
glacial deposits,
smoothed out by later
frost-action, lie on
solid rock. Man has
spread sea sand over
the area to replace a
poor soil with a fertile
one. On the right we
see cultivation in
unfenced strips.

Land Values

Land was valued in a systematic way in accordance with its productivity and its location. The very best land was capable of producing a wide variety of crops without manuring; it was level and free of persistent weeds. The weediness of land

was tested by turning a horse loose on it and seeing what weed fragments were caught on its legs; briars, thorns, burdocks and thistles lowered its value. Land yet to be cleared of trees was less valuable. The very best land was likely to have been in the east and south-east where today the extensive areas of grey-brown podzols provide versatile soils. Land unsuitable for cultivation included poorly-drained ferny low-lying land, mountain heathland and peat-bogs. Around the margins of the bogs and on the heathland, rough grazing was possible especially for sheep. It would have been essential, however, to guard the herds against predation by wolves. Land increased in value if it was close to a road or track, river, cattle pond, the seashore or mountain grazing. The presence of a mine on land enhanced its value also. It is important to stress that the land was privately-owned and common rights on land to hunting, collecting firewood or wild fruits were extremely limited. A neighbour could drive cattle across another's land if there was no other route. He could also cut a mill-race across a neighbour's land provided that he paid compensation and he could erect a fish-weir which abutted someone else's land. The emphasis on private property is an important one. Even for the lower grades of free farmer who only owned portions of a plough and its team and therefore were obliged to cultivate the land in common with neighbours, the farming was in no sense collective – each farmer retained ownership of his land and its produce.

A *cumal* of land seems to have been about 14ha (about 34 statute acres) in the Early Medieval Period. If it was of the best land it might have a value of twenty-four milch cows, less if the land was poorer. Bogland for example was worth eight dry cows for the equivalent area. As the word cumal is used both as a unit of value and of extent, it is not clear from the laws what was the minimum size of holding that a free farmer of the lowest grade possessed. One early eighth-century law of status states that the small farmer (*ocaire*) had land worth seven cumals on which he grazed seven cows – clearly he did not have an estate of 97ha. Something much less perhaps about 28ha (70 acres) may have been the norm, given that yields then were much lower than now.

Crops and Food

The *ocaire* is described as owning a quarter share in a plough and significantly he had only one ox. The plough was normally drawn by a team of four but we know nothing about how much ploughing actually took place each year. We do know that land was left fallow and that rested ploughland was grazed. It has often been assumed that the products of arable agriculture were much less important than those of the cattle and other animal herds in the food supply of the inhabitants but this is misleading. It is true that most excavated settlements yield substantial quantities of cattle and other animal remains and more rarely a quernstone for grinding corn or an iron ploughshare. It is however unsafe to conclude that arable agriculture was therefore significantly less important than pastoral. We know that water-powered mills were in use in Ireland from the seventh century and that ownership of a share in a mill was a requisite for even the lowest grade of free farmer. The remains of many of these mills have been found and we can conclude that grinding grain by hand was becoming less and less important as time passed.

The absence of iron plough parts is likewise misleading because the iron was valuable and the metal of broken shares and coulters would have been re-cycled rather than thrown away. The tilled land provided the grain for flour and for brewing which is mentioned so often in the laws of status. Wheat, which was greatly prized, barley, rye and oats were grown together with peas and beans. Woad for dye and flax for linen and oil were also cultivated. Sometime probably in the seventh or eighth century, the plough was fitted with a mouldboard which turned the soil cut in the furrow (*Illus. 137,138*). The new ploughs, perhaps introduced by monastic farm managers who had seen them in Europe, greatly increased productivity and enabled the heavier lowland soils to be ploughed more easily. Pollen studies from about 400 AD onwards are often complicated by the greatly increased outwash of sediments brought about by the added run-off created by expanded clearance and farming.

Vegetables added variety to the diet. Cabbages, onions, leeks, garlic and celery were grown although it is thought that these may have been mainly in the gardens of monasteries. Herbal remedies were used by both lay and monastic physicians and cultivated as well as wild herbs were used. A tap-rooted vegetable was also known together with apples and damsons. Wild fruits, including apples, were collected – it was possible in law for a productive tree in the wild to be appropriated. Bees were kept and there is a law devoted entirely to the complexities of bee-keeping. Chickens (so well illustrated in the Book of Kells), geese, cats and dogs were an important part of the farming livestock. Cats were pets but they also controlled pests such as mice which could do so much damage to stored grain. The chase added relatively little to the diet and red deer bones are a minor component on many sites. Deer were hunted and trapped and hunting was probably an aristocratic pursuit. A cross shaft from Banagher in Co. Offaly (almost certainly originally from Clonmacnoise) shows a stag caught in the sort of wooden trap which has often been found in bogs. Fishing – by means of fish-traps, netting, and spearing – is well-attested. Angling of a sort was practised and one of the most evocative objects of the period is a beautifully-decorated bronze fish-hook from Carrownanty in Co. Sligo. Collecting shellfish on the shore was an important source of food and the occasional windfall in the form of a stranded whale was a welcome if erratic source of both meat and whalebone, a material from which many objects could be fashioned – saddles are specifically mentioned as made from it. Whalebone was found at Marshes Upper in Co. Louth and at Rathmullan in Co. Down, both of them close to the seashore. Even on the shore, the ownership of what was collected and washed ashore was regulated by law.

Livestock

The laws also tell us that the livestock was made up of about equal numbers of cattle, sheep and pigs and this is certainly incorrect. The animal bones from many sites show a preponderance of cattle (often 65-80% of the bone recovered) over other beasts and the evidence of the animal bones supports the emphasis upon dairying which we have already noted. Surplus cattle were slaughtered in their second autumn. Calves were born in spring and the herds were driven to upland summer pastures where these were accessible. There, at the peak of milk production butter and pressed curds were made, the former for winter use. The herdsmen and their families often may have lived in temporary huts and traces of these from various periods are often to be seen on the uplands. This practice, 'booleying' as it was later called, persisted in Ireland into early modern times.

Pigs provided meat and their remains are always present on sites in proportions of about 14-25% of the total of bone recovered. When the numbers of individual beasts are calculated, the figures very often match those for cattle. At Rathmullan in Co. Down, overlooking Dundrum Bay, a raised rath had later been converted into a motte castle after the Anglo-Norman invasions. In the early medieval levels a number of successive phases yielded important assemblages of animal bones. In the second rath phase, the pig bones consisted mainly of mandibles and this suggested that hams were processed on site by either smoking or salting and then exported, the less-favoured cuts being retained. Pigs were mainly slaughtered around 36 months old and there is some evidence that many were killed at about the same time suggesting the harvesting of a flock rather than the occasional slaughter of single animals as the need arose. Rathmullan may have been a specialised production site.

Sheep are present in most excavated groups of bone, usually in quantities from as little as 4% to as much as almost 43% as in the first phase at Rathmullan. Sheep were kept for their wool and meat and the herds were managed to maximise the output. The Rathmullan sheep were mainly slaughtered by 42 months with a few before 18-24 months. It has been suggested that as well as on rough pasturage, sheep may also have been grazed in the immediate vicinity of sites of high status. The closely-cropped sward typical of their grazing habit would have provided a suitable playing surface for the games and exercises which we know from literature occupied a good deal of the time of the nobles and freemen.

Monasteries and Churches

The early medieval period saw the development of a sophisticated mixed-farming economy managed by kings, nobles and free farmers. The island was almost entirely settled – the distribution of raths and cashels are but part of the picture of settlement. Unenclosed houses, the largely undated huts of the uplands, monasteries and placenames all tell of a landscape that was almost wholly tamed. The ancient laws recognise the existence of wasteland and forest but as the period progressed, the amount of unclaimed waste must have diminished with rising population, appropriation of useful rough grazing, reduction of forest by clearance for agriculture and harvesting of timber. Monasteries may have played a central role in this process as many were located in areas which had relatively low agricultural potential. The monasteries survived and prospered and so some land reclamation and improvement must have been undertaken. Across the midlands in a broad band there is a concentration of famous monastic houses, many of them in bogland which had continued to grow around their locations. The appearance of remoteness is deceptive, however, as many monasteries were sited beside or at the junction of important routes. Clonmacnoise in Co. Offaly (*Col. 43*), on the east bank of the Shannon, is the focus for a number of routes along eskers which provided dry pathways through the extensive raised bogs of the area. Where the eskers are interrupted, there is some evidence that the routes were continued by artificial causeways such as that made of stone slabs at Bloomhill in Co. Offaly. The river itself was an important artery – Clonmacnoise was especially vulnerable to combined operations in Viking and later times – and north and south of the monastery are ancient fords. Monastic sites frequently occupy islands of relatively good land in the bogs and the placename *cluain* so often associated with many of them (Clonfert, Clonard, Clonmacnoise) seems to carry the implication of forest clearance. Many monasteries have placenames with the element *doire* (angl. derry) which explicitly refers to oak-woods – Durrow, Derry and Derrynaflan are examples. Derrynaflan occupies an island of about 26ha (65 acres) in the Littleton complex of bogs in Co. Tipperary. It lies in the townland of Lurgoe, a name derived from an Irish word which denotes a 'shin' or spit of land. Just such a spit provided the essential causeway to the dryland at the bog's margin. A seventh-century trackway connected Derrynaflan with a smaller bog island nearby while a reference in the *Life* of St. Ruadhan, who was traditionally connected with the site, speaks of the miraculous opening of a causeway to the island. Causeways across bogs are also referred to in the lives of St. Colman of Lann Elo, a monastery at the north end of Lough Ennel, and of Brigid of Kildare. Littleton Bog has a scattering of monastic sites around its margin on patches of good land now completely insulated by wetlands. At Derrynaflan, a ditch or fosse forming the monastic enclosure was completely inundated by the growth of bog since it was dug – a process no doubt hastened by clogging its drainage with the rubbish of the monastery. The great expansion in evidence for farming revealed in the pollen-diagrams for the period and especially from Littleton Bog itself almost certainly testifies to the monasteries stimulating the growth of farming especially in areas previously left waste.

The earliest church sites – by no means all monasteries – that we can identify, seem to have been simple, small enclosures sometimes containing inscribed pillar stones with simple crosses or other Christian symbols and perhaps the remains of a simple church. The classic stereotyped picture of early Irish monasticism is based on the wonderfully preserved remains to be found along the Atlantic seaboard where stone was the principal material of construction and where, as a result, the layout and often the standing buildings are clearly to be seen (*Illus. 148, 149*). These remains – notably those such as Skellig Michael (*Col. 15*), on a remote pinnacle of rock – promote the notion that the Irish church was dominated by ascetic hermits around whose cells or tombs the pious gathered to form monastic communities. There is no doubt of the importance of ascetic religious practices in the early Irish church but these models of monastic development are deeply unsatisfactory for very many reasons. The powerhouses of Irish Christianity in the seventh and eighth centuries were not in remote places; they were in the midlands, in prominent coastal settings north and south and in areas of agricultural and political significance elsewhere. Monasteries of outstanding importance such as Armagh, Kildare, Lismore, Durrow, Kells and Derry spring to mind. The remains of

these monasteries are now difficult to trace. Some such as Clonard are noticeable mainly as a series of earthworks, others have shrunk to little more than a graveyard sometimes still in use. Others are marked by substantial remains of quite late date, including round towers (built from the ninth to the beginning of the thirteenth centuries), stone churches (probably in no surviving case earlier than the ninth century), carved high crosses (also unlikely to be earlier than the ninth century), or successor Later Medieval or modern churches (*Illus. 150, Col. 44*). These remains represent the first really sophisticated architecture in stone, other than fortifications, which we have seen since early prehistoric times and there is little doubt that the impulse to build masonry towers and churches derived from the ecclesiastical architecture of mainland Europe. Wooden churches, however, built of substantial timbers or even of wattles continued to be erected as late as the twelfth century.

Many monastic and other church sites still show evidence of a surrounding rampart, intended more to mark the spiritual boundary of the foundation (*termon* from the Latin *terminus*) than to provide a practicable defence. Very often this takes the form of a roughly circular outer vallum or embankment with an inner eccentrically-placed smaller one, thus giving the better-preserved examples the characteristic 'fried-egg' plan. Traces of a substantial rectangular rampart can be seen at Clonmacnoise where excavation has shown that there were houses and workshop areas. Some monasteries constituted the cores around which a later accretion of houses formed to create towns and the original monastic lay-out can often be traced with great fidelity in the modern street-plan. Very good examples of this include Armagh, where excavation has revealed that settlement within the monastery existed at a considerable distance from its sacred core at the site of the present Church of Ireland cathedral. Kells and Duleek in Co. Meath and Lusk in Co. Dublin also preserve much of the plan of the original monasteries around which they developed (*Illus. 151*). Research suggests that there may be as many as two thousand ecclesiastical enclosures in Ireland. Of these, some were non-monastic small proprietary churches served by a secular priesthood but many were true monasteries with communities of monks and lay dependants.

The development of the church in Ireland was very dynamic and to freeze our view of it at any one stage would be misleading. Many small churches found it in their interests to ally themselves formally with larger foundations for protection and for economic reasons. Others were allied because they traced their origins to a common founder. In various ways, therefore, federations of loosely-linked foundations grew up. Monasticism was not invented in Ireland. When in the sixth century it became popular, it was as a mature institution with rules and practices already developed abroad. The Irish gave it a particular twist but the management of monasteries and monastic properties was already well-understood. In later centuries, the ecclesiastical and court administrators of the Carolingian empire wrote treatises on the management of estates. One of the most famous of these was for the monastery of Bobbio in northern Italy founded by St. Columbanus in 614 AD and closely connected with Ireland throughout the Early Medieval Period. It is inconceivable that the much-travelled churchmen of early Ireland would not

have had access to this literature of management theory and the growing wealth and importance of monasteries probably had as much to do with good administration as with other factors.

Monasteries became so important economically that the larger ones became closely allied with important kings and the cadets of leading dynasties often provided their abbots. The office of abbot became increasingly separated from purely ecclesiastical concerns and many were in effect great lay lords administering monastic properties and were accorded an honour price of fourteen cumals, the same as that of a provincial king or an archbishop. Monastic office frequently became hereditary and even where abbots were churchmen, they were often chosen from the kindred of the founding saint. The church was Ireland's first *institution* as we have seen and unlike the kings and secular landowners, it never died and thus its possessions tended to accumulate in contrast to those of lay potentates whose inheritance was divided and subject to the claims of a wide kindred. The monasteries rapidly became owners of extensive property. They had many tenants and in time the word *manac*, a monk, came to mean monastic tenant and the abstract noun derived from it, *manchuine*, came to mean the duties owed by a client or follower to a monastery or to a secular lord. The monasteries disposed of a great deal of manpower, they became depositories of secular wealth protected to some extent by sanctuary. Their farms, close at hand or far away, provided them

*Illus. 150
Ardmore,
Co. Waterford.
This ancient
monastic site was
founded by St. Declan
and briefly, in the
twelfth century, was
the seat of a
bishopric. The small
St. Declan's Oratory
is reputedly the grave
of the saint and is a
place of pilgrimage.
The cathedral is
Romanesque and the
round tower with its
elegant masonry was
perhaps the latest to
be erected in Ireland.*

Illus. 151

Kells, Co. Meath. A monastery was established here by the early ninth century when the community of Iona moved here as a result of the Viking threat. The settlement of Kells was important both in the pre- and post-Norman period and the layout of the modern town with its curved streetlines still preserves much of the plan of the Early Medieval monastic settlement. The core of that settlement – the Church of Ireland parish church, the round tower, high crosses and cemetery – can be seen just below the centre of the picture.

with a surplus and they naturally became centres of trade including long-distance trade. We have as yet very little direct evidence of monastic agriculture but at Church Lough on Inisbofin, a dramatic increase in cereal cultivation seems to coincide with the foundation of a monastery nearby at the end of the seventh century. Where they possessed important relics and were the sites of pilgrimage, their status and wealth increased significantly. In the Viking Age, many monasteries were raided repeatedly and this shows that they were capable of recovering quickly from a setback. Some of these raids probably coincided with feastdays and so harvesting the manpower of the monastery and its pilgrims for the slave trade may have been a major objective of the Vikings. Documentary sources reflecting the position in the tenth and eleventh centuries, speak of streets and suburbs at some monasteries such as Armagh, Kildare and Clonmacnoise. This has led to the view that some of the earliest towns in Ireland were in formation around the greater monasteries in late pre-Viking times and that the process of monastic urbanisation was boosted by the Irish experience of the first Viking townlike settlements from 840 AD onwards.

The debate is subject to great over-simplification led by the desire to provide pat answers to extremely complex problems and we shall return to it briefly later. The economic importance of Irish monasteries is not in doubt. They formed a significant factor in the worlds of politics and military strategy. As great lordships they had their interests to protect and their clients provided them with military levies to fight on their own account and on that of secular rulers. Indeed, if the monasteries had managed to obtain ownership of very extensive lands, no king could have tolerated their exemption from his service in time of war; he would have been greatly weakened had he done so. In this, as in so many other things, the early Irish monasteries were little different from contemporary religious houses in mainland Europe.

Francis John Byrne has suggested a fundamental way in which monastic foundations changed Ireland politically. If the monasteries of the midlands in Leinster and north Munster did much to reclaim wasteland and populate the region, they may well have opened a can of worms. By the early eighth century, the Eoganacht kings of Munster and the great Uí Neill dynasties of the north and midlands, previously separated by tracts of inhospitable land, came into conflict and began an intermittent struggle for domination which lasted until the Norman invasion. In time, the traditional historians developed a theory to explain this retrospectively. Ireland, they claimed, had been divided since time immemorial into two halves, a northern *Leth Cuinn* (Conn's Half) and a southern *Leth Mogha* (Mugh's Half) divided very roughly along the line of the Esker Riada. The opening of this land by monastic foundations may have brought about the direct conflict of interests which fuelled the rivalry.

It would be a mistake to over-correct the traditional, unworldly, saintly view of the church; the monasteries were a spiritual force, capable in the eighth and ninth centuries and again in the twelfth of generating important movements of spiritual renewal. They remained centres of learning and of piety and they provided sanctuary for those who needed it. Leading churchmen sponsored conventions to protect the church, the weak and non-combatants. The monasteries acted as a conduit for new and civilising ideas and to the very end of the native tradition, the ascetic impulse was valued and supported. Monasteries also became centres of craftsmanship – the wealth which they generated and the requirements of the church provided both the means and the stimulus. The cosmopolitanism of the church provided a window on novel technologies. The relative concentration of population afforded them opportunities to develop techniques of processing the products of their estates – fulling and leather-making spring to mind. The production of suitable skins for manuscripts indicates how extensive were the herds on which the monastic vellum-makers could draw; the Book of Kells was made from about one hundred and eighty-five uterine or very young calves, culled from a herd of perhaps twelve hundred cattle. With their emphasis on a predominantly vegetable diet for monks, monasteries may also have been instrumental in introducing novel food plants to Ireland and in time their kitchens may have seen the beginnings of a sophisticated cuisine – that is certainly the implication of a late satirical poem, the *Vision of MacConglinne*, which gives a pompous burlesque genealogy for the abbot of Cork reflecting the culinary reputation of his house:

> *Son of meat, son of juice, son of lard,*
> *Son of stirabout, son of pottage, son of fair radiant fruit,*
> *Son of smooth clustering cream, son of buttermilk, son of curds,*
> *Son of beer, glory of liquors, son of pleasant bragget,*
> *Son of twisted leek, son of bacon, son of butter,*
> *Son of full-fat sausage.*

(Bragget is a drink made of ale and honey.)

Had monasteries become towns by the beginning of the ninth century? The answer to such a question is likely always to be unsatisfactory. If there were a process of gradual urbanisation we might be able to establish it archaeologically when it had been completed, but at any given earlier stage in the process we should be faced with uncertainty. The argument from physical remains is very like the old question of how many hairs make a beard – how many houses, how many public buildings and places of assembly, how much evidence of long-distance trade is required to establish archaeologically the urban character of a site? Some of the secular functions of towns – trading and manufacture perhaps – were fulfilled by the monasteries in an otherwise rural society. Other more informal seasonal trading locations may also have existed, at suitable harbours and beaches, at important inland meetings of routes, at traditional assemblies and the like, but these had much less potential to develop as urban settlements than a large wealthy monastery which was the focus for year-round economic activity and the centre for a substantial population of dependants, however dispersed their homesteads might have been. We are probably entitled to view the greatest monasteries as some form of town by about the year 1000 AD, but by then true secular towns founded by the Vikings had already been in existence for over a century.

Early literature, especially saints' lives, speaks of the larger monasteries as cities and in the spiritual sense this is entirely understandable. We know that the early Irish church, once it had emerged from the relative isolation of the sixth century, produced many leaders who were preoccupied with Roman orthodoxy. In the past, the importance of the abbot has tended to obscure the ecclesiastical significance of the bishop in the Irish church – bishops were essential for the ordination of priests, the consecration of other bishops and for many other functions. The early liturgies were celebrated by bishops assisted by presbyters and bishops were par excellence the creatures of cities where elaborate celebrations, including processions, based on late Roman ceremony developed. In townless Ireland, the monasteries almost certainly provided the only appropriate setting.

This may explain a feature of Irish monasteries that has puzzled commentators and that is the building within them of many fairly small churches rather than a single large one. A number of explanations have been advanced for this: mass was celebrated in the open air, architectural skill was limited to small structures, congregations were small and only small oratories were needed for the monastic office. This is manifestly untrue at Clonmacnoise and Glendalough, for example, where the churches are relatively large. The explanation may lie in liturgy. At Rome – the model for the early Irish church – mass was celebrated at various *stations* throughout the liturgical year. A reminiscence of this is to be found in the Roman Missal prior to the Second Vatican Council where the appropriate basilica in Rome was prescribed. The Bishop of Rome led a solemn procession to the station where he was to say Mass and the liturgy was simultaneously celebrated in all the other major churches of the city. All the celebrations were linked symbolically together to form one congregation. This practice was followed in many of the other great cities of the early medieval world. A recent key-hole excavation at Clonmacnoise on the site of the South (High) Cross suggests that something like this may have been in mind there at the beginning of the tenth century. Heather King found evidence that an early phase of occupation was succeeded by a period of burial and finally by a phase when the stone cross was erected, perhaps as a successor to a wooden one. In the early tenth century, the cathedral was erected and in front of it was another High Cross, the Cross of the Scriptures. This suggests a major reorganisation of the layout of the holiest part of the monastery to provide a great church with a cleared area in front of it with important public sculptures; a fitting setting for the practice of a full episcopal liturgy on the Roman model. When the author of the *Martyrology of Oengus* speaks of Glendalough as a Rome, he may have intended a very precise meaning rather than a piece of hyperbole. What is true of Glendalough may also have been true of the many other important monastic sites with evidence of two or more churches and shrines within their enclosures.

7. THE WINDS OF CHANGE
840 – 1903 AD

THE VIKINGS

The arrival of the first Viking raiders at the end of the eighth century is often taken to mark a major shift in Irish political, social and economic life. The effects of the newcomers were doubtless dramatic – the first generation of raids by pirates had a significant impact on the morale of the Irish, unused as they were to external threat. The pattern of raiding seemed for almost forty years to fall heavily on the northern half of the island. This would have been expected with pirates originating largely in western Norway and finding their way along sea-routes to the Orkneys, Shetlands and rounding mainland Scotland, southwards past the Hebrides and so into the Irish sea. While the raids were a great shock especially to the monasteries which were targeted, they did not bring about a fundamental change in Irish polity and the resilience of many of the monasteries attacked is shown by the frequency with which they were the victims of repeat visitations, sometimes within the one summer's campaigning season. Fragments of gilt-bronze shrines and personal ornaments from Ireland and Scotland have turned up in the Viking-age graves of Norway and these trinkets and other pieces, while eloquent testimony to the extent of the depredations, were hardly the principal object of their voyages – slaves, as we have seen, and provisions may have been the target. Few of the genealogies preserved in the Icelandic sagas omit Irish slave women from the ancestry of their heroes.

In time, the Viking raiding parties began to overwinter and by the early 840s we begin to read of Viking settlements for example at Dublin (841-2 AD) and Cork. We read of Viking fleets on the Shannon and inland raiding bases and of the occasional occupation of monasteries. Irish resistance was stiff and often very successful. Indeed, it was during the earlier part of the Viking Age that Irish monasteries began to commission new buildings in stone – a sign not of disruption but of security and planning for the future. By the end of the ninth century, significant permanent Viking coastal settlements such as Wicklow, Arklow, Wexford, Waterford, Cork, Limerick and Dublin were established around the coasts at important harbours. The annals occasionally speak of Viking settlements in passing as ship-fortifications (the term used is *long-phort*) and it is always assumed that a long-phort is a half-rectangular or semi-circular enclosure with its open side to the sea-shore or a river bank, thus providing protection for settlement and for the ships moored beside it or beached within the enclosure. The truth is that we have no idea what is meant by the term long-phort and we have so far no clearly identified field monument which might be such a structure. It is always stated that the Vikings established the first true towns in Ireland and that the genesis of some of our coastal cities lay in the ship-fortifications of the first Scandinavians to settle. The concept of the secular town was assumed to have been in the minds of the leaders of the larger raiding parties of the mid-ninth century. This is very questionable because the Vikings who dominated the early phases of activity in Ireland were from Norway where towns did not then exist. Their experience of town-life was gained when they went voyaging to western Europe.

Dublin is an interesting case in point and the excavations there have generated so much of the theory about the origins of the Irish towns that it is worth looking at it a little more closely. The intense investigations in the vicinity of Christchurch Cathedral at the historic core of Dublin city have failed to reveal any traces earlier than the tenth century. We know that the Vikings established a settlement there in 917 AD, after they had been expelled some fourteen years before from a settlement or settlements in the Dublin area following a determined campaign against them. An extensive ninth-century cemetery was excavated at intervals from the nineteenth to the twentieth century at Kilmainham and Islandbridge to the west of Dublin city, and this was thought to have been the graveyard of the first settlement which was probably nearby. It has not been found. Viking burials were also found at College Green, at Donnybrook and probably elsewhere in the modern city at a considerable distance from Islandbridge. A scatter of monastic sites – at St. Patrick's Cathedral, beside Dublin Castle (at St. Michael-le-Pole where a round tower stood until the eighteenth century), off Kevin Street (at Old St. Kevin's) and an outer grouping at Kilmainham, Clondalkin, Tallaght and Finglas together with many smaller houses – provided a focus of native Irish settlement in the region of the Liffey estuary. Most of the monasteries in the Dublin area which appear in the historical record continued to function more or less throughout the Viking age.

So what should our model of the first Viking settlement of Dublin be: a single, highly-centralised and disciplined fortified proto-town which was planned as such from scratch and which dominated the area, or something much less tidy? The untidy model may be more convincing; there may have been some small concentrations of settlement at various points around the mouth of the Liffey and single homesteads established among the native Irish – sometimes by agreement sometimes not. Perhaps many of the earliest Scandinavian settlers lived in nerve-jangling proximity to occasionally hostile neighbours. The appearance of something like a town at Dublin in the ninth century may well have been brought about by a process of accretion and by some deliberate acts of political consolidation fostered by the opportunistic dynasty of Viking kings who established themselves there in the second half of the century. If the earliest types of settlement structures were taken over from the natives, they would be largely indistinguishable archaeologically from contemporary Irish sites. In any case, the first Viking habitations at Dublin have yet to be identified and the development of the first Viking town there is contentious.

None of the excavations at other Irish towns has yielded settlement evidence of the Vikings in the ninth century. Our knowledge of the impact of the

Scandinavians, therefore, is based on historical inference and occasional stray finds. There is no compelling evidence that extensive permanent inland Viking settlements existed in the ninth century. The distribution of artifacts suggests in the main that Viking-style material found in the countryside had fallen into Irish hands by way of trade, booty or tribute. The Scandinavians were regularly defeated in set-piece battles and their greatest military successes were primarily in raiding rather than attempted conquest as well as in trade when fighting was impractical. In time, trade became more important than plunder although there were significant, but ultimately unsuccessful, attempts at wider conquests by Viking armies in the tenth century. As early as the ninth century, some Vikings were in alliance with Irish kings and took part in the immemorial dynastic feuds of the island. Intermarriage seems to have been frequent and it is likely that each Viking enclave fitted fairly comfortably into the fractured polity of early Ireland. By the end of the ninth century, the population of the coastal settlements was probably a mixed Norse-Irish one, and the excavated domestic material of tenth century Dublin is virtually indistinguishable from that found in native Irish sites. In time, aspects of Viking technology – ship-building, military tactics and improved weaponry – were adopted by the Irish and to believers in a more gentle, innocent pre-Viking Ireland, the newcomers brought with them a ferocity which had not been seen before. Viking trade with the east via Scandinavia and the rivers of eastern Europe brought a great flood of silver to Ireland sometimes in the form of coins with Islamic inscriptions on them and there is strong evidence that the ancient native system of weights underwent change in the ninth century with the adoption of an ounce equivalent to that in use in Europe, a sure sign of the internationalisation of commerce. Early tenth-century silver hoards from Ireland testify to the wealth that trade and tribute brought to the strong Irish kings of the midlands from Viking sources at this time. A particular concentration around Lough Ennell, Co. Westmeath, contained in aggregate more than 30kg of the precious metal. Large quantities of Anglo-Saxon coin came into Ireland and the first Irish coinage was struck at Dublin in 995 AD by the Hiberno-Norse king, Sitric, stressing the mercantile importance of the Viking settlements.

We have seen that Dublin – or at least an enclosed core of settlement – was re-founded in the early tenth century on a site at the confluence of the Poddle and Liffey rivers. Excavation there over the last thirty-five years by Brendan Ó Riordáin and Pat Wallace has revealed the life of the inhabitants in remarkable detail. Enclosed within an embankment, the pathways, house types, domestic and luxury crafts dramatically illustrate the layout and functioning of an early medieval town in rich detail. The trade that made Dublin so important in western Europe in the period between about 920 AD and the Norman capture of the town in 1170 AD is marked by the amber, silk, imported pottery and walrus ivory found there. Vast quantities of wooden objects and the tools and detritus of wood-, leather-, antler- and bone-working have been recovered. The houses were rectangular made of post-and-wattle with thatched roofs, hearths and bedding. The cess-pits and food refuse provide a fascinating insight into the conditions under which people lived. Some of the houses along High Street had back gardens with apple trees growing in them.

The striking waterlogged preservation has yielded a sequence of superimposed houses constantly built upon which, combined with dendrochronological dating and coin finds gives us a detailed chronology for the period. Waterford, a smaller town like Dublin enclosed within fortifications, provides us with a remarkable townscape of the tenth and eleventh century. There, some of the houses were partly sunken into the ground and provided with stout stone cellars. The foundations of a simple church with an apse at the end of the chancel gives us a notion of what the more imposing public buildings might have been like in a late Viking-age Irish town. The evidence of Wexford, known only from two small investigations, mirrors closely that of Dublin.

Dublin was at the heart of an extensive settlement in the tenth and eleventh century which extended northwards to encompass much of Fingal (Territory of the Foreigners). It included the monastery of Swords but perhaps not that of Lusk nearby. The Viking settlers probably occupied the lands along the coast where their placenames are still to be found in Howth, Ireland's Eye, Lambay and Skerries. Southwards, they controlled a substantial strip along the coast perhaps continuous to Arklow. Inland, Leixlip (Salmon Leap) is a Scandinavian name and extensive lands in north Kildare may have been included in *Dyflinarskiri*, the Shire of Dublin, mentioned in some Icelandic sagas. We must imagine that the settlers were of mixed race and that suitable accommodations with Irish rulers and the Irish way of life had been made. We do not know precisely what the extent was of the settlements at the other Viking-age towns, but Anglo-Norman documents imply the existence of substantial lands controlled by the 'Ostmen' at Limerick, Cork, Waterford and Wexford (*Illus. 152*).

The towns, like the monasteries, could not be ignored by ambitious Irish kings most of whom never seriously threatened their existence. Instead, the

Illus. 152
Map showing the distribution of Hiberno-Norse settlement in the early twelfth century.

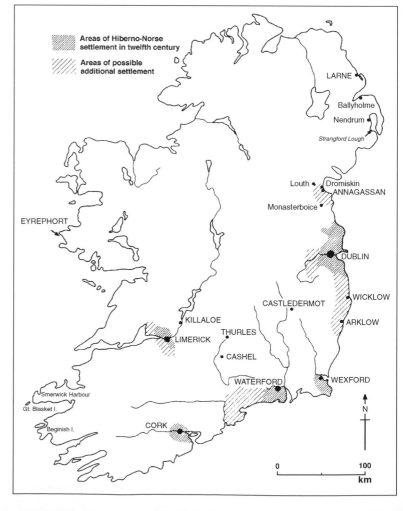

exaction of tribute from them seems to have been a major objective of policy. Dublin was frequently milked in this way but permitted to continue its commercial and political quasi-autonomy in the later tenth century. The one-thousandth anniversary of just one such extraction of protection money was used as the excuse for the Dublin Millennium celebration in 1988, which on any reckoning, should have been in 1841-1842. In time, Irish kings began to appoint officials to represent them in towns and in the eleventh century we hear of kings residing in them – surely a recognition of their strategic and commercial significance. The success of the towns, especially of Dublin, changed forever the location of political and economic power in Ireland.

At Knowth during the Viking age, a cluster of small houses with souterrains on the great mound was occupied before 1000 AD. The material found matched to a large extent the kind of finds made in Dublin and here we may have one example of an Irish settlement cluster albeit one within a dilapidated earlier enclosure. A few hints in literature might be taken to suggest that such open settlement clusters existed elsewhere, but they have not yet been found. The great Neolithic tombs were discovered about this time and Irish names appear as graffiti on their stones.

Ireland was undergoing change in the eleventh and twelfth centuries. Kings were beginning to behave more like their feudal contemporaries in Europe and asserting a dominance that cut even further across ancient custom than they had managed before. New ideas of fortification were adopted and a series of castles were built. These were almost certainly ring-work castles copied from examples in England, that is circular embanked enclosures of avowedly military purpose. They were sited so as to defend important crossings and to dominate territory. One at Athlone was built by King Turlough O'Connor. Although they may now be indistinguishable in appearance from some of the larger raths, they represent a clear departure from what went before. Christianity had changed the character of relations with the coastal towns while the native church began a long drawn-out process of reform and re-organisation which in the twelfth century culminated with the definition of territorial dioceses and the establishment of the episcopacy as the dominant governance of the church. A new monumental architecture, now bearing the hallmark of the Romanesque style, was adopted and a great revival in the decorative arts took place. The first of the regular religious orders to be established in Ireland, the Cistercians, arrived to found the monastery of Mellifont in Co. Louth in 1141 AD at the behest of the church reformers. Hard on their heels came the Augustinians and by the time of the Norman Invasion a generation later, a great network of regular religious houses had spread throughout the island. The Cistercians in particular brought with them new ways of managing estates and the beginnings of a new architecture. But above all, they provided a model of monastic rule which sounded the death-knell of the ancient native form.

The Markets of Medieval Dublin

In the same way as we formed some impression of eighth-century farming from the law texts relating to agriculture, we may get some sidelight on medieval farming from the refuse that accumulated in and around Dublin city and which has been brought to light by recent excavations. The refuse, dung and other litter was largely derived from the agricultural produce that reached the city markets. A narrow ridge of higher ground lies parallel with the River Liffey on its south side and the city was first founded on the eastern tip of the ridge. To the west, a route led away along the crest of the ridge and a market sprang up outside the west gate; the site is still known as the Cornmarket and as the name implies corn was certainly sold there. There would have been winter wheat for the production of fine white flour; there was also spring wheat, but this was probably heavily contaminated with the black seeds of the corn cockle (*Agrostemma githago*) which are much the same size as the cereal grains. The corn cockle seed was also farinaceous and for a long time it was quite happily accepted as part of the crop. It was ground up along with the wheat and speckled the flour with fragments of its dark seed coat. But the seed has a high content of saponin and can be injurious to health; modern seed cleaning methods separate the grain and the weed with the result that the corn cockle, formerly very common in Irish fields, has now almost totally disappeared. Barley was sold for baking and for brewing and oats and rye would probably have been on offer also.

In the city refuse there are large quantities of crushed seeds of goosefoot (*Chenopodium album*) and of various species of knotgrass or meld (*Polygonum*). Although these seeds are not eaten as human food in western Europe today, in prehistoric and in medieval times they formed a large part of the diet of the poorer classes either as bread or gruel and were almost certainly grown as crops in their own right and not just gleaned as weeds from the fallow. Buckwheat (*Fagopyrum esculentum*) sometimes known as sarrasin because of its eastern origin, is closely allied to *Polygonum* and is still widely eaten in eastern Europe. A German traveller in Ireland in 1828 records that buckwheat, potatoes and oats were the crops he saw most frequently and it is possible that buckwheat was still grown in the nineteenth century. Peas and beans would also have been for sale as well as cabbages and onions.

As in later times, dung-carts would have carried their loads out to the surroundings of the city where they would have been utilised in vegetable-gardens and in orchards. At the right season of the year, there would have been stalls offering pears and apples, plums, damsons and sloes, cherries, raspberries and strawberries. Some fruits came from farther afield: blackberries from fieldbanks, and bilberries or fraughans (*Vaccinium myrtillus*) from the slopes of the Dublin hills. Imported luxuries such as figs, raisins and walnuts would also have been on sale.

There were large numbers of dairies and piggeries in the city and these were a constant source of nuisance. However, they were tolerated and hay and straw together with bracken for bedding would also have been on sale. Goats were kept for their milk. Other stalls would offer rushes and sedges to strew on house floors. Moss served as toilet paper for the fastidious and bundles of moss collected on trees around the city were on sale. Butchers' stalls were probably confined to a special area, the Shambles, while the fishmongers would have been found, as the name makes clear, in Fishamble Street which still runs down to the river.

Conditions arising out of the meat trade and its associated offal were particularly noisome and the city ordinances of Anglo-Norman and later times are full of directions as to where guts should and should not be deposited. By studying both the refuse dumped behind the houses and the age of the animals that were slaughtered, we can see that urban demand had a strong influence on the type of cattle raised in the lands around the city. The older self-contained traditional dairy farm now found itself with a large market for beef. The response seems to have been to slaughter male calves and to retain females until they were more than three years old. These older animals would then have been driven to the city markets. There, many of them seem to have been bought by individual householders and held alive in the small plot behind the house until a group of people could be organised to share the carcass. The beast would then be slaughtered on the spot and the offal dumped. The large quantity of meat debris that must have been strewn around attracted carrion-eating birds and the raven was very common. (One site at Lough Gur was a farmyard of the thirteenth and fourteenth centuries and there raven bones were so common that the excavator thought they might have been exposed on gamekeepers' gibbets to discourage other birds.) There were also bones of buzzard, eagle and red kite. Crop debris included wheat, barley, oats and peas.

ANGLO-NORMAN FARMING AND ITS DECAY 1150-1550 AD

The feudal world wanted wealth and military power, and the land had to be the main source of wealth. Subsistence farming on indifferent land was no longer good enough, intensive farming of high quality land had to produce a handsome cash surplus. The great monastic orders were the first to bring this world to Ireland and of these the Cistercians with their emphasis on agriculture had the greatest impact on the Irish countryside. The Cistercians depended wholly on the land for their income and developed a system for selling their farm produce of cattle, horses and wool which did much to promote commerce in western Europe. Mellifont was consecrated in 1157 and within a few years daughter houses had sprung up in many parts of Ireland. The second impact, the military one, began in 1169 and soon great areas of the best agricultural land had been won, a task that was made the easier by the internecine strife that had been raging on a scale that was high even by Irish standards. 'There has been fighting in all provinces, endless campaigns, cattle-raids, burnings, atrocities – Ireland lies like a trembling sod.'

We are now less sure of how fundamental were the changes which were brought about by the Anglo-Norman invasions. Irish rulers had long ceased to be hidebound traditional priest-kings, if in truth they ever had been, and had exercised formidable powers for generations. Some had begun to form rudimentary household administrations and to appoint royal officials in a manner which prefigured the governments of feudal monarchs. (It is remarkable how medieval-style royal administration is replicated in many societies in so many ways. The Mafia bosses of America in our own century appear to have had 'officials' whose jobs originated in household functions.) Minor kings were gradually losing their distinctive positions and becoming in effect subsidiary lords although the title *rí* was tenaciously retained not just for a shadowy social cachet but because, at local level, it continued to bring with it tangible benefits in followers and exactions.

New ideas of military earthen fortification had appeared in Ireland before the invasion although discriminating between the new forts and older domestic structures which they may superficially have resembled has proved difficult. The towns founded by the Norse had established the beginnings of a mercantile trade which brought new wealth and luxury goods to the island. It is probably a great mistake to assume that by the eleventh and twelfth centuries agriculture in Ireland was essentially subsistence farming. Surpluses were created and the economy was capable of generating the resources to support the rulers in a fitting style. Agriculture likewise could finance extensive church-building with Romanesque structural and decorative features along with a great flowering of the arts which clearly reveals intimate knowledge of contemporary European style. A gradual slight warming in climate and the absence of recorded plagues in the period from the seventh to thirteenth centuries suggested to Lisa Bitel, who has written on Irish monasticism, that the population was rising in line with a steady increase in agricultural production.

The Norman conquest broadly took place in three phases. In the first phase, between the arrival of the first knights and about 1190, a vast area of land extending along the east coast – most of the counties of Wexford, Carlow, a large part of Laois, Kilkenny, east Waterford, parts of Tipperary, the better parts of Wicklow, Dublin and Meath – was taken and divided into important lordships. A second phase of conquest in the 1190s added much of the rest of Tipperary, north Cork and east Limerick to the lands of the conquerors. Outside these areas, smaller expeditions of conquest, often on individual initiative or following speculative grants by the crown, made significant inroads into the west midlands, Roscommon, Cork and parts of Kerry. In some of the richer areas, the settlement was intense and the conquerors left an indelible mark on the landscape and the people. In others, the newcomers, such as the de Burghs in Connacht, established successful and enduring overlordships in areas where the Irish population and significant elements of the native polity remained strong. In others, such as John de Courcy's spectacular inroads in east Ulster in the 1170s, an initial period of success led to the establishment of the great Earldom of Ulster (held by a branch of the de Burghs for a time). This really only proved lasting in a few areas close to the coast and rapidly dwindled into insignificance except for the establishment of a castle and town at Carrickfergus.

It was once thought that the principal archaeological marker of the advance of the Anglo-Norman conquest was the fortification known as the motte and bailey. The work 'motte' denotes a mound (often rendered *moat* in Irish dialects and placenames) while the term 'bailey' refers to its attached defended courtyard. A house was erected on the motte within a palisade. Weapon pits – foxholes from which weapons, probably crossbows could have been fired – have occurred on the summits of two excavated examples. The palisaded bailey was backed against the motte; it provided protection for followers and livestock. A protected causeway led from the bailey to the motte. Motte-and-bailey castles could be erected quickly;

many were raised on the sites of raths thus taking advantage of their position and capitalising on the amounts to which the raths were already raised by their original occupants and so saving labour. An additional advantage could well have been the message of dominance which the appropriation of a native potentate's house would have conveyed.

It has been assumed that the motte and baileys are par excellence the improvised fortification erected quickly to overawe and protect against a recently conquered people. If that is so, then it seems , strangely, not to have been used in all areas of the conquest in Ireland (*Illus. 155*), a fact which Terry Barry has explained by pointing to the variety of earthen fortifications used by the Anglo-Normans in Ireland, including ringwork castles which preceded the later stone castles at places such as Trim, Kilkenny and Athlone. In other places, the earthworks may have continued in use – excavation has not been sufficiently extensive to show this – or been abandoned in favour of stone castles on alternative sites. The town of Drogheda, once girdled by impressive town walls of which a magnificent towered gateway still stands, is still dominated by the massive motte, Millmount, now crowned by a ruined nineteenth-century fortification.

The dynamic of the conquest was the acquisition of land and its distribution among the followers and as long as manpower was available for fighting, the need to take in further and further territory dominated the thinking of the barons. The seizing of land meant that leaders of the conquest could accumulate capital assets which otherwise would not have been available to them and the building of their great works – castles and bridges for example – would not have been possible without this land bank. (In the United States in the nineteenth century, railroads, towns, schools and universities were financed by grants of land seized from the native population.) The impetus of conquest began to run out by the second quarter of the thirteenth century by which time, in the older conquered territories, the accumulation of capital by conquest had been replaced by a drive to ensure a continuing income from the land. It was in the management of that land and the means taken to hold it by peopling it with a reliable dependent population that the Norman conquerors made their most significant mark on Ireland's landscape.

What did Ireland look like to the invaders? We are fortunate that a Welsh travel correspondent, Giraldus Cambrensis, came to Ireland about 1185 and if we try to see Ireland through his twelfth-century eyes and not through our twentieth-century ones, we can get some vivid impressions. To adjust our vision we must remember first that he was a cleric accustomed to the sermonising of his day and apt to burst into theological excursions at any time; second, that with his contemporaries he believed all too literally in hell and its torments and saw the world as populated with monstrous beasts lying in wait both for the just and the unjust; and third, that he was a propagandist, always ready to flatter his betters including his kinsmen who were prominent in the conquest and to exalt the Welsh and denigrate the Irish. Giraldus certainly was an acute observer; he gives a word-picture of an illuminated manuscript that has never been bettered; in natural history, he gives a clear description of a dipper which he thought to be a variety of kingfisher. He refers to raths and cashels and reports that the Irish 'have no use for castles. Woods are their forts and swamps their ditches' – a comment that was to reappear in many subsequent dispatches from Ireland.

His report tells us that:

Ireland is the most temperate of all countries. Snow is seldom, and lasts only for a short time. There is such plentiful supply of rain, such an ever-present overhanging of clouds and fog, that summer scarcely gives three consecutive days of really fine weather. Winds are moderate and not too strong. The winds from the west-north-west, north and east bring cold. The north-west and west winds are prevalent, and are more frequent and stronger than other winds. They bend (in the opposite direction) almost all the trees in the west that are placed in an elevated position, or uproot them.

Ireland is a country of uneven surface and rather mountainous. The soil is soft and watery, and even at the tops of high and steep mountains there are pools and swamps. The land is sandy rather than rocky. There are many woods and marshes; here and there are some fine plains but in comparison with the woods they are indeed small. The country enjoys the freshness and mildness of spring almost all the year round. The grass is green in the fields in winter just the same as in summer. Consequently, the meadows are not cut for fodder, and stalls are never built for the beasts. The land is fruitful and rich in its fertile soil and plentiful harvests. Crops abound in the fields, flocks on the mountains, wild animals in the woods, it is rich in honey and milk. Ireland exports cow-hides, sheep-skins and furs. Much wine is imported. But the island is richer in pastures than in crops, and in grass rather than grain. The plains are well clothed with grass, and the haggards [farmyards] are bursting with straw. Only the granaries are without their wealth. The crops give great promise in the blade, even more in the straw, but less in the ear. For here the grains of wheat are shrivelled and small, and can scarcely be separated from the chaff by any winnowing fan. What is born and comes forth in the spring and is nourished in the summer and advanced, can scarcely be reaped in the harvest because of the unceasing rain. For this country more than any other suffers from storms of wind and rain.

Giraldus also offers detailed information on fish, amphibians, reptiles, birds and mammals, but this is so threaded through with medieval folklore that it is difficult to pick out fact from fable. He reports that salmon, trout, eels and lampreys are common in Irish rivers, but that many others, such as pike, perch, roach, chub, dudgeon, minnow, loach and bullheads are absent. Most of these do occur in Ireland today, but they have been introduced since Giraldus wrote. The Anglo-Normans introduced the rabbit and the fallow deer. What Giraldus has to say about wheat failing to ripen is of particular interest because a temperature curve shows he was writing at a time when mean annual temperature in England and presumably in Ireland also was rising to its thirteenth-century peak (*Illus. 153*). During that peak the Anglo-Normans certainly grew good wheat crops on the manorial estates they established in south-east Ireland. However, conditions for cereal crops became difficult again when the temperature fell once more in the late fourteenth century. It is not easy to pinpoint this effect; first, because of the consequences of the Bruce invasion early in the century, when the warring armies 'between them left neither wood nor lea nor corn nor crop nor stead nor barn nor church, but fired and burned them all'; and second, because of the Black Death in the second part of the century which reduced the population drastically, halving it according to some estimates. The outbreak of plague in Europe was preceded by decades of widespread famine and distress and Ireland was probably no exception.

Illus. 153
Graph to illustrate
the fluctuation of
mean annual
temperature in
England, by fifty year
averages, for the past
thousand years.

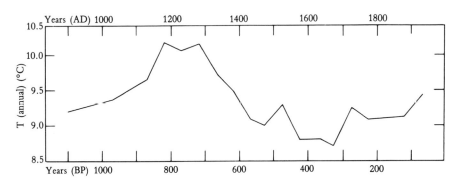

It was thus between 1170 and 1350 AD that Anglo-Norman influence was most clearly stamped on the Irish landscape. At first, the lightly equipped Irish soldiers could offer no resistance to the heavily-armed and well-drilled invaders who cut through the country smelling out the better lands like well-trained truffle hounds. The Anglo-Normans were prepared to expend capital on the organisation of their manorial farms and were only interested in land from which they could hope to draw a dividend on their investment. Fertile and well-drained soils were what attracted them. This was the first occasion on which financial considerations directly impinged on land use in Ireland. In the later periods of the Bronze Age, there had been a fairly regular distribution of sites throughout the country. It is the same with placenames containing such elements as rath and lios, most of which stem from the early centuries of the Christian era; these are scattered throughout the country avoiding only higher ground especially in western areas. In Ireland, there has always been land enough for all for farming at subsistence level and the Irish in the twelfth century, as at all times, reckoned their wealth in stock, principally in cattle. On the other hand the Anglo-Normans were hungry for commercial land especially ploughland and they reckoned their wealth in acres. Thus the distribution of Anglo-Norman sites is very different and the pattern of the sites is so closely related to the occurrence of good soils in Ireland today that it seems reasonable to assume that the soils we know today had developed by the time the Anglo-Normans reached the country. In the map of modern Irish soils (*Illus. 154*), we see the immediate contrast between the poorly-drained soils of the north and west (the gleys, peaty gleys and peats – including peaty podzols – shown in dark hues on the map) and the more freely-drained soils of the south and east (brown earths, acid brown earths, brown podzolics, grey-brown podzolics shown in

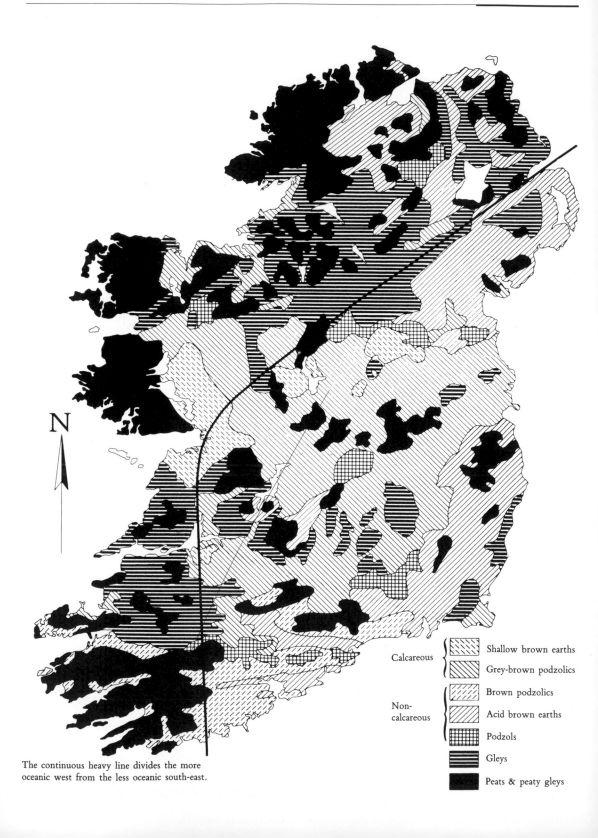

N

Calcareous
Shallow brown earths
Grey-brown podzolics

Non-calcareous
Brown podzolics
Acid brown earths

Podzols

Gleys

Peats & peaty gleys

The continuous heavy line divides the more
oceanic west from the less oceanic south-east.

lighter hues on the map). A continuous line on the map separates the two soil regions. If we look at a meteorological map (see *Illus. 71a*) that shows numbers of rain days, a very similar line divides a region with more than 175 rain days to the north and west from a region with less than that number to the south and east. In other words, in Ireland today the soil will be waterlogged if rain falls on at least half the days in the year. We can picture this as the edge of a cloud. If climate deteriorates (and the number of rain days increases), the cloud-edge will advance to the east and south; if climate improves (and gets drier), the cloud-edge will withdraw north-westwards. Meteorologists tell us that the Anglo-Normans arrived in Ireland during a phase of very favourable climate, but there is nothing about the distribution of their sites to suggest to us that at that time better-drained soils stretched farther to the north-west than they do today. Wherever they found soils to their taste or a strategic point worth defending the Anglo-Normans erected an earthen motte, or ringwork castle – later replaced by a stone castle in places of especial importance – and proceeded to settle themselves into the surrounding countryside (*Illus. 155*). On the whole, as we have seen, they did not advance beyond a line running from Skibbereen through Galway to Coleraine and settled most densely in Leinster and east Munster, an area of good land interrupted by only one large island of bad land, the uplands of the Wicklow Mountains, which were to prove a centre from which Irish forces would frequently emerge to harass the farms and towns of the surrounding lowlands.

The basic Anglo-Norman unit was the manor (*Illus. 156, 157*) with perhaps 1200ha (3000 acres) and here the lord would have his home-farm or stead, often protected by a moat, containing his house and his farm buildings surrounded by fields. Many of these moated manors appear to have been rectangular bank-and-ditch enclosures with the bank probably crowned by a palisade (*Illus. 159*). Sites of this type are widely distributed in the lands of the conquest but especially common in the south-east in counties Wexford and Kilkenny (*Illus. 155d*). The majority were plausibly house enclosures, but some may have been cattle pounds or even gardens – only excavation will tell. While in England many are associated with village settlements, in Ireland the majority of moated manors (but not all, for example Ballyduagh, Co. Tipperary (*Illus. 156,157*)) occur in isolation, prompting Terry Barry to suggest that they were most often built on good agricultural land near the margins of the Anglo-Norman expansion. They could be seen as providing protected habitation in what must have been hostile territory. The analogy of the later plantations of the sixteenth and seventeenth centuries springs to mind when the undertakers receiving large tracts of land were obliged to build fortified houses to guard against the displaced natives. Radiocarbon dating has dated a moated house at Kilmagoura in Co. Cork to about 1225 AD and late-thirteenth-century coins were found in another at Rigsdale also in Co. Cork.

Large farm units would be given to supporters – linked to the lord by allegiance as well as rent – to rent-paying individual farmers and to borough communities of burgesses with land in common and their own court and other privileges. The holders of these larger units came from outside Ireland. The favourable climate had brought about a population explosion in most of western

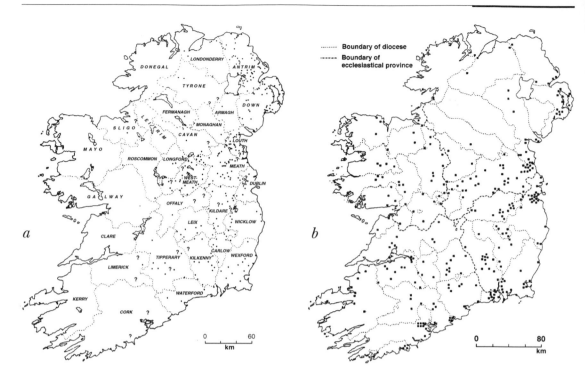

Illus. 155 The Anglo-Normans were great founders of religious houses, dedicated to high agricultural output and supportive of commercial activity. These maps show a close match between their settlements, markets and religious foundations, the distribution of favourable soils and the pattern of conquest:
*a Suriviving mottes1973, **b** New religious foundations 1169-1320, **c** Anglo-Norman boroughs, **d** Moated sites.*

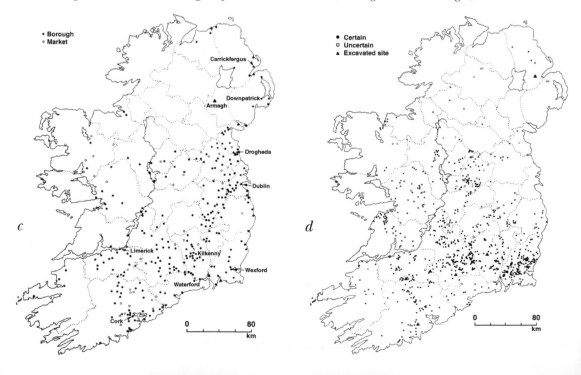

Europe, and in England, Wales and Flanders there were men anxious to get tenancies of good arable land in return for payments in money, in services and in kind. However, the supply of such men was not inexhaustible and the lord would endeavour to retain the Irish work-force that had originally occupied the lands. Where possible, he would reduce their status to that of villeins who would be his property both in their persons and in their goods. Some got small parcels of land, paying rent but with no security of tenure; others held cottages but no land; a third group certainly Irish, the betaghs, had land without tenure held mainly by service. As their service labour was largely communal, they tended to form a compact group probably living in close association in houses clustered together in a clachan. Even today we can find Ballybetagh as a placename and it is tempting to think that here we may have a link with the Anglo-Norman betagh villages or hamlets. In the list of the Bruce devastations we can identify the units of the Norman farm – stead, barn, corn, crop and lea – and other documents spell out the round of duties of those who owed service. The corn was usually wheat or oats and the service tenants had to plough, harrow, sow, weed, scare

Illus. 156
Illustration of
Ballyduagh,
Co. Tipperary, in the
thirteenth century. We
see the moated manor
and its farm buildings
at the bottom right. In
the centre we have
houses with gardens; at
the top there are
roadside cottages. At the
top left we have the
parish church, and on
the left margin we see
the ploughman
breaking up the stubble.

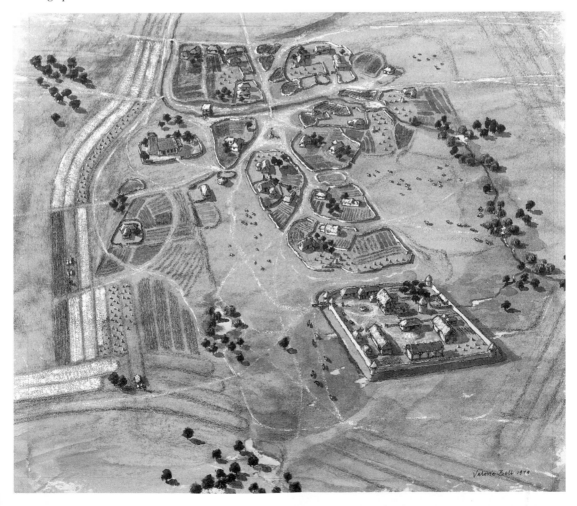

birds, reap, tie, stook, cart, stack and thrash in the course of their duties. Peas, beans and flax were also grown on the lord's land, but the poorer folk will have had meld and goosefoot in their rotation which will also have included periods when the land lay fallow.

It would be nice to think that on the manor in Ireland, the normal practice of crop sequence – winter corn, spring crop, fallow – was carried out in neat enclosed fields, but it is more probable that the smaller tenants at least

Illus. 157
Ballyduagh,
Co Tipperary.
On the right are outlines of houses and gardens with the manor house in the bottom right. In the top left a ring of of trees surrounds the site of the parish church. In the bottom left are the ruins of a later seventeenth-century house within a circular bank – a ringwork castle; the earliest type of Norman fortification.

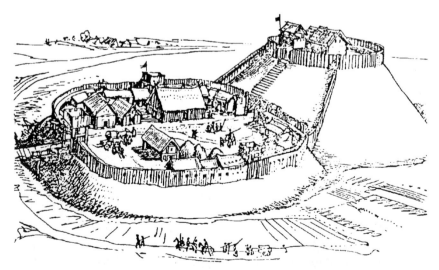

Illus. 158
Reconstruction of a motte and bailey, the ultimate defence for stock as well as houses.

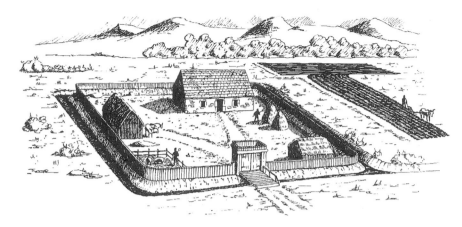

held separated strips scattered through large open common fields; this cannot have made for efficient working. Such strips have a long history in Ireland and up to 150 years ago, farms made up of such scattered strips could still be found; very often the plough furrow took on an arcurate form and this shape also survives in some modern Irish field-boundaries (*Illus. 161d*).

On the leas, if they had been shut up as meadows, the hay had to be made. The tenants had to scythe the grass, spread it, turn it and put it up in cocks and then carry it to the haggard. It is probable that the scythe made its first appearance in Ireland in Norman times. As well as the meadows, there was pasture and herbage, although what the exact difference was is unknown and here the length of the grazing period was carefully controlled. In the woods, rights to hunting, cutting timber, grazing and the eating of acorns by swine were spelt out in detail; swine had to be ringed to stop them grubbing up the trees. There was usually a rabbit-warren and a dovecote. The lord had a water-mill and if the tenants wished to grind their corn at home on a hand-mill, a fine had to be paid.

The colonists prospered for a time. Throughout Leinster and east Munster they took the flatlands, the rivers, the coasts and the Norse trading towns, leaving the hill-country, the woods and the bogs to the Irish. A network of walled towns, castles, villages and roads made the settlers secure and wealthy. Typically, the villages appear as a series of narrow house plots end on to a spine created by a street, sometimes a sunken-way. We must imagine simple, long, narrow houses often built gable-end towards the street. By offering burgess privileges, settlers were attracted to small clustered rural settlements – an experiment in plantation which has left us many deserted medieval village sites in Ireland (*Illus. 162*). These small planted settlements seem not to have survived the disaster of the fourteenth century. Oddly, although the historical record points to their early date, excavation so far of these village sites has been either disappointingly unproductive or has

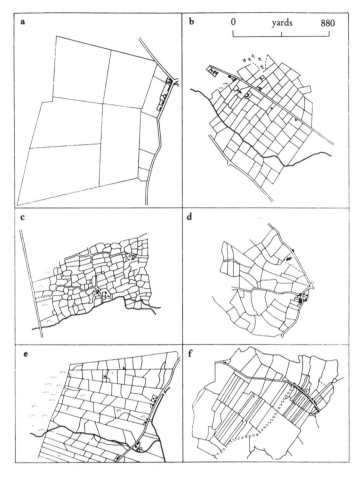

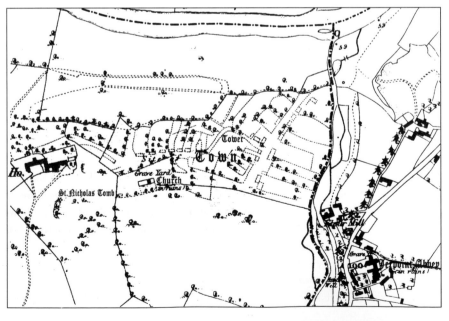

*Illus. 162
The deserted
medieval town of
Newtown Jerpoint,
Co. Kilkenny, as
shown on the first
edition of the OS
six-inch map (1839).*

Illus. 161
Some Irish field
systems:
a large regular fields,
  Jordanstown,
  Co. Meath;
b small regular
  fields, Ballykine
  Lower, Co. Down;
c small irregular
  fields, Glinsouth,
  Co. Kerry;
d curved strip fields,
  Nicholastown,
  Co. Kilkenny;
e ladder farms,
  Foriff, Co. Antrim;
f strips in common-
  fields, with
  surrounding ring
  of pasture, Dalkey,
  Co. Dublin,
  c. AD 1850.

sometimes yielded evidence of a later date. The larger older towns like Dublin, Wexford, Waterford, Cork and Limerick continued as centres of commerce with trade now focused on England and western France in particular. Trade and manufacture were highly regulated by guilds. New coastal towns, for example Drogheda, were founded and soon prospered. Towns like Kilkenny, already a centre of settlement around its important early monastery, thrived under the patronage of its Butler lords and developed into a town of great importance. In the older towns, Viking-age ramparts of earth revetted with stone were replaced by massive stone walls and often greatly extended to accommodate the growth during the economic boom of the thirteenth century. These town walls were provided with towers along their circuit and imposing fortified gates. Murage charters survive showing how the towns frequently financed the walls' construction by imposing duties on farm produce and other goods brought to market. Impressive stretches of town wall and towers survive in Waterford where excavation has also revealed some of the late Viking-age ramparts. In Dublin, only fragments of the walls can be seen above ground. However, the foundation levels of important towers and other features have recently been revealed by excavation (*Illus. 160*).

Smaller towns were often walled and excellent examples with standing remains can be seen at Fethard, Co. Tipperary, Kilmallock, Co. Limerick and Athenry, Co. Galway. Within the walls of the medieval towns of the twelfth- and thirteenth-century, only the castles, abbeys and churches survive above ground, although excavation often reveals the well-preserved traces of domestic dwellings and their contents. Our towns often contain later, fifteenth- and sixteenth-century stone houses in a good state of preservation – Kilmallock, Kilkenny and Galway have fine examples often partly concealed by modern plaster. Timber-framed houses of the period are likely to masquerade under a modern disguise in many towns to be revealed only by accident during alteration or, sadly, demolition. Other houses are more obvious such as the 'castles' of Dalkey, Co. Dublin and Ardee, Co. Louth.

Under favourable conditions, the economy boomed. Wool and hides were sent in large quantities to France, Flanders and Italy. Woollen cloth, linen and furs were exported and luxury goods – in food, wine, figs, raisins, walnut, and in fabrics, satins, silks and cloth of gold – were imported. However, the Bruce invasion, the Black Death and the deterioration in climate all combined in the fourteenth century to give the Anglo-Norman way of life a blow from which it never really recovered. Many of the colonists amalgamated with the Irish.

THE TUDOR PLANTATIONS 1550-1700 AD

Before the Tudors came to the throne, the kings of England had also been kings of western France and could afford to look on Ireland as a pleasant western annexe. The Tudors faced a potentially malevolent Europe and malevolence grew as religious differences deepened. To the Tudors, Ireland was the 'soft underbelly' of England and appropriate steps had to be taken to secure the western flank. What did Ireland look like to the Tudors? In Leinster they could see the well-kept Pale, a boundary ditch, and beyond the Pale the lands formerly loyal to the Crown but now in the hands of English rebels, lords of Anglo-Norman stock who had abandoned their allegiance and adopted many of the ways of Irish life. In the foreground were the well-wooded Wicklow Mountains; still a stronghold of the Irish enemies. In east Munster, there were the fortified towns of Waterford, Youghal, Cork, Kinsale and a few others and again the lands of the English rebels. The great valleys of the Blackwater and the Lee were still filled with dense oak-woods. This view stopped in west Munster where the soil got poorer and the hills crowded more closely together. It was cut off again at the Shannon basin, where woods and bogs lay on both sides of the ill-defined river channel. If they looked north, Ulster was hidden by the broad belt of drumlins that stretched south-west from Strangford Lough to the headwaters of the Erne and then followed the valley of that river north-west to the sea in Donegal Bay. Dense woods on the drumlin slopes and tops and lakes, bogs and sluggish streams between them made this very difficult country for the military man, as it had also been in the Iron Age.

However, land-patterns were changing in the Pale. In some communities, the medieval strip-holdings with scattered plots in common fields still survived, but enclosure and the disappearance of small plots held by labour-service in favour of large leasehold farms worked by almost landless labourers were rapidly under way. The staple crop was wheat, but barley and rye were also grown. Conditions were very different in the marchlands beyond the Pale and still more so in the Irish areas. There scrubby forest, lakes and undrained bog were still widespread. There was some tillage, mainly on a shifting or long-fallow basis, in small plots cultivated with a spade. The lands were constantly redistributed to co-heirs and so there was little incentive to intensive land-use, improvements or substantial buildings; even chieftains sometimes lived in cabins.

What impression of Irish farming and food can we form from the reports of Tudor observers, steeped in prejudice as most of them were? Cattle made the most impact. Milch-cows were prized; 'they will not kill a cow, except it be old and yield no milk.' Milk-products of all kinds continued to be eaten. Booleying was in full force; the people in summer lived in booleys; 'pasturing upon the mountain and waste wild places and removing still to fresh land … driving their cattle continually with them and feeding only on their milk and white meats [milk products]; it was a good thing that in this country of Ireland, where there are great mountains and waste deserts full of grass, that the same should be eaten down and nourish many thousand of cattle.'

Surplus cattle were readily killed and eaten and the large quantities of meat eaten without any accompanying bread was a constant source of surprise. Meat was eaten raw, boiled, roasted and used as an ingredient in soup. Blood was drawn and consumed after mixing with milk, butter or grains. Mutton, pork, hens and rabbits were also eaten. Venison appeared in pasties.

Wheat and rye were grown only on the better lands; barley was essentially for brewing and distilling; oats were dominant on poorer land in the west. The heads of grain were singed, not thrashed; such a practice looked primitive, but considerable judgement was needed to hit on the exact second at which to jerk the grain out of the burning stem. Ploughs were hitched directly to the horses' tails; this was a cruel practice by modern standards, but in days when hanging and quartering and breaking on the wheel were matters of everyday routine, definitions of cruelty were rather different. The practice certainly reduced the wear and tear on the plough. Slide-cars were drawn in the same way. People constantly on the move had little use for vegetable gardens and watercress and wood-sorrel served as salads. It was the easy-going wandering life of the Irish pastoralists that particularly irritated the Tudors, who thought that all would be well if the nomadic natives could be anchored on tillage-farms where a more settled round of duties would tire them out and leave them less time for mischief. Able-bodied men should have more to do than follow a few cows grazing '... for this keeping of cows is of itself a very idle life and a fit nursery for a thief.' If they were exhausted by working in the fields or gardens, they would have less energy for raiding; as it was, 'when it is daylight they will go to the poor village burning the houses and corn and ransacking of the poor cottages. They will drive all the kine and plow horses, with all other cattle, and drive them away.' To make wandering Irishmen into settled Englishmen was the goal. The back-breaking work of soil husbandry had few attractions for free warriors, who could on the other hand find an outlet for their skills more suited to their temperament guarding herds of cattle. The problem faced by many Irish chieftains in the sixteenth century was that of converting these men into settled rent-paying tenants. Most failed and the task was taken up with gusto by new-style colonial administrators who solved the problem largely by importing the kind of tenant-farmer they thought desirable and displacing the natives of all classes.

The Tudors were businessmen and they decided they could not afford to take Ireland by a single massive onslaught. They would open up the country by cutting passes through the woods, bridging the rivers, building roads and keeping the roads open by erecting forts and blockhouses along them. Military patrols and route-marches would impede the formation of native alliances in these frontier-lands. Apart from the good lands in the east and south and the coasts from Lough Foyle down the Irish Sea and round to Galway Bay, the geography of Ireland was little known and extensive surveys would be carried out to find out exactly what the country held. Internecine wars and risings against English authority would occur from time to time. These would be ruthlessly put down, the Irish enemies killed off or transplanted and English settlers and English ways brought in their stead wherever the land was of sufficient quality to support 'the English way of life'. The areas that were ultimately taken were essentially the same areas of good land that had appealed to the Anglo-Normans (*Illus. 155*) with in addition the good land in Munster. Irish resurgence was making life impossible for the open manor and the open village. The lord had to retire into the uncomfortable protection of the tower-house (*Illus. 163*) while the ordinary folk either fled back to Britain leaving their 'deserted village' behind them, or sought security in the walled towns which continued to operate – like mini Hong Kongs – in a countryside that was basically hostile yet tolerated their existence for the trading contacts that they brought. To give more shelter to crops and to make it more difficult to drive cattle off the lands, efforts were made to surround the fields with stone-faced banks and ditches; to encourage timber the banks were to be planted with ash trees.

By 1515, the remaining territory under English control, apart from the walled

Illus. 163 Castlegrove, Co. Galway. A fine example of a tower house. Defensive houses such as these were built predominantly in the fifteenth and sixteenth centuries, although a few examples may be earlier in date and some are known to have been built in the first half of the seventeenth century. Common in the southern half of the country, there are exceptional concentrations of tower houses in Tipperary, Limerick, Clare and Galway. They are relatively uncommon in Ulster.

towns, was now sadly shrunken to a coastal strip which itself had to be protected on its inland side by a bank and ditch – the Pale – which ran from Dundalk through Kells to Kildare and from there back east across the northern foothills of the Wicklow Mountains to reach the coast south of Dublin at Dalkey (*Illus. 164*). Outside the Pale, the remaining landlords of English origin no longer set their lands for money rents, but through share-cropping agreements advanced working-capital to their tenants, demonstrating in this as in many other ways their gradual adoption of Irish customs.

The first plantation came in the mid-sixteenth century when disturbances in Laois and Offaly, between the Pale and the Shannon, gave the English forces a chance to intervene. Victory was followed by the transformation of the area into King's County and Queen's County; the Irish were dislodged, their chief was pensioned off with 1300ha (3000 acres) and the rest was parcelled out to settlers

Illus. 164
Map of the extent of
the Pale in the
fifteenth century.

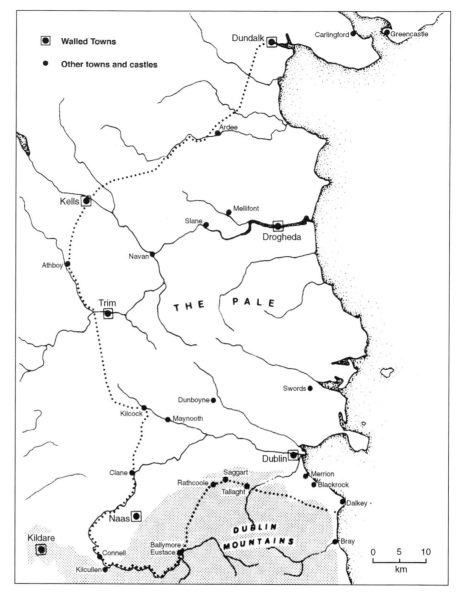

Illus. 164
Map of the extent of the Pale in the fifteenth century.

from England in lots ranging from 225 to 6ha (500 to 25 acres). The larger g: antees had to pay a rent, perform military duties, manage the local water courses and fords, introduce tillage, build houses and supply timber. To prevent their land becoming sub-divided in the Irish manner, the grantees had to undertake to leave it in tail-male to their eldest son.

Lack of adequate survey gave rise to difficulties in division and efforts were made to improve surveying methods. From such surveys we get glimpses of the landscape. Primary woodland was encountered round Athlone where the map-maker recorded extensive forests of great oaks in contrast to 'much small woods as crabtree, thorn, hazel, with such like.' In north Kerry, some of the woodlands were clearly secondary as they consisted of 'underwood of the age of fifty or sixty years, filled with decayed trees of ash, hazels, sallows, willows, alders, birches, whitethorns and such like.' The method of plantation in Laois/Offaly produced a state-sponsored quasi-military colony (*Illus. 165*). But new colonial ideas were developing as the Spanish conquistadors were carving up the Americas. Private enterprise could be encouraged.

The acquisition of Munster in 1585 came next and after the Desmond Rising had been crushed and the native population almost entirely dispossessed, about 600,000 acres (250,000ha) were available for new owners. Mouths were encouraged to open wide, and blocks of 4000 (1600ha), 6000 (2500ha) and even 12,000 acres (5000ha) were offered together with blueprint development layouts showing lots ranging from 1000 acres (400ha) for the demesne to 5.5 acres (2ha) for the cottages. Edmund Spenser got 3000 acres (1200ha). Favourites like Sir Walter Raleigh received 20,000 acres (8000ha) to whet his appetite for still greater plantations in north America. Richard Boyle, later Earl of Cork, subsequently purchased Raleigh's interest and by later transactions, many of them extremely dubious, amassed an enormous estate. In 1585, it was estimated that the plantation would bring eight thousand five hundred English settlers, but in 1590 their number was reckoned at about two thousand. They had brought ploughs and improved breeds of cattle and sheep with them and undoubtedly raised the standard of farming in the region. What with difficulties in securing settlers, difficulties in satisfying them when they did arrive and the partially successful efforts of the original owners to regain the land, Munster in 1600 by no means presented the happy picture, put forward by the prospectuses for the scheme, of contented English settlers farming enclosed fields on fertile farms protected by

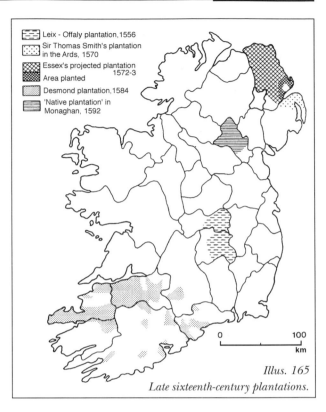

Leix - Offaly plantation, 1556
Sir Thomas Smith's plantation in the Ards, 1570
Essex's projected plantation 1572-3
Area planted
Desmond plantation, 1584
'Native plantation' in Monaghan, 1592

0   100
km

Illus. 165
Late sixteenth-century plantations.

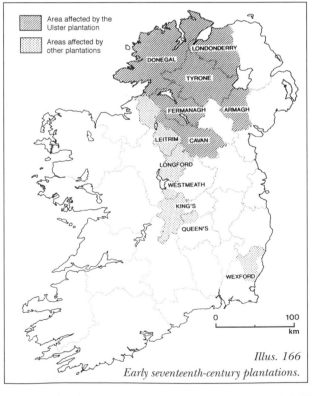

Area affected by the Ulster plantation
Areas affected by other plantations

LONDONDERRY
DONEGAL
TYRONE
FERMANAGH   ARMAGH
LEITRIM   CAVAN
LONGFORD
WESTMEATH
KING'S
QUEEN'S
WEXFORD

0   100
km

Illus. 166
Early seventeenth-century plantations.

Illus. 167
Tully Castle,
Co. Fermanagh.
A fortified house
within a defended
walled enclosure, a
bawn; early
seventeenth century.
The original gardens
have been restored.
The house had two
floors and an attic.
Giving greater
comfort than the
tower house, the
building with narrow
windows and turrets
was still clearly
intended to deter
attackers. To little
avail however, as it
was attacked and
plundered in 1641
and never reoccupied.

Illus. 168
Kanturk Castle,
Co. Cork. Built
around the year 1609
by McDonagh
McCarthy, Lord of
Duhallow, it was
never completed.
This style of castle
with more windows
reflected the desire for
a more comfortable
lifestyle than that
afforded by the tower
house. Nevertheless,
the flanking towers
and musket loops still
provided a means of
defence, just in case.

natural defences and near to the sea, a river or a town. The comment 'Enclosures are very rare amongst them, and then no better fenced than an old wife's toothless gums … as for the arable land it lies almost as much neglected and unmanured [unworked] as the sandy deserts of Arabia' is probably nearer the mark. But the plantation did throw the woods of Munster at the mercy of the new entrepreneurs and the commercial exploitation of the forests began in earnest. From the woods a continuous stream of timber flowed out – trunks from good large trees for ships and houses, branches from these trees and smaller trees for barrel staves, and lop and top and all other wood for charcoal for ironworks and glassworks (*Illus. 169*). It is hard to gauge the amount of large timber that was exported, but we can get some impression of the stave and charcoal trades from the information made available by Eileen McCracken. Her figures for barrel staves have been taken and cast into a crude and conjectural graphical diagram (*Illus. 170*). As can be seen, the production of staves made tremendous inroads on the oak-woods. Throughout the seventeenth century, the number of staves produced in Ireland rose steadily and over-production led to eventual exhaustion of the supply. After 1770, all necessary staves had to be imported.

       Eileen McCracken gives the years in which about one hundred charcoal-consuming ironworks started to operate and again these dates have been plotted in a crudely graphical form (*Illus. 171*). Production started in Munster shortly before 1600 and such was the consumption of woodland that after no more than a hundred years, parliament in 1698 was compelled to pass the first of a long series of acts both to conserve any remaining stocks and to encourage the planting of trees.

       While Ireland's woodlands were very greatly reduced, it did not follow that the fortunes of the entrepreneurs were correspondingly increased. Although Sir William Petty devastated the woods around Kenmare, his accounts show very little profit from the enterprise. Richard Boyle's figures for the Blackwater valley tell much the same story. The woods along the rivers of south-east Ireland were not only nearer to England, but were also safer; even here it was a constant struggle to recruit experienced managers of charcoal-kilns and superintendents of smelting-works – the experts, even if they could be coaxed to Ireland, were always looking over their shoulders and thinking how much more pleasant it would be in the Forest of Dean, the heart of English iron-working. Richard Boyle (later Earl of Cork) summed it up: 'God ordained my ironworks to be an endless trouble to me.'

Illus. 169
The curved timbers necessary for ship-building had to be selected with great care; the picture illustrates the timber possibilities of variously shaped oak trees.

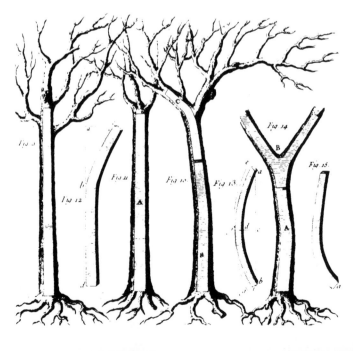

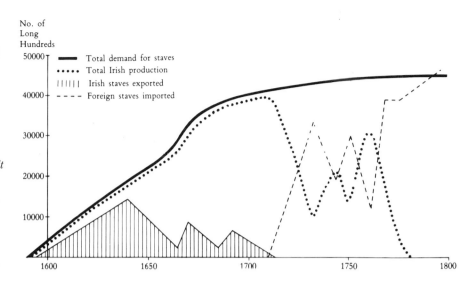

*Illus. 170
Production (and
export) of staves had
begun before 1600.
By 1615 staves were
going to the
Mediterranean for
wine casks. After
1640 home demand
for barrels to cask salt
meat for export rose
and export fell away.
When export of live
animals was
prohibited in 1665,
demand rose sharply.
Until 1710 the Irish
woods could meet the
demand, but in that
year staves were
imported for the first
time. Until about
1765 Ireland could
still meet half the
demand, but after
1770 there were no
more Irish staves.*

After 1593, there were nine years of general countrywide war until 1603, when an organised Irish army with foreign contingents was finally defeated by an Elizabethan army and the independence and isolation of Ulster was brought to an end. Here, 230,000ha (500,000 acres) were available for plantation, and this time the mistakes made in Munster were not repeated. Eight hundred hectares (2000 acres) was the upper limit on the blocks offered and those who accepted had to bring in tenants from Britain and build defences – a castle and a bawn – to protect their lands, tenants and goods. As a bait, the tenants were offered very generous leases. Roads and bridges were organised, towns and villages laid out and with growing commercialism markets, shops and local industries were established. A regular pattern of small enclosed fields for arable farming was established (*Illus. 172*). The Plantation of Ulster was more than the replacement of one group of farmers by another; it was truly an implantation of a different way of life, a difference that has maintained itself to the present day (*Illus. 166*).

Like Leinster, Ulster has its upland areas of poorer soils, the Sperrins and the mountains of Donegal. The displaced natives withdrew to these areas where tillage was still more difficult and there their nomadic habits became still more pronounced. Excessive sub-division of land as generation succeeded generation

*Illus. 171
Schematic diagram to
show the times at
which new charcoal-
burning ironworks
started to operate in
Ireland. Each dot
represents the opening
of a works. The
influence of military
and economic events
is clearly seen. The
sharp decline after
1750 indicates the
exhaustion of
supplies of charcoal.*

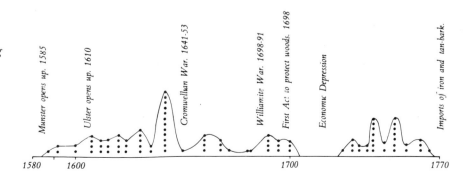

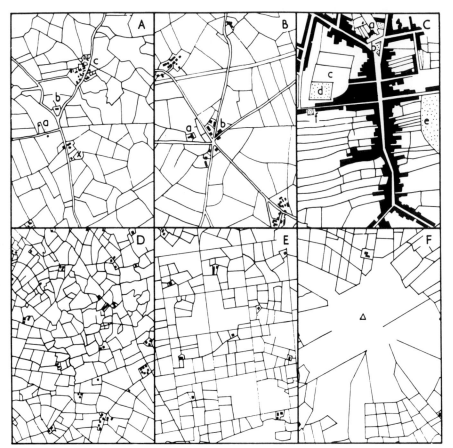

Illus. 172
Settlements and fields
stemming from the
Plantation of Ulster:

A Clachan;
   a church house,
   b church,
   c clachan,
   x site of rath.
B Roadside hamlet;
   a church,
   b local post office.
C Planned town;
   a technical
      institute,
   b open area,
   c brickfield,
   d fairgreen,
   e demesne,
   f linen factory.
D Small irregular
   fields.
E Regular fields
   with surveyed
   boundaries.
F Fields laid out to
   accord with hill
   slope topography.

and the constant fear of crops being burned or otherwise destroyed in raids and war had brought about still further concentration on livestock which escaped pillage if kept on the move. The seasonal booleying moves to summer pastures had always been strong and the more drastic practice of creaghting, whereby whole communities and their livestock kept more or less constantly on the move drifting from the protection of one lord to that of another, became more pronounced.

But when peace returned, agricultural output turned quickly upwards. Fish, hides and furs fell back in importance as exports and meat, butter and wool took their place. It may be that as the forests of Munster shrank, the numbers of cattle and sheep rose; certainly the ports of Youghal, Cork and Kinsale grew dramatically at this time (*Col. 46*). The bone content of some fifteenth to sixteenth-century ditches at Newgrange also demonstrated the rise in the importance of sheep at this time; sheep (or goat) provided almost one-third of all the bones found in the late medieval ditches, whereas in the prehistoric levels at the same site they only amounted to one-twentieth. The drastic action that had been taken in Ulster was followed by land confiscations in Connacht and the general hostility to these plantations, as well as to the strong central government in Dublin, provoked a further rising during the English Civil War in 1641. This led to a general countrywide war which lasted for twelve years before it was brutally terminated by

Cromwell's victories. Well over a million hectares (two and a half million acres) were involved in the population shifts which followed; the Irish landowners were pushed to the west to the wet and infertile lands beyond the Shannon; those of English extraction whose loyalties to England were considered sufficiently safe were retained on the best soils in the Southeast between the Boyne and the Barrow; between these two groups a colonial buffer zone with ex-soldiers and new settlers straggled down central Ireland on lands of varying quality. Nevertheless, the remarkable continuity of Irish family names – until very recently distributed in the localities occupied originally by their forebears – indicates that plans to shift the majority of the population were largely unsuccessful.

Once peace returned the country recovered quickly. An upturn in climate was bringing record harvests in Europe; Ireland concentrated on livestock. The markets and fairs that had been initiated in Ulster spread through the country and with an improving road system cattle easily found their way either to the docks or the slaughterhouse. Sheep went to stock the English sheepwalks. Even when the English market was closed by embargo, alternative overseas markets were readily to hand. Sugar produced by slave labour was now pouring out of the West Indies and meat was urgently required to feed the population there. Cork and its stockyards became the Chicago of Ireland and heavily salted beef was crammed into barrels for the West Indian trade. As we have seen, the export trade in barrel staves faded away as every barrel was needed for the trade. Generally it was a time of some prosperity. Petty reported that the general standard of clothing was equal to that of Europe. Chimneys were appearing in houses. Many people owned a horse. The emphasis on pasture rather than tillage left many people underemployed and cottage industries, the spinning and weaving of wool and flax, were a source of supplemental income. The short war that followed, from 1689 to 1691, was not altogether of Ireland's making, but she had to provide campaign fields for the Irish army of James II and the English army of William III. William's victory was followed by the reshuffling of at least 400,000ha (1,000,000 acres) of land and when that was over, only 15% of the land of Ireland was left in Irish ownership and the ascendancy of the English landlord was complete.

What did Ireland look like in 1700, 150 years after the first plantation? The population had probably doubled, though it is difficult to give exact figures; Petty reckoned the population in 1672 at 1,200,000 and if we think of 1,000,000 in 1550 and 2,000,000 in 1700, at least our order of number will probably be correct. In 1550, people still trusted in castles (*Illus. 173*), but these had been made obsolete by gunpowder and in the seventeenth century the castle began to transform itself into a house (*Illus. 174*). In 1700, confident estate owners were beginning to build houses with large windows through which they could admire the newly planted exotic trees in their demesnes (*Illus. 174*). When these new pollens appear in our pollen-counts, we bring the Destruction phase (ILWd3) to an end and open the Expansion phase (ILWe) when the slow process of restoring Ireland's woodlands takes its first tentative steps.

The road system still left a lot to be desired '... the great rain has made the ways almost impassable, the horse road which is most old causeway being broken up

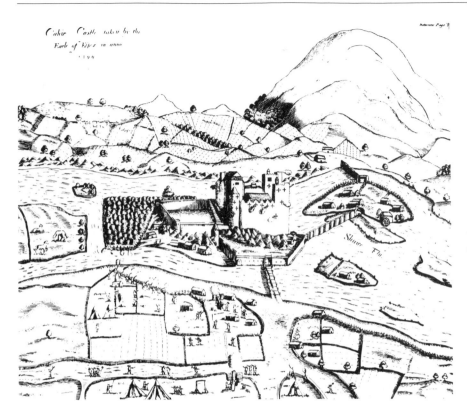

*Illus. 173
Cahir, Co. Tipperary.
This early
seventeenth-century
engraving shows a
landscape free of
trees, except on the
lower slopes of the
Galty Mountains.
The fields are
enclosed by banks,
walls and wattle
fences; within some
fields parallel lines
suggest cultivation-
ridges. The walls of
the castle, like those of
a tower house, are
pierced only by very
small windows.*

*Illus. 174
Coppinger's Court,
Co. Cork, as it may
have been in the late
seventeenth century.*

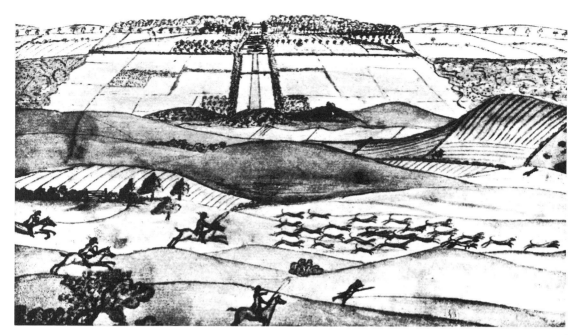

*Illus. 175
Near Castlepollard,
Co. Westmeath.
By the mid-eighteenth
century the large-
windowed mansion,
with its planted trees
and its formal
gardens, has replaced
the fortified castle
and the tower house.
The adjoining land
has been surveyed
and laid out in
regular fields; further
away there is
uncleared scrub.
Cultivation-ridges
are prominent
everywhere. In the
foreground the gentry
are enjoying a fox
hunt.*

and quite out of repair and the footway in the fields very boggy with abundance of ditches at that time full of water.' Despite this, the stage coach was beginning to appear. Stock could move easily to market and from there to the point of export. Banks to facilitate trade were coming into existence. The woods had shrunk out of all recognition and had been replaced by meadows and fields to support the larger population. The potato was beginning to take its place in the Irish diet. When did the potato appear in Ireland? At an early meeting of the Royal Society in 1662, Robert Boyle spoke in terms that suggested that the potato had already saved thousands from starvation in Ireland; but it may be that he was indicating what the potato could do rather than what it had already done, because at the same time his gardener was still struggling to produce the few potatoes needed to provide a delicacy in salads rather than an item of everyday diet. References to the potato in Ireland do not become common until the 1670s, and then they suggest that the potato was still a garden crop rather than a field crop. Dunton writes, 'Behind one of these cabins lies the garden a piece of ground sometimes of half an acre, and in this is the turf-stack, their corn perhaps two or three hundred sheaves of oats and as much peas; the rest of the ground is full of those dearly loved potatoes, and a few cabbages which the solitary calf never suffers to come to perfection.' At the end of the century the potato stood poised and ready to revolutionise life in Ireland.

CONSOLIDATION IN THE EIGHTEENTH CENTURY 1700-1785 AD

By comparison with the turbulent centuries which had preceded it, the eighteenth century was one of relatively uneventful development. By 1785, the population had doubled once more (*Illus. 176*) and trade had increased tenfold. A vigorous prog-ramme of road-building (accompanied by the full establishment of a stage-coach system) and the construction of canals both integrated the country and centred it on its capital, Dublin, to an extent hitherto unknown. The last Irish wolf had been killed. Unfortunately the now universal landlord-tenant relationship concentrated the new wealth in the hands of the landlords who erected the palatial houses looking out on well-wooded demesnes that are still such a feature of the Irish landscape. Outside the demesne, the lodgings of their tenants remained at their former miserable level. In the earlier part of the century, the interposition of a middleman who

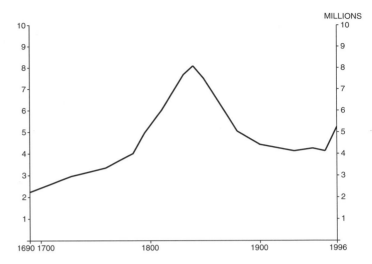

took large blocks of land on long lease from the landlord and let it in small blocks on shorter lease at higher rent to the tenant, ensured that such prosperity as escaped the landlord was siphoned off by the middleman and little or none of it was enjoyed by the tenant. The middleman was not entirely useless. He sometimes employed his capital in leasing dairy stock to tenants who could not afford their own and so took them into 'clientship' in a way that had been widespread in early Ireland. In this way, he exemplified that power to spring again from a cut-down stock that has typified much of Ireland throughout the ages. The cottage industries based on wool and flax continued to provide valuable supplements to family incomes and bleach greens became a feature of the Irish countryside. But Ireland was a backward agricultural country caught up in the rapidly developing British mercantile system and when that system was shaken either by harvest vagaries or by wars, then the fortunes of Ireland fluctuated also.

*Illus. 176
Graph to illustrate
population growth
and decline in
Ireland from 1690 to
1996.*

The agricultural revolution was slow to reach Ireland. Already in the middle of the sixteenth century, farmers in the Netherlands had eliminated the hitherto universal period of fallow. They replaced it with turnips and clover to feed increased numbers of stock whose larger output of manure was used to fertilise the land for the corn crops. Animal and crop husbandry were now united in one system capable of very intensive production. The weed problem was solved by the invention of the seed drill in 1700. With the young plants in neat rows, a hoe could be drawn between them and the weeds eliminated while the crop was growing. Ability to survive a hard winter on scanty rations was no longer the criterion by which stock had to be judged; with animal feed assured, it was now possible to breed for production of meat, milk and wool.

Eventually the wind of change did reach Ireland. A Linen Hall was founded in Dublin in 1711 to promote the growth of flax and oversee the weaving and sale of linen. The Royal Dublin Society was founded in 1731 for 'the advancement of agriculture and other branches of industry and for the advancement of science and art.' The society circulated agricultural books, imported implements and gave premiums for stock-breeding, tree planting, spinning, weaving and a host of other activities. It did much to stir up an interest in agriculture among the landlords who formed its membership and in the later part of the century the middlemen withered away as many landlords took a direct and improving interest in the management of their estates. An improvement was badly needed; each year the Cork stockyards alone slaughtered 300,000 head of cattle, but the cattle were small, averaging only 200-400kg against the 500-760kg of contemporary English breeds. If the quality of the cattle population was to be improved, controlled breeding was necessary. Improved pastures and hay and roots for winter fodder made it possible to carry bigger stocks and here also control was necessary. Hedged fields prevented stock from wandering, controlled the degree of grazing and manuring and provided shelter, while the ditch at the foot of the hedge improved drainage. Soon the landlords were hard at work, surveying and laying out new field alignments, digging ditches and throwing up banks which were then made secure by the planting of hawthorns along them. They 'improved' their tenants' lands as well as their own, in places breaking up the old clachans and building new houses well separated from one another. On flat ground the arrangement of fields might be highly regular, on isolated hills such as drumlins the layout would be adjusted to the slopes and on sloping ground a ladder pattern was often employed. Some landlords extended this activity to the settlements on their land, buying up plots and reorganising villages along planned lines. Some villages were completely reorganised in this way – Maynooth in Co. Kildare is a good example. Some such as Slane in Co. Meath were totally new.

After 1698, numerous acts of parliament promoted the planting of trees and in 1735 the Royal Dublin Society began to offer premiums for such planting. These stimuli appear to have been quite effective because by the year 1800 more than 52,000ha (130,000 acres) of plantations had been added to what native woods survived; between 1800 and the Famine another 85,000ha (210,000 acres) were added. Therefore, we had the paradoxical situation that while the landscape in the immediate vicinity of the estates was getting more and more densely crowded with trees, many of them exotic, the general countryside was getting barer and barer as the rising population was becoming more and more desperate for fuel.

In the 1780s, the pace of development began to falter. The new Corn Laws brought a swing from cattle to grain-growing and the population was entering on that period of staggering growth that was to bring it from four to eight millions in the course of sixty years. We are very fortunate to have a record of what the country looked like in the immediately preceding years in Arthur Young's account of his Tour in Ireland in 1776-9. Like Giraldus Cambrensis, Young was from Britain and not without prejudice; he was not very successful as manager of Lord Kingsborough's estate in Mitchelstown. He was conservative in outlook, he carried a large chip on his shoulder, but from his extensive travels and experiences we can build up a clear picture of the times. In Cavan, he found that Mr Clements had 'been very attentive to bring his farm into neat order respecting fences, throwing down and levelling old banks, making new ditches, double ones six feet wide and five deep, with a large bank between for planting.' He also approved of Lord Farnham who had farmed in Norfolk and sowed his turnips and cabbages with a drill and horse-hoed the weeds. The fields were drained and liberally fertilised with dung, ditch-earth and lime. There was a herd of Lancashire cows and although oxen were used for ploughing and general draft work, Lord Farnham also bred work-horses. The estate was well planted with Scots fir, silver fir, beech, oak and ash. 'Upon the whole Farnham is one of the finest places I have seen in Ireland.' Outside the demesnes the situation was different; Co. Galway 'is perfectly free from woods, and even trees, except about gentlemen's houses'. Near the cities things were worse; at Dunkettle, outside Cork, he reports 'Fuel; a very little coal, the rest supplied by bushes, stolen faggots, etc., as there is no turf in this part of the country.' He also approved of Mr Oliver, of Castle Oliver, Co. Limerick, but not of his tenants who raised bullocks on farms of up to 230ha (500 acres). 'The face of the country is that of desolation; the grounds are over-run with thistles, ragwort, etc. to excess; the fences are mounds of earth, full of gaps; there is no wood, and the general countenance is such, that you must examine into the soil before you will believe that a country, which has so beggarly an appearance, can be so rich and fertile.' At the bottom of the scale we hear 'great quantities of flax sown by all the poor and little farmers, which is spun in the country, and a good deal of bandle [narrow] cloth made of it. This and pigs are two great articles of profit here; they keep great numbers, yet the poor in this rich tract of country are very badly off. Land is so valuable, that all along as I came from Bruff, their cabins are generally in the road ditch, and numbers of them without the least garden; the potato land being assigned them upon the farm where it suits the master best. The price they pay is very great, from £4 to £5 an acre, with a cabin; and for the grass of a cow 20s to 45s. They are, if anything, worse off than they were twenty years ago. A cabin, an acre of land, at 40s, and the grass of two cows, are the recompense for the year's labour; but in other places they are paid by an acre of grass for potatoes at £5. Those who do not get milk to their potatoes, eat mustard with them, raising the seed for the purpose. The population of the country increases exceedingly, but mostly on the higher lands; new cabins are building everywhere.' It is clear that in Young's time the potato had become a field rather than a garden crop, that it was the principal item of diet for the majority of the population and that a rapid expansion of that population was making itself felt. What Young could not realise was that that expansion was going to produce a further sub-division of land into tiny potato patches and impede the orderly realignment of field boundaries of which he approved so highly.

The landlords, like Lord de Montalt at Dundrum in Co. Tipperary, might follow the advice of the Dublin Society and use Warwickshire and Shropshire ploughs, but elsewhere it was different, as at Castletownroche in Co. Cork. 'Four horses and three men to every plough, one to drive, one to hold, and another with a pole, bearing on the beam to keep it in the ground; but they do an acre a day, by means of leaving a great space untouched in the middle of each land, where they begin by lapping the sods to meet.' Such a ploughing scene can have changed little since the fourteenth century, though two men are now sharing the job the ploughman alone did then (*Illus. 138*). In the stony west everything was done with the spade. 'Upon asking whether they ploughed with horses or oxen, I was told there was not a plough in the whole parish, which was 12 miles long by 7 broad. All the tillage is by the Irish loy; ten men dig an acre a day that has been stirred before. It will take forty men to put in an acre of potatoes in a day.' He appreciated that spade cultivation was not necessarily to be despised as it could give a better return than the plough; at Belleisle in Co. Fermanagh, he reports 'Much corn, etc. by Poor People, put in with spades, which they call loys, because they have no horses, and one acre of oats dug, is worth one and a half ploughed; some do it on this account, though they have horses.'

Arthur Young saw Ireland from horseback or through the windows of a post-chaise. Were he touring today in a motor-car, he would be amazed at the hedges along the roadside, he would wonder where the masses of people had disappeared to, he would remark on the fanciful nature of many of the new houses, he would notice some trees, but much of the rest would still look familiar to his eyes.

THE POTATO AND THE POPULATION PEAK 1785-1850 AD

It is not easy to pinpoint the cause or combination of causes that drastically accelerated the rate of population increase in Ireland around 1785. We can picture that in 1741 the population was about three million, in 1785 it was about four million, while in 1841 when a census was taken shortly before the Famine the figure was 8,200,000. The death-rate was falling. As the 1840s approached, medicine was improving, vaccination for smallpox was adopted and a chain of hospitals and dispensaries was spreading through the country. Food was improving in quality and also in quantity; there was no major famine (apart from the Great Famine) after 1740 and the improved transport system made the movement of food within the country more easy. The birth rate was rising; more young people in the population meant more alliances and the better diet may have raised the fertility rate. In other European countries, the population was also rising, but not as fast as in Ireland. The potato was being eaten in other countries, but not to the same extent as in Ireland and it is difficult to resist the conclusion that the potato, not only by its dietary influence but also by its social influence, was the chief cause of the fantastic and disastrous rate of population growth in Ireland. During the Napoleonic Wars, there was money to be made in agriculture and land capable of producing corn provided a prosperous lifestyle and reliable rents. After the wars and the removal of incentives to grow corn, there was a drastic agricultural decline and many, including landlords, fell into difficulties. For those at the bottom of the heap, things were much worse and in western counties the decline was exacerbated by the collapse of the once-rich herring fisheries.

The potato is one of the great food crops of the world and alone of them finds conditions in Ireland entirely to its liking. The potato favours water-retaining soils and these are not in short supply in Ireland, particularly in the west and south. Conditions for wheat are minimal and those for barley are little better; oats and rye are more at home. The summer temperatures are rarely high enough for the sugar-beet to produce its full potential of sugar, but they are more than enough for starch production by the potato, whose homelands are the Andean uplands of South America. Though 75% of the tuber is water, the food value of an acre of potatoes is greater than that of an acre of any grain crop. The potato yields starch, amino-acids and Vitamin C and the consumption of 3kg (6lbs) per day provides an adequate diet. In Ireland, 0.4ha (1 acre) can be expected to yield about 9 tons, enough to feed six adult men for one year and more than adequate to support a relatively large family. It is thought that the consumption per head may have reached 3.6kg (8 lbs) a day. For most of us, forcible feeding in prison would seem preferable to thrusting half a stone of potatoes down our throats day in day out throughout the year. And for many this was all there was for months on end. We have only to read Arthur Young's litany as he perambulated the country. At Castletownroche; 'They live the year through upon potatoes, and for half the year have nothing but water with them; at Johnstown their food is potatoes for at least eleven months of the year, and one month of oat, barley or bere bread.'

For those with courage, there could be money in potatoes. W S Trench tells us how in 1846 he took 160 acres (65ha) of rough mountain pasture worth one shilling an acre. He scattered lime over it and then ploughed it into ridges five feet wide; the potatoes were sown, guano was added as manure and the ridges were further built up by hand. 'The potato grew to perfection in this rude description of tillage.' He expected to get a crop of potatoes worth £3000, 'at the very moderate price of 3d. per stone' and be left with the land with its value raised twentyfold to one pound an acre and ready to grow a good crop of corn or grass. But 1846 was the year of the blight and he lost all.

In Ireland as in other rural countries before farming was mechanised, the social pyramid was the landowners, the tenant-farmers and the landless labourers. We have seen the landowners in their elegant mansions, set in a tree-studded demesne which was now surrounded by a wall built as a relief measure by the local labourers. The tenant-farmers lived in a modest way; in his *Topographical Dictionary*, Lewis tells us; 'Farmhouses though varying in size are all built on the same plan, with an open chimney at one end, and at the other a small room separated by a partition, and serving both as a bed-chamber and as a storeroom. Few farm yards are attached to the houses, and these are very small and confined; the corn being frequently stacked on circular stages supported by upright capstones; barns are never used for any other purpose than thrashing, and are consequently built very small; the common farmer indeed is often unprovided with either stage or barn, and thrashes his grain in the open air.'

We can liken the social pyramid to a stratified beehive in which the three layers ought to be in appropriate proportions. Unfortunately after 1785, the boards containing the base of the beehive burst outwards and the labourers began to expand beyond the confines of the hive. The bee builds flimsy cells of wax, the labourers built their rickety cabins wherever they could find a sufficiency of square feet free from obstruction and if possible one wall was already provided against a field-bank, in a ditch or against a rock-face (*Illus. 177*). On the hillsides (far above the present level of cultivation) there were still patches of ground on slopes where lazy-beds could be laid out and a cabin set up. With luck there would be blanket bog not too far away and an easier supply of fuel to compensate for the harder struggle on higher ground. On rougher ground, stones could be cleared away. And as a last resort, there was the bog surface itself. Both on the raised bogs in the midlands and

Illus. 177
A nineteenth-century sketch from the Illustrated London News. *The cabins have mud walls and thatched roofs. In front of each cabin is a small 'garden' surrounded by low banks; here vegetables were grown. The background is completely free of trees.*

on the blanket bogs in the west, lazy-beds can be seen. Apparently only the thinnest skin of added sand or earth was necessary before the bog surface could be brought under cultivation. Near the coast, seaweed could be collected for manure. In the east, sub-divisions of land at first sufficed to produce the necessary acre per family. In 1830, the Royal Dublin Society was offering premiums for schemes to divide up land so that there would be allotted 'to the greatest number of cottages a quantity of land not less than one acre, Irish,' and also 'for the best account, of actual experience, of the quantity of land required to support a labourer's family with vegetables and potatoes, and to enable him to keep a pig and a cow all the year.' Those at a level higher up in the hive saw no reason to object to such fragmentation; the farmer by splitting some of his fields and letting the land at £5 or more per acre automatically received cash to make the payment of his own rent secure and the landlord was delighted to get prompt payment. Lest any suggestion should arise that the labourer should acquire even a shadow of title to the land he rented, he often got it on conacre or possession for eleven months only which made its reversion clear beyond doubt.

But where was one to get the money to pay the rent? There can have been no sale for surplus potatoes; in Ireland, potatoes are always a rags to riches crop. If the harvest was a light one, hunger might loom before the next harvest came round and the pressure to eat the seed stock might be impossible to resist. If the crop was a bumper one, there was no market for the surplus. Home spinning could bring in some cash and if the dwelling was substantial a loom could be set up. Estate cottages in the east often had a special room for looms. A bonham could be purchased and reared on family scraps for later sale as bacon. In addition to the acre of land, sometimes the £5 rent would bring the right to graze a cow for the year, and milk and butter would make a welcome supplement to the potato diet. Only at planting-time and at harvest was any serious labour required by the crop and the able-bodied members of the family were able to migrate in search of paid work. But the more the population increased, the more candidates there were for the jobs and the farmer had no difficulty in moving his wage-rate down.

A family was probably an asset rather than a liability once some of the children had reached the age of seven or eight. Capital outlay was almost nil. There were no agricultural implements needed beyond a spade for everyone big enough to use one (*Illus. 178*). There were no farm buildings because the potatoes could lie quite happily in a clamp in the field. A roof over the cabin, fuel for the fire and straw to lie on were essential. Clothes were patched beyond all recognition and handed down from one to another. Boots and shoes were for adults only and then only on special occasions. If necessary, the potatoes could be roasted in the ashes of the fire. It was subsistence-existence in the fullest sense of the word.

Illus. 178
Drawing of Irish labourer with spade in one hand and shoes in the other, c.1850.

The larger children could assist in the spade work. The others could gather herbs to flavour the potatoes, tend the cow and the pig, forage for manure – because the potato was a greedy crop – and most important of all, scour the countryside for fuel leaving no bush, bog or marsh unattacked. Nineteenth-century writers take up the tale where Arthur Young left off; in Co. Dublin 'the hedges are demolished without mercy, and, in many places they gather the dung from about the fields, and even burn straw.' Both the raised bogs and the blanket bogs were being heavily cut for fuel and even the swamps and marshes were being robbed of their muds. The mud was dug or dredged up, spread on the surrounding lands, tramped underfoot to a uniform consistency, moulded into lumps, dried and burned. West Cork today shows many small ponds; if we look at them closely we can see the still-jagged peat-cuttings that form their margins. Before the Famine they were closed marshes; their open-water was created by peat-cutting, just as the Norfolk Broads are the product of medieval peat-cutting on a much larger scale. It is hard to realise today just how serious the struggle for fuel was. Even in Arthur Young's time, hedges and fences were being stolen for firing. How much worse must it have been when the population was approaching its maximum. The countryside must have presented an extraordinary appearance. There were the walled demesnes with their trees, like oases in a desert. The boughs of the trees hung down over the walls, but inside the walls there were mantraps to deter timber poachers. There were the farmers' houses surrounded by shelter-belts of trees and the farmer would have had a blunderbuss to protect them. And then there was nothing, not a tree nor a bush, to break the view of the bare landscape dotted over with cabins and endless potato-patches.

Everything was done with the spade and every region had its own variety of spade. At one time, a spade factory at Monard in Cork used to produce at least seventy-five different forms of spade-blade. As we have seen, to use the spade rather than the plough is by no means a sign of inferior husbandry. The user of the spade gives to his work the detail of the gardener rather than the broader stroke of the plough and yields will usually be higher from the spade-plot than the ploughed field. If excess of labour allowed wage-rates to drop below a certain level, it would have been cheaper for the farmer to use teams of men with spades rather than the plough with its attendant cost of keeping the draught animals. And hand-in-hand with the spade went the cultivation-ridge or lazy-bed and we have seen that this method of cultivation is of high antiquity in Ireland. Though lazy-beds today are largely confined in distribution to the poorer west and in crop to the potato, they were formerly in use throughout the whole country, and a wide range of crops was raised on them. The width of the bed and the height to which it was built up, varied both with the nature of the soil and the requirements of the crop to be grown. The plough was sometimes used in the first laying out of the bed, but after that the spade took over and the shape of the bed might be adjusted to the needs of the crop at various stages of its growth. After the bed had been in use for some time it was divided down its centre; what had been the ridge-crest became the new furrow. As already commented, the general connotations of the word lazy are quite inappropriate here because the careful management of the cultivation-ridge is a sophisticated method of coaxing the best out of a soil that is often wet and unpromising to begin with. The water content can be improved by suitable proportions of ridge and furrow and the fertility can be raised by manuring. As a result, a low-grade soil can often be brought to a reasonable level of productivity.

In the west, the lazy-bed ruled all and the plough was unknown (*Illus. 179, 180, 181, 186*). In the early years of the nineteenth century, a detailed survey of the boglands of Ireland was made and Alexander Nimmo, a Scottish engineer very sympathetic to the plight of the peasantry, did a lot of work in the south-west. Speaking about the barony of Iveragh in south-west Kerry, he says there was not a single plough or proper spade in the whole area. All cultivation was done with 'an implement the iron blade of which is about five inches broad, and nine long, with a socket making an obtuse angle with the blade, into which a long wooden handle is fitted: the socket does not cover the base of the handle, which is fitted on by a wedge and nails: the edge admits of the appliance of the right foot only; the handle has no cross piece to draw it back or turn it. The implement admits not in any way being used as a lever, and may in its action be rather considered a peculiar kind of

Illus. 179
Bunnyconnellon,
Co. Mayo.
Cultivation-ridges
going back at least to
the earlier Bronze Age
are revealed when
blanket bog is cut
away.

plough than as a spade. It appears particularly adapted to the cultivation of sloping and stony ground; but its effect in digging or removing the soil being small, it is used in conjunction with a small triangular kind of shovel, which is fitted with a handle similar to the spade and employed for spreading the earth, which has been previously stirred by the spade in the trench, over the intervening beds; this being the universal mode of cultivation, at least in this part of Ireland.' He goes on to say

Illus. 180
Near Manor Kilbride,
Co. Wicklow. The
house foundations of
a long-abandoned
clachan lie beside an
extensive area of old
cultivation-ridges; the
varying shapes and
proportions of the
ridges show that a
variety of crops was
being grown in them.

that the implement is 'totally unfit for the purpose of cutting turf' and that 'if the cultivator is still to be kept without a plough, cart or team, at least the spade should be as highly improved to him as the instrument will admit.'

Nimmo's language is somewhat stilted, but he does give a picture of poverty and hard work. The same implement appears in Scotland as the cash-crom where it was used by groups of men to turn over the soil, in the way that a plough would have been used in less populated parts. In the west of Ireland, we can picture groups of men turning out of their clachan to the arable common-field each morning, ten to the acre if lazy-beds were to be set up, forty to the acre if potatoes were to be planted. There was no special factor controlling the shape or size of the field and a number of people would own either separate blocks within the field or, much more sensibly, rights on a certain number of lazy-beds in the field. Here we see a version of the common-field system that had flourished on the better land of eastern Ireland when the mouldboard plough appeared; it may go back to still earlier times. Cultivation in common withered away in the planted east of the country, but may well have survived in the native west and blossomed out again into the rundale system when eighteenth-century population pressures developed (*Illus. 176*).

In rundale there was the common arable field and nearby the clachan was a cluster of modest houses with outbuildings and small enclosures. Around the perimeter was the outfield, used for pasture and periodic cultivation and perhaps farther away the meadows, the mountain-grazing and the bogs, all of which were shared in common. With a balanced community, such a system was viable and could stand limited expansion. More potatoes could come into the arable field and the productivity of the outfield could be raised. But once population-growth exceeded a certain rate, the system had to collapse. Holdings and rights fragmented under succession in severalty. As the potato expanded to take up the whole of the arable

Illus. 181
Lenankeel,
Co. Donegal.
This small clachan is
still inhabited. Strips
of unenclosed
common-field are in
the background. Note
the lack of trees and
bushes.

field, it left no aftergrass to feed stock and to receive the dung in return. If stock numbers were reduced, the total amount of manure available for the arable field fell. Ultimately if everyone was not to be reduced below the subsistence level, there had to be movement either to higher levels up the hill-slopes to the east, where potato-patches could still be rented to the further detriment of the existing fields, or out of the country altogether to England or America.

The population of an overfull beehive can be relieved in two way. Swarms can carry large numbers away in search of new feeding grounds, or disease can decimate the colony. Long before the Famine, swarms of emigrants had begun to leave Ireland and by 1830 the rate of population growth was beginning to slacken off. But this was not enough and when in 1845 potato blight finally caught up with the potato in Ireland, disaster was inevitable. During the Famine years (1845-51), about eight hundred thousand people died and twice as many emigrated. The heart was knocked out of Ireland and the population continued to fall from a maximum of eight million without interruption until 1930, when it was only four million and Ireland was one of the emptiest countries in Europe (*Illus. 178*).

THE AFTERMATH OF THE FAMINE 1850-1900 AD

If we were to look back to 1850 BC, we would see a well-wooded Ireland and in clearings we would see a Bronze Age population enjoying a standard of life equivalent to that of anywhere in western Europe. If instead we were to look back to 1850 AD, we would see a ruined landscape almost destitute of any woody growth with the fertility of much of its soils grossly depleted by endless repetitions of potato crops. Those of its people in whom any element of *élan vital* had survived had only one goal – to seek a higher standard of living elsewhere. It is on the foundations of that ruined landscape that much of what we see around us today has been built.

One thing was clear: the land had to be rebuilt into larger units which might have some hope of economic survival. Some holdings fell back into the landlord's hands when the former tenants emigrated and he rapidly repossessed himself of others by means of eviction if the tenants fell into arrears with their rents. For the landlord himself was now facing ruin. Relief measures, both indoor and outdoor, had been organised for famine victims and these were charged on the local rates; not only had the landlord to pay his own dues, but if his tenants failed to pay and their valuation was less than £4 – there were vast numbers of such tiny holdings – then he had to pay their dues as well. It was only good sense for him to buy the family emigrant tickets to America and demolish their cabin lest another occupant should revive his liability for rates. Programmes of tree-planting were abruptly terminated. Many estates collapsed under the strain and in 1849 legislation made it possible for estates encumbered by debts to pass into new hands. But whereas many of the older landlords had lingering strains of paternalism towards their tenants, the newcomers had not and for many small land-holders it was 'out of the frying pan into the fire'.

After 1850, things improved rapidly. Increasing population and increasing prosperity in England meant good prices for Ireland's farm produce. The tenant farmers prospered on their larger farms and continued emigration of younger men meant that the services of those that remained were in demand and wages rose; at the top the landlord was happy. A railway boom was opening up the country; before the Famine there were 105km of rail, twenty years later there were over 32,000km. Imported manufactured goods and foodstuffs could reach all parts of the country with the result that shops thrived while local industries decayed.

But the essential dichotomy persisted between the more favoured and more accessible east and the poorer and more distant west. Paradoxically, it was the east that provided the bulk of the emigrants; in the west, a still dispirited population lacked the initiative to go further than seasonal work in Britain and the population obstinately remained at a level that was too high for the local resources.

The self-perpetuating flame of Irish resistance to British domination that had been encouraged to flare up by the Act of Union in 1801 had almost flickered out during the distresses of the Famine, but it gradually warmed to life again and England was forced to adopt, through the person of Mr Gladstone, a policy that has been aptly described as 'a nauseous mixture of slaps and sops'; the slaps being the coercion of political unrest and the sops being the bringing about, as a first step, of co-partnership between the landlord and tenant and as a second step, of the transfer of ownership from landlord to tenant. The Land Act of 1870 was the first important sop: if a tenant surrendered his farm he was entitled to be compensated for any improvements he had made; if he was put out for any reason other than non-payment of rent, he was entitled to compensation for disturbance; if he wished to purchase his holding, he could borrow money from the state.

The all-too-brief good times ended abruptly in the middle seventies when bad weather brought crop failures on a massive scale. Prices for what modest home produce there was did not rise, because the new generation of large cargo steamers was carrying in cheaper supplies from overseas. Rents could not be paid, evictions started up again and political agitations accompanied them. A further dose of coercion was accompanied by Mr Gladstone's second Land Act, that of 1881, with its famous 'three Fs': fair rents, fixity of tenure and free sale. A few years later, it was supplemented by an act by which the State would advance the whole of the purchase price of a farm to be repaid by annuities and about 25,000 farms soon changed hands.

From 1850 on, the process of realigning field boundaries, enclosing new fields and planting their boundaries with trees and bushes had gone steadily on, but landlords were no longer able to afford new plantations of trees on the scale that had existed before the Famine. Planting was balanced by cutting to finance it and the acreage under plantations remained the same. The Land Act of 1881, which brought nearer the transfer from landlord to tenant, had disastrous effects on the attitude of the landlord to his estate; he could no longer see it as something to be husbanded so that it could be passed on in tail-male in perpetuity and he decided to turn his estate into money while the going was good. As always, timber was turned to a source of cash and many landlords sold their stands of timber to travelling sawmillers who came over from England and moved across the country from estate to estate, again leaving devastation in their wake (*Illus. 182*). As a footnote we may add that the woods which survived this cutting

enjoyed only a brief respite before they vanished in World War I and when that was over, 80,000ha (200,000 acres) of woodland had disappeared and less than half of one per cent of Ireland was covered by forest.

The grim cycle came round again in the late eighties; poor yields at home, cheap imported foreign goods, rent arrears, evictions, violence, coercion and more Land Acts. Tenant protection was further extended and more money was made available for farm purchase. Economic conditions improved again in the nineties and from this time on, the more favoured east was economically viable and was beginning to develop the appearance that we know today. Some trees had survived on some estates, the trees that had been planted in the field-banks were growing to maturity and while the total number of trees was still minute, the view across the landscape did contain some trees and the ghastly dreariness of immediately post-Famine times was fading away, though numerous house ruins and shrunken clachans were still evidence of the vanished population.

The west remained on the precarious edge of subsistence and special attention was given to its improvement. In 1891, a Congested Districts Board was set up to help those western regions where the density of the population manifestly outstripped the local resources. The Board built roads, bridges and harbours and much of the modern tourist traffic enjoys the benefits of its activities. It stimulated

Illus. 182
Glendalough,
Co. Wicklow.
In the early
nineteenth century
the valley was
stripped of timber, as
wood for fuel and
charcoal for smelting.
The monastic
buildings stand out
like ruined teeth in a
bare gum. See Col. 44
for the same view
today.

*Illus. 183
Connemara,
Co. Galway. An
isolated farm
established in rocky
terrain by clearing
stones into field walls
and bringing in sand
and seaweed. The
round fields were
worked with spades;
we see potatoes in
cultivation-ridges
and a patch of oats.*

fishing, gave agricultural advice and encouraged cottage industries. Added income was vital and this came from the cottage industries and seasonal earnings in Britain, now made easier of access by the new roads and railways. But as the historian, Louis Cullen, points out, even before the Board had been set up, emigration rates from the west and the age of marriage had both started to rise. These were positive moves, portending better than the palliative remedies of the Board. New cash sent home in remittances from emigrants may well have exceeded new cash generated by the Board and the modernisation made possible by the new money probably tended to promote more emigration in search of still higher standards rather than to stem it.

Foreign food products were now flooding into the English markets and it was no longer sufficient for Ireland to produce in quantity, she must produce in quality also. In 1894, Horace Plunkett founded the Irish Agricultural Organisation Society to promote joint purchases and sales and to bring the dairy industry to a level where it could meet competition from Denmark and New Zealand. He followed this up in 1899 by securing the creation of a government Department of Agriculture and Technical Instruction to raise the general standards of farming in Ireland.

The year 1903 marks a turning point in the history of the Irish landscape. In that year, the new department established its first forestry centre and assumed responsibility for the management of its first block of woodland. Here we have the first step at national level to restore to Ireland a substantial area of woodland and the first step to alter drastically the appearance of the Irish landscape. It was also the year of the culminating Land Act – the Wyndham Act – which, when there had been added to it the power of compulsory purchase, made the completion of Gladstone's ambitions possible. Entire estates, not just piecemeal holdings, could now be offered for sale and very generous financial terms made easy purchase possible. When the possibilities of the Wyndham Act had worked their way through the system, Ireland was indeed a land of small farmer proprietors.

*Illus. 184
Brideswell,
Co. Roscommon.
Here there is thin soil
on limestone.*

Within modern square walled fields we see similar older enclosures and cultivation-ridges now being invaded by scrub. The smaller enclosures may have been worked with spades; the walls both protect a space and provide a dump for field stones.

8. MODERN IRELAND 1903 TO PRESENT

When the transfer of land was complete, all vestiges of early and of feudal Ireland had disappeared. In their stead authority was represented by institutions of government, both at national and at local level and the land was held by farmer proprietors who clung with a vice-like grip to their small units of inefficiently worked fields. Even today, half the Irish farms are of 12ha (30 acres) or less. But at least at the national level the landscape could now be viewed and managed on a countrywide basis rather than operated as a patchwork of estates farmed at various levels of interest and efficiency.

It was realised that the soil was a matter for nationwide concern and soil investigation units were added to the Geological Survey. The absolute deficiency of timber had to be rectified and a State forestry programme was initiated. Because of the virtual absence of coal, the winning of peat on an industrial scale had already attracted attention by the middle of the nineteenth century and one hundred years later this operation was placed on a national basis. The soil of a country is its most important single resource. Unlike other resources such as oil or metallic ores, the soil is or should be inexhaustible and no nation can afford to ignore its management. In Ireland, because the humid climate encourages soil deterioration, such management is a matter for special concern.

In coastal districts since at least the twelfth century, man has been drawing shelly sand and seaweed from the shore and spreading it on his fields to improve both the fertility and the drainage of the soils. It was only this practice that made farming possible along much of the western and southern fringe of Ireland. Here the soils had first degenerated to peaty podzols and had then become smothered by blanket bog. As the population pressures grew in the late eighteenth century, much of the peat was cut for fuel to reveal the poorest of soils. But if the soil was stripped down to the iron pan and the latter was broken up with crowbars, it was again possible for water to move downwards. Sea sand and seaweed were spread over the soil, which then ceased to be the surface layer (*Illus. 185*). Over the years, the otherwise idle hours of winter were spent in drawing and spreading more material until in some places as much as a metre had been deposited. Sometimes the sand was first used as bedding for cattle, where it absorbed large quantities of dung and urine. In the Aran Islands, such soils were built up on bare rock. In this way, a first-class soil replaced a very poor one (*Illus. 186*). The practice has been largely abandoned today, but the improved properties of the man-made soils remain; the agricultural activity in the vicinity of Castlegregory in Co. Kerry is entirely based on the soils that were laboriously built up by past generations.

As the twentieth century opened, another agricultural revolution was taking place, this time consequent on the introduction of the so-called artificial fertilisers which made it possible to directly replace calcium, potassium, nitrogen and phosphorus in the soil. External and internal wars then distorted this gradual development. World War I and especially the two years after it were among the most hectic periods of agricultural prosperity in Ireland's history, surpassing even the

Illus. 185
Collecting seaweed,
Brittany, France.

Illus. 186
Aran Islands,
Co. Galway.
Until very recently,
soil for cultivation-
ridges like these was
made by bringing in
sand and seaweed
and spreading them
on bare limestone
rock.

best years of the Napoleonic wars. Food and timber were in unlimited demand. The soil's reserves of fertility were heavily drawn on, while timber stocks were butchered. With the aid of artificial manures the soil could be replaced relatively quickly, but it was a matter of many years before the scars on the landscape could be healed. The difficulties of the post-war crash were intensified by military activities at home, first against British forces and later on an internecine level, but the first Dublin government was strongly in favour of agriculture and prices in general were kept low to encourage agricultural exports. The aftermath of the Great Depression of 1929 was intensified in Ireland by an economic war with Britain which pushed agricultural prices down still further. But if agriculture came under fire, the protective tariffs, which were part of the campaign, provided the screen in whose shelter the industrialisation of the south of Ireland was born.

World War II again created demand for agricultural products, but this time the government control of prices and other matters was more rigorous and the bonanza of 1914-18 was not repeated. Once again, production was increased at the expense of reserve-fertility and once again there was wholesale felling of park trees, hedgerow trees, woodlands and plantations creating a new generation of landscape scars. The end of hostilities left the land of Ireland in such poor shape that intervention at government level was necessary. The European countries whose lands had been ravaged by war were in the same position and received generous American aid through what came to be known as the Marshall Plan and although Ireland had been neutral, she also was helped. Large grants were made available for field improvement, both by the cutting of drains and by the removal of tree stumps and large boulders, but through the enthusiasm of contractors and other interested parties, grandiose schemes were often embarked on which expended money on a scale far beyond the benefit that might be expected.

To restore the calcium that had been leached from the soil, ground limestone was made available at subsidised prices; the innovation brought about the final demise of one of the characteristic features of the Irish landscape, the lime-kiln, where small quantities of limestone had been burned with peat or coal at least since the eighteenth century. To restore the other nutrients, an ambitious and expensive scheme was launched whereby a farmer could have the necessary amount of fertiliser applied to his fields by undertaking to pay an annuity over a period of years, in the same way as the land purchase annuity was being paid. Most soils were found to be heavily deficient in phosphorus and in many cases an overdose of this type of fertiliser was applied making further applications unnecessary for many years.

None the less, the farmer continued to apply his habitual fertilisers of phosphorus, potassium and nitrogen. Current spreading of phosphorus amounts to 60,000 tons per annum at a cost of £25 million. Much of this phosphorus is not absorbed by the soil, but is carried by rain-flow on the surface to rivers and lakes where it promotes algal blooms. Such blooms are deleterious both to fish stocks and the amenity value of the waterways. The amount of nitrogen applied is also excessive and makes its way down into the ground waters. If the ground waters are drawn off for drinking water, the nitrogen content may reach a level dangerous to health.

Part of the American grant was used to found an Institute of Agricultural

Research, An Foras Talúntais, now absorbed into a larger organisation, Teagasc, and this has been of the greatest importance in furthering agricultural development. The institute launched a national soil survey to discover the real capacity of Irish soils. Short-sightedly, this programme was interrupted before it was completed, but there are indications that its vital work may be resumed. But by the middle nineteen-fifties, post-war developments were beginning to run out of steam, the country was stagnating and the tide of emigration was beginning to flow again. Revitalisation was necessary and this was provided by the Whitaker Plan for Economic Development, which was accepted by the government in 1958. This plan was to transform the Irish scene.

We still prize Arthur Young's record of late-eighteenth-century Ireland and the detail he gives of new and old farming practices. T W Freeman first published his very valuable book, *Ireland: A General and Regional Geography* immediately after the war in 1950 and a second revised edition followed in 1960. The book presents an Ireland that had drifted along almost unchanged since the twenties, but which in the subsequent twenty-five years vanished almost as completely as Young's Ireland. In the book, the Grand Canal still carried commercial loads and only two pleasure boats had ventured onto the Shannon; today there are more than one thousand cabin cruisers on the Shannon waterways. Freeman's *Geography* will stand beside Young's *Journal* as a record of a vanished time.

The Whitaker Plan stressed the need to capitalise on Ireland's greatest natural resource – the grassland which covers 80% of Ireland's utilised agricultural area – and to boost cattle, sheep and milk production. But the main thrust was in the industrial area and the challenge of free trade was accepted. A second seven-year programme was adopted in 1963 and was equally successful. In the sixties, economic growth was faster and more sustained than in any previous period in Irish history. Living standards rose by more than 50% and the tide of emigration was reversed. Private motor-cars rose from 250,000 in 1958 to 700,000 in 1970. But somewhere along the line, as John Healy pointed out, the people's eyes turned away from the country, as a land to be cherished and looked instead to the economy as a source of privilege.

In the same period, such growth was not unique to Ireland nor entirely achieved by Ireland's own efforts. Much of the momentum was derived from the general economic upswing that Europe enjoyed in the sixties. But the golden age ended in 1971 when the United States would no longer issue gold metal in exchange for paper dollars and sustained economic progress faded away as monetary instability developed.

1973 brought two further developments as different from one another as the two poles of a magnet. The first was accession to the EEC (now the EU) after which another agricultural bonanza was launched. Farmers received steadily increasing prices for their products, the Common Agricultural Policy swallowed up all that was produced, financial institutions fell over one another to press loans on the farmers, land prices rocketed to heights that defied all reason, farm buildings proliferated on all sides and no one stopped to think that 'with eager feeding food doth choke the feeder.'

With the EEC milk price 40% above world level, it was so easy just to shovel the butter into cold store and not think of adding value to the milk by developing alternative dairy products. It was just as easy to push the sides of beef into intervention without much attention to quality and not think of butchering and packaging. Ultimately, there had to be a limit to what the storage caves of the Common Market could engulf.

This transient prosperity masked the second development of 1973, the creation of a cartel by the world's most important producers of oil. At first, increased energy costs were absorbed easily as prices for farm products continued to rise. But international prosperity and above all economic expansion were dealt very deadly blows. The cartel has since collapsed and oil prices have fallen dramatically carrying energy costs down with them. But the extinction of the cartel did not restore the status quo of 1973. The Common Agricultural Policy (CAP) was very severely pruned and excess production was penalised.

9. THE PRESENT

Discontent with the European Union's policy of subsidising agriculture continues. A policy of restriction can no longer be sustained or defended either on financial or on moral grounds. One half of the world should not produce excess food which it cannot eat and cannot afford to sell while the other half of the world starves. But it must be remembered that Europe does not stand alone in its policy of selfish subsidisation. In 1994, lengthy labyrinthine international negotiations between powerful groups of nations, each with its own type of subsidisation, were necessary to attain the GATT agreement on agricultural policies.

How will Ireland, which did very well under the unreformed CAP, fare in the new climate? Further radical revisions of the agricultural grant system are needed. The EU has called a halt to grants to increase milk production and a severe quota system is in operation. As a result, a good dairy farmer in eastern Ireland will produce his restricted quota of milk from fewer acres than he is using for this purpose at present; what is he to do with his surplus land? At first it was thought that the milk quota was inalienably tied to the land. But a decision in a Dutch Court ruled that quota and land were separate entities and that quotas could be bought and sold. So the big farmer in the east buys milk quotas from small farmers in the west, thus depriving the latter of their best cash crop and making their lifestyle still more vulnerable.

Grassland best suited for milk production is concentrated in the high rainfall areas of Ireland and the west of Great Britain. Ireland has 95% of the best grassland in the Union and dairying will always be important in Ireland. With the quota system the price of milk is artificially high (standing at 105p a gallon in 1996) and, surprisingly, varies between member states, even between Northern Ireland and the Republic. As a result, Northern Ireland producers are beginning to invade the Dublin milk market, offering the supermarkets cartoned milk at a price below that of the local suppliers.

Even today, farmers in western Ireland are still seeking EU grants to reclaim hill land and turn it into grassland which they will use to feed dairy cows. However, very much less land as well as very much less milk is what the EU wants. The high agricultural prices of the CAP encouraged farmers to improve their efficiency and less and less land can now produce the same amount of food. John Lee of Teagasc looked at this question and he reckoned that by the year 2000 the EU will have five million hectares of surplus grassland, and up to ten million hectares of surplus arable land, an area almost twice the size of Ireland. A scheme of compulsory 'set aside' will reduce the number of hectares under production, but will not bring about a proportionate reduction in output. In the United States some years ago, a policy of paying farmers to set aside a land-bank meant that they took the poorer land out of use, accepted the set aside money, spent it on more fertiliser and raised the output of the good land still in production.

The making of hay has virtually ceased in Ireland and silage rules the land. It is a convenient way of grass storage, but it brings at least two main hazards: the poisoning of rivers and the widespread dispersal of scraps of plastic. Silage effluent is deficient in oxygen and when it reaches a stream it greedily draws down the content of oxygen in the water to a level at which fish and other forms of wildlife asphyxiate with disastrous consequences. Baling silage in plastic sheeting has two advantages: it conserves the grass well and makes the fodder available in easily handled units. But the farmer rips off the sheeting which together with fertiliser bags and other fragments of plastic is often carried far and wide by the wind. Parts of the countryside are becoming badly disfigured, but in some areas there are further more serious consequences.

In areas of bare limestone, such as the Burren, much of the rainwater is carried off by underground streams with tortuous channels. A considerable quantity of plastic fragments is carried down swallow-holes and through winding channels to join the river below. Inevitably, some plastic will be trapped in the bends and ultimately the drainage channels will become irretrievably constricted and severe maintained surface flooding will occur. In 1995, flooding in some parts of the Burren in Co. Clare and parts of Co. Galway was extremely severe and the water was slow to drain away. Many relatively new houses were badly affected; it seems that in some cases because of the possibility of flooding, initial planning permission had been refused, but this was overturned by a county council vote and the buildings went ahead with inevitable results.

However, the rain that is welcome for grass creates problems for tillage. Because of poor soil-drying conditions, the Irish farmer has to carry out tillage operations on days that are less than favourable with resultant damage to the soil structure and increased machinery costs. The swing to winter wheat will continue because it is easier to work heavy soils in autumn than in spring. None the less, Irish cereal yields are well above the EU average in quantity, though perhaps not in quality, even though the country only has 4% of the best arable land in the community.

Arable farms will continue to increase in size and the role of the specialised contractor will grow. The all-round farmer has virtually disappeared and the large specialist will sit in his office and make arrangements for preparing the seed-bed, spraying the young crops and harvesting them when ripe using various contractors. But the EU tide has turned against grain surpluses and restrictions on production will become more severe.

Ireland is traditionally a land of potatoes, although a yield of 26 tonnes per hectare is below the EU average and far below Holland at 36 tonnes. Ireland's potato farmers will have to give great attention to quality and packaging if they are to hold even the home market.

At present because the price of sugar is at an artificially high level in the EU, sugar beet is a profitable option for Irish farmers. In order to prevent the erection of a sugar mountain, land under the crop is restricted by a quota system and there is no prospect of expansion here. In any case, in a rational world sugar production would be left to the West Indies and areas of similar climate which might then enjoy some prosperity instead of being pushed down into misery by the subsidised production of sugar elsewhere.

The livestock industry is the other bastion of Irish agriculture, but here too the limitation of production is high on the agenda. There are two possible destinies for the beef cow on the farm – the factory or the boat – and the balance between them is precarious. The packing of meat for export brings both added value and more employment and needs to be encouraged. Prices in live export markets, principally the Near East, rise and fall and the prospect of prompt payments varies. If prices fall then the cattle are offered to the factories, which on the other hand want a steady flow-through of animals if the plant is to operate efficiently; contracts for steady supply are difficult to enforce. Obviously live transport over long distances puts a strain on animals and a movement is growing to ensure that they have tolerable conditions throughout the journey. Quite rightly, animal welfare groups are growing more vociferous and tighter international control of transport conditions are promised. Tighter oversight is also affecting the dead-meat trade as the EU insists on higher and higher standards of hygiene in the factories.

Fifty years ago foot-and-mouth, a bovine disease easily transmitted to humans, was a serious health threat. Today, two sinister and fatal diseases, Bovine Spongiform Encephalopathy (BSE) and Creutzfeld-Jacob Disease (CJD), which cause a spongy deterioration of the brain in cattle and man respectively are causing acute alarm. In both diseases there appears to be a very long incubation period, and it is difficult to see at what point the counter-attack will be most effective. BSE is acute in Britain, and British beef is being banned in many countries. So far the incidence in Ireland has been low, but a grave cloud hangs over the whole cattle industry. The catastrophic decline in beef sales following the admission by the British Minister of Health in March 1996 of a possible link between BSE and CJD, shows how vulnerable a primary commodity-based agricultural industry can be to unforeseen political events. There is, however, evidence that consumers internationally were turning away from beef before the BSE crisis began. The serious short-term effects of the disease may have masked a longer term trend in consumption which must be taken into account in future planning for the cattle industries. The discussion of the future of the beef industry in Britain has aroused a great deal of resistance in the marketplace to political discourse. What discourse there is is based mainly on economic considerations and hardly at all on the health of the consumer. A greater exposure to the variations of the marketplace may well impose new thinking on the managers of our agri-industries. It can be argued that the government agencies concerned with food should be detached from the Department of Agriculture and Food, which has been accused – not entirely fairly – of being a prisoner of the producers.

Obviously all these trends have important implications for the Irish farmer and the Irish landscape. In 1996, the State will have spent more than £55 million on long-term development aids to agriculture. These want to be looked at with a new eye. The State will have spent £10 million on arterial drainage in addition to the many, many millions it has spent on such drainage in the preceding years. Almost none of this money has gone on further improvement of good land; the bulk went to achieve a modest improvement in very poor land and neither Ireland nor Europe wants more poor land; they have more than enough of it already. What then should we do with the poor land we already have?

Numbers of sheep in Ireland have increased enormously in recent years – from 3.3 million in 1980 to 8.8 million in 1991 – encouraged by excessive EU subsidies, and the problem of overgrazing (*Col. 52*) has already been referred to. The profit margins on sheep are difficult to forecast as prices in France, Britain and Ireland show short-term fluctuations. The pig market is also very difficult, but the universal practice of confining pigs indoors makes this an industrial rather than an agricultural problem. The difficulty of preventing their manurial effluent reaching rivers and lake is a major one. Hens too have disappeared from the open countryside and factory farming rules the day. Disposal of their excreta also gives rise to problems.

Pollution of rivers and lakes brings the pig and the poultry people into immediate conflict with anglers, their rod-lines and their nets. But this is a mere skirmish compared with the problem of sea-fishing, both inshore and offshore. Shellfish stocks are becoming exhausted; larger and larger trawlers supported by floating processing-factories are sweeping the oceans clear of fish. The whole concept of countries claiming exclusive fishing-rights for a certain distance out from their shores, with a free-for-all beyond that limit, has been made completely obsolete by the development of modern large-scale fishing techniques. A further mockery arises when a Spanish-owned boat operating out of Vigo can register as British or Irish, fish in 'their' waters and then return to Vigo with the catch. However, while in Irish waters they are pursued by Irish naval vessels and if the mesh of their net is below the internationally recognised standard, they can be prosecuted in an Irish court. These courts hear other fishery cases usually referring to the use of illegal monofilament nylon nets which take a high toll of salmon migrating from Greenland to warmer waters further south. Salmon are also farmed in floating coastal cages and an unresolved battle runs as to whether the sea-lice which infect the enclosed fish also attach themselves to migrating fish heading for the inland rivers in which they will spawn.

For many of the practices of modern farming, the oversufficiency of rain in Ireland is a major problem. The debate on what to do with the wet soils of western Ireland has now been in progress for more than a century and a half. Most authorities agree that of the 8 million hectares (20 million acres) of land in Ireland about 2.5 million hectares (6 million acres), say one-third of the whole, are unfit for profitable agriculture; the bulk of this unprofitable land lies in the west. In 1845, Griffith in his Valuation Report said that half the unprofitable land should be planted with trees. In 1883, Gladstone invited a Danish forester, Howitz, to report on the possibilities of reafforestation in Ireland; his report echoed that of Griffith: 2 million hectares (5 million acres) were more suited to forestry than anything else and 1.2 million hectares (3 million acres) lay along the western seaboard.

From modest beginnings and despite the setbacks of two world wars, the annual rate of planting in Ireland has been pushed up to over 8000ha (20,000 acres). Today, 8% of the land is covered by trees and the goal is to reach 24%, the EU average. But this is a minefield in which economics and environment are engaged in a pitched battle. The planters are powerfully armed. First, the planting grants are generous, at up to £3000 per hectare for hardwoods. Second, it is recognised that the income raised in the early years will be small and annual grants varying between £100 and £300 per hectare per annum are paid for a period which may be up to twenty years in length. These grants are available to all, but to wealthy individuals or companies which regard the matter as a paper investment and may never see a tree, there is much more. All income arising is free from income tax and this is followed by exemption from capital gains tax and stamp duty as well as a relief on capital acquisitions tax. For the wealthy this offers a very handsome form of long-term investment. But what of the environment? Vast timber processing factories are in operation in Leitrim and Waterford; what of their effect on pollution of air and water?

Much of the planting hitherto has been on the uplands above the recognised limit for cultivation or on blanket bog, but sooner or later the main question must be answered. Are the low-lying poorly-drained soils of western Ireland to be taken bodily out of marginal agriculture and transferred instead to timber production where the yield can be expected to be generous?

Recently, attention has been focusing on the drumlin belt, a broad swathe running from coast to coast through Down, Armagh, Monaghan, Fermanagh, Leitrim and Sligo. Drumlins are low, elongated, isolated hills built up of glacial till which make very poor farmland (*Illus. 35*). The till is rich in clay and was extruded under heavy ice pressure and so it is very dense in texture. Water cannot easily percolate through it and soils are wet and very difficult to drain. The sloping flanks are in many cases too steep for farm machinery to manoeuvre easily. Leitrim is the worst off of all the counties; only one-tenth of the soils are well drained, six-tenths are poorly drained and much of this is on steeply-sloping drumlin sides. The remainder is bog, lake or river occupying the low ground between the drumlins. Farms are small, and the vast majority of them cannot produce a family income which is comparable to that of a family of industrial workers. Population loss by emigration has been heavy. Much of the land is held by unmarried elderly folk, both men and women. It would seem impossible for agriculture, even if efficiently practised, to give an adequate return for investment here. But there is no doubt that trees grow well on drumlin soils and large-scale afforestation has been proposed.

But poor though his land may be, the Irish small farmer due to a subliminal recollection of 'Landlord' days has a passionate attachment to it. As a result it is almost impossible to acquire parcels of land to build up into adequately-sized units for commercial forestry. Proposals for long leasings have not been taken up either. There may be some further psychological block here. For more than a hundred years Ireland has been a treeless country and every viewpoint shows a wide expanse of landscape. Transfer an Irish farmer to an Irish Black Forest and he may suffer from claustrophobia. The farmer may want to lean on a gate and look out over rushy fields with wandering bullocks; he may not want to sit in a cottage blanked off by conifers even though his wealth is augmenting itself around him as he sits.

Frank Convery has looked in detail at the position in Leitrim where A O'Rahilly has been growing trees for some time and has a first crop approaching maturity. There is no doubt that spruce from the west coast of North America, *Picea sitchensis*, will grow well in Leitrim. The only question is does it grow too rapidly? Will its wood produce planks of necessary strength? Windthrow may be another difficulty; when the trees are approaching maturity, the soil may not have sufficient strength to anchor the roots. But acquisition is the main problem as blocks of some extent have to be built up. If an adequate pilot scheme can be shown to be successful, then the wealthy investors will move in. After oil, wood is the largest single import by value into the European Union.

However, it is not simply a case of planting trees anywhere you can get land sufficiently cheaply – a policy which has tended to colour the activities of State forestry in the past. The plantings should be on good forestry land below 240m in elevation and great care should be taken of the young trees in their first critical years. Because of windthrow, peat – either as upland blanket bog or cutaway lowland bog – should be avoided. To maintain landscape variety, small blocks of hardwoods such as oak should be scattered through the conifers. The hardwoods attract generous 'start-up' grants and though they will take a long time to come to maturity, they will pay handsomely when they do. In addition, we must nurture the stocks of native trees and ensure that these are well-represented in the plantings.

But great areas of blanket bog have already been planted or marked down as areas for future afforestation. In north Mayo, where the blanket bog is remarkably extensive and continuous, the generation of electricity in peat-fired power stations is in operation (*Col. 49*). World War I had created a demand for native fuels and considerable experimentation sought to generate electricity efficiently from peat. In 1946, bog development was nationalised under the auspices of Bord na Móna and by 1970, 55,000ha (135,000 acres) of bog, nearly all raised bog, were yielding over 4,000,000 tons of peat per annum, produced either as surface moss for horticulture or milled peat for the power station.

Elimination of unnecessary handling of the peat has been the goal and more than three-quarters of the total is won by tearing up the surface with a harrow, allowing the debris to dry and then sweeping it into a ridge along the bog from which a light railway carries it to the power station. The dry ridges are protected by enormous lengths of polythene sheeting and seen from a distance, the shimmering ridges create the illusion of a vast and unexpected lake. If the windmill has disappeared from the Irish countryside, the cooling towers of the bogside power stations have added a new feature. There is also a trade in baling the mossy surface layers and selling the bales for horticulture; but the green lobby is beginning to oppose this practice. At the outset of the programme, it was decided in principle that the exhausted boglands would be turned into farmlands or forests. Today, we have the cutaway bogs and no one knows what is the best thing to do with them. Will they revert to wetlands, wilderness areas or rubbish dumps? It will be difficult

to make them commercially viable. With the exploitation of the bogs has gone a huge loss in our archaeological heritage. Nowadays when you walk on to the surface of a Bord na Móna bog being harvested mechanically, you will more than likely stand on a level laid down not later than the beginnings of the Later Bronze Age – say about 1200-1000 BC. Except for around the margins, everything of later times has gone forever. The loss of archaeological heritage through afforestation of uplands is equally worrying, especially as most of it remains entirely unrecorded. Mechanical winning of peat is also carried out on a smaller, private enterprise scale (*Illus. 187, Col. 50*).

Illus. 187
Peat macerator on tractor at Corstown bog, Co. Meath. A rotary cutter is below the bog surface and sods are being extruded to the right of the macerator.

The Shannon is the country's greatest source of hydroelectric power, yet the farmer is constantly calling for a major drainage scheme, even though much of the land liable to flooding is of poor quality. Here again we have a zone where politics and economics overlap. In the east, it was proposed to develop the River Boyne for hydroelectric purposes and expensive preliminary works were undertaken. Then the decision was reversed and it was agreed to undertake a main drainage scheme even though the simplest of cost-benefit-analyses would have shown that money expended on drainage would never be recouped by increased agricultural output. However, the sight of a great excavator crawling up and down a river bed – even if it is ruining the landscape by degrading the river to the status of a half-filled canal, destroying its fish and piling up spoil-banks along its margins – is a much greater winner of local rural votes than the idea of a distant power-station bringing benefit to faceless city-dwellers. The concept of an unspoiled wetland with its accompanying wildlife as a local, national or even international resource is one which it is equally difficult to sell to the rural voter. However, perhaps even here the tide is turning as the value of such renewable environmental assets is beginning to be accepted.

Irish seas have a considerable tidal rise and fall and the west coast has powerful waves built up by winds crossing the Atlantic. Much international research has been done to achieve schemes which would harness waves and tides in the economic production of electricity, but so far without significant result. The Irish coast has been scoured for sites where tidal flow might be utilised, but again there has been no development. Strangford Lough immediately attracts the eye as a potential site, but the importance of the Lough as a wildlife paradise cannot be overlooked.

There is now more interest in wind of which again there is aplenty in Ireland as a source of power. One wind farm is already in operation in Bellacorick bog in north-west Co. Mayo (*Col. 51*) and planning permission has been given for a second farm in Kerry. The state has indicated that it will buy up to 75 megawatts of new-sourced electricity and here there is considerable scope for wind power. But wind farms are unsightly and noisy establishments. The turbines stand on towers up to 40m high with slightly shorter rotor blades and they are uneconomic unless built in clusters of at least twenty turbines; in short the farm is ugly. The noise created is tremendous. The Australian aborigine has his 'bull-roarer', a short flat stick with an attached string. If the stick is whirled rapidly round, it produces a low, moaning sound. A turbine in action sounds like several million aborigines twirling their roarers in unison.

It is clear that an adequate supply of wind cannot be the only criterion by which a site is selected. The Irish Planning Institute has suggested that each county should prepare a list of sites where such stations should be prohibited. Most would wish to be near the windy west coast, but this includes some of Ireland's most scenic areas which are hugely attractive to locals as well as tourists. In autumn 1996, for example, a proposal to erect a wind farm at the dramatic Barnesmore Gap in Co. Donegal, provoked strong opposition from environmental groups, but was approved of in the end. All applications for permission to erect wind farms should be accompanied by an environmental impact study especially referring to general scenic aspect, sites of archaeological importance and areas of ecological interest. However, the effort to find renewable sources of energy which do not pollute widely is to be welcomed.

10. THE FUTURE

When we have reached a stage where tillage is concentrated in drier south-east Ireland, the dairy herds are on the good grasslands, overgrazing has been eliminated and forests have been established wherever they can form profitable wood, what is to become of the rest of the landscape and of its people? This is a problem that is not confined to Ireland, but exists equally in many parts of rural Europe. There is an especially close parallel between the problems of Brittany and Ireland.

In Ireland in 1900, everyone was rejoicing that the tyranny of large estates was over, and that the land now belonged to the small farmers. But almost a hundred years later, the horrid thought is beginning to arise that perhaps there was something to be said for large estates, such as still survive in England. There, they often no longer belong to greedy landlords, but to shrewd insurance companies or pension funds. These owners offer parcels of land on lease and so make it possible for a young person to begin farming, first by being able to get land, and second by getting it without being crippled by having to borrow the money necessary to purchase it. In Ireland, it is still next to impossible to rent land on a lease of sufficient length to make improvements and where land can be bought, it is often in small parcels at too high a price. On the other hand, small parcels are no longer so objectionable now that farming is specialised and nearly every family has at least one car. Ireland is the land where almost nobody, except a tourist, walks. Cows are intelligent creatures, and learn to obey the horn of a tractor just as well as the bark of a dog. The farmer no longer has pigs, hens are rarely kept and the milk comes in cartons from the supermarket, so why live on the farm? It is much nicer to live in a ribbon-development outside a town with municipal water and sanitation and the possibility of company. The farmer can then go off in the car to visit his scattered parcels of land! Access to work, services of all kinds and entertainment have encouraged the drift towards towns. This has been intensified by policies which favour the car over affordable public transport resulting in long-term serious consequences for our countryside and cities.

The poorer soils of Ireland must face not only usage at a less intensive level, but also habitation at a still lower level (*Col. 47*). In addition to the move of farmers to the local towns, there is an overall drift to the eastern half of the country, in particular to the conurbations of Belfast, Dublin and Cork. Limerick, Waterford and Galway will also continue to grow. Greater Dublin now holds 35% of the population of the Republic and is set to grow much larger (*Illus. 188*); in comparison, Paris holds only 20% of the population of France.

And lurking behind these modern local trends are the modern population upheavals. In the Republic in 1995, and for the first time since 1937, the number of

Illus. 188
Blanchardstown,
Co. Dublin. Today
the Irish landscape is
in a state of flux.

children presenting themselves for the national Junior Certificate examination fell. In 1996, 7000 fewer pupils sat the national Leaving Certificate examination than in 1995. Entries to primary schools were 11,000 lower in September 1996. As the birth rates decline and medicine advances, the proportion of people over 65 years rises steadily.

Even more of Ireland's land will fail to produce an income which will allow the lifestyle that the city dweller has achieved and the country dweller has come to expect. Unfortunately, our lifestyle is supported as much by foreign borrowing and EU transfers as by domestic productivity. Either new income sources will have to be found for the country dweller, or an income subsidy will have to be paid, if considerable areas in Ireland are not to become wilderness land.

Farming has always had a major influence on the appearance of the countryside and here slovenly rather than tidy practices have tended to rule. But with the assistance of EU funds, a determined effort is being made to raise standards. The Rural Environment Protection Scheme (REPS) is comprehensive and it is to be hoped that it will succeed – even if only for a short time. For the small farmer the financial considerations offered are very generous and the scheme should be well taken up. However, they are less attractive to the large farmer, who can often be the source of major pollution.

The REPS scheme has three main thrusts. The first deals with a problem already mentioned, that is the control of the amounts of phosphorus and nitrogen being applied and the elimination of the pollution of both surface and ground water. The second sets stocking rates to avoid overgrazing and prohibits the escape of pollutants from the farm; holding-tanks for silage effluent must be built. The third provides that the landscape features of the area must guarded by the protection of water courses, the maintenance of hedges and walls and the removal of derelict materials and machinery. As initially offered, a grant of up to £25,000 may be claimed over a period of five years as long as the standards set are fully attained. One unfortunate feature of its announcement has been the rush in some areas to get work that would otherwise be discouraged by the schemes carried out in advance of REPS. Particular examples of this have been documented in the Burren where the unique, ancient landscape has been under threat from well-intentioned but misguided reclamation. Farming interests argue that the schemes impose a bureaucratic burden on applicants and that this has resulted in a less than enthusiastic take-up. In mid-1996, only 15,000 farmers and 200,000 hectares were covered by REPS; this is clearly insufficient.

A similar scheme named Environmentally Sensitive Areas operates in Northern Ireland. To benefit from it, a farmer must limit both stocking rates and fertiliser applications, avoid pollution, make no major changes in general appearance and protect historic monuments.

Farm income can also be increased by tourism, either by taking paying guests or providing accommodation. France has established an elaborate system of gîtes, that is self-catering holiday accommodation on bona fide farms. We say bona fide because in Ireland an establishment describing itself as a farmhouse may prove on arrival to be a bungalow outside a small town. Such gîtes have great attraction to visitors with a special interest such as natural history or archaeology, and these visitors are increasing in number.

The REPS scheme should improve the appearance of farmland, but what about access to the land? This issue is a minefield and new control legislation is in the pipeline. Under the law as it stands, it seems that if a farmer asks someone who is wandering on his/her lands without permission to leave and if in the course of leaving the trespasser trips over a stone and injures himself, then the intruder can claim damages from the farmer. Until a few years ago such a claim would never have been made, common sense prevailing. However, more and more people today have become aware of the possibilities of a damages claim, sometimes aided and abetted by a lawyer acting on the principle of 'no damages no fee'. In the motoring world, for example, numerous claims for damages for alleged soft-flesh injuries, that is injuries which cannot be pinned down by medical examination, are constantly being pursued and often with success. A reasonable balance must be struck between access to the countryside and the rights of the farmer. We must remember that today because of artificially high prices, the cash value of stock and crops is much higher than in former times and that if the visitor should cause damage to these, the farmer's loss will be the greater. On the other hand, reasonable access to the countryside for the town dweller is essential. All taxpayers contribute heavily to the supports for agriculture and if we are to promote a healthy understanding between town and country dwellers, then all who wish to go out into the countryside must feel welcome there.

Access for walkers, particularly hill-walkers, is also threatened from another direction. In former times when grazing pressure was light, much of the uplands were jointly held by a number of participating farmers under the principle of commonage. It is estimated that the remaining area under commonage could be several hundred thousand hectares in extent, but there are no accurate figures. In commonage there is mutual agreement as to the number of stock each participant can put on the common. However, higher prices for livestock have greatly increased the number of beasts on the commons which are as a result being seriously overgrazed. If the commons are fenced, with the division being proportionate to the stock entitlement, then at least some of the farmers will not overgraze their share. But this spells serious problems for the hill-walker, who will be incommoded by the fences which, with the aid of EU grants, will be constructed to a standard that should prove impassable even to the wiliest of hill sheep.

Tourism is widely hailed as a source of national income, but not one that can be expanded indefinitely. Tourism can be a many-headed hydra and we must decide which heads we wish to feed and which we wish to lop off. Do we want casinos? Do we want Disneylands? Given the uncertainties of the Irish weather, visitors must be offered some indoor facilities. Given its *panache*, a giant Disneyland may succeed, but this success cannot be achieved on a small budget and a small scale or replicated in multiple locations. Theme-parks and heritage centres offer alternative possibilities. Provided they are situated in appropriate locations and are adequately funded and researched, the addition of such features to the Irish tourist trail is to be welcomed. But local enthusiasm, which is to be commended, is often not matched by adequate funding and appropriate development plans. In an area where the visitor demands high standards, evidence is beginning to accumulate that many of the heritage developments are not winning their approval – tourists have visited similar attractions elsewhere and find the placing of repetitive experiences close together increasingly oppressive especially if tour operators stop at each one. The natural and undeveloped countryside with its accessible 'unpackaged' landscapes and monuments remains the best attraction for the tourist.

Our tourists fall mainly into three groups, the urbanite, the golfer and the open air person. On the whole the countryside is safe from the urbanite, but we do not want to see our city street-scapes marred by plastic fronts to casinos and night-clubs and by shoddy looking apartment blocks. It is clear, however, that most of our urban tourists have a sophisticated interest in our towns and cities, and attempts in the past to please them by meretricious development have been seriously misguided. Interesting towns, well-presented cultural heritage, good entertainment and good food are the hallmarks of successful urban tourism, and these are demanded by our own people also. Much of this seems now to be accepted, even if implementation has some way to go.

Dublin is a city of wide streets with many dignified buildings. Because of suburban growth urban decay was setting in along some streets and tax incentives were offered for building construction. This provoked a rush by developers to crowd as many pint-sized apartments as possible onto a quart of site; buildings sadly lacking the quality of earlier years. The urban development incentive schemes have placed our archaeological heritage under great stress – the country was frankly unprepared for the great riches of archaeological evidence preserved under our ancient towns. Rushed campaigns of salvage excavation have reduced the potential yield of historical information and left little place for considered programmes of conservation in association with sympathetic development. Terrible things are also done in the name of improvement by well-intentioned but misinformed restorers. An example is the current misguided fad for stripping older houses to reveal the underlying rubble masonry which was never intended to be seen. Resources and space must be found to redress the balance in future urban renewal schemes. Some few projects have pointed the way, but on the whole the picture is disappointing. It is, however, reassuring to note that all our political parties have adopted the conservation of our architectural heritage and our towns as their policies.

Cities depend on municipal refuse collections, but few authorities make any serious attempt to insist on pre-collection sorting of different types of refuse; instead they scour the countryside for sites for further massive dumps. Tidy Towns competitions do bring about improvement in smaller centres and do encourage general awareness of the litter problem, but much more needs to be done. For the outdoor visitors, their general impression of the countryside must be one that senses that it is a land of which its inhabitants are proud. But there is little evidence of such pride in Ireland, and the problem of litter and unauthorised dumping of refuse remains a constant embarrassment (*Col. 48*).

Golfers play an important role in Irish tourism; 170,000 golfers spent about £60 million in Ireland in 1993. Golf courses alter the landscape, but provided the alteration is done sympathetically and does not threaten natural habitats for rare species, the substantial quantities of money that golf courses bring into the country can only be welcomed. However, landscape alteration on a grand scale is to be avoided. A golf course was recently created in Cavan, in a setting where the natural landscape was small rush-filled fields. The developer was not to be deterred and he brought in 160,000 tons of sand and gravel to create his well-drained fairways. Nobody asked the question: What did the source of the gravel look like after that quantity had been removed?

Quarrying of this kind is a serious problem which as yet has not attracted much debate. In many parts of the northern half of Ireland, the retreating ice deposited vast quantities of unsorted sand and gravel, often with pleasantly undulating surfaces later clothed with grasses and bushes. Developers extract the sand but leave the coarser material – anything bigger than a tennis-ball – behind in unsightly heaps and craters which are slow to reclothe themselves in vegetation. Examples are all too common, but are especially ugly in the vicinity of Blessington in Co. Wicklow where the pleasant setting of an estate village has been ruined, and on many roads around Omagh in Co. Tyrone where the extraction of gravel has created a devastated landscape.

Many eskers have already disappeared; few are left relatively intact. Esker robbers are quite shameless. Planning permission is currently being sought for the removal of a length of a very important esker, Castlesampson, in Co. Roscommon. It is important geologically, ecologically and historically and its significance has been noted by the Geological Survey, the Department of Arts, Culture and the Gaeltacht, the County Development plan and numerous local groups. Are its graceful contours to disappear and leave only a bare trail of rough boulders?

Efforts to give protection to areas of environmental importance interesting to the open-air enthusiast have not had a happy history in Ireland because they were often open to legal challenge. A new start has been made in the North and is in train in the Republic, where Natural Heritage Areas (NHA) will soon be defined by statute. The right of a farmer within an NHA to alter his lands at his own discretion will be preserved, but he must give prior notice to the National Monuments and Historic Properties Service (NMS) and he will not receive any EU grants. The EU is preparing a list of areas deemed as of 'community importance' for conservation. The list will appear as *Natura 2000* and Ireland must set out in the list the areas it will conserve.

Some time ago, the Office of Public Works (now partly subsumed in the Department of Arts, Culture and the Gaeltacht as the NMS and the National Parks and Wildlife Service) embarked on massive developments at two sites of great environmental importance, one in the Burren in Co. Clare and the second in the Wicklow Mountains. The site at Mullaghmore in the Burren provides the most important view of the main Burren features, rocks and plants. It was proposed to build an information centre consisting of large buildings and several car-parks. Environmentalists reacted loudly and efficiently to the project and after several years of struggle, the courts ruled that the project could not proceed. The site in Wicklow was within the area of the long-proposed Wicklow National Park and the information centre was to be visually less obvious as it was to lie within a long-established coniferous plantation, itself an anomaly within a national park. The principal objection was that here we had an area of rich and varied natural beauty with mountains, valleys and lakes, best explored by small groups and that it would be wrong to concentrate visitors in a large information centre, again with large car-parks, when the centre could be in a nearby village such as Roundwood. The courts ruled against the development.

This reaction to development promises well for the environment, but what about sites and areas of archaeological importance? Efforts have not always had a happy history in Ireland, but new legislation offers new possibilities. A recent controversy emerged as the NMS (formerly OPW) embarked on a massive development in the Boyne valley with the excellent intention of trying to reduce tourist pressure on the jewel of the Boyne valley – the great passage tomb at Newgrange – by building a visitor centre nearby. Unlike Lascaux in France, Newgrange has no paintings at risk, but the long-term effect of the day-after-day procession of visiting groups can only be similar. Each group entering the tomb exudes both heat and moisture and the see-saw alternations in heat and humidity must affect the stones of the chamber. Mechanical damage – the rubbing of the stones by 170,000 pairs of shoulders, abrasion by striking wristwatches, cameras and the like – is also taking a severe toll on the monument.

The information centre is to be sited at some distance on the opposite side of the river and will contain a replica of the Newgrange chamber as well as other features. The hope of the NMS is that many casual visitors will be satisfied with the replica and with a general introduction to the landscape and will not proceed further, while the distance from the tomb itself is not so great as to deter the serious visitors to the Boyne valley. These will generally visit in controlled groups in minibuses provided. The plan also calls amongst other things for visitors to be diverted to Knowth and introduced also to the wider landscape. George Eogan has been excavating at Knowth for more than thirty-five years and as his work proceeds the NMS follows, making more and more of this fantastically rich site available to visitors. Already, Knowth is drawing pressure away from Newgrange. Voluntary agreements with some local landowners on whose land are sited important features also point the way forward for sensible management of the ancient monuments.

Hard things had often been said about the OPW in archaeological circles – that it was too big, that it was monolithic, that it was too secretive about its intentions. The appropriateness of its inclusion in the Department of Finance had been questioned while its activities had in recent years been organised into smaller units, each charged with specific tasks. Its functions in relation to the natural and built environment are now exercised within the Department of Arts, Culture and the Gaeltacht. For one hundred years, the OPW and its British predecessor worked hard to preserve Ireland's archaeological heritage and a very great deal had been accomplished. Monuments were acquired and conserved, excavations were carried out and the country's stock of antiquities, as far as they had been recognised, were listed and so granted legal protection. Under current policies, two survey volumes are to be produced for each county: one providing a simple list (now completed), and a second amplifying the list using notes, plans and illustrations. The lists are extending legal protection to new sites under the National Monuments (Amendment) Act 1994 which has established a Register of protected sites. When developers or farmers are made aware of the existence of the lists, then they cannot plead ignorance if they deface a listed national monument. With goodwill and proper resources this work can continue under the new dispensation and contribute greatly to the enrichment of our lives. It is most important that in its new guise, the National Monuments Service is enabled to continue its vital national task.

There is no doubt of the widespread public interest in our natural and man-made environment. The support and enthusiasm of local and community groups have helped to build a constituency for environmental issues which can only be welcomed. There are some areas where enthusiasm has led to problems – the unsupervised 'clearing up' of ancient graveyards and the unsympathetic restoration of buildings spring to mind. These are all problems that can be resolved by better liaison with official bodies, better supervision and circulation of more information. Looked at generally, the achievements of local and national, environmental, historical and archaeological societies, community groups and small single-issue pressure groups have been decisive in changing attitudes throughout the country for the better.

For many years, the ½" Ordnance Survey map (1/126,000) has been the vade-mecum for those wandering in the Irish countryside, but its sheets show only a limited number of antiquities. This scale is now being supplanted by a new series at 1/50,000 on which listed antiquities are shown. These maps will not only be of the greatest interest to the visiting antiquarian, but will further identify to the farmer some of those monuments which have legal protection.

Public awareness of the value of our environment is growing and the state has been forced by the activities of An Taisce in the Republic and the National Trust in the North to set up its own agency, ENFO, the Environmental Information Service. The establishment of a statutory Heritage Council in 1995 with responsibilities for the natural and built environment was a welcome development; time will tell if the resources necessary to accomplish its tasks will be made available and if the Government in the south will listen more carefully to its own advisors. We must demand proper environmental control as a right for ourselves and our descendants in the first instance and not merely as a bait for tourists. However, if we are to achieve this, we have to put an end to our penchant for disfiguring our environment by erecting ugly buildings on prominent sites, by polluting its waters or by scattering litter. The United Nations have designated 17% of Ireland as areas of outstanding natural beauty, but for how long will we hold that position?

As the rural population continues to fall, public transport diminishes and local post-offices close, how can we maintain the status quo of the countryside? We like its current appearance, perhaps because it is entirely the work of our immediate predecessors. If there was a modern resurrection of some of our earlier ancestors, who lie at rest in the Bronze Age cemeteries of 3500 years ago, they would be amazed by and completely lost in today's landscape.

Continuing depopulation is most acute in the west. Are we prepared to pay a direct subsidy to chosen western farmers to stay on the land and work it at a deliberately low level so as to save the landscape from first falling into desertion and then being overwhelmed by trees and bushes? Could we pay them a salary as litter wardens and give them power to inflict on-the-spot fines to those who desecrate the countryside? Can we give them mobile cranes to collect abandoned cars (*Col. 48*) Or can we work together to provide for all our people a dignified, meaningful working life?

It may seem curious to talk of encouraging low-level output, even in a restricted area and with a definite purpose, since low-level output is our national disease. We expect a European standard of income from an Irish standard of output. There are twenty-two member countries of the Organisation for Economic Co-operation and Development and these have recently been ranked in order of international competitiveness; Ireland stands sixteenth in the list with the UK only two places ahead at fourteenth. At a recent conference in Dublin, the chief executive of a large Irish corporation said that we should not rest until we have raised our standard of living to that of Germany or Holland; this is dangerous nonsense, because our standard of living is already too high to be sustained by the world's current resources. Despite the remarkable performance of the Irish economy in the 1990s, it is doubtful if his dream can come true. Much of our economic growth has been based on imported technologies or primed by significant EU transfers for structural development. Ireland however remains an open economy and its native resources provide only a limited protection against the vagaries of world commerce, trade and monetary fluctuations. New, high-technology industries have, notionally, unlimited potential growth but Ireland cannot rely on continuous technology transfers from other countries indefinitely, and our own research and development establishment is miniscule by international standards and poorly funded. World environmental pressures may soon oblige us to limit our expectations. Of the two countries which our industrialist chose as the summit of his ambitions for us, one has a huge domestic market and a history of centuries of industrial development, the other has enjoyed a long period of social consensus, nearness to very large markets and for about 350 years, vast transfers of wealth from colonial possessions. The comparisons are not appropriate. Small nations from the east of Europe are beginning to hope that some portion of EU largesse may come their way. If their hopes succeed, Ireland will have to pull in its belt.

Do we need or deserve a still higher standard of living when the Third World is starving? Can we reproach the Third World for causing damage not only to their agricultural land but also to the general environment by introducing more CO_2 into the atmosphere as they cut down their local forests, when we are busy polluting our atmosphere, our land, our lakes and our rivers and sweeping away our field monuments for the sake of short-term gain? Some development must be bridled in our long-term interests. Preaching to the third world about environmental concerns evokes cynicism – the rich north has had its industrial development bought to some extent at the expense of almost three hundred years of pollution and colonial exploitation; why should developing countries practise self-denial before they have reached something like our standards of living?

The eighteenth century saw the agricultural revolution, the nineteenth century saw the industrial revolution and as the twentieth century draws to a close we are whirled along at ever increasing speed in the technological revolution. The ground is shaking below us and only fools will make predictions about the future. Institutions on which we have depended for decades will change dramatically, and with them the familiar face of the Irish countryside. The traditional Post Office will lose ground to e-mail. The Electricity Supply Board that bestrode the Irish landscape for seventy years is threatened by amputations. Farming, already very different from what it was thirty years ago, will change still further. Some areas now farmed will be covered in forest. Small schools will close as pupil numbers decline. Towns already glutted will grow even larger.

Not all is gloomy – the welcome signs of a revival of interest in our landscape, the inclusion of meaningful teaching of environmental and human history at all levels in our schools and growing signs that the environment has become politically important hold out the hope that a balanced husbandry of our Four Green Fields might yet be achieved.

BIBLIOGRAPHY

This bibliography of the environment past and present does not attempt to be comprehensive, but endeavours to suggest sources for further reading. Emphasis is concentrated on recent publications as far as possible and many of these themselves contain detailed bibliographies of the sphere of interest in question. References to articles in *Proceedings, Journals* etc give only the year and the volume number, they do not give page references.

GENERAL
AALEN, F H A. *Man and the Landscape in Ireland.* Academic Press, London, 1978

COMMON, R (ed.). *Northern Ireland from the Air.* Queen's University Belfast, 1964

D'ARCY, G and HAYWARD, J. *The Natural History of the Burren.* Immel, London, 1992

FEEHAN, J. *The Landscape of Slieve Bloom.* Blackwater, Dublin, 1979

FEEHAN, J and O'DONOVAN, G. *The Bogs of Ireland.* The Environmental Institute, University College Dublin, 1996

FOSTER, J W and CHESNEY, H G C (eds.). *Nature in Ireland: A Scientific and Cultural History.* Lilliput Press, Dublin, 1996

FREEMAN, T W. *Ireland* (2nd edition). Methuen, London, 1960

GILLMOR, D (ed.). *The Irish Countryside.* Wolfhound Press, Dublin, 1989

GILLMOR, D. *A Systematic Geography of Ireland.* Gill & Macmillan, Dublin, 1971

GRAHAM, B J and PROUDFOOT, L J (eds.). *An historical geography of Ireland.* Academic Press, London, 1993

HAUGHTON, J P (Chairman). *Atlas of Ireland, prepared under the direction of the Irish National Committee for Geography.* Royal Irish Academy, Dublin, 1979

HICKIE, D. *Evaluation of Environmental Designations in Ireland.* Heritage Council, Dublin, 1996

KIELY, B. *The Aerofilm Book of Ireland from the Air.* Weidenfeld and Nicolson, London, 1985

MITCHELL, G F (ed.). *The Book of the Irish Countryside.* Blackstaff Press; Town House, Dublin, 1987

MOODY, T W and MARTIN, F X (eds.). *The Course of Irish History.* Mercier Press, Cork, 1984

MOULD, DAPHNE D C POCHIN. *Ireland from the Air*. David & Charles, Devon, 1972

NELSON, E C and WALSH, W F. *Trees of Ireland.* Lilliput Press, Dublin, 1993

NOLAN, W (ed.).*The Shaping of Ireland: The Geographical Perspective.* Mercier Press, Cork, 1986

ORME, A R. *The World's Landscapes: Ireland.* Longman, Essex, 1970

PRAEGER, R L. *The Way that I Went.* Allen Figgis; Methuen, London, 1937

RYAN, M (ed.). *Irish Archaeology Illustrated.* Country House, Dublin, 1994

STEPHENS, N and GLASSCOCK, R E. *Irish Geographical Studies.* Queen's University Belfast, 1970

1. THE GROWTH OF THE ROCK FOUNDATION

DAVIES, G L, HERRIES and STEPHENS, N. *Ireland, Geomorphology.* Methuen, London, 1978

HOLLAND, C H (ed.). *A Geology of Ireland.* Scottish Academic Press, Edinburgh, 1981

JENNINGS, J N. *Karst Geomorphology.* Basil Blackwell, Oxford, 1985

MITCHELL, G F. 'The Search for Tertiary Ireland', *Journal of Earth Science* Vol. 3. Royal Dublin Society, 1980

MITCHELL, G F (revised 1990). *The Irish Landscape.* Michael Joseph; Country House, Dublin, 1986

MITCHELL, G F. *Man and Environment in Valencia Island.* Royal Irish Academy, Dublin, 1989

MITCHELL, G F. *The Way that I Followed.* Country House, Dublin, 1990

MITCHELL, G F. *Where has Ireland Come From?* Country House, Dublin, 1994

NAYLOR, D and SHANNON, P M. *The Geology of Offshore Ireland and West Britain.* Graham & Trotman, London, 1982

WHITTOW, J B. *Geology and Scenery in Ireland.* Penguin, Middlesex, 1974

2. THE ICE AGE

BOWEN, D Q. *Quaternary Geology.* Pergamon Press, Oxford, 1978

BOWEN, D Q et al. 'Correlation of Quaternary glaciations in the Northern Hemisphere', *Quaternary Science Review* Vol. 5, 1986

COXON, P. 'Irish Pleistocene Biostratigraphy', *Irish Journal of Earth Science* Vol. 12, 1993

EDWARDS, K J and WARREN, W P. *The Quaternary History of Ireland.* Academic Press, London, 1985

McCABE, A M and HIRONS, R K. *Field guide to the Quaternary of South-East Ulster.* Quaternary Research Association, Cambridge, 1986

PREECE, R C (ed.). *Island Britain: A Quaternary Perspective.* Geological Society of London Special Paper 96, 1995

SHACKLETON, N J and OPDYKE, N D. 'Oxygen isotope and palaeomagnetic stratigraphy of Equatorial Pacific core V28-238', *Quaternary Research* Vol. 3, 1973

SUTCLIFFE, A J. *On the Track of Ice Age Mammals.* British Museum (Natural History), London, 1985

3. THE END OF THE ICE AGE

ANDRIEU, V et al. 'Late-glacial Vegetation and Environment in Ireland', *Quaternary Science Review* Vol. 12, 1993

BLANCHON, P and SHAW, J. 'Reef drowning during the last deglaciation', *Geology* Vol. 23, No. 1, 1995

FOSSIT, JULIA. 'Late-glacial and Holocene Vegetation History of Western Donegal, Ireland', *Proceedings of the Royal Irish Academy* Vol. 1, B, 1994

GODWIN, SIR HARRY. *History of the British Flora* (2nd edition). Cambridge University Press, 1975

JESSEN, K. 'Studies in Late Quaternary deposits and flora-history of Ireland', *Proceedings of the Royal Irish Academy* Vol. 52, B, 1949

MITCHELL, G F. *Littleton Bog, Tipperary: An Irish vegetational record.* Geological Society of America Special Paper 84, 1965

PENNINGTON, W. *The History of British Vegetation* (2nd edition). English Universities Press, London, 1974

SINGH, G. 'Late-glacial vegetational history of Lecale, Co. Down', *Proceedings of the Royal Irish Academy* Vol. 69, B, 1970

4. RESPONSE TO WARM CONDITIONS

BELLAMY, D J. *The Wild Boglands; Bellamy's Ireland.* Country House, Dublin, 1986

COSTELLO, M J and KELLY, K S. *Biogeography of Ireland.* Irish Biogeographical Society, 1993

DE BUITLÉAR, É. *Ireland's Wild Countryside.* Boxtree, London, 1993

DEVOY, R J N. 'The problem of a late Quaternary landbridge between Britain and Ireland', *Quaternary Science Review* Vol. 4, No. 1, 1985

O'CONNELL, M, BERGLUND, B E et al (eds.). 'Ireland: Palaeoecological events during the last 15,000 years', *Regional synthesis and palaeoecological studies of lakes and rivers in Europe.* John Wiley and Sons, Chichester, 1996

MOORE, P D and BELLAMY, D J. *Peatlands.* Elek Science, 1974

O'ROURKE, F J. *The Fauna of Ireland.* Mercier Press, Cork, 1970

PREECE, R C, COXON P and ROBINSON, J E. 'New biostratigraphic evidence of the post-glacial colonization of Ireland and for Mesolithic forest disturbance', *Journal of Biogeography* (in press)

ROHAN, P K. *The Climate of Ireland.* Stationery Office, Dublin, 1975

SLEEMAN, D P, DEVOY, R and WOODMAN, P C. *Post-glacial Colonisation of Ireland.* Irish Biogeographical Society, Cork, 1986

WEBB, D A. *An Irish Flora.* Tempest, Dundalk, 1943

WEBB, D A. 'The flora of Ireland in its European context', *Life Science* Vol. 4. Royal Dublin Society, 1983

WOODMAN, P C. *The Mesolithic in Ireland.* British Archaeological Reports, Oxford, 1978

5. THE FIRST FARMERS

This bibliography of the impact of man on the environment does not attempt to be comprehensive, but endeavours to suggest sources for further reading. The sources for many of the observations made in the text are scattered in a variety of learned and popular journals and no appreciation of Irish archaeology is possible without recourse to them. The reader is particularly directed to the volumes of the *Archaeological Survey* (Stationery Office, Dublin) (NMS) and to numerous privately-commissioned surveys. Important new discoveries frequently appear for the first time in the magazine *Archaeology Ireland*, making it indispensible. The following journals are the primary publications of records of Irish archaelology: *Proceedings of the Royal Irish Academy, The Journal of the Royal Society of Antiquaries of Ireland, The Ulster Journal of Archaeology, The Cork Historical and Archaeological Journal* and *The North Munster Antiquarian Journal.* Two journals which specialise in theoretical or speculative articles of value are *The Journal of Irish Archaeology* and *Emania* (the journal of the Navan Research Group). The volumes of the *Irish Wetland Unit Reports* and the *Discovery Programme Reports* are also essential reading.

BERGH, S. *Landscape of the monuments: a study of the passage tombs in the Cúil Irra region.* Riksantikvarièämbetet, Stockholm, 1995

CLARKE, D V, COWIE, T G and FOXON, A. *Symbols of Power.* HMSO, Edinburgh, 1985

COONEY, G and GROGAN, E. *Irish Prehistory: a social perspective.* Wordwell, Dublin, 1994

COONEY, G and MANDAL, S. 'Getting to the core of the problem: petrological results from the Irish Stone Axe Project', *Antiquity* Vol. 69, No. 266, 1995

COXON, P and O'CONNELL, M (eds.). *Oileán Cliara agus Inis Bó Finne: Clare Island and Inishbofin.* Irish Association for Quaternary Studies Field Guide No. 17, 1994

Discovery Programme Reports 1. Royal Irish Academy, Dublin,1993

Discovery Programme Reports 2. Royal Irish Academy, Dublin, 1995

EDWARDS, RUTH D. *An Atlas of Irish History* (2nd edition). Methuen, London, 1981

EOGAN, G. *Excavations at Knowth.* Royal Irish Academy, Dublin, 1984

EOGAN, G. *Knowth.* Thames & Hudson, London, 1986

EOGAN, G. 'Prehistoric and Early Historic culture change at Brugh na Bóinne', *Proceedings of the Royal Irish Academy* Vol. 91, C, 1991

EOGAN, G and ROCHE, H. 'A Grooved Ware wooden structure at Knowth, Boyne Valley, Ireland', *Antiquity* Vol. 68, 1994

EVANS, J G. *The Environment of early man in the British Isles.* Paul Elek, 1975

GOWEN, M (ed.). *Three Irish gas pipelines: new archaeological evidence in Munster.* Wordwell, Dublin, 1988

HAMLYN, A and LYNN, C (eds.). *Pieces of the Past.* HMSO, Belfast, 1988

HARBISON, P. *Pre-Christian Ireland.* Thames & Hudson, London, 1988

HERITY, M and EOGAN, G. *Ireland in Prehistory.* Routledge & Kegan Paul, London, 1977

LYNCH, A. *Man and environment in south-west Ireland 4000 BC – AD 800.* British Archaeological Reports, Oxford, 1981

MALLORY, J P and MACNEILL, T E. *The archaeology of Ulster.* The Institute of Irish Studies, Queen's University Belfast, 1991

MOUNT, C. 'Aspects of Ritual Deposition in the Late Neolithic and Beaker Periods at Newgrange, Co. Meath', *Proceedings of the Prehistoric Society* Vol. 60, 1994

NORMAN, E R and ST JOSEPH, J K. *The Early Development of Irish Society.* Cambridge University Press, 1969

O'BRIEN, W. *Mount Gabriel: Bronze Age mining in Ireland.* Galway University Press, 1994

O'CONNELL, M. *Connemara: vegetation and land use since the last Ice Age.* Office of Public Works, Dublin, 1994

O'CONNELL, M (ed.). *An Boireann: Burren, Co. Clare.* Irish Association for Quaternary Studies Field Guide No.18, 1994

O'KELLY, M J. *Newgrange: Archaeology, Art and Legend.* Thames & Hudson, London, 1982

O'KELLY, M J. *Early Ireland: an introduction.* Cambridge University Press, 1989

Ó NUALLÁIN, S. *Stone Circles in Ireland.* Country House, Dublin, 1995

RAFTERY, B. *Trackways through Time.* Headline Publishing, Rush, Co. Dublin, 1990

RAFTERY, B. *Pagan Celtic Ireland: the enigma of the Iron Age.* Thames & Hudson, London, 1994

REEVES-SMYTH, T and HAMMOND, F. *Landscape Archaeology in Ireland.* British Archaeological Reports, Oxford, 1983

RYAN, M (ed.). *Irish Archaeology Illustrated.* Country House, Dublin, 1991

STOUT, G. 'Embanked earthern enclosures of the Boyne region', *Proceedings of the Royal Irish Academy* Vol. 91, C, 1991

SWEETMAN, P D. 'A Late Neolithic/Early Bronze Age pit circle at Newgrange, Co. Meath', *Proceedings of the Royal Irish Academy* Vol. 85, C, 1985

SWEETMAN, P D. 'Excavation of a Late Neolithic/Early Bronze age site at Newgrange, Co. Meath', *Proceedings of the Royal Irish Academy* Vol. 87, C, 1987

VAN WIJNGAARDEN-BAKKER, L. 'The animal remains from the Beaker settlement at Newgrange', *Proceedings of the Royal Irish Academy* Vol. 74, C, 1974

WADDELL, J and SHEE-TWOHIG, E. *Ireland in the Bronze Age*. Stationery Office, Dublin, 1995

WEIR, D. A 'Palynology and environmental history of the Navan area', *Emania* Vol. 3, 1987

WEIR, D.A 'Palynological study of landscape and agricultural development in Co. Louth from the second millennium BC to the first millennium AD: final report', *Discovery Programme Reports 2*. Royal Irish Academy, Dublin, 1995

6. THE BEGINNINGS OF HISTORY

BELL, J . 'A contribution to the study of cultivation ridges in Ireland', *Journal of the Royal Society of Antiquaries of Ireland* Vol. 114, 1984

BITEL, LISA. *Isle of Saints: Monastic settlement and Christian community in early Ireland*. Cornell University Press, 1990

BRADLEY, J (ed.). *Settlement and Society in Medieval Ireland*. Boethius Press, Kilkenny, 1988

BYRNE, F J. *Irish Kings and High Kings*. Batsford, London, 1973

CLARKE, H, Ní MHAONAIGH, M and Ó FLOINN, R. *Ireland and Scandinavia in the Early Viking Age*. Four Courts Press, Dublin (in press)

DE PAOR, L. *St. Patrick's World*. Four Courts Press, Dublin, 1993

EDWARDS, NANCY. *The Archaeology of Early Medieval Ireland*. Batsford, London, 1990

FLANAGAN, DEIRDRE and L. *Irish Place Names*. Gill & Macmillan, Dublin, 1994

HARBISON, P. *Pilgrimage in Ireland: the monuments and the people*. Barrie and Jenkins, London, 1991

HERITY, M. *Studies in the layout, building and art in stone of early Irish monasteries*. Pindar Press, London, 1995

HUGHES, K and HAMLIN, A. *The Modern Traveller to the Early Irish Church*. SPCK, London, 1977

KELLY, F. *A guide to early Irish law*. Institute for Adanced Studies, Dublin, 1988

MACNIOCAILL, G. *Ireland before the Vikings*. Gill & Macmillan, Dublin, 1972

MANNING, C. *Early Irish Monasteries*. Country House, Dublin, 1995

MEEHAN, B. *The Book of Kells*. Thames & Hudson, London, 1994

MYTUM, H. *The origins of Early Christian Ireland*. Routledge, London, 1992

RYAN, M (ed.). *The Derrynaflan Hoard I: a preliminary account*. National Museum, Dublin, 1983

STOUT, M. 'Ringforts in the south-west midlands of Ireland', *Proceedings of the Royal Irish Academy* Vol. 91, C, 1991

THOMAS, C. *Christianity in Roman Britain* (2nd edition). Batsford, London, 1981

WHELAN, K. *Wexford: History and Society*. Geography Publications, Dublin, 1987

7. THE WINDS OF CHANGE

BARRY, T B. *Medieval Moated Sites in Ireland.* British Archaeological Reports, Oxford, 1977

BARRY, T B. *The Archaeology of Medieval Ireland.* Methuen, London, 1987

BARRY, T B, FRAME, R and SIMMS, K. *Colony and Frontier in Medieval Ireland.* Hambledon Press, London, 1995

BRADLEY, J. *Walled Towns in Ireland.* Country House, Dublin, 1995

COSGROVE, A (ed.). *Medieval Ireland 1169-1534.* Oxford University Press, 1987

CULLEN, L M. *The Emergence of Modern Ireland, 1600-1900.* Batsford, London, 1981

ELLIS, S G. *Tudor Ireland.* Longman, London, 1985

GRAHAM, B J. *Anglo-Norman Settlement in Ireland.* Group for the Study of Irish Historic Settlement, 1985

LYONS, F S L. *Ireland since the Famine.* Charles Scribner & Sons, 1973

MACCARTHY-MORROGH, M. *The Munster Plantation.* Clarendon Press, Oxford, 1986

MCCRACKEN, EILEEN. *The Irish Woods since Tudor Times.* David & Charles, London, 1971

MACCURTAIN, M. *Tudor and Stuart Ireland.* Gill & Macmillan, Dublin, 1972

NICHOLLS, K. *Gaelic and Gaelicised Ireland in the Middle Ages.* Gill & Macmillan, Dublin, 1972

Ó CORRÁIN, D. *Ireland before the Normans.* Gill & Macmillan, Dublin, 1972

SIMMS, A and ANDREWS, J H. *Irish Country Towns.* RTE/Mercier Press, Dublin and Cork, 1994

STALLEY, R. *The Cistercian Monasteries of Ireland.* Yale University Press, 1987

SWEETMAN, D. *Irish Castles and Fortified Houses.* Country House, Dublin, 1995

WALLACE, P F. *The Viking Age Buildings of Dublin.* Royal Irish Academy, Dublin, 1992

YOUNG, A. *Tour in Ireland.* George Bell, 1780 (edited in 1892 by Hutton, A W republished in 1983 by Blackstaff Press, Dublin)

8. MODERN IRELAND

FANNING, R. *Independent Ireland.* Helicon, Oxford, 1983

FITZPATRICK, H M. *The Forests of Ireland.* Society of Irish Foresters, Dublin, 1965

FOSTER, R. *Modern Ireland 1600 – 1972.* Allen Lane, London, 1995

GILLMOR, D A (ed.). *Irish Resources and Land Use.* Institute of Public Admimistration, Dublin, 1979

LEE, J. *Ireland 1912-1985: Politics and Society.* University Press, Cambridge, 1989

MOODY, T W, MARTIN, F X and BYRNE, F J (eds.). *A New History of Ireland III: Early Modern Ireland.* University Press, Oxford, 1976

MURPHY, J A. *Ireland in the Twentieth Century.* Gill & Macmillan, Dublin, 1975

WHITAKER, T K. 'Economic development – the Irish experience', *Irish Times, 28.9.82*

9. THE VIEW IN 1996

LEE, J (ed.). *Ireland: Towards a Sense of Place.* Cork University Press, 1985

QUINN, J (ed.). *The Tinnakilly Senate.* RTE, Dublin, 1993

10. THE FUTURE

AALEN, F H A. *The Future of the Irish Rural Landscape.* Geography Department, Trinity College Dublin, 1985

BLACKWELL, J and CONVERY, F J. *Promise and Performance: Irish Environmental Policies Analysed.* Resource and Environmental Policy Centre, University College Dublin, 1983

CONVERY, F J. *Farming and the Environment: Cost and Opportunities.* Resource and Environmental Policy Centre, University College Dublin, 1986

CRUICKSHANK, J G and WILCOCK, D N. *Northern Ireland: Environment and Natural Resources.* Queen's University Belfast and the New University of Ulster, 1982

LEE, JOHN. 'European Land', *Farm & Food Research,* 17, 1986

LEE, JOSEPH. *Reflections on Ireland in the EEC.* Irish Council of the European Movement, 1984

MOORE, M J. 'A Bronze Age settlement and ritual centre in the Monavullagh Mountains, Co. Waterford, Ireland', *Proceedings of the Prehistoric Society* Vol. 61, 1995

O'CARROLL, N. *The Forests of Ireland: history, distribution and silviculture.* Turoe Press, Dublin, 1984

List of Acknowledgements of Photographs and Illustrations

LIST OF ACKNOWLEDGEMENTS OF COLOUR PLATES

INDEX

This index does not record every mention of common plants and animals; significant entries are noted. Where the caption of a photograph, illustration or colour plate amplifies the text, a reference is given in italics.